Communicative Efficiency

All living beings try to save effort, and humans are no exception. This groundbreaking book shows how we save time and energy during communication by unconsciously making efficient choices in grammar, lexicon and phonology. It presents a new theory of 'communicative efficiency', the idea that language is designed to be as efficient as possible, as a system of communication. The new framework accounts for the diverse manifestations of communicative efficiency across a typologically broad range of languages, using various corpus-based and statistical approaches to explain speakers' bias towards efficiency. The author's unique interdisciplinary expertise allows her to provide rich evidence from a broad range of language sciences. She integrates diverse insights from over a hundred years of research into this comprehensible new theory, which she presents step-by-step in clear and accessible language. It is essential reading for language scientists, cognitive scientists and anyone interested in language use and communication.

NATALIA LEVSHINA is a postdoctoral researcher at the Neurobiology of Language Department, Max Planck Institute for Psycholinguistics. She is the author of the best-selling book *How to Do Linguistics with R* (2015).

Communicative Efficiency
Language Structure and Use

Natalia Levshina
Max Planck Institute for Psycholinguistics, The Netherlands

CAMBRIDGE
UNIVERSITY PRESS

Shaftesbury Road, Cambridge CB2 8EA, United Kingdom

One Liberty Plaza, 20th Floor, New York, NY 10006, USA

477 Williamstown Road, Port Melbourne, VIC 3207, Australia

314–321, 3rd Floor, Plot 3, Splendor Forum, Jasola District Centre, New Delhi – 110025, India

103 Penang Road, #05–06/07, Visioncrest Commercial, Singapore 238467

Cambridge University Press is part of Cambridge University Press & Assessment, a department of the University of Cambridge.

We share the University's mission to contribute to society through the pursuit of education, learning and research at the highest international levels of excellence.

www.cambridge.org
Information on this title: www.cambridge.org/9781108743945

DOI: 10.1017/9781108887809

© Natalia Levshina 2023

This publication is in copyright. Subject to statutory exception and to the provisions of relevant collective licensing agreements, no reproduction of any part may take place without the written permission of Cambridge University Press & Assessment.

First published 2023
First paperback edition 2025

A catalogue record for this publication is available from the British Library

ISBN   978-1-108-84079-8   Hardback
ISBN   978-1-108-74394-5   Paperback

Cambridge University Press & Assessment has no responsibility for the persistence or accuracy of URLs for external or third-party internet websites referred to in this publication and does not guarantee that any content on such websites is, or will remain, accurate or appropriate.

To my teachers

Contents

List of Figures	*page* x
List of Tables	xii
Preface	xv
Acknowledgements	xvi
List of Abbreviations	xvii

Part I Different Types of Efficiency in Language 1

1 Communicative Efficiency: Main Concepts 3
  1.1 What Is Communicative Efficiency? 3
  1.2 Benefits and Costs in Communication 8
  1.3 How to Be Efficient? 18
  1.4 Three Principles of Efficient Communication 23
  1.5 'Good-Enough' Efficiency 29
  1.6 Conclusions 34

2 Efficiency and Formal Length 36
  2.1 Efficient Length Asymmetries 36
  2.2 Accessibility of Referents and Length of Referential Expressions and Markers 37
  2.3 Grammatical Coding Asymmetries and Splits 46
  2.4 The Use and Omission of Clause Connectors 50
  2.5 Same-Subject and Different-Subject Constructions 55
  2.6 Zipf's Law of Abbreviation 57
  2.7 Phonetic Reduction and Enhancement 61
  2.8 Conclusions 65

3 Efficiency and the Order of Meaningful Elements 66
  3.1 Efficient Order 66
  3.2 Factors Determining Efficiency of Order 66
  3.3 Cross-Linguistic Manifestations of Efficient Order 76
  3.4 Star Wars and Violations of Conventional Word Order 90
  3.5 Conclusions 93

Contents

4	**Other Ways of Saving Effort**	**95**
4.1	Efficiency Beyond Coding Length and Word Order	95
4.2	Preference for Accessible Units and Interpretations	95
4.3	Analytic Support	97
4.4	*Horror Aequi*, or Avoidance of Identity	100
4.5	Entry Place for New Referents	102
4.6	Conclusions	103

Part II Efficiency and Language Evolution — 105

5	**Emergence of Efficient Language Patterns**	**107**
5.1	Changes Leading to Efficient Patterns	107
5.2	Efficiency-Driven Formal Reduction	109
5.3	Efficiency-Driven Formal Enhancement	111
5.4	Causal Models of Formal Reduction and Enhancement	118
5.5	Suppletion, Compositionality and the Competition of Meanings for Forms	128
5.6	Word Order Optimization	130
5.7	A Note on Teleology	132
5.8	Conclusions	134
6	**From Trade-Offs to Causal Networks**	**136**
6.1	Trade-Offs in Linguistics	136
6.2	Problems with Trade-Offs	139
6.3	From the Trade-Off between Case Marking and Word Order to a Multivariate Causal Network	144
6.4	Conclusions	151

Part III Case Studies — 153

7	**Efficient Form–Meaning Mapping in Causative Constructions**	**155**
7.1	The Causative Continuum	155
7.2	More Than Just Direct and Indirect Causation	161
7.3	Competition between Formal Parameters	175
7.4	Diachronic Evidence	182
7.5	An Artificial Language Learning Experiment	187
7.6	Conclusions	191
8	**Differential Case Marking and Efficiency**	**193**
8.1	Differential Case Marking	193
8.2	Cross-Linguistic Generalizations Related to Differential Case Marking	195
8.3	Explanations of Differential Case Marking	203
8.4	Reverse Engineering: Cross-Linguistic Generalizations and Corpus Data	208
8.5	Development of Differential Case Marking	223
8.6	Experimental Evidence from Artificial Languages	226
8.7	Conclusions	228
9	**Efficient Use of Function Words in English Alternations**	**230**
9.1	Construction–Filler Predictability and Efficiency	230
9.2	Stay *(at) Home*, Save Lives!	232

9.3	Efficient Use of *Help (to)* Infinitive	234
9.4	Alternation *Go (and)* Verb	240
9.5	Conclusions	244
10	Conclusions and Perspectives	245

Appendices 250
Appendix 1 List of Languages in the Typological Sample Used in Chapter 7 — 251
Appendix 2 Corpus Frequencies of Different A and P from Previous Studies Used in Chapter 8 — 253
References 256
Index 288

Figures

1.1	A hierarchy of benefits in linguistic communication	*page* 10
1.2	Different types of costs in linguistic communication	10
2.1	Spearman's rank correlation coefficients between word length and self-information, and between word length and contextual informativity	59
3.1	A sentence with crossing dependencies, according to the Universal Dependencies style	86
3.2	Proportions of nominal objects (horizontal axis) and pronominal objects (vertical axis) after verbs in the Universal Dependencies corpora	90
5.1	A pragmatic causal model of language change	119
5.2	A causal model of language change based on Zipf's Rational Artisan	123
5.3	A causal model of language change based on Bybee's usage-based approach	127
6.1	A Pareto frontier based on imaginary data with two different costs	137
6.2	A causal graph showing relationships between clarity, ease and context in communication	140
6.3	A graph displaying causal relationships between four types of cues	149
7.1	Percentage of the total number of causative situations in corpora of three languages	170
7.2	A conditional inference tree for French	172
7.3	Fragments of a video clip used in the experiment	189
7.4	Counts of short and long causative forms in the responses	190
8.1	Probabilities of different features of A based on corpora of spontaneous conversations in five languages	219
8.2	Probabilities of different features of P based on corpora of spontaneous conversations in five languages	220

8.3	Probabilities of the role A given different features based on corpora of spontaneous conversations in five languages	221
8.4	Proportions of marked object forms produced by different pairs of participants in the online communication game	228
9.1	Effect of informativity on the chances of *go and* Verb vs. *go* Verb, based on a Generalized Additive Model	243

Tables

5.1	Different properties of language use and change	*page* 133
7.1	Correlation between formal compactness and semantic and syntactic parameters according to Dixon (2000)	161
7.2	Different types of causation in the typological sample, the meaning of the less compact form	164
7.3	Semantic variables used in the study based on the parallel corpus	171
7.4	Variables participating in splits that separate analytic from lexical causatives	173
7.5	Variables participating in splits that separate morphological from lexical causatives	173
7.6	Variables participating in splits that separate analytic from morphological causatives	174
7.7	Formal parameters associated with (in)directness of causation: number of contrasting pairs	180
8.1	Cross-linguistic distribution of differential transitive subject marking in AUTOTYP 0.1	199
8.2	Cross-linguistic distribution of differential object marking in AUTOTYP 0.1	200
8.3	Number of languages that fit (violate) the scales in the cross-linguistic differential and optional marking database	202
8.4	Reverse-engineered predictions for the distribution of features of A and P in discourse	211
8.5	Distribution of features of A (transitive subjects) within the role	214
8.6	Distribution of features of P within the role	216
8.7	Distribution of the roles within the features (only A shown)	217
8.8	Reverse-engineered predictions and the data	222
9.1	Frequency and informativity of the top twelve verbs most frequently used with locative *(at) home*	234

9.2 Frequencies of different subschemata of the construction with *help*	239
9.3 Spearman's coefficients representing partial correlations between the proportions of *to*-infinitives and the informativity measures	240

Preface

This book is a result of two anachronisms. The first one is the old German tradition of writing a postdoctoral thesis. It is part of the habilitation process, which enables a researcher to become a professor. This intention has not materialized yet, but I really enjoyed the process itself when I was writing my habilitation thesis back in 2018. I found that the large format allowed me to put together many different things that I have been thinking about, so I decided to develop the thesis into something better and more comprehensive. And then suddenly came the second anachronism, the pandemic of the dangerous virus, which has been plaguing us since 2020. Never had I thought that such a thing would be possible in the twenty-first century. The shutdown, however, did have the proverbial silver lining, giving me the time and mental space necessary for thinking about the big picture.

Of course, a book may also be an anachronism these days, when important debates happen on Twitter or Facebook. I really hope we are not there yet, but for those who do not have time to read the whole text, the individual chapters should be sufficiently accessible. Some of them provide overviews of specific types of efficiency, while others are centred around a well-known linguistic phenomenon, such as causative constructions or differential case marking.

Thanks to my unconventional career path, or rather, stochastic Markov chain, I have had an opportunity to pursue different research directions and learn about different theories and methods from typology, functional and cognitive linguistics, psycholinguistics, neuroscience and corpus linguistics. I hope that this collection of findings from diverse disciplines will be useful to researchers from different frameworks and backgrounds, and will inspire more (and better) interdisciplinary research in language sciences.

Acknowledgements

An African proverb says, 'It takes a village to raise a child.' To paraphrase, it takes a research community to do science. This book is inspired by encounters with many brilliant people, face-to-face and more recently on Zoom. I could not possibly do justice to all of them here, to my colleagues and ex-colleagues in Leipzig, Nijmegen and around the world. Still, I must mention Martin Haspelmath, whose generous intellectual and practical support enabled me to start with this project when I was working in his Leipzig lab in 2016–2019. My work on this book has continued at the Max Planck Institute for Psycholinguistics in Nijmegen, where I have been working since 2019. I am particularly grateful to Peter Hagoort, the head of the Neurobiology of Language Department, who has given me a chance to learn about psycholinguistics and neuroscience, which are indispensable for efficiency research, in a very friendly and intellectually stimulating environment.

I have also learned a lot from my interactions with such experts on efficiency and closely related topics as Mira Ariel, Gertraud Fenk-Oczlon, Martin Haspelmath, John Hawkins, members and ex-members of Ted Gibson's lab at the MIT, and many, many others. My special thanks go to all colleagues in the Language in Interaction Consortium, who have helped me to understand better the cognitive processes involved in human communication. Of course, all mistakes in this book are solely mine.

Financially, this research was possible thanks to the European Research Council (ERC) under the European Union's Horizon 2020 research and innovation programme (grant agreement No. 670985) and later thanks to the Dutch Research Foundation NWO (Gravitation grant Language in Interaction, grant number 024.001.006).

I also want to thank my husband Björn for his unfailing faith in me and also for supporting me in my attempts to keep *mens sana in corpore sano*, which has been especially important and challenging in these strange times.

Abbreviations

1	1st person
2	2nd person
3	3rd person
1+2	1st person plural inclusive
A	grammatical role corresponding to the Agent
ABS	absolutive
ACC	accusative
AGT	agentive
ART	article
ASP	aspect
CAUS	causative
CONV	converb
DAT	dative
DEC/INF	declarative informal
DEF	definite
DIM	diminutive
DIR	directional
ERG	ergative
EXP	experiential aspectual particle
F	feminine
FOC	focus
FUT	future
GEN	genitive
IM.P	immediate past
IND	indicative
INF	infinitive
INTR	intransitive
LOC	locative
M	masculine
NAR	narrative
NOM	nominative
NPST	non-past

OBJ	object
Q	question particle
P	grammatical role corresponding to the Patient
ℙ	probability
PART	particle
PERF	perfect
PFV	perfective
PL	plural
POSS	possessive
PRES	present
PRO	pronoun
PST	past
REC.P	recent past
S	grammatical role corresponding to the intransitive Subject (in ergative languages)
SBJ	subject
SBJV	subjunctive
SFP	sentence-final particle
SG	singular
SUP	supine
TNS	tense
TR	transitive

Part I

Different Types of Efficiency in Language

1 Communicative Efficiency
Main Concepts

1.1 What Is Communicative Efficiency?

Generally speaking, efficiency means minimization of a cost-to-benefit ratio. In other words, being efficient means not spending more effort than necessary in order to achieve something. This idea is popular nowadays. We are taught to work smarter, not harder. We are advised to keep only things and human contacts that are meaningful to us. We are expected to practise time management and use energy-efficient cars and gadgets.

Efficiency is an inherent property of living organisms. It is a product of biological evolution. Individuals who behave efficiently will be more fit and ultimately will leave more copies of their genes (Ha 2010). There is plenty of evidence that humans and other animals behave efficiently in foraging, parental investment, cooperation and sibling rivalry. For example, the kinematic paths of motion of humans minimize the energy costs of movement (Anderson and Pandy 2001). Penguins waddle because it conserves energy. If they did not, this would result in more work being required from the muscles (Griffin and Kram 2000). Zach (1979) found efficient foraging behaviour in Northwestern crows, who feed on whelks (sea snails) by dropping them from a height in order to break them. The birds preferred the largest whelks, which have a higher caloric content and broke more readily than medium and small ones. Since ascending flight was energetically expensive, the crows minimized the total amount of ascending flight required for breaking whelks by choosing the optimal height of drop. As a result, they achieved a large positive difference between the amount of calories gained from whelks and the amount of calories spent flying.

But efficiency is not only a result of biological evolution. It also comes with practice. For example, professional runners position their heels in such a way as to lower metabolic energy consumption (Scholz et al. 2008; see also Napoli and Liapis 2019). Since language is a very old and frequent human activity, we have had many opportunities to optimize it, both in phylogeny and ontogeny.

Human language as such can be regarded as a very efficient tool because it helps us to save time and effort when we need something from others.

Language has created huge benefits for us as a species, allowing us to build large and complex societies and cope with many challenges. At the same time, we tend to save our articulatory and processing effort while using language. For example, during the COVID-19 pandemic, people all over the world started using abbreviated names for *coronavirus*. The clipped form *corona* is particularly popular, being used in many languages, such as Bengali, Hebrew, Indonesian, Malayalam and Romanian. In Dutch, as well as in German, Danish and Swedish, *corona* is particularly frequent in compounds. The Dutch, for example, speak about *coronapatiënten* 'corona-patients', *coronadoden* 'corona-deaths' and *coronatests*. They must adhere to *coronaregels* 'corona-rules' and deal with the *coronacrisis*. In short, we are living in the *coronatijd* 'corona-time' at the moment. Speakers of Australian English are probably the champions in least effort. They have come up with a radically shortened form, *rona*. One would say, *I'm in iso [self-isolation] because of rona*.[1]

Moreover, we are aware of our tendency to save effort. We can even use it as an excuse. For example, at one meeting Donald Trump called Tim Cook, the Apple CEO, 'Tim Apple'. After the media started making fun of his gaffe, Trump posted a message on Twitter, saying that he had been trying to 'save time & words':

At a recent round table meeting of business executives, & long after formally introducing Tim Cook of Apple, I quickly referred to Tim + Apple as Tim/Apple as an easy way to save time & words. The Fake News was disparagingly all over this, & it became yet another bad Trump story! Donald J. Trump (@realDonaldTrump) 11 March 2019

Thus, efficiency is an important aspect of language communication. But it is not easy to study. Unfortunately, it is impossible to tell exactly how efficient a particular utterance is in a specific context. The reason is that we cannot measure all costs and all benefits of communication (see more in Section 1.2). Instead, we can compare alternative expressions that convey similar meanings and say which one is more costly, and which is less. In many situations the speaker[2] can choose between expressions of different length. Some examples are given in (1). In (1a), one can use the lexical causative *stop* or the periphrastic causative *get X to stop*. Example (1b) illustrates the use of different referential expressions: the longer proper name *Jennifer*, and the shorter pronominal form *she*. In (1c), the difference between the sentences is

---

[1] I thank Peter Austin for this example. See more information in the MPI TalkLing blog: www.mpi-talkling.mpi.nl/?p=36&lang=en (last access 4 June 2022).

[2] In this book I discuss mostly spoken languages. Still, I expect the general principles and strategies of efficient spoken or written communication to be applicable in many cases of signed communication (but see Section 1.3). To what extent this working hypothesis holds is a question for future research.

1.1 What Is Communicative Efficiency?

in the use or absence of the complementizer *that*. In (1d), the speaker can choose between the clipped form *maths* and the full form *mathematics*. The example in (1e) contrasts the analytic and synthetic comparative forms of adjectives, which can sometimes be used interchangeably in English. The example in (1f) illustrates variation in pronunciation of *I don't know*. The variants differ in the total length, the presence or absence of the pronominal subject and amount of articulatory detail. The example in (1g) is an instance of the genitive alternation, where the Saxon genitive with *-'s* is shorter than the Norman genitive with *of* and also allows for omission of some determiners.

(1)   a.   *John **stopped** the car. – John **got** the car **to stop**.*
        b.   ***Jennifer** entered the room. – **She** entered the room.*
        c.   *She believes you are here. – She believes **that** you are here.*
        d.   *I'm studying **maths**. – I'm studying **mathematics**.*
        e.   *Ann is **cleverer** than Mary. – Ann is **more clever** than Mary.*
        f.   *Dunno [dəˈnəʊ]. – I don't know [aɪ dəʊn(t) ˈnəʊ].*
        g.   *the emperor**'s** family – the family **of the** emperor*

In all these pairs, the costs of articulation are lower if the speaker uses the shorter variant. It also costs less time. But the shorter variant is not always the best one. Sometimes one needs to use a more effortful expression in order to make sure that the intended meaning is conveyed. For example, if there is a chance of phonetic misinterpretation, one will use hyperarticulation: *It's not a pin, it's a bin*. Also, when talking to a stranger, a local is unlikely to use an abbreviated variant of a toponym. For example, if a Berliner says *Alex* instead of *Alexanderplatz* when giving directions to a tourist, they are likely to be misunderstood. We speak about efficiency if people use less costly expressions, at the same time conveying the intended meaning. In many cases, this means using shorter forms to convey easily accessible meanings, and longer forms to convey less accessible ones. More examples of such contrasts can be found in Chapter 2.

But efficiency is not only about saving articulation effort and time. Different structures can be more or less efficient from the perspective of language processing. For example, (2) illustrates variation in the order of syntactic constituents. According to some theories, the sentence in (2a), where the short prepositional phrase precedes the long object, requires less processing effort than the sentence in (2b), where the order is reversed. The reason is that (2b) has longer syntactic dependencies, which create higher memory costs. These issues are discussed in detail in Chapter 3.

(2)   a.   *I met [on the street] [my eccentric aunt from San Francisco].*
        b.   *I met [my eccentric aunt from San Francisco] [on the street].*

In the above-mentioned examples, users have choice between more and less costly expressions. Very often, these choices become conventionalized and associated with different meanings, grammatical categories or registers. They become obligatory. A typical example is the singular–plural distinction. Cross-linguistically, singular forms are less often marked formally than plural forms (Greenberg 1966), as illustrated by the pair *book – books* in (3a). In (3b), the shorter form *furniture* has a collective use, whereas the longer form *a piece of furniture* has a singulative meaning. In (3c), the comparative forms of adjectives are more costly than the positive forms.

(3)   a. *(one) book-Ø – (five) book-s*
        b. *furniture – **a piece of** furniture*
        c. *nice – nicer, expensive – **more** expensive.*

Unlike in (1) and (2), the speaker has no choice because the constructions convey different categories and meanings (although one can find languages where number marking is optional, for instance). Still, these asymmetries are efficient because more frequent meanings and categories are expressed by less costly forms. This saves the total amount of effort and time in the long run.

Finally, we can compare the costs of expressions which are not functionally or formally related at all, provided we can also compare their accessibility. According to Zipf's (1965 [1935]) Law of Abbreviation, more frequent words tend to be shorter than less frequent ones. Compare, for example, short and frequent words *I, in* and *be*, with long and rare words *harpsichord, archaeopteryx* and *gongoozle* 'to watch the passage of boats'. Although one can also find many pairs of words in which the frequent member is longer than the rare one (e.g., the word *understand* is more frequent in everyday language than a physics term *quark*, but the former is longer than the latter), any text of sufficient length will yield a significant negative correlation between frequency and length (see Section 2.6).

The idea of minimizing the costs of communication while keeping the benefits has a long tradition in linguistics. In fact, already in the 19th century similar ideas were used to explain the processes of grammaticalization and sound change. For example, Georg Curtius (1820–1985), a German philologist, explained phonetic attrition (*Verwitterung* 'weathering') by the drive to *Bequemlichkeit* 'comfort'. This drive is counterbalanced by the tendency to preserve meaning-bearing sounds and syllables, which resist attrition in order to be recognizable (Delbrück 1919: 143–144). Therefore, language users try to minimize their effort, at the same time making sure that the meanings are conveyed. Similarly, William Dwight Whitney (1875: 69) wrote about the tendency towards ease and economy as a driving force of the process of assimilation. He also mentioned that what is easy to the 'practised speaker' is not necessarily what is easy for second language learners and children, thus pointing to the potential conflict with learnability – another important factor in language evolution.

1.1 What Is Communicative Efficiency?

Zipf not only formulated the Law of Abbreviation (see above), but also contemplated the causes of efficient behaviour. He argued that language users act as rational 'artisans', who follow the Principle of Least Effort (Zipf 1949; see also Section 5.4.2). Among more recent approaches, one can mention the following closely related principles and hypotheses:

- Haiman's (1983) principle of economy;
- Du Bois' (1985) dictum 'Grammars code best what speakers do most';
- Cristofaro's (2003) principle of Information Recoverability;
- Hawkins' (2004) principle 'Minimize Forms';
- Givón's (2017: 157) code–quantity principle;
- Haspelmath's (2021a) form–frequency correspondence hypothesis.

Efficient word order has also received substantial attention. One of the earliest contributions is Behaghel's (1909) law of growing constituents, which says that of two constituents of different length, the longer constituent follows the shorter one. This provides advantages both for production and comprehension. Later, Yngwe (1960) wrote about efficient word orders generated by a formal language model, which put less demands on working memory. Hawkins (2014) formulated the principles 'Minimize Domains' and 'Maximize On-line Processing'. One manifestation of word order efficiency which has received a lot of attention recently is so-called dependency distance minimization (Ferrer-i-Cancho 2006; Liu 2008; Futrell, Mahowald and Gibson 2015b; see also Chapter 3).

The speaker's efficient choices are also discussed in pragmatics. In particular, they are captured by some of the Gricean and Neo-Gricean principles, maxims and heuristics (Grice 1975; Horn 1984; Levinson 2000), as will be shown in Section 1.4. I should also mention here Keller's hypermaxim 'Talk in such a way that you are socially successful, at the lowest possible cost' and maxim 'Talk in such a way that you do not spend more energy than you need to attain your goal' (Keller 1994: 107).

In the recent decades, these and similar ideas have been tested on large and typologically diverse corpora with the help of advanced quantitative methods (see Levshina and Moran 2021 for an overview). Examples are phonological studies of language production, focusing on duration of words and articulation or omission of certain sounds (e.g., Cohen Priva 2008; Bell et al. 2009; Seyfarth 2014), use and omission of optional grammatical markers, such as complementizers or relativizers (e.g., Jaeger 2006; Wasow, Jaeger and Orr 2011), or the above-mentioned dependency distances. In addition to corpora, we can rely on other methods, such as computational modelling, artificial language learning, communication games and traditional psycholinguistic experiments. In many studies, an important role is played by information theory (cf. Gibson et al. 2019).

All this wealth of ideas and evidence requires systematization and explanation, as well as some critical re-evaluation. In particular, the following questions require an answer:

- What are the different costs and benefits in language communication?
- What efficient linguistic strategies are there?
- What are the pragmatic and cognitive mechanisms of efficient linguistic behaviour for the speaker and the addressee?
- How do efficient conventionalized linguistic form–meaning pairings develop?

This book addresses these questions and provides many examples of efficient linguistic structures and patterns of use. Note that we will only speak here about communicative efficiency, that is, minimization of the cost-to-benefit ratio in language use, and leave out other possible types of efficiency in language (e.g., learning efficiency).

1.2 Benefits and Costs in Communication

1.2.1 Types of Benefits

If efficiency is minimization of a costs-to-benefits ratio, what are the costs and benefits of using language? We will begin with benefits. Surprisingly, they are rarely discussed in the literature on communicative efficiency.

Speaking very generally, the ultimate goal of all our activities as an organism is survival. For this purpose, we need to collaborate with some people and compete with others. This involves influencing other people, so that they give us some material goods, help us, attack our rivals or simply leave us alone. We also benefit from useful information that we request and obtain because it helps us to adjust our behaviour and adapt to the environment better. These are the benefits of communication in a very broad sense.

Following Relevance Theory (Sperber and Wilson 1995; Wilson and Sperber 2004), we can also speak of benefits as positive cognitive (or contextual) effects for the addressee. Positive cognitive effects are worthwhile differences between the old (before communication) and new (after communication) representation of the world. They represent new conclusions based on the utterance and context, but also strengthening, revisions and abandonment of already available assumptions. Cognitive effects are similar to updating of prior beliefs in Bayesian inference. Human cognition is geared towards maximizing cognitive effects (Sperber and Wilson 1995). The changes in beliefs correspond to diverse cognitive processes in the addressee: learning new information or confirming previous beliefs about the world, bonding with the speaker, deciding to perform an action, empathizing with the speaker, enjoying the style or accepting new linguistic conventions. These diverse processes illustrate Jakobson's referential, phatic, conative, emotive, poetic and metalingual functions of language use (Jakobson 1971 [1960]). Importantly, cognitive effects and the resulting processes represent benefits not only for the addressee but also for the speaker, who is interested in evoking them.

In order to evoke desired cognitive effects in the addressee, the speaker needs to ensure that the linguistic units and their functions (that is, lexical meanings, grammatical categories, roles and other information) are transferred more or less successfully. Using Relevance-Theoretic parlance, we can say that successful communication requires a recovery of what is explicitly said, or explicatures. This information is obtained by a combination of decoding and inference, with the help of such operations as reference resolution, semantic narrowing, loosening, speech act identification and others. Explicatures form the basis for recovery of implicated premises and conclusions, which represent cognitive effects for the addressee.

Of course, this is an idealization. We do not always recover all units and all meanings; nor do we need to. First of all, communication happens in a noisy channel, using Shannon's terminology (1948). Faithful transfer of linguistic units can fail due to physical impediments (e.g., speaking in a crowded pub) or processing difficulties (e.g., see F. Ferreira [2003] on 'good-enough' processing of sentences). Our language seems to be protected against noise by redundancy (cf. Hengeveld and Leufkens 2018), which means that not all units must be transferred perfectly. At the same time, it is obvious that linguistic units must be of some use for communicators. If we speak about the grammatical function of a case marker, for instance, we assume that this meaning helps the addressee to understand who did what to whom, even if this information can be partly inferred from other linguistic cues (e.g., lexical or semantic properties of the arguments). The working hypothesis is that human languages develop and retain conventionalized cues because these cues are normally useful for evoking cognitive effects.

The benefits, from more specific to very general ones, are displayed in Figure 1.1. We will assume that in most cases the transfer of linguistic units is successful, helping the addressee to obtain intended cognitive effects and adjust their own behaviour, as a result. From the speaker's perspective, triggering desirable cognitive effects in the addressee helps to influence the addressee's behaviour in a useful way. Finally, influencing other people's behaviour or adjusting one's own increases the chances of the language user's survival as a living organism.

1.2.2 Types of Costs

Communication costs have received more attention than benefits in the literature. They can be classified into several types, as shown in Figure 1.2. First of all, we can speak about costs related to the effort involved in communication. Two major types are processing and articulation (including sign languages) or

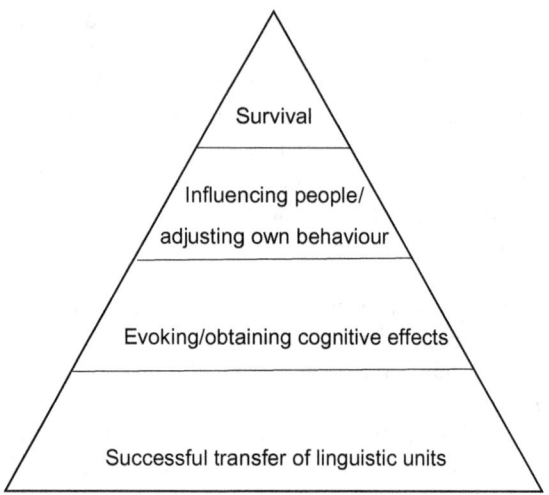

Figure 1.1 A hierarchy of benefits in linguistic communication

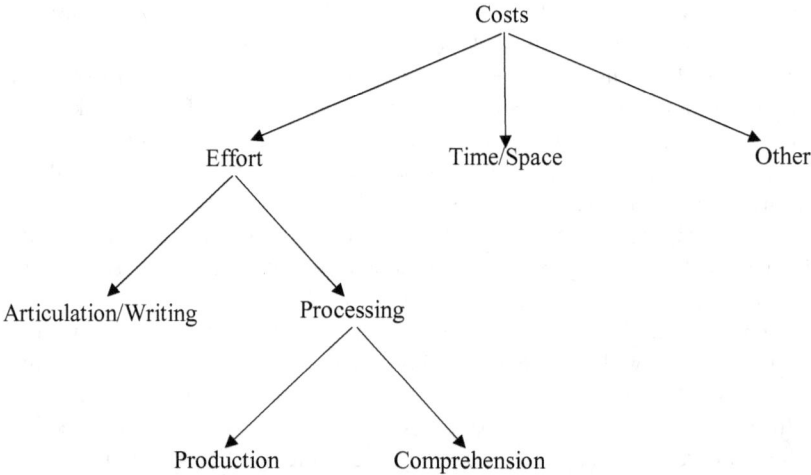

Figure 1.2 Different types of costs in linguistic communication

writing. Processing costs are associated with different cognitive processes required for language comprehension and production.

Time (or space in writing) is another type of cost. According to V. Ferreira (2008), speakers have the responsibility not only to say things their addressees can understand, but also to say things quickly. Similarly, Clark's (1996) 'temporal imperative' says that speakers need to use time in the conversations wisely and responsibly. Since articulation takes time, these costs usually go together. However, there are situations in which time has an independent value. An important aspect of efficient use of time has to do with word order. Speakers tend to produce first the constituents that are more accessible. Accessibility is influenced by a range of factors, including frequency, givenness and animacy. By producing accessible material first, the speaker buys time for planning less accessible units (see more in Section 3.2.2).

Most studies of efficiency focus on the amount of effort and time, but other costs can be important, too. For example, poor communication can have severe social consequences, including loss of face, ruined reputation and broken relationships. Politicians know this all too well. For example, when the current US President Joe Biden once said, *I'm Irish but not stupid*, many Irish people were not amused. Why? The use of *but* signals that the speaker thinks that both he and the addressee are familiar with the cultural stereotype that Irish people are generally stupid. From that, it is easy to conclude that Biden actually thinks that his audience shares the stereotypical belief that the Irish are stupid.

It is difficult to measure social costs, but there are ways of quantifying the degree of miscommunication with the help of information theory. For example, Kemp, Xu and Regier (2018) operationalize what they call communicative costs as the difference between the speaker's and the addressee's probability distributions over referents that can be represented by a certain referential expression. See more on this approach in Chapter 6.

Social costs are closely related to effort. Misunderstanding can lead to additional articulation costs and loss of time, from a simple repair in a dialogue to extensive explanations and press releases. Articulatory and social costs can also be in conflict, as one can see in the current debate about the use of feminitives in German. In particular, the masculine plural form of nouns referring to human beings is considered ambiguous in the sense that it is not clear whether it names men only or both men and women. For example, *die Kollegen* 'the colleagues' and *die Lehrer* 'the teachers' can be interpreted in both ways. In order to be gender-inclusive, avoiding the male-only interpretation, it is considered appropriate by many people to use these forms along with the plural feminine forms, e.g., *Kolleginnen und Kollegen* 'colleagues (female) and colleagues (male)'. This can lead to very long forms, especially if there are attributes. For example, in a job advertisement, one would write something like this:

(4) *Wir suchen ein-e erfahren-e Buchhalter-in*
 We search ART-F.ACC experienced-F.SG.ACC accountant-F
 / ein-en erfahren-en Buchhalter.
 ART-M.ACC experienced-M.ACC accountant
 'We are looking for an experienced accountant (male or female).'

In this example, the costs of writing and space are particularly high.

There have been attempts to make the forms gender-inclusive but more compact. For example, one can use the so-called *Gendernstern* 'gender-star', an asterisk followed by the feminitive suffix, as in *Lehrer*innen* 'teachers (male or female)'. Alternatively, one can use a gap or a slash, e.g., *Lehrer_innen* and *Lehrer/innen*. Also, the suffix can be written with a capital -I-: *LehrerInnen*. In order to reflect this in spoken language, the feminitive suffix is separated by a glottal stop. It is also possible to avoid gendered nouns with the help of passive constructions, relative clauses or participles, e.g., *Studierende* 'the ones who study' instead of *Studenten und Studentinnen* 'students (male and female)'.[3] The attempts to make the German language more gender-equal with the help of these forms are a matter of heated debate.

Another negative correlation between social costs and articulation costs is associated with politeness and etiquette. Commonly, expressions that are appropriate in formal situations are long. For example, in Japanese, when asking someone for a favour, one says *yoroshiku onegaiitashimasu* in very formal situations, *yoroshiku onegaishimasu* in less formal situations, and simply *yoroshiku* when speaking to one's friends. Similarly, formal and distant V-forms are often longer than informal and intimate T-forms, e.g., French *vous parlez* vs. *tu parles*, Russian *ty znaeš* 'you.SG know.IPF.PRES.2SG' vs. *vy znaete* 'you.PL know.IPF.PRES.2PL'. If one uses the form that is shorter than required, one will save articulation costs but risk substantial social costs.

Let us now turn to articulation costs, which play a major role in studies of efficiency. Unfortunately, the current state of research does not allow us to measure articulation costs precisely (ideally, in calories or other units of energy). Usually, their estimations are based on the number of phonological segments, or even letters. This is not unproblematic, of course. While in contrasts like *cat* vs. *crocodile* or *cat – cats*, the latter wordform is obviously more costly than the former, it is easy to find less clear cases. For example, take the wordform *cups* [kʌps] with four segments, which include a short vowel and voiceless consonants, and *calm* [kɑːm], which has three segments, but a long vowel and a sonorant. Which one is more costly (cf. Martinet 1963: 169)? The costs associated with stress and pitch are still waiting for a more precise estimation, as well.

Articulation effort is not a property of spoken languages only. It also includes kinematic effort in sign languages and gesture communication. If a signer moves more joints, this means that they also move greater mass and therefore expend more articulatory effort in comparison with moving fewer joints. Also moving one's shoulders or elbows – that is, joints that are more

---

[3] See www.duden.de/sprachwissen/sprachratgeber/Geschlechtergerechter-Sprachgebrauch (last access 4 July 2022).

proximal to the torso – is more effortful than moving one's wrists or fingers (Napoli, Sanders and Wright 2014).

As pointed out by Levinson (2000: 28), human speech encoding is the slowest stage in human communication, due to the physiological constraints on articulation. It also consumes muscular energy. All other aspects of speech production and comprehension can run at a much higher rate, including inference. So,

inference is cheap, articulation expensive, and thus the design requirements are for a system that maximizes inference. (Levinson 2000: 29)

But this does not mean that processing comes at zero costs. In order to measure processing costs, we can use different behavioural and neural indicators. For example, extra effort in language production can be accompanied by disfluency markers (e.g., *um*, *eh*) and longer planning times (Beattie and Butterworth 1979). Another kind of effort marker is speech errors, such as blends, e.g., 'Don't shell so loud', where *shell* is a blend of *shout* and *yell* (Hockett 1967). These reflect difficulties in choosing between lexical items with similar semantic features (Fromkin 1973).

Another important behavioural marker is reaction times. For example, Britt, Ferrara and Mirman (2016) found that language users were fastest to name pictures that only had one appropriate name, slower when selecting among synonymous names (e.g., *gift* and *present*), and slowest when selecting between closely related names, which were near semantic neighbours (e.g., *jam* and *jelly*). This suggests that lexical choice can be costly.

Similarly, production of grammatical structures can be more or less complex. F. Ferreira (1991) showed that it took participants longer to initiate an utterance when sentences were more complex from a syntactic point of view, as measured by the number of nodes in a phrase-structure tree. Also, if a sentence had a syntactically complex subject and a syntactically complex object, speakers tended to pause at the subject–verb phrase boundary. The duration of pauses increased with upcoming complexity.

Another type of production cost is associated with the use of memory. If the speaker has to keep some elements of the utterance in the memory buffer before dispatching them, it will create additional memory costs. More on that follows in Chapter 3.

Processing costs in comprehension can be detected by poor comprehension accuracy, slower reading times and greater activation of brain areas. In particular, one can detect deflections in the EEG (electroencephalogram) signal, which serve as indicators of extra effort in language processing.

An important cause of processing costs is low predictability, which corresponds to low averaged cloze probability in a norming task, or high surprisal (unpredictability) based on *n*-grams (that is, neighbouring words) or more sophisticated neural network models trained on large corpora. More predictable words are pre-activated by previous context. As a result, it is easier to retrieve their lexical information. Words that are less predictable have longer reading times (e.g., Demberg and Keller 2008; Frank and Bod 2011; Smith and Levy 2013; Merkx and Frank 2020; Wilcox et al. 2020). They also trigger a deflection with greater amplitude in EEG in comparison with predictable words (Frank et al. 2015). This happens approximately 400ms from the onset, which is why this effect is called N400. Units that do not fit semantically or violate our expectations based on encyclopaedic or contextual knowledge generate N400, due to more effortful unification of the unit with the context (see Baggio and Hagoort 2011 for an overview).

A different type of neural response is called P600. This represents a positive deflection reaching its peak around 600 milliseconds after presentation of the stimulus. This effect is associated with syntactic reanalysis, and in particular with garden-path sentences. Osterhout, Holcomb and Swinney (1994), for instance, observed a P600-effect in response to sentences like 'The lawyer charged the defendant was ...', in contrast to 'The lawyer charged that the defendant was ...'. Similarly, a positivity between 300 and 600ms post onset was observed in sentences that required a reversal of the thematic ordering between the arguments (Bornkessel, Schlesewsky and Friederici 2003). Another trigger of P600 is syntactic anomaly, e.g., an error in subject–verb agreement or word category, such as noun and verb (Hagoort, Brown and Groothusen 1993). At the same time, one should be aware that readers do not always engage in reinterpretation of the input. They are often satisfied with shallow and incomplete interpretations (Ferreira 2003). This approach is known as 'good-enough' processing, which can be considered efficient because it saves processing effort, and works just fine in most cases.

Memory costs play an important role in comprehension. The addressee often needs to store in the memory parts of the input that may be integrated later with upcoming units (Gibson 1998, 2000). Compare (5a) and (5b). The sentences contain the same words and meaning. However, (5a) does not represent a problem for processing, whereas (5b) is unprocessable for most people. The reason is that the memory load is too heavy (Gibson and Warren 2004; Grodner and Gibson 2005; Bartek et al. 2011). See more in Section 3.2.1.

(5)   a. [The intern [who [the nurse supervised]] had bothered the administrator [who [lost the medical reports]]].
           b. # The administrator [who [the intern [who [the nurse supervised]] had bothered]] lost the medical reports.

There is evidence showing that pragmatic processing can be costly. In particular, comprehension of intended ironic meanings caused processing costs during late phases of processing indicated by P600 in Regel's (2009) study.

An example of a target sentence in German is *Das ist ja großartig* 'That's great!', which was used in either ironic or literal sense. Interpretation of irony requires suppression of some aspects of the literal meaning, and computation of the intended meaning, which involves contextual information and speakers' communicative intentions. As shown by Bašnáková et al. (2014), processing of indirect speech acts requires activation of several brain regions usually responsible for mentalizing and empathy and for discourse-level language processing.

At the same time, the literal interpretation is not always the most accessible. For example, Giora, Givoni and Fein (2015) show that negative understatements of the type *He is not the smartest president* in Hebrew are processed faster than negative literal utterances (e.g., *He is not the smartest president. John Adams was the smartest one*), as well as affirmative sarcastic utterances (e.g., *He is the smartest president. So don't use any difficult words when talking to him*). In fact, in the absence of any context, negative sentences *X is not the most Y* are by default interpreted sarcastically (e.g., 'He is stupid'), which means that they should be treated as constructions – that is, conventionalized form–meaning pairings (Goldberg 1995).

Of course, human language involves many other costs. In particular, the costs of learning a linguistic system can play an important role in explaining why human languages are the way they are. These costs are beyond the scope of this book. Also, we will focus mostly on articulation, time and processing costs because they have been investigated in greater detail.

1.2.3 Cooperation or Selfish Behaviour?

An important question is whether the speaker and the addressee each try to minimize their individual costs or they both minimize their joint costs in a collaborative effort. There is a long tradition of regarding communication as a conflict of the speaker's and the addressee's interests. In particular, Zipf (1949) wrote about them as opposing forces. The interests of the speaker are represented by the force of unification. The speaker 'has the job of not only selecting the meanings to be conveyed but also the words that will convey them' (Zipf 1949: 20). The highest economy for the speaker would be if the vocabulary consisted of only one word that would mean anything the speaker wanted to mean. There would be no effort to acquire and maintain a large vocabulary and to select the words with a particular meaning from that vocabulary. In contrast, the addressee is interested in diversification, that is, having a distinct word for each meaning to be verbalized. A popular view is that the speaker's and the addressee's efforts represent a trade-off. As V. Ferreira puts it,

A speaker can expend little effort when constructing an utterance ('the thing'), leaving much of the burden for understanding to their listener. Or, speakers can work harder ('the red Honda on your left'), leaving less work for their addressees. (Ferreira 2008: 209)

At the same time, it is obvious that participants are forced to cooperate. If speakers are too 'stingy', they will not get their message across and fail to reach their goals. Alternatively, the speaker will have to produce a repair, which will result in even more effort in total. So, it is in the best interest of the speaker to make life not too difficult for the addressee.

Another question is, how costly is ambiguity? According to available experimental evidence, lexical ambiguity represents a challenge for processing in the absence of disambiguating information. During natural reading, the duration of fixation times has been shown to be longer for ambiguous words compared with unambiguous controls (Frazier and Rayner 1990). Also, EEG studies with word-by-word presentation reveal a sustained frontal negativity for ambiguous words presented in a semantically neutral context compared with unambiguous words (Hagoort and Brown 1994). These findings show that processing of ambiguous words is more effortful than processing of monosemous words, which supports Zipf's ideas. However, there are no clear indications that ambiguity is costly in normal language use, where contextual disambiguating information is usually abundant (see also Section 6.2.1):

what is surprising ... is not that people *sometimes* [my emphasis] experience difficulty with ambiguity, but that they experience difficulty so rarely. (MacKay 1987: 133)

In other words, ambiguity as a threat to communication is overrated (Wasow 2015). We become aware of it only in jokes, as in the examples below.

(6)   a. *Call me a taxi! – OK, you're a taxi.*
        b. *Time flies like an arrow, fruit flies like a banana.*
        c. *How do you make a turtle fast? Take away his food.*

Similarly, syntactic ambiguity is sometimes presented as evidence that the speaker's interests are more important than the addressee's. In particular, V. Ferreira and Dell (2000) had their participants produce sentences as in (7):

(7)   a. *The coach knew (that) I missed practice.*
        b. *The coach knew (that) you missed practice.*

If the speakers took seriously the addressee's needs, they would avoid creating garden-path sentences in contexts like (7b), where the pronoun *you* could be first understood as the direct object of *knew*, by using the complementizer *that* more often than in the unambiguous (7a). However, this is not what the participants did. The omission rate of *that* was nearly identical in the potentially ambiguous and unambiguous contexts (see similar results in Jaeger 2010).

Notably, when Ferreira and Dell (2000) compared the rates of *that*-omission in different sentences exemplified in (8), they found that the participants omitted

1.2 Benefits and Costs in Communication

that more often when the subject of the embedded clause was coreferential with the subject of the main clause and therefore more accessible, as in (8a) and (8d), in comparison with the different-subject sentences in (8b) and (8c).

(8)   a. *I knew (that) I would miss the flight.*
        b. *I knew (that) you would miss the flight.*
        c. *You knew (that) I would miss the flight.*
        d. *You knew (that) you would miss the flight*

Again, disambiguation pressure did not play any role. Note that (8d) with the sequence *You knew you* was unlikely to be interpreted as a transitive clause because one would then use the reflexive pronoun for the coreferential object, *You knew yourself*, so the only potentially ambiguous sentence was (8b), but this difference did not play any role. One can conclude that the grammatical encoding process works in a speaker-centred rather than addressee-centred way. As argued by V. Ferreira (2008), there is a division of labour between the speaker and the addressee. The former takes care of minimizing time, the costs of formulation and articulation, whereas the latter is supposed to do the rest.

The experimental task involved sentence recall without actual communication, so it is difficult to interpret the results in favour or against the addressee-centred linguistic behaviour, in the first place. Another problem is that ambiguity is understood as the existence of several possible interpretations disregarding language users' expectations based on the context. But, as argued above, we can perfectly manage ambiguous words and structures if there is enough context. In the examples from Ferreira and Dell, the chances that *you* can be interpreted as a direct object of *knew* are in fact very small. A search for the sequence *knew you* in a segment of the spoken subcorpus from the Corpus of Contemporary American English (COCA, Davies 2008–) reveals that contexts where *you* is the subject of a complement clause are five times more frequent than contexts with *you* as the direct object of *knew*. So, there are few reasons, if any, to provide additional marking in order to avoid the interpretation of *you* as a direct object.[4]

In fact, ambiguity is highly beneficial both for the speaker and the addressee. First of all, it is advantageous for the speaker to save articulatory effort by using shorter words. Since short words are limited, ambiguity provides a convenient way to minimize the costs without jeopardizing message transfer very seriously, thanks to rich contextual cues (Piantadosi, Tily and Gibson

---

[4] In their post hoc analyses, Ferreira and Dell took into account the probability of different verbs to be followed by a complement clause or a direct object, but found no consistent correlations between those probabilities and the use or omission of *that*. Their findings are contradicted by more recent multifactorial analyses in Jaeger (2010); see also Section 2.4.2.

2012; see also Section 6.2.1). Moreover, using ambiguous but short words and constructions helps the addressee to save time, too.

It is likely that 'participants in a contribution try to minimise the total effort spent on that contribution – in both the presentation and acceptance phases' (Clark and Schaefer 1989: 269). This is known as the Principle of Least Collaborative Effort (see also Clark and Wilkes-Gibbs 1986). There are some indications that this is indeed true. For example, there is no immediate benefit for the addressee to say *yeah*, *mm-hm,* nod or even systematically blink when listening to the speaker (so-called backchannel communication). But this is what hearers do all the time, signalling to the speaker 'I'm here with you, please continue' (Hömke, Holler and Levinson 2017). If there are problems, they quickly ask for repair (e.g., *huh*?), which means 'I'm not with you, please don't continue.' All these costs, however, seem to save everyone's effort in the long run.[5] Without these signals, the speaker does not know if they are on the right track and runs the risk of spending a considerable amount of time and effort in vain. Constant feedback is essential.

So, is communication a cooperative action or selfish behaviour? The most likely answer is 'both'. The speaker and the addressee cooperate because it is in their best interests.

1.3 How to Be Efficient?

In this book I argue that we use language efficiently, trying to minimize the cost-to-benefit ratio of communication. But how to achieve this in practice? First of all, the speaker can save time and effort by not expressing irrelevant information that will not produce useful cognitive effects. An example is the deletion of the agent in passive sentences and the patient in anti-passive sentences. This strategy is so natural that we hardly ever think about it. It only becomes obvious when the speaker violates it by providing information that is irrelevant, for example, to distract or confuse the interlocutor. Experienced politicians are very good at creating a smokescreen in order not to answer difficult questions directly.

Another efficient strategy is to save costs by omitting information that is highly accessible, available, predictable, expected, typical, and so on. In this book I will use the term **accessibility**, in order to highlight the role of the cognitive state of the speaker and the addressee in efficient language use. Accessibility reflects the ease with which some mental representations or forms can be activated in or retrieved from memory (Bock 1982; Bock and Warren 1985). If a mental representation or a form is highly accessible, it is

---

[5] I thank Mark Dingemanse (p.c.) for drawing my attention to the important role of these small but ubiquitous interactive signals in efficient communication.

1.3 How to Be Efficient?

either activated in discourse, or it can be easy to access due to high frequency, salience, relatedness to the activated information, etc. The notions of activation and accessibility are closely related. If some information has low accessibility, it is normally not activated. But accessibility is not reducible to activation. For example, Bill Gates is accessible as a referent because he is famous, but he was not activated in the context before this sentence.

The notion of accessibility has been successfully used for explaining why some referential expressions are long (e.g., *the old schoolteacher*) and others are short (e.g., *she*) in Accessibility Theory (Ariel 1990, 2001). According to Ariel, more informative, less ambiguous and longer forms help to identify less accessible referents. Accessibility of referents has been shown to depend on a variety of factors, including recency of mention in discourse, topicality, syntactic role, the presence of competing referents, and others (see Section 2.2.1).

In addition to length differences, accessibility has been argued to affect the order of syntactic constituents. Different flavours of accessibility – conceptual, lexical, semantic and phonological – are important in this regard. For example, referents that are more accessible due to their previous mention or high imaginability tend to appear before less accessible ones (cf. Bock and Irwin 1980; Bock 1982; Bock and Warren 1985; see also Section 3.2.2). Factors including animacy, concreteness, shortness and discourse-givenness play an important role in the choice between near-synonymous constructions, e.g., particle placement, the English double-object vs. prepositional dative constructions, and the active–passive alternation (Weiner and Labov 1983; Gries 2003; Bresnan et al. 2007). Different parameters of accessibility usually overlap (e.g., *she* normally refers to a discourse-given and animate referent, and is also a highly frequent and short wordform, which is easy to retrieve), but they often have independent effects on language production (e.g., Bresnan et al. 2007).

In Relevance Theory (Sperber and Wilson 1995), accessibility is a property of the contextual assumptions needed for recovery of the intended meaning. The more frequently a certain assumption is used for inference, the greater its accessibility. For example, for an average European, stereotypical assumptions like 'Germans love rules' or 'Italians talk with their hands', which are often used in jokes, are probably more accessible than stereotypes describing Canadians or New Zealanders. Also, the fewer steps one has to take in order to get from the immediate context to certain information for deriving cognitive effects, the higher the accessibility of this information.

In this book, the term 'accessibility' will be used in a broad sense, covering diverse kinds of intended information: referents, lexical and grammatical meanings, syntactic functions, connotations, and so on. I believe that the observed manifestations of efficiency in different areas of linguistics have more in common than has been acknowledged so far, and that we can speak of accessibility asymmetries in phonology, lexicon, morphology and syntax, which are correlated with different levels of costs.

In many cases, accessibility can be measured quantitatively, although the measures may vary from one case to another. For example, Haspelmath (2021a) uses the relative frequencies of contrasting grammatical meanings (e.g., singular and plural) to explain many efficient formal asymmetries (see Section 2.3). Accessibility (or rather, inaccessibility) can also be discussed in terms of surprisal, or informativity, which are popular in studies taking an information-theoretic perspective on efficiency (e.g., Cohen Priva 2008; Levy 2008; Piantadosi, Tily and Gibson 2011; Seyfarth 2014). These measures are often estimated with the help of n-gram frequencies in large corpora, or, more recently, with the help of neural network models, which often show higher correlations with measures of brain activity and human behaviour in language processing than simpler n-gram models (e.g., Heilbron et al. 2019). There is substantial evidence that informativity is correlated with formal length (see Chapter 2).

Crucially, accessibility depends on common ground. For example, in studies of the production of referential expressions in a joint activity, speakers rely on the knowledge that they believe they share with the addressee. In particular, Clark and Marshall (1981) speak about three possible sources of common knowledge:

- preceding linguistic context;
- beliefs about the communities the speaker and the addressee belong to (see also Isaacs and Clark 1987);
- particular interaction, physical context, common past experience.

Common ground plays a vital role in minimization of effort. For example, in a director-matcher experiment where the participants had to describe irregular geometric shapes (tangrams), speakers used short referential expressions more often in the subsequent interactions than in the very beginning (Clark and Wilkes-Gibbs 1986).

While the effects of situational and linguistic context on the formal properties of linguistic expressions have been studied extensively, there is less research that focuses on the role of encyclopaedic knowledge as a factor that influences accessibility. There are attempts to quantify our knowledge of everyday scenarios and scripts, such as eating at a restaurant or cooking food (Venhuizen, Crocker and Brouwer 2019), but this information is still not easy to obtain for every situation.

A popular idea in the literature on communicative efficiency is that an efficient speaker will provide information at a constant rate. This hypothesis was first formulated by Fenk and Fenk (1980), who argued that an efficient communication system should distribute the information (understood in an information-theoretic sense and measured in bits) as uniformly as possible across small time spans. More recent formulations are known as the Smooth Signal Redundancy Hypothesis (Aylett and Turk 2004) and the Uniform Information Density Hypothesis (Jaeger 2006; Levy and Jaeger 2007). In a noisy communication channel like language, efficiency is maximized when the rate of information is distributed as uniformly as possible throughout an utterance. Crucially, it should not be distributed too densely for perception, because that would lead to a breakdown in communication. But it also should not be distributed too sparsely because that would result in a waste of time.

This claim is supported by positive correlations between informativity (the opposite of contextual predictability) and duration or orthographic length of linguistic units. For example, Aylett and Turk (2004) show an inverse relationship between surprisal of a syllable and its duration. However, it is more challenging to test the uniformity of information carried by more complex meaningful units, such as words or syntactic constituents. In some studies of grammatical variation, it has been shown that language users tend to add optional function words to avoid a peak in surprisal when the upcoming word or construction is not very predictable from previous context (Jaeger 2006; Levy and Jaeger 2007; Jaeger 2010), or omit function words in predictable contexts (e.g., Bouma 2016). Yet the correlations between informativity and length can also be interpreted by the tendency to spend less effort and time on more accessible information, and more effort and time on less accessible information. In a similar vein, Ferrer-i-Cancho (2017) argues that uniform information density and similar principles are not needed to explain the correlation between length and informativity: the principle of compression (that is, minimization of coding length in bits) in standard information theory will perfectly suffice.

Moreover, there is not much direct evidence showing that information is indeed distributed uniformly across time. A noteworthy exception is the study by Coupé et al. (2019). Using spoken corpora of seventeen diverse languages, they show that languages have similar information rates (approximately 39 bits per second), which is computed on the basis of information per syllable and speech rate (number of syllables per second). This evidence supports the idea that there is a certain optimal quantity of information per second, which is advantageous under communicative pressure and can probably be explained by neurobiological constraints. To what extent this can be extrapolated to units that express lexical and grammatical meanings is an open question.

At the same time, there are some indications that language users tend to avoid processing overload. For example, human languages have restrictions related to the number of new referents that need to be integrated into discourse (Du Bois 1987). One of the restrictions is that a clause should contain at most only one new referent that needs to be integrated into discourse (see more in Section 4.5). So, language users may indeed be sensitive to having too much new and inaccessible information. When the cognitive load is too high, processing can break down, and the interlocutors will have to start anew, which means higher total costs.

Similarly, language users can decrease processing effort by putting semantically and syntactically related linguistic units next to each other, thereby avoiding the costs of storing and integrating long dependencies. This also helps to avoid high surprisal (another cost component) because if one word is strongly associated with its neighbours, its surprisal is low. Also, language users tend to produce accessible information as early as possible, which helps to save time needed for planning of less accessible elements. Examples are discussed in Chapter 3.

Even poetry contains relatively accessible words, contrary to what one might expect. An empirical study of Russian poetry and prose revealed that surprisal of words in poetry and prose is surprisingly close (Manin 2012). Poetry has indeed less conventional lexical choices and word order than prose, but the choice of the next word in verse is restricted by metric, rhythmical and other formal constrains. As any person with some experience in writing verse should know, it is often very difficult to find a good replacement for a word in a poem. Even avant-garde poetry is more formally constrained than prose. This suggests that there is a certain level of accessibility that needs to be reached for communication to be comfortable for all participants.

To summarize, we can formulate the following principles for an efficient communicator:

- the principle of positive correlation between benefits and costs, which means that language users should spend more effort and time on information that provides more benefits, and less effort and time on less useful information. If information is useless, no effort and time should be spent;
- the principle of negative correlation between accessibility and costs, which means that language users should spend less effort and time on highly accessible information, and more effort and time on less accessible information;
- the principle of maximization of accessibility, which tells language users to maximize accessibility of information at every point in communication.

The principles interact. For example, if the principle of maximization of accessibility fails, e.g., due to the choice of a particular word order, this will lead to higher articulation costs according to the principle of negative correlation between accessibility and costs. The first principle is more important than the other two. For instance, a message should be informative enough to justify the time and articulation costs needed for articulating it (the first principle).

This is why the message still has to be somewhat surprising, despite the pressure to maximize accessibility (the third principle). Also, if some information is not accessible but useless, such information will be omitted, contrary to the second principle, which posits negative correlation between accessibility and costs. An example is omission of some arguments, as in agentless passives (see more in Section 2.2.1).

The strategies formulated above are mostly based on available data from spoken languages. Signed languages can have their own ways of being efficient. Importantly, signers can represent information about different referents and their actions sequentially or simultaneously, whereas speakers have to arrange the elements only sequentially. For example, if one needs to encode 'A woman is holding a child', a signer can do it sequentially, by using lexical units for 'woman', 'hold' and 'child'. Alternatively, it is possible to express this event simultaneously by using a specific head direction, face expression and eye-gaze directed to an imaginary child, at the same time bending the arm and hand, as if holding the child. According to Slonimska, Özyürek and Capirci (2020), simultaneous encoding of complex events helps to reduce the cognitive load. Semantically related information is represented simultaneously, which is analogous to dependency length minimization and similar principles of efficient order in spoken languages (see Chapter 3). As a result, the working memory costs are minimized, as well as the time needed for encoding the event.

Notably, there is evidence that the use of gesture with speech can reduce processing costs in spoken communication. For example, Goldin-Meadow et al. (2001) asked children to solve a maths problem. The children were then given a list of unrelated items to remember while explaining how they solved the problem. It turned out that the children did better on a memory task when they gestured while explaining their solution than when they were told not to gesture. This means that gesturing lightened working memory. How different channels of communication and their costs interact is an open question which requires further investigation.

1.4 Three Principles of Efficient Communication

1.4.1 The Principle of Positive Correlation between Benefits and Costs

This section discusses the principles of efficient communication formulated above in more detail. According to the first principle, benefits and costs should be positively correlated: high costs are associated with high benefits, and low costs are associated with low benefits. On the low-cost, low-benefit side, this idea is similar to Givón's principle 'Unimportant information need not be mentioned' (2017: 3). For example, if one uses a passive construction with an explicit agent, as in (9a), we can assume that the information about the agent (*a moped gang*) plays a certain role in the story. The addressee will probably expect the speaker to discuss a new form of street crime. If the speaker mentions the object of the crime (*his Rolex watch*), as in (9b), the addressee may think that the speaker wants to talk about the careless victim, who wore an expensive watch while travelling. Finally, if the location *near the police station* is mentioned, as in (9c), the addressee is likely to conclude that the speaker will complain how daring criminals have become.

(9)   a. *A tourist was robbed by a moped gang.*
            b. *A tourist was robbed of his Rolex watch.*
            c. *A tourist was robbed near the police station.*

The idea is similar to a recommendation that is often attributed to Anton Chekhov, a famous Russian playwright and writer: 'If in the first act you have hung a pistol on the wall, then in the following one it should be fired. Otherwise, don't put it there.' If the audience in a theatre see a pistol hanging on the wall, they will expect that it will be used later in the play. Similarly, if the speaker introduces a new piece of information, the addressee will expect it to play a part in the story.

This principle is closely related to Grice's Maxims of Quantity, 'Make your contribution as informative as required (for the current purposes of the exchange)', and 'Do not make your contribution more informative than is required' (Grice 1975: 45), as well as to Horn's (1984) Q-principle: 'say as much as you can', and the R-principle: 'say no more than you must'.

At the same time, there may be cultural reasons for omitting some information. In particular, some arguments of a verb can be omitted because they are taboo, or out of politeness. Examples are provided in Section 2.2.1.

In some communicative situations, the costs can be higher than normal. This usually happens in communication where the primary focus is on the form, rather than on the content, of the message. Consider performance dance, a non-linguistic form of communication. In performance dance, the movements are enhanced, not reduced, which creates greater metabolic costs for performers, but gives the audience extra aesthetic pleasure (Napoli and Liapis 2019). Therefore, the high costs are justified by the high benefits.

1.4.2 *The Principle of Negative Correlation between Accessibility and Costs*

This principle reflects the tendency to use shorter forms to express more predictable, expected, typical, etc. meanings, and longer forms to express less predictable, expected, typical, etc. meanings. Numerous examples are given in Chapter 2.

The principle is somewhat similar to the supermaxim of Manner in Grice (1975), which says, 'Be perspicuous'. It is related to how something is said (not to 'what is said'), and includes several submaxims: 'Avoid obscurity of expression', 'Avoid ambiguity', 'Be brief (avoid unnecessary prolixity)' and 'Be orderly' (Grice 1975: 46). If we interpret ambiguity as lack of accessibility of a single interpretation due to insufficient linguistic cues and context, and unnecessary prolixity as using costly expressions for transfer of highly accessible information, we can see that Grice's supermaxim of Manner subsumes the principle of negative correlation between accessibility and costs.

Probably more directly relevant, however, is the account proposed by Levinson (2000) because it involves the notion of typicality, which can be directly linked to accessibility. One of Levinson's main principles is called the I-heuristic: 'What is expressed simply is stereotypically exemplified' (Levinson 2000: 37). Consider the following example:

(10) John: *I cut a finger*

Under normal circumstances, this utterance communicates that the finger belongs to John, although this information is not encoded in the sentence. This is an instance of generalized conversational implicatures, which can be triggered normally (in the absence of special circumstances) by the use of certain forms in an utterance (Grice 1975). If the finger belongs to someone else, a longer expression will be used (e.g., *I cut my brother's finger*). We are speaking about an implicature here because it still depends on the context. One can imagine a situation where the most natural interpretation could be that John cut someone else's finger. That would be the case, for instance, if John were a manicurist speaking to his colleague (Levinson 2000: 17).

Another example is implicated gender. For example, *a nurse* implicates 'a female nurse' because female nurses are the norm in many countries.[6] If one speaks about male nurses, one often adds the adjective, as in the following scene from the film *Meet the Parents* (2000) with Ben Stiller and Robert de Niro:

(11) Jack Byrnes: *Is your name Gaylord Focker, yes or no?*
      Greg Focker: *Yes.*
      Jack Byrnes: *Are you a male nurse?*
      Greg Focker: *Yes.*

Also, English nominal compounds, which are formally 'lean', tend to have highly accessible interpretations. For example, *a bread knife* is a knife for cutting bread, *a steel knife* is a knife made of steel, and *a kitchen knife* is a knife used in the kitchen. When the intended interpretation is less accessible, a longer expression is used. For instance, one can speak of a *knife made of ice* when the interpretation of material is intended, rather than of an *ice knife*, which normally represents a tool for cutting and carving ice (cf. Hawkins 2004: 47).

---

[6] See the statistics at https://realmanswork.wordpress.com/2012/05/05/male-nurses-worldwide/ (last access 5 July 2022).

From the efficiency perspective, I-implicatures can be accounted for by the principle of negative correlation between accessibility and costs. In the examples above, there is a default interpretation which involves some typical relationship or scenario. The intended interpretation has the highest accessibility given the linguistic cue. For example, female nurses constitute the overwhelming majority of the entire population of nurses, a fact known both to the addressee and the speaker.

Levinson also formulated the Q-heuristic: 'What isn't said, isn't' (Levinson 2000: 35). This means, in other words, that the lack of extra information or a stronger statement is informative. The Q-heuristic helps the speaker to spare effort because it enables them to omit additional restrictions. In Examples (12) and (13), the (a) version, where this principle is exploited, is shorter than the (b) version, which the speaker would need to produce if language users could not rely on the Q-heuristic.

(12)   a. *Her dress was red.*
        ($\rightarrow$ not red and blue or red and any other colour)
       b. *Her dress was red, and only red.*

(13)   a. *I've eaten some chocolates.*
        ($\rightarrow$ not all).
       b. *I've eaten some chocolates, but not all.*

The knowledge required for inferring these implicatures is the knowledge of the existing alternative expressions, such as 'red and X' for (12a), where X stands for any other colour, and 'all' for (13a). The addressee derives the implicatures because they understand that the more informative expressions are not selected (Levinson 2000: 40–41). The examples in (b) can also be motivated by the principle of positive correlation between benefits and costs. In particular, (12b) and (13b) can be efficient if the speaker wants to override the addressee's false belief that the dress was in different colours, or that all chocolates were eaten. Cancelling old beliefs and creating new ones implies greater cognitive effects, which justifies the higher costs.

Finally, Levinson also formulated the M-heuristic. In the short version, it is expressed as follows: 'What's said in an abnormal way isn't normal' (Levinson 2000: 38). There is also a longer version, which may be somewhat easier to understand:

(14)   The M-heuristic

       Speaker's maxim: Indicate an abnormal, nonstereotypical situation by using marked expressions that contrast with those you would use to describe the corresponding normal, stereotypical situation.

       Recipient's corollary: What is said in an abnormal way indicates an abnormal situation, or marked messages indicate marked situations.
       (Levinson 2000: 136)

1.4 Three Principles of Efficient Communication

Consider some examples, where both I- and M-implicatures are present:

(15)   a. *Sue smiled.*
           (I-implicature → Sue produced a nice happy expression.)
     b. *The corners of Sue's lips turned slightly upward.*
           (M-implicature → Sue produced a smirk or grimace).

Another pair of examples illustrates the contrast between forms like *go to school* and *go to the school*, which involves highly conventionalized inferences:

(16)   a. *She went to school/church/university/bed/hospital/sea/town ...*
           (Conventionalized I-implicatures → She went to do the stereotypical activity associated with this location.)
     b. *She went to the school/church/university/bed/hospital/sea/town ...*
           (M-implicatures → She went to the place, but not necessarily to do the associated stereotypical activity).

Other examples of the contrast between more typical and less typical expressions which involve implicatures of stereotypical and non-stereotypical situations, include litotes (e.g., *happy* vs. *not unhappy*, where the latter implicates 'less than happy'), lexicalized forms of periphrasis (*pink* vs. *pale red*, i.e., an untypical pink), nominal compounds (e.g., *a matchbox* vs. *a box for matches*, i.e., an untypical one), some prepositions (e.g., *on the table* vs. *on top of the table*). Another well-known case is the contrast between lexical and analytic causatives, as in the example below:

(17)   a. *Susan stopped the car.*
           (I-implicature → in the usual way, i.e., by putting her foot on the brake pedal).
     b. *Susan got the car to stop.*
           (M-implicature → in an unusual way, e.g., by using the emergency brake or crashing into a lamppost).

The notion of markedness is not unproblematic, though. Marked forms are more morphologically complex and less lexicalized than the corresponding unmarked forms; they are also more prolix or periphrastic, less frequent, or less neutral stylistically. One can see that these are very diverse features (cf. Fenk-Oczlon 1991, 2001; Haspelmath 2006). As far as the meaning is concerned, marked forms imply some additional meaning or connotation absent from the corresponding unmarked forms (Levinson 2000: 137).

Thus, we can also regard M-implicatures as inferences based on the principle of negative correlation between accessibility and costs. When confronted with a costly form, the addressee chooses the less accessible interpretation.

For an M-implicature to be derived, it is crucial to have a conventionalized typical expression. If a periphrastic causative does not have a corresponding lexical causative, the implicature of doing something unusual does not emerge, according to Levinson. For example, the expression *make someone laugh* does not generate such an implicature because English has no lexical causative with a similar meaning (McCawley 1978: 250). It is an open question whether language users are likely to evaluate the meaning of *make someone laugh* as having low accessibility, even if they do not consider the causation unusual or strange. A more detailed discussion of causative constructions can be found in Chapter 7 of this book.

1.4.3 The Principle of Maximization of Accessibility

Finally, the principle of maximization of accessibility reflects the tendency to minimize processing effort by producing accessible (given, salient, frequent, etc.) meanings and forms early in the sentence, by putting semantically and syntactically related words next to each other, or by integrating referents in discourse by linking them with previous information. This helps to minimize processing costs related to surprisal and memory (Futrell and Levy 2017). Therefore, the addressee can expect that at each point in discourse, the information presented next will be maximally accessible given the rules of grammar, unless this is in conflict with the principle of negative correlation between accessibility and costs.

The principle corresponds closely to V. Ferreira and Dell's (2000) Principle of Immediate Mention, which is driven by the pressure of producing fluent speech efficiently. According to this principle, speakers tend to choose syntactic structures that allow accessible lemmas to be mentioned early. As a result, the speaker buys some time to retrieve the less available material. Similarly, MacDonald (2013) speaks of the Easy First Bias: easily retrieved words and phrases tend to appear earlier in the utterance. Time is an important resource for both the speaker and the addressee. According to the unwritten rules of communication, the speaker is responsible for using time wisely.

Not only can specific words be more or less accessible, but also abstract grammatical structures. Speakers tend to reuse recently executed sentence plans, as one can see from experimental evidence and corpus-based studies of morphosyntactic priming (Pickering and Branigan 1998; Pickering and Ferreira 2008; Szmrecsanyi 2006). With every use, a morphosyntactic plan becomes more likely to be reused in the future. MacDonald (2013) argues that the source of rigid word order lies in the preference for easy, more practised plans of utterances, which is called Plan Reuse. It encourages us to reproduce highly familiar structures. Both principles – Plan Reuse and Easy First – help to optimize language production, the former at the level of abstract schemas, the latter at the level of specific words and phrase elements. Human languages rely on both principles, but the preference for Plan Reuse is stronger in languages with rigid word order and weaker in flexible languages.

1.5 'Good-Enough' Efficiency

Addressees also process language as if they have expectations of maximal accessibility. This can be seen from the following example provided by Gibson (1998):

(18)   *The bartender told the detective that the suspect left the country yesterday.*

The adverb *yesterday* can be linked to two verbs. One candidate is the local verb *left*. The other one is the more distant verb *told*. The local attachment to the verb *left* is strongly preferred. According to Gibson, this preference is explained by the fact that it is less costly to reactivate the verb *left* in the memory than to reactivate the verb *told* when integrating the adverb into the syntactic structure. The reason is that the activation of *left* has decayed less than the activation of the more distant verb *tell*. More information about the costs of syntactic integration is provided in Chapter 3. In the presence of ambiguous parses, the addressee will choose the structure that minimizes the costs of keeping the unit in the memory and reactivating it (in addition to other factors, such as plausibility of an interpretation, usage frequency and others). In other words, the addressee will prefer the most accessible interpretation.

Moreover, the fact that the addressee buys into garden-path sentences like *The horse raced past the barn fell* and other misleading expressions, instead of wisely suspending the choice between possible interpretations until the end of the sentence, suggests that the addressee expects that the speaker will adhere to this principle. These sentences can mislead the addressee exactly because they are different from structures used in everyday communication. The addressee knows from experience that the most accessible interpretation is nearly always correct. The use of such misleading sentences is like a betrayal of this trust (although sentences like these are often produced for humorous effect, so the addressee is in fact rewarded with additional cognitive benefits).

1.5   'Good-Enough' Efficiency

Language users tend to behave efficiently, following the principles formulated in the previous section. But how is this possible? What kind of cognitive processes are involved?

According to the pragmatic theory of Grice (1975) and the more recent Rational Speech Act model (Frank and Goodman 2012), language users behave rationally and cooperatively, and expect the same from their interlocutors. They follow the Cooperative Principle, which says:

Make your contribution such as is required, at the stage at which it occurs, by the accepted purpose or direction of the talk exchange in which you are engaged. (Grice 1975: 45)

In a similar vein, we can also formulate the Principle of Communicative Efficiency:

(19)   The Principle of Communicative Efficiency
        Communicate in such a way as to minimize the cost-to-benefit ratio.

Similar to the Cooperative Principle, the Principle of Communicative Efficiency can be treated as an implicit and mutual assumption shared by interlocutors. The speaker knows that the addressee believes that the speaker behaves efficiently. This is why when using a particular linguistic expression, the speaker will rely on the addressee's ability to interpret this expression in the intended way. In cases when this principle is obviously violated, the addressee can derive inferences that are similar to Gricean implicatures. For example, if one asks a question and gets a completely irrelevant answer (e.g., *Why aren't you married? – Nice weather, isn't it?*), this means that the question was possibly stupid or tactless. The inference is based on the principle of positive correlation between benefits and costs.

In the absence of obvious violations, the addressee can make inferences intended by the speaker, as well. For example, when hearing a message with a certain referential expression, the addressee can engage in pragmatic reasoning of the sort, 'The speaker uses the form F_1 to refer to some referent R_i. There are two referents, R_1 and R_2, that fit this description. The speaker is acting efficiently, and she expects that I know that. The referent R_1 is more accessible than the referent R_2. If she wanted to refer to the less accessible referent R_2, she would be using the more costly form F_2. But she is using the less costly form F_1. Therefore, she should mean R_1'.

I believe that this type of reasoning, which involves complex mental recursion with several levels of embedding, is possible, but infrequent. It is too effortful. The number of phonological, lexical and grammatical choices a language user makes during language production is so large that we will be quickly overwhelmed. Somewhat paradoxically, trying to be maximally efficient is inefficient. Using Daniel Kahneman's (2011) terms, we use 'fast' (that is, sloppy, automatic, stereotypic, unconscious and easy) thinking way more often than 'slow' (deliberate, logical and effortful) thinking. In other words, our rationality is bounded.

I argue that efficient communicative behaviour is usually automatic, unconscious and therefore not very costly from the processing perspective. Language users adhere to simple shortcuts whenever possible, treating the efficient strategies as heuristics, or rules of thumb, similar to Levinson's (2000) heuristics described in Section 1.4.2.

Once successful, efficient linguistic choices are reproduced over and over again, requiring even less effort than previously (cf. Diessel 2019: 37). This kind of recycling is efficient by itself because it saves our effort and produces desired effects most of the time. Communicative efficiency is only 'good enough', like most of our thinking and language processing (cf. Ferreira 2003). Although language users can engage in the recursive reasoning exemplified above, this happens rarely, when the principles of efficient communication are obviously violated, for example.

This view is supported by the results of experiments in Turnbull (2019), who found no consistent relationship between efficient phonetic reduction driven by predictability and individual differences in theory of mind. Individuals with high scores on the autism-spectrum quotient (AQ) questionnaire and low scores on other theory-of-mind tasks did not show less efficient behaviour in language production than participants with greater theory-of-mind abilities. This suggests that theory of mind is unlikely to be strongly involved in efficient management of communication costs, at least, as far as efficient reduction is concerned. However, note that all participants were neurotypical, which leaves open the question how autistic individuals with even weaker theory-of-mind abilities would perform in this respect.

At the same time, there is some empirical evidence that the principles of efficient communication formulated above can trigger pragmatic inferences. For example, the use of more costly forms signals that something unexpected is going on, which needs more attention and effort. In contrast, when less costly forms are chosen, this signals to the addressee 'business as usual', nothing special is going on. In this way, costly and cheap forms can also be seen as tools for attention management, directing the processor's cognitive effort to where it is needed most. Gordon and Chan (1995) showed that reading times increase when a repeated long referential expression is used for a highly accessible referent. Consider the following example:

(20)　　*Susan decided to give Fred a hamster. She/Susan was questioned at length by Fred about what to feed it.*

When the referential expression was longer (*Susan*), the self-paced reading times were longer than when the pronoun *she* was used. The proper name is supposed to introduce a new referent, but this is not the case. The readers get confused, which slows down their reading times. These results indicate that there are certain expectations based on the principle of negative correlation between accessibility and costs.

Similarly, it was demonstrated by Engelhardt, Demiral and Ferreira (2011) that overspecification of referential expressions leads to longer processing times and negativities in the event-related brain potentials (ERP, N400), which usually indicate different types of semantic and syntactic anomalies during language comprehension. For example, a participant in an experiment can see a red star and a red square side by side on the screen. If the participant hears 'Look to the red star', this results in slower reaction times and ERP negativity in comparison with the situation where the participant can see a red star and a blue star. This means that over-descriptions with an unnecessary modifier impair comprehension performance. More information does not mean more clarity.[7]

There is also evidence that uninformative utterances are costly for pragmatically competent language users, as well. For example, processing of trivial sentences like *Some people have lungs* triggered a pragmatic N400 effect (Nieuwland, Ditman and Kuperberg 2010). Although accessible information is normally easier to process, language users expect a certain degree of inaccessibility from their interlocutor if a substantial amount of effort and time is used. Similarly, Rohde, Futrell and Lucas (2021) found shorter self-paced reading times for more newsworthy and informative expressions (e.g., *chopping carrots with a shovel*) in comparison with less newsworthy and informative ones (e.g., *chopping carrots with a knife*).

To summarize, this evidence suggests that language users have certain expectations about the relationships between the accessibility of information and the costs and benefits of its transfer. These expectations may be based on pragmatic reasoning, but it is more likely that they operate in form of simple heuristics, e.g., 'Don't waste time and effort on useless information', or even abstract constructional schemas representing pairings of form (e.g., a proper name) and function (e.g., a low-accessibility referent), which emerge as a result of frequent occurrence in language use.

A related question is how much 'audience design', or adjustment of one's message to take into account the addressee's perspective (Bell 1984), is needed for efficient communication? The evidence is mixed. For example, in an experiment by Isaacs and Clark (1987), pairs of participants were asked to work together to arrange pictures of New York City landmarks by talking about them. Some of the participants knew the city well; others did not. The experiment demonstrated that the participants assessed each other's level of expertise very quickly and automatically, adjusting their choice of descriptions. In particular, the directors, who were describing the pictures, used fewer words on average when the matchers were familiar with the city than when they were not. For example, a director would say 'the Citicorp building' (now 'Citigroup center') to an expert and 'the tall building with the

---

[7] One should be careful when estimating the usefulness (informativeness) of additional cues. For example, if the choice is between a yellow banana and a yellow apple, the description *yellow banana* is overspecified and unlikely to be chosen. But if the participant sees a yellow banana and a red apple, the expression is more informative because the colour helps to identify the referent, as well. Finally, if the picture contains a blue banana and some other fruit, the expression is informative because blue bananas are very untypical and are poor representatives of the category, so using the noun only would not be sufficient (see Degen et al. 2020). So the notion of redundancy is not as simple as it seems at first glance.

1.5 'Good-Enough' Efficiency

triangular top' to a novice. The experts often introduced the proper name after the match. This allowed the novices to become experts, too. As a result, the total number of words decreased in the course of interaction. However, Isaacs and Clark also hypothesize that in more naturalistic settings, where the criteria of success are less stringent than in the experiment, language users would spend less effort by accommodating less and exchanging less expertise.

In some cases, language users take into account the other's perspective, but they do so inconsistently. For example, Vanlangendonck, Willems and Hagoort (2018) investigated situations where the speaker and the listener have access to the same or different information. In their experiment, the speaker described one object from a set of objects shown in a picture, and the listener was supposed to select it. Some objects on the pictures were visible only to the speaker, while some others were visible to both participants. For example, if the speaker saw three glasses, one small, one medium-sized and one large, while the addressee saw only the large and the medium-sized ones, we could expect that the speaker would refer to the medium-sized one as 'a small glass', provided that they took into account the addressee's perspective. The participants indeed chose the pragmatically more felicitous description most of the time, but not always.

Fukumura and van Gompel (2012) investigated if speakers choose pronouns or full noun phrases depending on whether the addressee also heard an immediately preceding sentence that made the target referent more accessible to the addressee. Although in general the proportion of pronominal reference was higher in the shared condition (i.e., when the addressee heard the preceding sentence) than in the privileged condition (i.e., when the addressee did not hear the sentence), as one could expect based on Accessibility Theory (Ariel 1990, 2001; see also Section 2.2.1), the difference was small and did not reach statistical significance. Moreover, this tendency was observed regardless of whether the preceding sentence mentioned the target referent or the competitor. More exactly, the speakers used pronouns slightly more often when the preceding sentence was shared with their addressee than when it was not. However, they did not take into account whether this sentence made the referent or the competitor accessible to the addressee. It is likely that the speakers experienced difficulties combining two types of information: the fact that the sentence was shared with the addressee, and the content of the sentence.

Experimental evidence suggests that the extent to which a speaker engages in audience design, taking into account the addressee's perspective, depends on the cognitive load in a specific task (Pate and Goldwater 2015). If it is low, then the speaker adjusts to the addressee's needs. If it is too high, the speaker fails to do so. If it is in-between, the speaker tries to evaluate the situation and make a choice. For example, speakers can adjust their language to the listener's needs only if they see that the listener is engaged in interaction. This selectivity can be seen as efficient behaviour.

Pate and Goldwater (2015) found that predictability given preceding context affects word durations in adult-directed speech, but not in infant-directed speech. Also, when interlocutors saw each other and could use the visual channel, they used less phonetic redundancy in communication. The conclusion is that language users modulate predictability effects according to very coarse, salient, and easy-to-track characteristics of the addressee and the channel of communication.

It is also possible that the speaker and the addressee evaluate the costs, benefits and accessibility in many situations automatically, based on their own cognitive states rather than the addressee's. This should work well when the speaker and the addressee create common ground in social interaction. Performing joint actions or simply discussing different issues, they align their conceptual representations and even synchronize their neural patterns (Stephens, Silbert and Hasson 2010). This helps to evaluate the accessibility of certain information for the partner correctly and easily. In the absence of such alignment or under cognitive pressure, language users fall back on their previous communicative experience, reproducing linguistic strategies that were previously successful with similar interlocutors or in general.

To summarize, the Gricean behaviour of the speaker and the addressee, involving full-scale pragmatic reasoning for making efficient choices, is possible, but unlikely in most situations of language use. The pragmatic principles described in the previous sections normally operate as heuristics and are likely to become conventionalized. If an efficient strategy is found, it can be recycled in future communication under similar circumstances, leading to 'good-enough' efficiency. The amount of the speaker's effort required for estimating the accessibility of some information for the addressee is restricted by the cognitive resources the speaker has at the given moment.

1.6 Conclusions

This chapter has introduced the main concepts that will be discussed in this book: communicative efficiency, costs, benefits and accessibility. It was also proposed that language users' behaviour is guided by several principles, which explain how they can behave efficiently in everyday communication. The three main principles are as follows: the principle of positive correlation between benefits and costs, the principle of negative correlation between accessibility and costs, and the principle of maximization of accessibility. I also argued that it is unlikely that these principles are normally realized in fully rational behaviour. It is more probable that the principles work as heuristics, or rules of thumb, which operate automatically and unconsciously most of the time, and do not involve full-scale mind reading and perfect audience design. A crucial role is played by previous experience of using language. Successful linguistic choices are recycled again and again.

These concepts and principles will be exemplified in the following chapters, which describe different manifestations of efficiency in language structure and use. In Chapter 2, I will discuss longer and shorter alternative forms which can be used efficiently. The main focus will be on the principle of negative correlation between costs and accessibility. Chapter 3 focuses on efficient order of meaningful elements and deals mostly with the principle of maximization of accessibility. Chapter 4 will show several less frequently discussed types of efficiency, which help to maximize accessibility as well.

2 Efficiency and Formal Length

2.1 Efficient Length Asymmetries

This chapter describes efficient use of linguistic units with different lengths. Length represents articulation costs, but it can also be interpreted as time expenditure. It is difficult to separate articulation costs from time costs. In phonological studies, one often measures the duration of units (e.g., Aylett and Turk 2004), while in studies of lexicon and grammar, which are often based on written corpora, the focus is usually on the number of words, segments or letters (see examples below). Although articulation effort also depends on stress and amount of articulatory detail, which require carefully annotated spoken data, I will focus here on length, which is easier to measure and compare.

As mentioned in Chapter 1, articulation is the slowest and most energy-consuming stage in human communication. The speaker can spare effort and time by omitting or shortening the forms that represent accessible information – that is, the information already available to the addressee, or easily inferable from the context and general knowledge. In contrast, more effort should be spent on information that is less accessible. This behaviour corresponds to the principle of negative correlation between accessibility and costs. We speak of an efficient length asymmetry when there is a negative correlation between formal length and accessibility of information. The sections below illustrate diverse formal asymmetries that display this correlation.

Formal length asymmetries are extremely diverse. Some efficient asymmetries are fully conventionalized, as, for example, zero marking of singular and non-zero marking of plural, e.g., *book – books*. Some asymmetries are context-dependent and require pragmatic inference. For example, when someone says their address to a taxi driver, they in fact exploit the principle of negative correlation between accessibility and costs. An expression like *Park Street, 23, please* is efficient, unlike saying *I need to get to Park Street, house number 23, in this city. I want you to take me there in your cab now and promise to pay you a certain amount of money in return if you get me there.*

The principle of negative correlation between accessibility and costs is also responsible for so-called bridging implicatures. For example, if your friend says, *I bought a new bicycle yesterday. The saddle is very comfortable*, you will understand that the saddle belongs to the bicycle that your friend has bought. You friend relies on your ability to access the knowledge that a typical bicycle has a saddle. This allows your friend to spare effort instead of saying *The saddle of the bicycle I bought yesterday is very comfortable*. This type of efficiency is pervasive in discourse.

Importantly, by opting for a longer or shorter expression, the speaker signals how accessible the intended interpretation is. The length itself represents an instruction for where to search for the interpretation. For example, the pronoun *she*, as discussed in the next section, means that the referent is not only female and singular, but also highly accessible, whereas the definite description *the friend* means not only a 'close acquaintance', but also that the referent has a relatively low degree of accessibility (Ariel 2001: 29). In this sense, every linguistic expression the speaker chooses is also a marker of the accessibility of its interpretation (cf. Ariel 2001). Some marking of this type involves the speaker's choice, as in the referential expressions mentioned above (see Section 2.2), while some is fully conventionalized, as in the obligatory marking of grammatical categories (see Section 2.3). I argue that the emergence and maintenance of obligatory marking follows the same pragmatic principle as the speaker's choice between different coding possibilities in optional marking – namely, the principle of negative correlation between accessibility and costs.

2.2 Accessibility of Referents and Length of Referential Expressions and Markers

2.2.1 *Efficient Use of Referential Expressions: Hierarchy of Explicitness*

An important type of efficient context-dependent asymmetries is observed in referential expressions. One can formulate a hierarchy of explicitness of such expressions (Ariel 1990, 2001; Arnold 2010, see also Givón 1983, 2017), as shown in (1):[1]

(1)   Hierarchy of explicitness:
        Most explicit
                Semantically rich expressions (*the most popular teacher at our school*)
                Shorter nominal expressions (*Ann, the teacher*)
                Pronouns (*she*)
                Zeros
        Least explicit

---

[1] See a more detailed hierarchy in Ariel (1990: 73) and Ariel (2001).

This variation is constrained by the degree of accessibility of mental representations of the referents. The notion of accessibility was introduced in Chapter 1. Highly accessible representations are expressed by shorter forms than less accessible ones. Note that there can be more subtle accessibility distinctions within these broad categories, which cannot be explained by length alone. For example, *James* as a surname can signal lower accessibility than *James* as a first name (Ariel 2001). In Russia, colleagues would refer to me using the full patronymic form *Natalja Gennadievna* in front of the students, and would say *Natasha* when speaking with other colleagues, although the accessibility of me as the referent could be the same. As discussed in Section 1.2.2, social costs often interact with formal length.

The level of accessibility of referents in discourse depends on several factors (Ariel 1990, 2001, 2008; Arnold 2010), which can interact in complex ways (see Ariel 2001). A crucial factor is previous discourse. The referents that have been introduced in discourse have more activated representations than the referents that have not been mentioned. This is why full nouns are typically used to introduce new referents, while pronouns or zeros are usually reserved for the referents already introduced in the discourse. Moreover, the more recent the mention of the referent, the more accessible the mental representation is. For example, Arnold (2010) provides data to show that the chances of pronominal reference decrease with distance from the last mention of the referent (measured in clauses). Paragraphs and episode boundaries also decrease accessibility. A related factor is density of mention. The higher the density of mention of a referent in previous discourse, the more activated its mental representation is and therefore the higher the chances of short (pronominal) expressions (Levy and McNeill 1992). In addition, topical referents are more accessible and therefore expressed by less explicit forms than non-topical ones.

The syntactic function of the referent is another important factor. A referent is more accessible if it has been mentioned previously in the same syntactic function. This parallelism makes it easier for the addressee to identify the referent. This explains why reduced forms are more likely if the referring expression and the previous mention of the referent are in the same syntactic position (Levy and McNeill 1992). Consider an example:

(2)   *Ann invited Sue to the conference.*
    a. *She asked Sue to present her new research on metaphors.*
    b. *Sue asked her to tell more about the event.*

According to Arnold (2010), the preference for the pronoun *she/her* that refers to *Ann* should be stronger in (2a) *She asked Sue...*, than in (2b) *Sue asked her....* . Also, the current thematic role of the referent can be important. For example, Arnold (2001) shows that goals of verbs of transfer, e.g., *give/send/ bring to Sue*, are more frequently referred to by shorter pronominal forms than sources, e.g., *accept/get/borrow from Sue*. Language users also refer more to goal referents than to source referents in discourse, as Arnold's story-telling experiment and corpus analyses reveal. This frequency asymmetry is also observed for inanimate goals and sources (e.g., *to London/the market/a village* is more frequent than *from London/the market/a village*), which accounts for the cross-linguistic differences in the length of marking of goals and sources (Michaelis 2017). The higher probability of goals means their higher accessibility, which explains why they are expressed by shorter forms than sources.

The presence of competing referents in the context decreases accessibility. Tily and Piantadosi (2009) found, in particular, that participants were less likely to guess the upcoming referent correctly if there were many referents in the previous text. Notably, the presence of other referents plays a role even if there is no direct need for disambiguation. For example, Arnold and Griffin (2007) performed an experiment with cartoons, on which the subjects could see either one character or two different-gender characters. The first line of the story was, for example, *Daisy went for a boat ride {with Mickey} on the lake*. Next, the second picture was shown, which displayed one character doing something (e.g., Daisy rowing away). The second character was either present or absent. Participants generated another line for the story (e.g., *Daisy left Mickey behind;* or *She rowed into the sunset*). Interestingly, pronouns were more common in the one-character than two-character stories, despite the obvious fact that there was no risk of confusability, since the characters had different genders. The competition between the characters in the speaker's mental model results in greater cognitive load and, importantly, in lower activation of each referent.

Finally, we should mention the interaction between the speaker and the addressee. Wilkes-Gibbs and Clark (1992) show that descriptive nominal expressions tend to become shorter when the speaker and the hearer develop and expand their common ground – the information they believe they share. Interestingly, even subtle differences in the status of the hearer, e.g., from being able to overhear or watch the previous interactions to being totally new to the scene, determine the amount of coding in the subsequent interaction.

To summarize, the more accessible a referent is due to the immediate context, interaction settings, syntactic role or previous experience with language, the less costly the referential expression will be. As pointed out by Ariel (1990), the choice of the specific form helps the addressee to identify the location of the referent in their mental representation. The use of a shorter variant signals that the referent is accessible. Longer forms signal low accessibility. Section 1.5 discussed experimental evidence showing that processing costs increase if there is a mismatch between the length of a referential expression and the accessibility of the referent. This supports the idea that the pragmatic processes captured by the principle of negative correlation between accessibility and costs play a role in the processing.

As for zero anaphora, different languages have different rules with regard to which constituents can or should be omitted in discourse. Yet, there are a few general tendencies. First, given and topical referents, which are restorable from previous discourse, are more frequently omitted than new and focal ones. In many languages, including Chinese, Japanese, Korean, Hindi, Hungarian and Lao, any given, non-focal argument can be omitted, whereas no language omits focal elements (Goldberg 2005). As defined by Lambrecht (1994: 218), the focus relation relates 'the pragmatically non-recoverable to the recoverable component of a proposition and thereby creates a new state of information in the mind of the addressee'. This is why focal elements need to be overtly expressed.

In Gilligan's (1987) cross-linguistic study, imperative subjects can be omitted in nearly all languages, followed by subjects and then by direct objects. Other constituents (indirect objects, possessive pronouns and adpositional objects) are very rarely omittable. Note that this hierarchy is observed in languages without agreement (see Section 2.2.2). The hierarchy can be explained by the different average levels of accessibility of different arguments. Imperative subjects are easily restorable from the context, and therefore highly accessible. They are followed by other subjects, which are more frequently thematic, given, and therefore more accessible than objects (Lambrecht 1994: 262; see also Chapter 8). Some languages display variation within a specific argument. For example, in Ancient Greek, it was natural to omit definite objects if they were highly accessible (Luraghi 2003). Notably, their omission depended on the degree of conventionalization and grammaticalization of the information helping the addressee to access the object referent. In highly grammaticalized constructions with conjunct participles,[2] object omission was obligatory. It was also common in coordinated clauses, followed by answers to yes–no questions. In other cases, omission was discourse-conditioned and optional. It affected highly accessible topical objects.

The examples of obligatory zero arguments demonstrate that efficient behaviour motivated by accessibility of a referent in context can become conventionalized, becoming obligatory. This mechanism is efficient by itself, as it makes language production more automatic and reduces the processing load.

English represents an interesting case as far as zero objects are concerned. Although it generally does not allow for object omission, there are a few lexically specific exceptions (Fillmore 1986). Consider the following contrasts:

- *She won Ø* can be said when the person in question won an election/game/race, but not if she won the gold medal or the first prize.
- *She lost Ø*, again, can be said if she lost some competition, but not if she lost her wallet or keys.

---

[2] The conjunct participle construction consists of one or more participles that depend on another verb form which has the same subject. This construction was very frequent in Ancient Greek.

2.2 Length and Accessibility of Referents

- *We've already eaten Ø* can be said in the situation when we have had a meal, but not when we have eaten something specific.
- *I forgot Ø*, e.g., to fix something, but not if the speaker forgot the keys.

Interestingly, the object cannot be omitted even if it is previously mentioned or clear from the context (e.g., *Where're the keys? I forgot *(them)*).

One might think that abstract entities and events are more commonly omitted than concrete physical objects. However, this is not quite true. If we take verbs of motion with a specific destination or point of departure, the object can be omitted if it is a physical location, and cannot be omitted if it is abstract and metaphorical:

- *She was approaching Ø* (e.g., *the speaker, the town*), but not if *she approached the solution*.
- *She arrived Ø* (e.g., *at the summit*), but not if *she arrived at the answer*.

The elliptical use is supported by conventionalized inferences based on the principle of negative correlation between accessibility and costs. This is obvious in the case of motion verbs, where the interpretation of the physical motion (approaching a location and arriving at a certain place) is the stereotypical interpretation, and the metaphorical extensions (approaching a solution or arriving at an answer) are less accessible. In other cases, the interpretation that allows the ellipsis is on average more probable than the interpretation that does not.

Consider the verb *win*. In a random sample of 100 examples of the verb from the Corpus of Contemporary American English (COCA, Davies 2008–), 90 were instances of *win* as a verb followed by a direct object or used without any complement. The majority of these instances (61) were about winning some competition (elections, sports, social conflicts, etc.), as in (3a). We will call this sense win_1. Only 26 were about winning something for oneself (a prize, confidence, support, more rights, a Senate seat, etc.), as in (3b). This usage will be called win_2. In three instances, it was difficult to classify the examples semantically.

(3)   a. *Everything counts, everything has to be perfect for you to win the game.*
            (COCA, News, Denver, 2005)
     b. *Guess what? You can win a cruise at home as well.*
            (COCA, Spoken, NBC: Today Show, 2017)

The meaning of win_1 (i.e., winning some competition) is more common and therefore more restorable from context than win_2 (i.e., winning some objects or other benefits). Also, the information about winning a competition is often mentioned previously or clear from context. Consider (4a and b):

(4)   a. *If this is a big chess game, did you win or lose?*
            (COCA, Spoken, CBS_48Hours, 2007)
     b. *How are you doing in the polls? How are you going to win in New Hampshire?*
            (COCA, Spoken, CBS_Early, 1999)

So, the information about the competition X wins (win_1) is often accessible. It is discourse-given and topical. In contrast, the information about the prize X wins (win_2) is usually not accessible. It is often focal. This is why the intransitive use of win_2 has not become conventional, even if the object is accessible in a given context, e.g., *Where did he get ten million dollars from? – He won$_2$ *(them) in a lottery*. This example demonstrates how an efficient strategy becomes conventionalized and becomes a categorical grammar rule.

Omission can also be due to reasons different from saving articulation effort or time. For example, taboo objects, such as bodily emissions (spit, piss) are usually omitted for reasons of politeness (from Goldberg 2005):

(5) a. *Pat sneezed (mucus) onto the computer screen.*
     b. *The hopeful man ejaculated (his sperm) into the petri dish.*
     c. *Pat vomited (her lunch) into the sink.*

These are cases of the so-called Implicit Theme Construction (Goldberg 2005). At the same time, the object is highly accessible to the addressee from general knowledge, so its omission helps to save effort, as well.

Next, the object can also be irrelevant if the attention is on the action itself (Goldberg 2005):

(6) a. *Tigers only kill at night.*
     b. *She gave and gave, and he took and took.*

These are instances of the so-called Deprofiled Object Construction (Goldberg 2005). This agrees with Givón's (2017: 3) principle of cataphoric zeros: 'Unimportant information need not be mentioned.' Probably the most famous example of this principle at work is omission of the agent in passive constructions:

(7) *An English tourist was robbed of his Rolex watch (by Ø).*

This type of argument omission is efficient, as well. The speaker does not spend effort on transfer of information that will bring no communicative benefits (see Section 1.4.2).

Goldberg also explains conventionalized habitual uses like *She drinks/ smokes/writes* as a result of such deprofiling of the object, with subsequent lexicalization of the intransitive use. A similar perspective is taken by Givón (2017: 198). Indeed, what is important is that the person in question is an alcoholic, a smoker or a writer.

Although this interpretation is perfectly reasonable, accessibility of the object may also play a role. In particular, Huang (2007: 48–49) classifies uses like *John doesn't drink* in the sense 'John doesn't drink alcohol' as cases of lexical narrowing based on an I-implicature (see Section 1.4.2). Alcohol is a highly accessible interpretation if one is speaking about a habit, as the present simple form suggests. So it can be omitted as a typical object. Similarly, one can say *John smokes*, implying that he smokes tobacco (cigarettes, cigars or a pipe). Smoking other substances would be a less likely interpretation. One might wonder, however, if this inference will be made in a community where other plants are preferred.

Resnik (1996) investigated the use of English verbs with and without objects in corpora and in human subject norms. He also measured selectional preference strength, which reflects the strength of association between the verbs and semantic classes of their objects.[3] The stronger the preference, the more biased a verb is to objects of certain semantic classes. Resnik found that the percentage of omitted objects positively correlated with selectional preference strength. For example, *drink* and *sing* had the highest rates of object omission, as well as the strongest selectional restrictions. In contrast, verbs like *get* and *make* had zero object omission rates and weak selectional restrictions. He concluded that strong selectional restrictions are a necessary condition for object omission. Notably, Glass (2020) does not find strong support for this claim in general-interest conversations on Reddit.[4] However, when the data are taken from specific-interest threads, an interesting pattern emerges: verb objects are more frequently omitted in the communities where they are more strongly associated with a routine. For example, fitness enthusiasts frequently omit the object of the verb *lift* (weights), whereas home-brewers do not mention the object of *bottle* (beer). This demonstrates the importance of social and situational expectations for efficient use and omission of arguments.

It is possible that all the factors mentioned above play a role in determining if the argument can be omitted: its level of accessibility (based on diverse sources), the communicative benefits of naming it, and politeness concerns. The interaction of these factors requires further investigation.

2.2.2 Dependent Forms of Arguments

In addition to the factors discussed in the previous section, argument omission also depends on the presence or absence of agreement. In a cross-linguistic survey by Gilligan (1987: Section 3.4), languages where the verb agrees with a specific argument nearly always allow for omission of that argument. An example is subject agreement in Pashto:

(8)   Pashto: Indo-European (Huang 2007: 142)

        Ø   mana   xwr-əm.
                apple   eat-1.M.SG
        '(I) ate the apple.'

---

[3] More exactly, Resnik computed relative entropy, which measures how much on average the probability of a verb with an object that belongs to a certain semantic class deviates from the reference probability of that semantic class.

[4] Reddit is an American social media site where users post content and discuss it in threads.

Languages without agreement allow pro-drop less frequently. As far as subject expression is concerned, this claim is supported by a recent study by Berdicevskis, Schmidtke-Bode and Seržant (2020), who report that languages that have subject indexation tend to allow for omission of the pronominal subject. They interpret that as evidence for an efficient trade-off: the subject should be coded only once, either as an independent form or as an agreement marker (see a critical evaluation of this claim in Section 6.2.1). There are some indications of a similar trade-off in case of object agreement: some languages (Arabic, Bantu and Iranian) have so-called pro-indexes, which are in complementary distribution with object nominals (Haspelmath 2013a; Haig 2018). In other words, the indexes cannot occur when the object is explicit (although they may occur in the case of dislocated objects). However, object indexing often depends on diverse semantic and pragmatic factors, which are parallel to those relevant for differential case marking of objects (see Chapter 8). This can lead to patterns opposite to pro-indexing.

Consider Ruuli, a Bantu language, which has differential object indexing. In (9), the index *-bu-* corresponds to the noun class of the object (traps).

(9) Ruuli: Bantu (Just and Witzlack-Makarevich, Forthcoming: 2)

Obuterega   o-bu-maite?
trap(14)   2SG.SBJ-14.OBJ-know.PFV
'Do you know these traps?'

The indexing is probabilistic: 1st and 2nd-person, human and given objects are more frequently indexed than 3rd-person, non-human and new ones (Just and Witzlack-Makarevich, Forthcoming). This is efficient because new, indefinite/non-specific, nominal and 3rd-person referents are more likely to be objects than subjects, while given, definite/specific, pronominal and 1st or 2nd-person referents are biased towards the subject role (see the data in Section 8.4). So, arguments with a more accessible interpretation in terms of their grammatical role are less likely to be marked than arguments with a less accessible interpretation.

Another example is Maltese (Just and Čéplö 2019). An object index is always present if the object is pronominal and given, and always absent if it is new and non-specific (in typical VO sentences). Thus, arguments whose grammatical role is less accessible are indexed, and those whose role is more accessible are not. Also, an index is always used in sentences with OV order, which is less typical than VO. By providing an object marker, the speaker helps the addressee to process a sentence with a non-canonical order (see another example in Section 8.3.1).

We can also find efficient patterns at a more general level if we compare different arguments. Siewierska (2004: 43–46) observes a cross-linguistic correlation between the two scales in (10), which describe types of person markers.

(10) a. Scale of phonological reduction/dependence of person markers:
      Zero > Bound > Clitic > Weak
   b. Scale of argument prominence:
      Subject > Direct object/Theme > Indirect object > Oblique

In the vast majority of languages that she examined (89 per cent, to be exact), more phonologically reduced and/or dependent person markers according to the scale in (10a), are used for arguments higher on the argument prominence hierarchy in (10b). Siewierska explains this correlation by the differences in accessibility of typical arguments in different syntactic positions:

since dependent person markers involve less encoding than independent ones, the expectation is that they should be characteristic of syntactic functions which tend to realize highly accessible referents. (Siewierska 2004: 46)

Therefore, we can observe efficient asymmetries both on a global level (between person forms of different arguments), and on the level of specific arguments (as in differential indexing). As we will see below, such 'recursive' organization of efficient patterns is very common.

2.2.3 *Expression of Coreferential Objects*

Coreferentiality allows us to see two types of efficient correlations between accessibility and formal length. First, reflexive pronouns coreferential with the subject are either as long as or longer than corresponding forms with disjoint reference, e.g., English *himself* vs. *him*, Dutch *zich* or *zichzelf* 'him/herself, themselves' vs. *hem* 'him', and Mandarin Chinese (*tā*) *zìjǐ* 'him/herself' vs. *tā* 'him/her' (Haspelmath 2008a). This has to do with the fact that in the overwhelming majority of cases, the subject and the object have disjoint reference (Ariel 2001: 37; Ariel 2008: 218–219). For example, the Book of Genesis in Hebrew contains no direct objects coreferential with their subjects, out of approximately 4,500 clauses. This means that a disjoint reference interpretation of an object is more accessible than a coreferential one, which explains why the corresponding forms are often shorter. A diachronic account of the emergence of reflexive pronouns is offered in Section 5.3.1.

Second, similar to what we saw in the previous section on agreement markers, some languages display efficient asymmetries also at a more local level. There is variation within coreferential uses, which depends on the semantics of the verb. A language can have different coreferential forms for objects of verbs that usually represent self-directed actions, which include grooming verbs (e.g., *wash*, *shave* or *dress*), and for objects of verbs normally representing other-directed actions (e.g., *hate*, *see* or *envy*). Coreferential objects of self-directed verbs tend to have forms that are as long as or shorter than coreferential objects of other-directed verbs (Ariel 2008: Ch. 6;

Haspelmath 2008a). For example, in English it is possible to omit the object when the action is self-directed, e.g., *He shaved and dressed*. In contrast, one cannot omit the object of an other-directed verb, e.g., *He hates himself*. This formal difference is efficient because a coreferential object of a self-directed verb is highly accessible, while a coreferential object of an other-directed verb has low accessibility. The different degrees of accessibility are supported by corpus frequencies (Haspelmath 2008a).

Thus, on the global level, coreferential objects are usually less accessible than objects with disjoint reference. This is why reflexive pronouns are often longer than non-reflexive ones. Moreover, at a local level, coreferential objects of verbs like *wash* are more accessible than coreferential objects of verbs like *hate*, for which disjoint reference is more typical. This is why coreferential objects of verbs like *wash* are shorter than coreferential objects of verbs like *hate*. The multiple layers of efficiency we observe here are similar to global and local markedness patterns and coding splits (Haspelmath's 2021b), which are discussed in the next section.

2.3 Grammatical Coding Asymmetries and Splits

2.3.1 Global Markedness

Grammatical coding asymmetries are observed in members of contrasting grammatical categories that are expressed by markers of different length (Greenberg 1966; Haspelmath 2021a). Below are some examples.

(11) a. singular vs. plural nouns (e.g., *book – books*)
      b. positive vs. comparative and superlative degrees of comparison of adjectives (e.g., *nice – nicer – the nicest*)
      c. cardinal vs. ordinal numerals (e.g., *ten – tenth*)
      d. indicative vs. subjunctive (e.g., *I go – I would go*)
      e. active vs. passive verb forms (*I called X – I was called by X*).

It is a robust cross-linguistic tendency that the first member in these pairs is formally unmarked (or has a shorter marker), whereas the second (and third) one is formally marked (or has a longer marker). These coding asymmetries became important in structuralist linguistics after Roman Jakobson (1971 [1932]) extended the notion of markedness from phonology to grammar. In binary oppositions, the shorter member is considered the unmarked one, whereas the longer one is referred to as marked. The unmarked member appears in neutralization contexts. For instance, in the opposition between singular and plural, as in *cat – cats*, the singular form is used to express the generic meaning, e.g., *The cat is a night wanderer*. Therefore, it is considered unmarked. With time, the notion of markedness has become so broad, being understood as non-naturalness, cognitive complexity, language-specific or cross-linguistic rarity, etc., that it can hardly be considered a useful scientific concept (see Haspelmath 2006). As argued by Fenk-Oczlon (1991, 2001) and later by Haspelmath (2006), markedness phenomena can be reduced to frequency effects, which provide a more parsimonious explanation and a causal mechanism for many interesting facts. For example, the unmarked members in the examples above usually have higher inflectional and syntagmatic potential than the marked members (Croft 2003: Chapter 4). This and other observations can be explained by the fact that the unmarked members are more frequent than the marked ones (some corpus evidence is provided in Greenberg 1966).

Importantly for the efficiency account of these asymmetries, the marked members are usually expressed by longer forms than the unmarked ones. According to Haspelmath, the unmarked categories are more frequent, and therefore, their meaning is more predictable:

Speakers can afford to use short shapes or zero coding for predictable meanings, but they have to make a greater coding effort for unpredictable meaning. (Haspelmath 2021a: 19)

Using the notion of accessibility, we can say that a singular interpretation of a nominal is in general more accessible than a plural one. This allows language users to spare effort when speaking about singular referents. The same logic applies to the other coding asymmetries.

2.3.2 Local Markedness

The examples in (11) illustrated global markedness, where the markedness contrast is the same for all instances of the categories (e.g., singular is unmarked, while plural is marked). Local markedness, in contrast, represents a markedness reversal for some members of the contrasting categories. Tiersma (1982) discussed such exceptions in the paradigm levelling in Frisian and some other languages. Markedness theory predicts that the levelling of paradigmatic alternation will favour the unmarked form. However, as some nouns in Frisian undergo change, the originally 'marked' plural form becomes the basis for the singular form, rather than the 'unmarked' singular. For example, *goes/gwozzen* 'goose/geese' becomes *gwos/gwozzen*. Thus, the plural stem can be seen as unmarked. Tiersma showed that this markedness reversal happened to those nouns that are frequently used in the plural ('arm', 'goose', 'horn', 'stocking', etc.). Some examples from Slavic languages and Bavarian dialects are given in Fenk-Oczlon (1991).

In some cases, the frequency effects can be even stronger and trigger a reversal of the formal marking. There are a few languages, for example, that can have both overt plural marking (e.g., *day – days*) and overt singular marking (e.g., Welsh *pys-en* 'pea' – *pys* 'peas'), depending on the noun. Haspelmath and Karjus (2017) distinguish between 'individualist' nouns, which tend to occur with uniplex meaning, e.g., *day*, and 'gregarious' nouns, which are usually associated with multiplex meaning, e.g., *pea*. Gregarious nouns are often the names of fruits and vegetables, e.g., Russian *kartofel'* 'potatoes (mass noun)' – *kartofelina* 'potato'; small animals, e.g., Welsh *adar* 'birds/flock of birds' – *aderyn* 'bird'; and body parts, e.g., Cushitic *farró* 'fingers' – *farri-t* 'finger'. Corpus data from different languages demonstrate that the nouns that tend to have overt singular cross-linguistically are also predominantly gregarious. That is, they are used in the multiplex sense.

It would be efficient if all languages were like Welsh, marking the plural of individualist nouns and the singular of gregarious nouns. However, this is not what we see in the world's languages. For example, English individualist and gregarious nouns behave similarly, e.g., *day – days, pea – peas, potato – potatoes, bee – bees, eye – eyes*. There is a strong competing factor, namely the systemic pressure, which explains why such efficient strategies are not very frequent cross-linguistically. A system with simpler rules is easier to learn (Haspelmath 2014).

2.3.3 Coding Splits

A famous example of coding splits is differential object marking. If a language formally marks some objects and does not mark others, prominent (e.g., animate and definite) objects tend to be formally marked, while less prominent (inanimate and indefinite) are usually unmarked. Differential object indexing was discussed in Section 2.2.2. Differential case marking of subject and object will be addressed in detail in Chapter 8. In all these cases, languages tend to mark more frequently those arguments for which the interpretation of an object or subject is less accessible given some semantic and pragmatic features or other contextual factors.

Coding splits can also be found in locative marking (Haspelmath 2019). If a language has a split depending on the semantics of locative noun phrases, then place names are likely to be unmarked, inanimates can be either unmarked or marked, and animates tend to be marked. The explanation is that place names represent typical locations, while animates are untypical locations. In other words, the interpretation of a location is the most accessible for place names, and the least accessible for animate beings.

Another example is adnominal possessive constructions, e.g., *John's house* (Haspelmath 2017). In some languages, different possessive constructions are used, depending on whether possession is alienable or

2.3 Grammatical Coding Asymmetries and Splits

inalienable. For example, in Abun, a West Papuan language, there is the following contrast:

(12) Abun: West Papuan (Berry and Berry 1999: 77–82, cited from Haspelmath 2017: 194)
    a. alienable possession
       ji   bi   nggwe
       I   GEN   garden
       'my garden'
    b. inalienable possession
       ji syim
       I arm
       'my arm'

This example illustrates a cross-linguistic tendency for inalienable possession constructions, as in (12b), to have shorter coding than alienable possession constructions, as in (12a). Haspelmath's corpus data demonstrate that entities that are usually inalienable (kinship terms, body parts) more frequently occur in the possessive constructions (e.g., 'my hand', 'his sister') than alienable objects, such as a house, a garden or a knife. In other words, the interpretation of inalienable entities as possessed is more accessible. Since nouns that are more frequently mentioned as possessed objects receive less formal marking than those that are less frequently mentioned as such, this coding split can be regarded as efficient. More details about the diachronic development of such patterns follow in Sections 5.2 and 5.3.3.

Differential marking of Recipient can be found in English. It can be expressed by a zero-marked form in the double-object dative (e.g., *Sue gives her colleague the memory stick*), and by a case-marked form in the prepositional dative (e.g., *Sue gives the memory stick to her colleague*). The two constructions have different word orders, namely, Recipient + Theme in the double-object construction and Theme + Recipient in the prepositional dative (although there can be exceptions, especially in dialects (Hawkins 1994: 214; Gast 2007)). There is substantial evidence that language users switch between the constructions in order to manage the flow of information and optimize processing, as will be shown in Section 3.2.2. For example, Bresnan et al. (2007) show that the double-object construction is preferred when the Recipient is animate, definite, given and pronominal, whereas the Theme is non-given, non-pronominal and indefinite and has a low rank on the animacy hierarchy. The prepositional dative is preferred in the reverse situations (see also Hawkins 1994: 212–214; Goldberg 1995: 91ff). In addition, according to Goldberg (1995: Chapters 5–7), the prepositional dative construction is a metaphorical extension of the caused motion construction 'X causes Z to move to Y' (e.g., *I sent the letter to my parents/to her old address*), while the double-object construction means 'X causes Y to receive Z'. This semantic difference is also supported by the distinctive collexeme analysis in Gries and Stefanowitsch (2004).

Yet, the constructions differ not only with regard to the order of their constituents and semantics, but, crucially, also in the amount of formal coding. Haspelmath (2021b) argues that the shorter variant in alternations is normally used if the referential prominence of arguments corresponds to their roles, while the longer variant is used if there is some deviation from such canonical relationships. In particular, if an argument is animate, given, definite and pronominal, it is more likely to be Recipient than Theme. And conversely, if an argument is inanimate, new, indefinite and nominal, it is more likely to the Theme than Recipient. The features that provide strong cues to the roles (namely, animate, given, definite and pronominal Recipient, and inanimate, new, indefinite and nominal Theme) are associated with the shorter double-object construction, according to the data in Bresnan et al. (2007). Therefore, we can interpret the division of labour between the two dative constructions as an efficient coding split in the marking of Recipient: the construction with more formal coding (that is, the prepositional dative) expresses the less accessible assignment of roles to arguments than the construction with less formal coding (the double-object dative).

Interestingly, the frequency of the *to*-dative rose dramatically in Middle English, when formal marking on verbs and nouns was substantially reduced. Zehentner (2022) uses corpus data to show that the more costly *to*-construction was preferred in contexts with semantically atypical Recipient and Theme – that is, if Recipient is inanimate and/or Theme is animate. These findings can be regarded as support for the idea that the additional marking is used to facilitate a less accessible interpretation.[5]

2.4 The Use and Omission of Clause Connectors

2.4.1 *Omission of Adverbial Clause Connectors*

In Relevance Theory (Sperber and Wilson 1995), an important distinction is made between conceptual (representational) and procedural (computational) information. The former is information about concepts or conceptual representations to be processed, and the latter is information about how to process them (e.g., Blakemore 1987; Wilson and Sperber 1993). For instance, the conjunction *so* plays such a role:

(13) *She's got a PhD, so she'll be able to fill in this form.*

---

[5] In addition, the *to*-dative was also preferred in contexts with morphologically identical Agent and Recipient, but it is not clear at the moment if this effect is due to nominal (and therefore less accessible) caseless Recipients, or a result of ambiguity avoidance, as Zehentner (2022) argues.

2.4 The Use and Omission of Clause Connectors

Such connectors indicate the type of inference process that the addressee is expected to go through. In (13), the connector *so* indicates that the second clause should be interpreted as a conclusion. As Blakemore points out, expressions like *so* contribute to relevance by guiding the addressee towards the intended cognitive effects. In Grice (1975), such inferences, which are associated with specific expressions, are called conventional implicatures. The connector *so* conventionally implicates, according to Grice, that the first clause explains the second. In spite of the differences between the theoretical interpretations, there is one common idea: the speaker guides the addressee's inferential process by providing an instruction about how to process the propositions in the first and second clauses. Other examples of such cues are the connectors *but, and, therefore, on the other hand* and *after all*.

Importantly, connectors can be omitted when the intended inference is expected or easy to make. For example, Blumenthal-Dramé and Kortmann (2017) investigate the use and omission of causal and concessive adverbial connectors *therefore* and *still*, as in the following examples:

(14)   a. *Ann didn't read the essay questions properly and therefore failed the exam last January.*
        b. *Ann didn't read the essay questions properly and failed the exam last January.*
        c. *Peter studied a lot and still failed the exam last January.*
        d. *Peter studied a lot and failed the exam last January.*

It is argued that there is a general tendency for concessive relations to be marked overtly, as in (14c), while causal relations are more often left implicit, as in (14b). The reason is that concessive relationships are more cognitively complex. As a result, implicit concessivity is more disruptive to discourse processing than implicit causality.

Taking the efficiency perspective, we can say that a causal interpretation is generally more accessible in discourse than a concessive one. This claim is supported by the counts from the Penn Discourse Treebank obtained by Asr and Demberg (2012), who also show that causal relations are much more often implicit (62% to 69%, depending on the order of cause and effect) than concessive relations (8% to 19%). Therefore, the omission of a connector signals that the more probable (causal) meaning is intended. In addition, we cannot exclude that humans have a cognitive bias towards establishing causal links between events, even if these events are not causally related, e.g., the logical fallacy *post hoc ergo propter hoc*. If this is true, it makes a causal interpretation more accessible.

2.4.2   Omission of Complementizers and Relativizers

Similar reasoning can be applied to other clause-linking elements, such as complementizers and relativizers. They help the addressee to identify the syntactic and semantic role of elements in discourse. In a language with optional clause-linking elements, the speaker can use them if the function of the clause they introduce is more difficult to identify, and omit them if the function is more accessible. An important role is played by their heads – i.e., nominal phrases and predicates. If they are often followed by a clause, the interpretation is easier to access, which allows the speaker to omit the function word. For instance, as shown by Wasow, Jaeger and Orr (2011), the relativizer *that* in non-subject relative clauses is more likely to be omitted when the nominal phrase is definite (e.g., *the colleague I'm replacing*) or contains a superlative adjective (e.g., *the most interesting subject I've ever studied*) because such nominal phrases are more commonly followed by a relative clause than indefinite nominal phrases (e.g., *a secret that I don't want to tell anyone*).

A similar pattern has been observed for *that* as a complementizer (Jaeger 2006, 2010):

(15)   a. *I think (that) alternatives exist.*
        b. *I'll show ?(that) alternatives exist.*

The corpus data show that the odds of *that* are lower when the matrix verb is frequently followed by a complement clause (*think, guess, suppose*, etc.) and higher with matrix verbs that are rarely followed by a complement clause (e.g., *teach, see, show*). Thus, the omission of *that* is more likely in (15a) than in (15b).

This variation has been explained by the Uniform Information Density hypothesis, which predicts that speakers aim to transmit information uniformly close to, but not exceeding, the channel capacity (Jaeger 2006; Levy and Jaeger 2007; see also Section 1.3). Adding extra markers in more informative contexts helps to keep the information flow even and uniform, avoiding peaks and canyons. Mentioning the complementizer *that* at the onset of a complement clause distributes the same amount of information over one more word, thereby lowering information density.

As was argued in Section 1.3, the explanation of these effects in terms of the negative correlation between accessibility and effort would be sufficient. The speaker provides additional formal cues to help the addressee to make inferences in those situations when the interpretation is less accessible, and omits them when it is more accessible.

As one more illustration, consider the use or absence of the particle *to* after *help*. More information about this alternation is provided in Section 9.3. According to Rohdenburg (1996), the chances of the *to*-form increase with linguistic distance (in words) between *help* and the infinitive. For example, the use of *to* is more likely in (16b) than in (16a):

(16)   a. *You should help him (to) overcome his fears.*
        b. *You should help this troubled teenager with many complexes and difficult childhood ?(to) overcome his fears.*

2.4 The Use and Omission of Clause Connectors

This variation has been explained by the principle of (reduction of) cognitive complexity:

(17)   The principle of cognitive complexity (Rohdenburg 1996: 151):

> In the case of more or less explicit grammatical options the more explicit one(s) will tend to be favored in cognitively more complex environments.

Rohdenburg also mentions other formal asymmetries, which, according to him, support this principle. They include inflected and uninflected present-tense forms in non-standard varieties of English (e.g., *My mother and father drink/drinks*), optional prepositions (e.g., *time spent (in) doing something*) and prepositional substitutions (e.g., *She was prevailed on/upon to write another letter*). In addition to linguistic distance, which was discussed above, higher complexity is also attributed to passive constructions.

The effect of linguistic distance in (16) can be explained by the principle of negative correlation between accessibility and costs. As the linguistic distance increases and there are more and more words between the matrix verb and the infinitive, the mental representation of the matrix verb becomes less accessible, which makes it more difficult to identify the infinitival complement as a part of the construction with *help*. At the same time, the addressee may have less experience of using and processing such constructions in discourse because structures like (16b) are quite rare. Therefore, the speaker is more likely to choose the more costly expression in this case.

2.4.3   Resumptive Pronouns

Another illustration is the use of resumptive pronouns in relative clauses. Keenan and Comrie (1977) found that languages use relative clauses according to the following scale, known as the Accessibility Hierarchy[6]:

(18)   Subject > Direct Object > Indirect Object > Oblique > Genitive > Obj. of Comparison

For example, if a language has oblique genitive clauses, e.g., *I see an equation, the solution to which is well known*, it can also have subject clauses, as well as direct object, indirect object and oblique clauses, as in the examples below.

(19)   a. *I see the woman who works in the room next to mine* (Subject RC)
        b. *I see the woman I admire* (Direct Object RC).
        c. *I see the woman who I sent my manuscript to* (Indirect Object/Oblique RC).

---

[6] This use of the concept 'accessibility' is different from the one accepted in this book, as well as in Ariel (1990, 2001 and other works) and the psycholinguistic works discussed previously.

English has all types of relative clauses, although Object of Comparison RCs can be uncomfortable, e.g., *the girl who Sue is taller than*.

More directly relevant for the topic of this chapter, however, is another finding by Keenan and Comrie, namely that the same hierarchy constrains the use of resumptive pronouns in relative clauses. Consider an example from Hebrew:

(20)   Hebrew: Afro-Asiatic (Keenan and Comrie 1977: 92)

   ha-isha   she-David   natan   la   et   ha-sefer
   the-woman   that-David gave   to-her   OBJ   the book
   'the woman that David gave the book to'

Here, *la* is a resumptive pronoun in the indirect object position. According to the hierarchy, if a language has resumptive pronouns in the subject position, the pronouns will also be used in all other positions. If a language requires or allows them in the indirect object position, it will also require or allow them for obliques, genitives and objects of comparison.

Keenan (1975) provided corpus data from English to demonstrate that the order in the hierarchy correlates with the frequency with which different positions occur. In a sample of more than 2,200 relative clauses, subjects were the most commonly relativized (e.g., *the girl who is playing a computer game*), and objects of comparison were never relativized. There were only a few examples of relativized genitives (e.g., *the gate of which the hinges were rusty*).

These findings have not been met uncritically, however. In particular, Fox (1987) argued that instead of Subject on the left end of the scale in (18), one should speak about arguments P or S (that is, objects and intransitive subjects, respectively). In some ergative languages (e.g., Dyirbal and Mayan), ergative subjects (A) are not relativized.[7] Moreover, object relatives are as frequent as subject relatives in conversational English. Fox explains this finding by the important discourse function played by object relatives. Namely, they anchor the head noun phrase with new information, often with the help of pronominal given subjects in the relative clause, e.g., *Have you heard about the party we threw in Las Vegas?*

One should also mention here a famous debate about the relative complexity of processing of subject and object relative clauses, as in the examples below (from Levy, Fedorenko and Gibson 2013; see also references therein):

(21)   a. *The reporter who attacked the senator hoped for a story.* (Subject RC)
       b. *The reporter who the senator attacked hoped for a story.* (Object RC)

It is received wisdom that object relatives are more difficult to comprehend than subject relatives. Numerous accounts have been given. One relevant

---

[7] A language is considered ergative, or ergative-absolutive, if transitive subjects (A) are marked with a special ergative case marker, whereas intransitive subjects (S) and objects of transitive verbs (P) are in the absolutive case, which almost always has no overt marker.

factor is the memory load, which increases with the number and length of open syntactic dependencies, in particular, with the number of intervening words between the relative pronoun and the verb (see Section 3.2.1). This is why (21a), where the verb follows immediately after the relative pronoun, is easier to process than (21b).

However, this seems only to hold in artificial sentences with full noun phrases. For example, Reali and Christiansen (2007) demonstrated that object relative clauses can be more easily processed (that is, require shorter reading times) when they begin with a personal pronoun, e.g., *The consultant that you called*, than similar subject clauses, e.g., *The consultant that called you*. They were also more frequent than subject relative clauses in a large corpus. Object clauses with personal pronouns are much more natural than ones with nouns (cf. Fox 1987), which may explain the different results. Thus, the relative complexity of subject and object clauses strongly depends on the specific linguistic cues and the language users' experience with them. We process more easily what we are frequently exposed to and what we expect to encounter. See also Diessel (2019: Section 10.5).

Regardless of whether the Accessibility Hierarchy is correct or not, the use or omission of resumptive pronouns can be explained by the principle of negative correlation between accessibility and costs. Ariel (1990: Section 7.21) argues that the use and omission of resumptive pronouns in Hebrew is driven by the accessibility of their referents. Resumptive pronouns are omitted when the referent is highly accessible and used when it is less accessible. Accessibility depends on different factors, such as the distance from the head noun. Even Subject RCs, which normally do not allow for resumptive pronouns in Hebrew, can contain them if the distance is long. Resumptive pronouns are better in non-restrictive relative clauses (e.g., *The foreign students, whom the university accepted, are very hard-working*) than in restrictive ones (e.g., *The foreign students who the university accepted are very hard-working*), because the former are less semantically and pragmatically dependent on the main clause than the latter. Non-restrictive relative clauses are also intonationally (and, at least in English, with the help of punctuation) separated from the main clause. This may reduce the accessibility of the referents in non-restrictive clauses.

In addition, resumptive pronouns can help to ease the memory load and lower the processing costs (see Hawkins 2004). All this makes the use and omission of resumptive pronouns relevant for efficient communication.

2.5 Same-Subject and Different-Subject Constructions

According to Cristofaro (2003: 250), if the participants of the main clause and subordinate clause are shared, the reference to them in the subordinate clause is likely to be missing. If the situations expressed by the main and dependent clauses have different participants, they are likely to have overt participant reference in the subordinate clause. We can think of overt participant reference in subordinate clauses as a switch-reference device, which signals that the participants are different from those in the main clause, while the absence of participant reference signals that the participants are the same (cf. Ariel 1990: Section 7.1). All this means that highly accessible participants obtain less coding than less accessible participants. Frequently, some coding material is added to facilitate the interpretation, as well.

For example, the subject of the verb *want* and the complement it controls is usually the same (Haspelmath 2013b). That is, the meaning 'X wants to do Y' with the same subject is more frequent than the meaning 'X wants Z to do Y' with different subjects. When the subject is the same, in most languages it is not mentioned again, as in (22a) from German. If the subjects are different, both of them are mentioned. Moreover, additional coding is often used, such as complementizers and finite verb morphemes, as in (22b).

(22) German (own knowledge)

    a. *Ich will zuhause bleib-en.*
       I   want at.home stay-INF.
       'I want to stay at home.'
    b. *Ich will, dass du zuhause bleib-st.*
       I   want that you at.home stay-2SG.PRES
       'I want you to stay at home.'

In some languages (e.g., Samoan and Korean), a longer verb form is used for the different-subject *want*. A few languages have the same construction for the same-subject and different-subject meanings, so no coding asymmetry is observed (e.g., Modern Greek). Most importantly, however, the cross-linguistic sample in Haspelmath (2013b) contains no languages in which the same-subject *want* would be expressed by a longer construction than the different-subject *want*.

Another example is *intend* (Comrie 1986). Intentions usually involve our own future actions, as in (23a), where an infinitival clause is used. But if we speak about intentions with regard to someone else's actions, a finite clause is required, as in (23b).

(23)   a. *Sue intends to stay at home.*
       b. *Sue intends that Joe should stay at home.*

But this is not the whole story. We can find some 'local markedness' examples again. If the verb in the main clause has two human arguments, and one of them appears in the subordinate clause, the use of the short and long forms depends on the lexical semantics of the verb. Take the verb *promise*. We usually promise someone to do something because we can control our actions more easily. This is why (24a) is shorter than (24b).

2.6 Zipf's Law of Abbreviation

(24) a. *Sue promised Joe to stay at home.*
      b. *Sue promised Joe that he would stay at home.*

Now consider the verb *persuade*. When we persuade someone, we expect that they will perform some action. In English, this is expressed by an object-control construction with an infinitival clause, as in (25a). But if the agent of the action is the person who persuades, as in (25b), then a finite clause is used.

(25) a. *Sue persuades Joe to stay at home.*
      b. *Sue persuades Joe that she should stay at home.*

This formal length asymmetry is efficient because the more accessible interpretation is conveyed by a shorter form than the less accessible one. Although in general the principle observed by Cristofaro (2003) is true, the examples with *promise* and *persuade* show that languages can have local formal asymmetries which depend on the expectations triggered by a specific verb in the main clause.

2.6 Zipf's Law of Abbreviation

This section addresses one of the most famous manifestations of language efficiency, namely, the fact that more frequent words tend to be shorter than less frequent ones. This correlation is known as Zipf's Law of Abbreviation (1965 [1935]). Bentz and Ferrer-i-Cancho (2016) have tested the law on 986 languages from 80 families, using massively parallel corpora of Bible translations. They found a negative correlation between word length in characters and word frequency for all languages. The Law of Abbreviation is thus an absolute language universal, although it is statistical in each separate language because the correlation is not perfect.

According to Zipf (1965 [1935]), this correlation is explained by the general pressure to save time and effort. The linguistic mechanisms responsible for this correlation include truncations, e.g., *gas* instead of *gasoline*. There is a lot of evidence for this strategy, e.g., *app* for *application,* or German *Auto* for *Automobil.*

We should also mention here formal erosion. This often happens as a result of grammaticalization (e.g., Lehmann 2015: Section 4.2.1), for example when full verbs become auxiliaries (the Old English *willan* 'want' > *will* and *'ll*), full pronouns become clitics (e.g., *them* and *'em*) and bound person markers, *because* becomes *'cause* and *coz*. A more detailed discussion of the diachronic mechanisms that lead to formal reduction is provided in Chapter 5.

The second strategy, according to Zipf, is to use permanent or temporary lexical substitutions. Temporary substitutions are anaphoric pronouns, which were discussed in Section 2.2. Examples of permanent substitutions are *car,* which is used instead of *automobile* or, in more specialized domains, *juice* for electricity or *soup* for nitroglycerine (at least in Zipf's times).

There have also been some sceptical opinions about the interpretation of Zipf's Law of Abbreviation in terms of efficient organization of language. Miller (1957) noted that a correlation between word length and word frequency is also observed if someone randomly types characters on a keyboard with letters and a space character. A randomly typing monkey would produce a sequence of meaningless strings of characters, whereby shorter strings would appear more frequently than longer ones. At the same time, Howes (1968) argued that the assumptions of Miller's model are not applicable to natural language. Obviously, we do not form words from randomly reshuffled letters to express some random meanings. More recently, Ferrer-i-Cancho, Bentz and Seguin (2020) showed that Miller's random typing itself represents an optimal encoding system from the perspective of standard information theory, which means that it is not surprising that the results of random typing are similar to Zipf's. Moreover, there are multiple indications that efficient formal reduction is an important type of language change. Section 1.1, for example, discussed the shortened forms for 'coronavirus'. It is impossible to see this and numerous other examples (see Chapter 5) as a result of random processes.

Word length correlates not only with frequency but also with how predictable a word is from its context. In an experimental study, Manin (2006) showed that word length is correlated with the average probability of guessing the word in context. Informativity can be also inferred from very large corpora. Using *n*-grams from several Germanic, Romance and Slavic languages, Piantadosi, Tily and Gibson (2011) found out that the average informativity, i.e., the negative logarithm of the conditional probability of a word given its previous context (1 to 3 words on the left), is even more strongly correlated with word length than simple frequency. These findings were complemented and extended by Mahowald et al. (2013), who examined such pairs as *exam – examination*, *chimp – chimpanzee* and *math(s) – mathematics*. Their corpus-based analysis demonstrates that the shorter forms had on average lower informativity given their left context. An experiment with forced-choice sentence completion also revealed that the shorter forms are preferred in more predictive contexts.

These conclusions, however, have been challenged recently by Meylan and Griffiths (2021), who showed that the dominance of informativity is no longer observed when one encodes strings in UTF-8, which is more fit for languages other than English than the ASCII standard, and excludes words that are not found in the dictionaries of the specific languages. Moreover, one may wonder if the results will hold if more diverse languages are taken into account.

In order to answer this question, I investigated corpus data from nine languages: Arabic, Czech, English, Finnish, German, Hindi, Hungarian,

2.6 Zipf's Law of Abbreviation

Indonesian and Russian. The data are online news corpora with 30 million tokens from each language taken from the Leipzig Corpora Collection (Goldhahn, Eckart and Quasthoff 2012). The length of words was measured in UTF-8 characters. For each language, 4,000 wordforms (only alphabetic characters) with frequency greater than 20 were selected randomly for analysis. This frequency cut-off was used in order to avoid typos and other spurious hits. Frequency was represented by self-information. That is, the frequency is divided by the corpus size and then the negative logarithm is taken. The higher the frequency of a word, the lower the self-information value. Informativity represents the average probability of a word given one previous word, also negatively log-transformed. The more predictable a word on average from preceding words, the lower the contextual informativity value.

Next, Spearman's rank correlation coefficients were computed for each language (a) between word length and self-information, and (b) between word length and contextual informativity. The results are shown in Figure 2.1. Partial correlations were also computed, such that the correlations between length and self-information were controlled for contextual informativity, and the correlations between length and contextual informativity were controlled for self-information. The partial correlations are represented by symbols (dots and triangles) on the same plot.

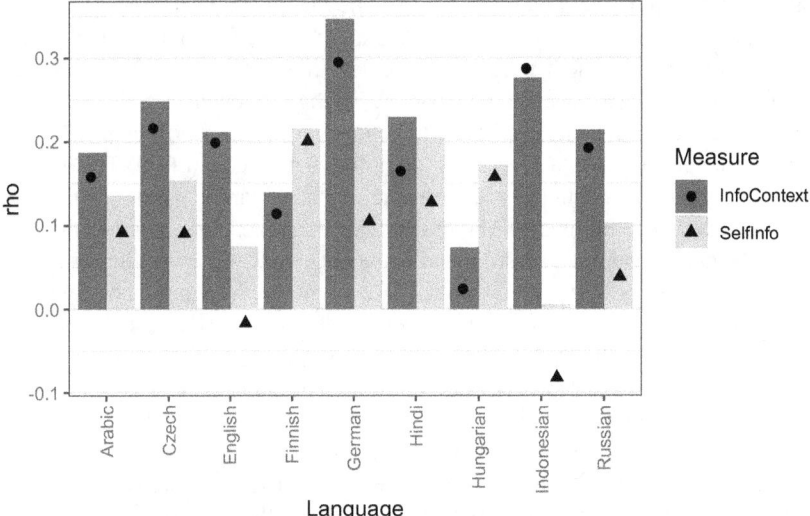

Figure 2.1 Spearman's rank correlation coefficients between word length and self-information, and between word length and contextual informativity. The dots and triangles stand for partial correlations.

The plot shows that in most of the languages, contextual informativity is indeed more strongly correlated with word length, following Piantadosi et al. (2011). The dominance of informativity is particularly striking in highly analytic languages: Indonesian and English, especially if we look at the partial correlations. However, in Finnish and Hungarian, which are highly synthetic, the opposite is the case. Self-information based on simple frequency is more strongly correlated with word length than contextual informativity is. Note that, unlike in Meylan and Griffiths (2021), words absent from dictionaries were not excluded; however, a follow-up study based on cleaned data reveals divergent correlations between informativity measures and length across languages, whereas the Zipfian correlation between frequency and length remains consistent (Levshina 2022b).

How can we interpret the findings? If we look at the distribution of word frequencies and bigram frequencies, we will see that Finnish and Hungarian tokens and bigrams have the highest number of hapax legomena (that is, units that occur only once). This is not surprising. Because of their rich morphology, Finnish and Hungarian have very many different forms of content words. The grammatical relationships are expressed by word-internal grams rather than by function words. The individual tokens (individual wordforms) are more difficult to predict from other content wordforms, which are rare. This means that the measures of contextual surprisal can be less reliable in those languages. Yet, even if we remove the hapax legomena when computing the surprisal (or, alternatively, all context words with frequency less than 5), the results change very little. This suggests that the results are not an artefact of data sparseness. The relatively infrequent neighbours are less reliable as cues for infrequent wordforms. Another reason is word order: in languages with rich morphology, word order tends to be less rigid and therefore less predictive of the next words than in languages with a less rich morphology (see Section 6.3). This makes the neighbouring tokens less reliable predictors of target words. Moreover, individual constructions also play a role. For example, some postpositions in these languages can be quite long and at the same time highly predictable from the previous word with a specific case form, e.g., Hungarian *keresztül* 'through, across', *érdekében* 'for the benefit of', *kapcsolatban* 'in connection with', *kapcsolatos* 'in relation to' and *köszönhetoen* 'due, thanks to'.

Thus, there is no clear evidence that either frequency or informativity is more strongly correlated with length. One of the reasons is that informativity as a psychological construct representing the accessibility of a word for a language user is very difficult to estimate from corpora.[8] Moreover, different strings of characters have different degrees of wordhood, and the results will

---

[8] I thank Steven Piantadosi (p.c.) for this observation.

depend on orthographic conventions. Despite the debate about which measure is the most appropriate one for measuring the accessibility of words, the correlations reported above can be regarded as evidence for communicative efficiency.

2.7 Phonetic Reduction and Enhancement

Speakers tend to reduce articulation effort while at the same time producing a signal which shows sufficient acoustic distinctiveness for the addressee to correctly identify the linguistic content of the message (Lindblom 1990). There is ample evidence in the literature that more accessible linguistic units (words, syllables and individual sounds) undergo reduction more frequently than less accessible ones. Bolinger (1963) observed that words are durationally shorter when they occur more frequently on their own or in combinations with other words. For example, the relatively new word *robot* is pronounced longer than the more familiar *rowboat*, whereas verbs can be pronounced shorter when followed by more typical complements or adjuncts.

The measures of accessibility that determine the degree of phonological reduction can be of different kinds. One of them is the context-free frequency of a given unit in discourse. Another factor is the conditional probability given the left or right context, e.g., *n* words on the left or right from the target word. Frequency can be measured across different texts or only in previous discourse. Similarly, conditional probability can be measured in a specific context where the unit of interest is used, or it can be averaged across all contexts where the unit occurs (see Section 2.6 for an illustration). In studies inspired by information theory, the probabilities are often made negative and logarithmically transformed, such that the resulting number represents the informativity of the unit in bits (or nats, depending on the logarithm base). Higher probability means lower informativity, and vice versa. Pointwise Mutual Information, which reflects how much more information is obtained about a word upon seeing its neighbour, and the other way round, has also been shown to be relevant for different types of reduction in language production (e.g., Gregory et al. 1999).

Bell et al. (2009) studied the relationships between pronounced durations of words in a spoken corpus and several factors: frequency, conditional probability and repetition. They looked separately at content and function words. Both in content and in function words, there was a significant effect of different types of conditional probability – given the previous context or the next context. Moreover, word frequency and repetition led to reduction of content words. Similarly, Fowler and Housum (1987) found effects of repetition on the duration of content words in a narration.

Phonetic reduction can manifest itself not only in formal shortening but also in the loss of phonetic detail. For instance, Aylett and Turk (2004) report that highly predictable phrase-medial syllables are shorter than less predictable ones. At the same time, there is a loss of articulatory detail. In particular, vowels undergo centralization of their first and second formant frequency values. As a result, the vowel space is reduced (Aylett and Turk 2006).

Both context-specific and average predictability play a role in reducing the acoustic duration of a notional word, many other factors being controlled for (Seyfarth 2014). Therefore, formal reduction is to some extent stored in the lexicon. Similar results are obtained by Cohen Priva (2008), who finds that oral and nasal stop deletion in English is influenced by the phones' average informativity. This demonstrates again how the use of a unit in particular contexts percolates into language structure.

Pierrehumbert (2001) proposes an exemplar-based model in order to explain why high-frequency words undergo reduction faster than low-frequency words. For example, the middle schwa is deleted before /r/ and /n/ in high-frequency words, such as *evening* and *every*, but is retained in rare words, such as *mammary* and *artillery* (Hooper 1976; see also Fenk-Oczlon 2001). According to Pierrehumbert, this difference can be explained by the systematic production bias towards lenition (Lindblom 1984), or 'undershooting' the phonetic target to the extent that it does not disrupt understanding. Since high-frequency words are used more often than low-frequency words, their stored exemplar representations are more affected by this persistent bias. This explains why high-frequency words are more reduced than low-frequency words synchronically and why the former undergo this reduction faster than the latter in diachrony. It does not seem very plausible, though, that there is a certain constant rate of lenition that is applied to every use of a word or sound in every context. Frequent words are also highly accessible on their own and across individual contexts, which is why they can be reduced in the first place.

Speakers also enhance linguistic forms under some circumstances, e.g., when they believe that the addressee may need help to disambiguate between two similarly sounding words. This has been shown in studies of hyperarticulation. For example, when the hearer has to choose between two similarly sounding words, e.g., *dose – doze*, the speaker tends to increase the voicing of the final consonant in *doze* more often than in situations when such ambiguity is not present (Seyfarth, Buz and Jaeger 2016). Speakers also hyperarticulate when their communication partners misunderstand instructions (Stent, Huffman and Brennan 2008). Hyperarticulation is observed immediately after the speaker finds out that they were misunderstood, and then decays gradually over several turns in the absence of further misrecognitions.

Explanation of these effects has been a controversial issue. First, they can be explained by audience design (Bell 1984), which means that language users proactively adjust their message in order to increase their communicative success while at the same time reducing their efforts any time they can.

2.7 Phonetic Reduction and Enhancement

But this is not the only explanation that can be found in the literature. A popular view in usage-based linguistics involves the phenomenon of chunking. According to Bybee, for example, each instance of use further automates and increases the fluency of a sequence of words, leading to their fusion (Bybee 2007: 324; see also Section 5.4.3). A frequently repeated stretch of speech becomes automated as a processing unit due to neuromotor routines. Further repetition leads to reduction and overlapping of articulatory gestures. All this shortens the duration. For instance, Bybee and Scheibman (1999) found that reduction of the vowel and the consonants in *don't* in spoken English is particularly frequent after the pronoun *I* and before the verbs *know* and *think* because this contraction occurs particularly frequently in phrases *I don't know* and *I don't think*. The process of automatization is not restricted to language alone and is largely unconscious.

If the automatization account is the only true one, then the joint probability of neighbouring units (i.e., the frequency of these units together, divided by the sum frequency of all other sequences) would be the only important factor in predicting formal reduction. However, empirical evidence reveals that conditional probability is more important than joint probability in that regard. In particular, Bell et al. (2003) investigated the effects of conditional probabilities and joint probabilities on the duration and phonetic reduction of function words in spoken English. They found that the conditional probabilities have either the strongest or the only significant effect in the predicted direction (i.e., more predictable target words are more frequently reduced than less predictable ones). Joint probabilities, which basically represent the frequencies of possible chunks and their degree of routinization, sometimes have an effect in the opposite direction. Also, Barth (2019) shows that reduction of *be* and *have* in highly grammaticalized contexts is due to the high conditional probabilities rather than the joint probabilities of these words with their neighbours (most importantly, the words that follow *be* and *have*). This can be regarded as evidence that accessibility due to high contextual predictability is more important than the process of chunking, at least, in these cases of formal reduction.

Another popular explanation is that the speaker buys time for planning by using a longer expression. As shown by Bell et al. (2003), planning problems, which are represented by disfluencies either preceding or following a function word, increase the chances of longer or fuller variants of words in language production. Planning issues were also one of the explanations offered by Szmrecsanyi (2003) to provide an account for the preference of the construction *be going to* in syntactically complex environments (in comparison with *will/shall*), which are more demanding in terms of processing resources (see Section 4.3).

While planning issues may well play a role, they fail to explain many instances of reduction and enhancement. For example, Jaeger and Buz

(2017) argue that the link between the contextual predictability of a linguistic form and its own realization is not very clear if one accepts the 'buying-time' explanation. There is also evidence that backward transitional probabilities (i.e., those that predict the target unit given the following context) play a role that is at least as important as the role of forward transitional probabilities (i.e., the ones that predict the target unit from the preceding context), if not more important (Seyfarth 2014; Barth 2019). Moreover, speakers adapt subsequent productions towards less reduced variants if previous use of more reduced variants resulted in communicative failure (Stent et al. 2008; Buz, Tanenhaus and Jaeger 2016). As Jaeger and Buz (2017) argue, this is incompatible with the idea that the degree of reduction depends solely on production ease.

One cannot exclude the possibility that routinization, 'stalling for time' and other production-related and speaker-centred explanations are relevant in some situations (cf. Ernestus 2014). I argue that the effect of production factors should be ultimately constrained by the communicative need of the speaker to get the message across, although some of the lower-level reduction or enhancement processes can be caused by cognitive processes unrelated to the addressee's needs (cf. Lindblom 1990). This constraint becomes obvious if we listen to human (not previously recorded) announcers at a railway station. When the speaker announces that the platform number has been changed, the number will be highly accessible to him or her. However, the numeral representing the platform number is unlikely to be reduced because this information is highly important and not accessible to the travellers who need to catch the train.[9] Notably, numbers tend to be very stable phonologically across languages (Diessel 2019). We can think of at least two reasons for this. First, confusion can be costly in many linguistic and extralinguistic ways. Second, numbers are often used in similar contexts (e.g., *X costs two/five/ten/... euros*), which makes them on average less predictable from context. We need more research in order to obtain a conclusive answer and to disentangle these competing motivations and explanations.

A final word of warning should be said against a potential misunderstanding that an account based on audience design should only display effects based on context-specific accessibility. There is no conflict between this account and the evidence of entrenchment effects, which can last for a while, or even become conventionalized. For example, the voice-onset time of words with initial voiceless stops that have minimal pairs, e.g., *cod – god*, is greater in comparison with words without such a pair, e.g., *cop – *gop*. Baese-Berk and Goldrick (2009) found that this difference is observed even if the minimal pair is not

---

[9] In German, the emphatic form *zwo* instead of *zwei* 'two' is used in order to avoid confusion with *drei* 'three' at railway stations, over the telephone and in other situations where faithful transmission is important.

present in the context (i.e., there is no need of disambiguation). They conclude that this effect is not driven by what they call 'listener–modelling'. We know from Cohen Priva (2008), Seyfarth (2014), which were mentioned above, and other studies, that units that frequently occur in reducing contexts also become more reduced in general, i.e., usage percolates into the system. Therefore, units that are frequently hyperarticulated or reduced in some contexts may become hyperarticulated or reduced across the board. This may lead to short-term or long-term effects. In the study mentioned above, Stent et al. (2008) show that hyperarticulation is a targeted and flexible adaptation to a specific situation, which decays with time. At the same time, reduced or enhanced forms can be entrenched and conventionalized in their conjunction with specific communicative situations. As a result, whole special registers can emerge, e.g., child-directed speech, foreigner-directed speech, etc. (Jaeger and Buz 2017). As in the previous examples of efficient formal asymmetries, we can observe different kinds of efficiency, from context-sensitive language use, where audience design is probably the strongest and most precise, to conventionalized patterns, which are coarser, but do not require much thinking and produce the desired cognitive effects most of the time.

2.8 Conclusions

We have seen many different manifestations of efficiency as a descriptive phenomenon in all domains of language – lexicon, phonology, morphosyntax and discourse. Some of them lend themselves easily to the efficiency explanation, while some others also have alternative accounts. Chapter 5 will discuss some of them and others in greater detail.

Formal length is related to processing costs. Longer expressions can be used to make processing easier for the addressee. For example, the use of resumptive pronouns (see Section 2.4.3) in some types of relative clauses can help the addressee to process the sentence. This does not automatically mean, however, that shorter expressions mean more processing effort for the addressee, and longer expressions mean less processing effort. First of all, as we saw in Section 1.3, overly informative expressions create problems for comprehension. Second, the use of short and ambiguous expressions does not result in processing difficulties, provided that there is enough relevant context. See more on this topic in Section 6.2.1.

3 Efficiency and the Order of Meaningful Elements

3.1 Efficient Order

The order of linguistic units is another important source of cost minimization. Efficient word order has received a lot of attention in the literature, in particular in the typological work by John Hawkins (e.g., 2004, 2014) and in numerous experimental and corpus-based studies, which are discussed below. In addition to word order, I will also discuss efficient order of bound morphemes.

There are very many theories, especially in psycholinguistics, which argue that some word orders are more costly than others. The costs that are discussed in the literature are usually related to processing effort, especially to memory load. Many accounts give an advantage to word orders that allow for using time most efficiently, in particular, when accessible words and constituents are produced first. I will argue here that different ways of minimizing processing costs can be interpreted as maximization of accessibility, according to the principle discussed in Section 1.4.3.

First, I will discuss which factors can, according to different researchers, make word order more or less costly, based on existing evidence (Section 3.2). Next, I will provide well-known examples of efficiency observed across languages (Section 3.3). Finally, Section 3.4 will discuss the costs and benefits of violating word order conventions, using word order produced by Yoda in *Star Wars* as an example.

3.2 Factors Determining Efficiency of Order

3.2.1 Minimization of Memory and Surprisal Costs

It is uncontroversial that memory plays a crucial role in determining the costs of syntactic processing. As early as 1960, Yngve proposed an idea for measuring processing complexity by counting the open dependencies that need to be kept in working memory. He postulated that memory capacity limits, such as Miller's 'seven plus or minus two' determine the maximum depth (that is,

3.2 Factors Determining Efficiency of Order

the number of open dependencies) of a structure that can be processed. Yngve expected these limits to shape the grammars of human languages.

Memory costs were discussed in great detail in dependency locality theory (Gibson 1998, 2000). According to this theory, the costs arise due to two tasks. The first one is related to storage of the structures built so far, as well as predictions about the following element until it appears. The second one has to do with integration of the new material into the structure. Integration requires reactivation of the word in the previous context that has a dependency relationship with the current word. The activation of the word decays as more and more words are added between the previously mentioned word and the current word, so more effort is needed to reactivate the former. Therefore, syntactic predictions held in memory over long distances are costly, which matters both for production and comprehension.

Memory costs should not be too high for a sentence to be processable. For example, sentences with double centre-embedded clauses, as in (1a), are problematic because there is a state during its parse that exceeds the available memory resources (Gibson 1998: 16).

(1)   a. *The administrator who the intern who the nurse supervised had bothered lost the medical reports.*
        b. *The nurse supervised the intern who had bothered the administrator who lost the medical reports.*

According to Gibson, this state occurs at the noun *nurse*. There are too many predictions that the processor needs to keep in mind at this point: predictions about the empty category positions of the first *who* and the second *who*, as well as predictions of the verbs in both relative clauses.[1] Avoiding centre-embedded clauses, as in (1b), helps to avoid the breakdown.[2]

As for integration costs, they are highest at the second lexical verb *bothered*. This is also the point where reading times are predicted to be the longest. Here, the processor has to perform two particularly long and costly integrations. The first one is to assign a thematic role from *bothered* to *the intern*. The second is to link the empty argument of *bothered* to the first instance of *who*.

By minimizing dependency distances, language users minimize memory costs. This is called the Principle of Dependency Locality. The processing costs are also lower when the speaker minimizes the domains necessary for the recognition of constituents (Hawkins 2004). See more on this in Section 3.3.1.

---

[1] In Gibson's theory, prediction of the matrix verb (here: *lost*) does not have memory costs.
[2] An alternative explanation of why double centre-embedded clauses are problematic is discussed in Section 4.4, which has to do with avoidance of similar constituents in close proximity (Lewis 1996).

These considerations can also be explained in terms of maximization of accessibility. Long dependencies decrease the accessibility of preceding words because their memory traces fade with time. More effort is needed to reactivate them.

Dependency locality can be seen as a special case of a more general principle, which is called information locality. According to Futrell and Levy (2017), processing is difficult when any elements with high mutual information (that is, which are strongly associated, based on the previous linguistic experience) are far from one another, not only members of syntactic dependencies. Efficient order then means that strongly associated words are placed close to each other.

This approach unifies two seemingly unrelated processing costs: the memory-based costs associated with dependency distances, and the expectation-based costs associated with high surprisal. Surprisal (that is, unexpectedness) of a word given its context is a contributor to processing costs. Numerous studies have shown that surprisal is a good predictor of online processing difficulty (see Section 1.2.2). By minimizing distances between semantically and syntactically related words, language users not only minimize storage and integration costs, but also minimize surprisal, because neighbouring words become more predictable. As the distance between two related words increases, the preceding word becomes a less effective cue for predicting the other word. As a result, the latter becomes more surprising, which creates processing costs. Since high surprisal means low accessibility, we can say that the principle of information locality (including dependency locality) reflects the principle of maximization of accessibility.

Locality effects can interact with other factors. In particular, the processing costs associated with increasing dependency distances can be modulated by context that helps to predict the upcoming word (Konieczny 2000; Vasishth and Lewis 2006). For example, the sentence in (2b) is more plausible than (2a) because the information about cutting onions makes the verb *cried* more expected than in (2a). This makes the verb easier to interpret (Grodner and Gibson 2005).

(2)   a. *The fisherman cried.*
         b. *The fisherman who was cutting onions cried.*

The discourse status of noun phrases inside long dependencies also plays a role. Warren and Gibson (2002) found that reading times at crucial verbs were faster when the referents introduced by intervening nouns were discourse-given and therefore easily accessible. In the example below, sentences with the 1st-person pronoun (*we*) were processed the most easily, as can be measured by the reading times on the main verb *advised* together with the following word. Sentences with a famous person's name (*Elon Musk*) were more costly, followed by sentences with definite descriptions (*the chairman*). Finally, sentences with an indefinite description (*a chairman*) required the longest reading times in the crucial region.

(3)   *The consultant who we/Elon Musk/the chairman/a chairman called advised wealthy companies.*

According to Warren and Gibson (2002), given and accessible referents, which are easier to integrate in discourse, also make the syntactic integration of the verb and arguments easier – probably, the resources used in processing of syntactic arguments and integration of discourse referents are not independent.

Locality effects interact with articulation effort. If a sentence has structures with low accessibility due to long dependency distances, for example, the processing costs can be mitigated by using longer forms. This can explain the cognitive complexity hypothesis by Rohdenburg (1996) discussed in Section 2.4.2, which explains the tendency to use function words when the memory of syntactically related words decays. The example provided there was the use of the particle *to* in the *help* + (*to*) infinitive construction, in situations where there are many intervening words between *help* and the infinitive. Low accessibility triggers the use of more costly expressions, while high accessibility allows the speaker to use less costly expressions. Another option is to use word order that helps to minimize dependency distances or syntactic domains. This strategy is discussed in Section 3.3.1.

3.2.2   Producing Accessible Elements First

Another criterion of processing ease is directly related to the principle of maximization of accessibility. When more accessible units are produced first, and less accessible ones are produced later, this helps to save processing effort and time. As already discussed in the previous chapter in relation to the expression of referents (Section 2.2.1), accessibility is determined by multiple factors: previous mentioning of the referent and the lexeme, recency in discourse, topicality, predictability from context, and others. There is substantial evidence that more accessible concepts are produced first, if this is allowed by the grammar (Bock and Irwin 1980; Bock and Warren 1985). In particular, language users place given before new (e.g., Bock and Irwin 1980 for English and Ferreira and Yoshita 2003 for Japanese) and animate before inanimate (Tanaka et al. 2011 for Japanese).[3] Consider (4a) and (4b). Both SO and OS orders are possible in Dutch. Which one will be preferred depends on the relative accessibility of the referents expressed by the arguments. Under normal circumstances, (4a) will be preferred because the referent expressed

---

[3] Note that animacy is strongly correlated with givenness, according to my experience with conversational corpora in different languages.

by the personal pronoun *zij* is animate and given and therefore more accessible than the referent expressed by the indefinite noun *appel*.

(4)   Dutch (personal knowledge)
   a. *Zij   heeft   een   appel   gegeten.*
      she   has   an   apple   eaten
      'She has eaten an apple.'
   b. *Een   appel   heeft   zij   gegeten.*
      an   apple   has   she   eaten
      'She has eaten an apple.'

Why does this help to save costs? First of all, we need to go beyond the boundaries of a sentence, which has been the traditional unit of analysis in many psycholinguistic theories. Referents, events and other pieces of information in discourse are connected by cohesion relationships, which can be seen as a kind of dependency. By mentioning a referent early, we decrease the memory costs required for integration of this referent. We can also save articulation costs because the referent will be more accessible, and therefore a less costly form will be used (see Section 2.2).

Moreover, putting accessible information first helps to save time. According to Levelt's (1989) model, language production consists of several stages: Conceptualization (determining the contents of the message), Formulation (building the necessary grammatical and phonological structures) and Articulation (uttering the phonetic representations). Importantly, sentence generation is incremental and can run in parallel, both between the stages and within the stages (De Smedt 1994). Because of the competition between different conceptual content at the Formulation level, the segments that are formulated faster can be sent to Articulation sooner. Heavy components, which usually have low accessibility, are also more time-consuming for Formulation than light components. When light and highly accessible elements are formulated and articulated first, and heavy and less accessible ones are produced later (cf. Arnold et al. 2000), this saves time required for speech production. While formulating and articulating more accessible and lighter constituents, the production mechanism is busy with processing less accessible and heavy ones.

Consider binomial expressions, e.g., *land and sea, bride and groom, fame and fortune*. Fenk-Oczlon (1989) argues that the order in such expressions is best explained by frequency. The first element is normally more frequent than the second one. Since more frequent words are more accessible than less frequent ones, this order is efficient. Note that semantic relations also help to explain the data to some extent. In particular, an important role is played by iconicity of order, e.g., *past and present, birth and death*. This principle will be discussed in Section 3.2.4. Similar reasoning can also explain the so-called right dislocation, when the heavy component, which requires a lot of time for formulation, is uttered last. See an example in Section 3.3.5.

3.2 Factors Determining Efficiency of Order

As another illustration, consider English dative alternation, which was discussed in Section 2.3.3. The choice is between double-object dative, as in (5a), and prepositional dative, as in (5b).

(5)   a. *The teacher gave me an interesting book.*
      b. *The teacher gave them to the smartest student.*

Bresnan et al. (2007) demonstrate that the choice between the constructions is determined by a number of factors. In particular, the double-object construction, in which the recipient is followed by the theme, is more likely to be chosen than the prepositional-object construction if the Recipient is pronominal, animate, definite, discourse-given, 1st or 2nd person and relatively short in comparison with the Theme, and the Theme is not given, not pronominal, and not concrete. The reverse holds for the prepositional-object construction. Therefore, the more accessible and shorter element (Recipient or Theme) tends to come first, and the less accessible and longer one is usually placed second. In addition, the word order helps to minimize dependency distances, which saves memory costs. Note that processing efficiency again interacts with articulation efficiency. The prepositional dative has more coding material (the additional preposition *to*) than the double-object dative, which can be explained by the fact that the former represents less accessible configurations of participants (see Section 2.3.3).

There are some other factors determining which constituent will come first. In particular, Clark and Chase (1974) show that figures are better starting points than grounds. Compare two pictures in (6). The star is the figure, and the line is the ground.

(6)   (a)   *   (b) -
      -                    *

When describing (6a), language users predominantly mention *the star* first: *The star is above the line*, rather than *The line is below the star*. As for (6b), they prefer beginning with the star, too. So, *The star is below the line* is produced more often than *The line is above the star*. At the same time, the figure-first preference for (6b) is weaker than for (6a). The reason is another bias: speakers prefer to identify with objects 'above' rather than in the marked relation 'below'. This identification is the starting point for building mental representations and sentence production (MacWhinney 1977). It is deeply rooted in our early sensorimotor experience (Piaget 1952). This asymmetry is echoed in the tendency to describe vertical relationships such that the 'point of reference' is at the bottom. For example, it is more natural to say *Jack is taller than Bill* than *Bill is shorter than Jack*. Similar asymmetries are observed for the pairs 'in front of' – 'in back of', 'ahead' – 'behind' and 'before' – 'after'. Agents are also easier to identify with than Patients, which explains why the active voice is more frequent than the passive across languages (Greenberg 1966). Also, animate entities are more accessible than inanimate ones, as was already mentioned.

The tendency to mention accessible units first is called the 'Easy First' bias by MacDonald (2013). She also argues that this bias competes with another principle, which she calls 'Plan Reuse'. Speakers favour 'easy', more practised or recently used utterance plans. This explains effects of structural priming (Weiner and Labov 1983; Bock 1986; Pickering and Branigan 1998; see an overview in Pickering and Ferreira 2008). For example, if the speaker has recently uttered, heard or read a passive sentence, they are more likely to produce it again. According to MacDonald (2013), structural priming is part of long-term learning, so there is no principled difference between accessibility of a plan in long-term memory and as a result of activation in a recent usage event. While Easy First operates at the level of words and constituents, Plan Reuse involves more abstract sentence schemas, e.g., SOV or SVO. If Plan Reuse strongly dominates language production in a language, the order of constituents will be rigid, as in English or Mandarin Chinese. If it is weaker, then Easy First has more room for action, and word order will be more flexible, as in Russian or Czech. Both Easy First and Plan Reuse maximize accessibility, but they do it at different levels of abstraction.

3.2.3 Avoidance of Reanalysis

An efficient order will enable the recipient to interpret a sentence correctly (for example, to determine who did what to whom) from the first try. If the analysis has to be done again, it creates additional processing costs. This is why so-called garden-path sentences, e.g., the famous *The horse raced past the barn fell*, are costly. The processor would first interpret the participle *raced* as a finite past-tense form, which is reanalysed after the unambiguous verb form *fell*. This results in a waste of processing resources for the recipient.

The criterion of early and correct access can be linked to the principle of maximization of accessibility, as was argued in Section 1.4.3. The speaker leads the addressee up the garden path because the addressee is used to the fact that the most accessible interpretation is the best one in most cases.

That said, it is necessary to mention that language users do not always engage in reanalysis. Experiments demonstrate that language processing often yields a merely 'good-enough' rather than a detailed linguistic representation of the meaning of a sentence (Ferreira 2003).

Closely related to the requirement to avoid reanalysis is Hawkins' (2004) principle called Maximize On-line Processing. According to this principle, the speaker should use word order that provides the earliest possible access to as much structure as possible. For example, antecedents precede anaphor cross-linguistically, e.g., *John adores himself* is preferred to *Himself adores John*. The former order helps the addressee to identify the referent of the anaphoric expression (*himself*) easily. This can also be regarded as a strategy for maximization of accessibility, because the referent of the reflexive pronoun is immediately accessible if we use the standard order.

In addition to word order adjustments, early access can be secured by case marking and semantic cues. For example, verb-final languages tend to have case marking of the main arguments and a strong association between the syntactic roles and the semantics of the nominals that can fill them (Hawkins 1986; Levshina 2020b). This information helps us to understand who did what to whom early in the sentence, avoiding the costs of reanalysis. See more on this in Section 6.3.

3.2.4 Diagrammatic Iconicity of Order

Linguistic iconicity refers to the correspondence between the conceptual structure and the linguistic structure (Haiman 1985; Croft 2003: Section 7.2). This section focuses on diagrammatic iconicity where the order of linguistic units corresponds to the conceptual relationships between the elements they represent. This correspondence is also known as the semantic principle of linear order (Givón 1990: 92). For example, the order of verbs in the phrase attributed to Julius Caesar, *Veni, vidi, vici* 'I came, I saw, I conquered', corresponds to the order of their conceptualization. An iconic order is efficient because it is easier to produce and to process. For example, it should be easier to process *I moved from Berlin to Amsterdam* than *I moved to Amsterdam from Berlin*. Other examples include frozen binomial expressions, e.g., *birth and death, there and back, past and present* or *kiss and tell*[4] (cf. Benor and Levy 2006), although a major role in determining the order in binomial expressions in general is played by the frequency and therefore accessibility of their components (Fenk-Oczlon 1989; see also Section 3.2.2). Moreover, since the default interpretation in the absence of connectives is the sequential one, additional coding should be added in order to override it, in accordance with the principle of negative correlation between accessibility and costs, e.g., *I conquered after I saw after I came*.

The order does not have to be temporal. Consider the ascending order in numbering, e.g., *Each steak needs 6–7 minutes to cook*, where the lower estimate is followed by the upper estimate. Sequence relationships can also be very abstract and related to the cognitive and communicative space shared

---

[4] The expression *kiss and tell* usually means telling about one's sexual exploits, especially with a famous person.

by the interlocutors. For example, in many languages (but not in all) old information usually precedes new information. This corresponds iconically to the development of knowledge and cognition from known to new information, as in (7A) and (7B):

(7) Russian (personal knowledge)

A: *Nu,   čto   ty   kupila   segodnja?*
well   what   you   bought   today?
'Well, what have you bought today?'

B: *Ja   kupila   novoje   platje.*
I   bought   new   dress
'I've bought a new dress.'

B′: *Novoje   platje   ja   kupila!*
new   dress   I   bought
'I've bought a new dress!'

However, new and newsworthy information can also be put first, followed by old information, as in (7B′), which is more emotionally coloured. The speaker simply cannot wait to boast about her new dress. The old information can in principle be omitted, but it can be added, as in the example, in order to remind the hearer about the continuing topic.

This shows that the pressure for iconicity of information flow can be overridden by the pressure for iconicity of urgency. In some languages more newsworthy (discourse-new and indefinite) nominal constituents are usually put first. Examples are polysynthetic languages Cayuga, Ngandi and Coos (Mithun 1987). However, these languages have obligatory bound pronouns that represent the main arguments, so given information is usually not expressed by separate nominal constituents.

Another very abstract type of iconicity is called iconicity of contiguity, using the classification from Haspelmath (2008c). This means that elements that belong together semantically also tend to occur next to each other in speech. Here, the distance between linguistic units in speech iconically corresponds to the conceptual distance between concepts. This is why most constituents, e.g., nominal phrases, are usually not interrupted by other units, e.g., *We listened to a very interesting lecture*, and not *We a very listened interesting lecture to*. At the same time, spontaneous speech is known for exceptions, e.g., in Russian it is possible to say, *My ocen' interesnuju slusali lekciju* (literally, 'We very interesting listened to lecture'). Similarly, modifiers are located close to their heads. For example, the intensifier *very* is placed next to the property it intensifies, e.g., *a very interesting lecture*, and not *an interesting lecture very*.

It is possible to interpret many of the examples provided above as the tendency to put more accessible information first, following the principle of maximization of accessibility (see also Section 3.2.2). For example, the word order variation in (7) can be explained by higher accessibility of given information in the emotionally neutral utterance (7B) and higher accessibility of newsworthy, subjectively important information in the emotionally coloured version (7B′). Similarly, we can say that continuous constituents are motivated by the higher accessibility of semantically related elements, which can be overridden by other factors, such as emotional salience. In accordance with the principle of information locality, closely related words or constituents should also be put close to each other in the sentence (see Section 3.2.1).

One difficult problem with iconicity as an explanatory factor is that it is not always easy to access a conceptualization independently from its linguistic expression. We do not have access to the language of thought and cannot compare the isomorphism of conceptual and linguistic structure directly (cf. Croft 2003: 203). Moreover, there is evidence that conceptualization of events may depend on the preferred word order in a specific language, as we learn from eye-tracking studies. For example, speakers of subject-first languages, such as Dutch, first look at the agent before starting to describe a transitive event. Quite differently, speakers of Murrinhpatha, an Australian Aboriginal language with very flexible word order, do not show a preference for either the agent or the patient in the earliest stage of speech planning (Nordlinger et al. 2022). Notably, speakers of Tzeltal, a predominantly VOS language, direct their eye-gaze first to the agent (grammatical subject) when describing transitive events, although the preference is weaker (Norcliffe et al. 2015). This might sound surprising, given the fact that the subject in most sentences occurs last. A possible explanation is that the Tzeltal verb carries subject agreement markers. All this means that conventional order influences the order of conceptualization in language production, in accordance with Slobin's (1987) thinking-for-speaking hypothesis. The causal relationships between conceptual and linguistic structure are likely to be bidirectional.

3.2.5 *Uniform Information Density*

The Uniform Information Density (UID) hypothesis and similar proposals, which were discussed in Section 1.3, say that information (in the information-theoretic sense) should be distributed evenly throughout an utterance, avoiding high peaks and canyons. Usually, these ideas are used to explain formal variation, e.g., phonetic reduction or the use or omission of function words. This approach can also help to explain the cross-linguistic distribution of word order. Fenk-Oczlon (1983) argued that word orders are more efficient if they lead to more uniform distribution of information. In particular, objects can be highly informative. However, when introduced later in the sentence, they become more predictable due to previous context, so that a peak in informativity is avoided. With subjects, the situation is reverse. This explains why SOV and SVO are the most popular orders cross-linguistically. Maurits (2011) tested this hypothesis empirically, evaluating which of possible permutations of Subject, Object and Verb leads to the smallest differences between the entropy scores of each word, given the previous words. More on this follows in Section 3.3.4.

Also, avoidance of too high surprisal as a desideratum of the UID hypothesis overlaps with the information locality principle described in Section 3.2.1. According to that principle, closely related words appear together, which helps to minimize the processing costs associated with high surprisal. Therefore, we can interpret this aspect of the UID hypothesis as the fulfilment of the principle of maximization of accessibility, which manifests itself in word order. As for another aspect of the UID hypothesis, namely, the enhancement and reduction of the speech signal, this is explained by the principle of negative correlation between accessibility and costs (see Section 1.3).

3.3 Cross-Linguistic Manifestations of Efficient Order

3.3.1 Minimization of Dependency Distances and Domains

Language users tend to minimize distances between syntactic heads and their dependents (Ferrer-i-Cancho 2006; Liu 2008; Gildea and Temperley 2010; Futrell, Mahowald and Gibson 2015b). An example is so-called heavy-NP shift. In English, the direct object nominal phrase (NP) is usually followed by the prepositional phrase (PP), as in (8a). However, when the NP is heavier than the PP, the preferred order is reversed, as in (8b).

(8) a. *I've read $_{NP}$[the fascinating paper on nominal classifiers, which you sent me last week], $_{PP}$[with great interest].*
  b. *I've read $_{PP}$[with great interest] $_{NP}$[the fascinating paper on nominal classifiers, which you sent me last week].*

Using the Universal Dependencies conventions (Zeman et al. 2020), the dependency distance between the verb *read* and the object *paper* in (8a) is 3 words (*the, fascinating, paper*). The distance between the verb and the head of the prepositional phrase *interest* is 15 words. If we add up these numbers, we get $3 + 15 = 18$ as the sum dependency distance with regard to these two dependencies. In (8b), the dependency distance between *read* and *interest* is 3 words, and the distance between *read* and *paper* is 6 words, which makes the sum distance of 9 words. Since the sum of dependency distances in (8b) is shorter than in (8a), the word order in (8b) is more efficient than the order in (8a). Note that the preposition *with* is regarded as the head of the prepositional

3.3 Examples of Efficient Word Order

phrase *with great interest* in many theoretical frameworks (Osborne and Gerdes 2019), but this approach will lead to similar results.

The principle of minimization of dependency distances is closely related to the law of growing constituents formulated by Behaghel (1909) on the basis of text data from Indo-European languages. If there are two constituents of different length, the longer constituent follows the shorter one. Corpus evidence (Wasow 1997) and experimental data (Stallings and MacDonald 2011) support this claim for English. The higher the ratio of length of an NP and a PP, the more likely it is that speakers of English will put the shorter PP before the longer NP.

According to the dependency locality theory (Gibson 1998, 2000), longer-distance attachments, as in (8a), involve higher integration costs. As for storage costs, they are involved if both complements are obligatory and therefore expected. For example, Gibson (1998: 51) argues that (9a) is more memory-expensive than (9b) because the verb *give* creates an expectation of Recipient and Theme coming later in the sentence:

(9)   a. *The young boy gave $_{NP}$[the beautiful green pendant that had been in the jewellery store window for weeks] $_{PP}$[to the girl].*
        b. *The young boy gave $_{PP}$[to the girl] $_{NP}$[the beautiful green pendant that had been in the jewellery store window for weeks].*

Recent corpus-based studies, however, usually do not make the distinction between obligatory and non-obligatory constituents (which is very difficult due to the absence of this information in most corpora, and also theoretically problematic because this distinction is gradient). Also, there is normally no distinction between storage and integration costs. In addition, Gibson's theory takes into account the number of new referents that need to be integrated into the structure. In corpus-based studies, processing difficulty is usually represented by the number of all words between the head and the dependent. The assumption is that different measures are highly correlated with each other, so that the differences between them are not substantial (Wasow 2002; Futrell, Levy and Gibson 2020).

Interest in measuring dependency distances has been boosted by the emergence of large corpora annotated for syntactic dependency relations, especially the Universal Dependencies corpora (Zeman et al. 2020). But the preferences in the examples above can also be explained if we focus on syntactic constituents (e.g., NP, VP or PP) instead of dependencies. Most prominently, Hawkins (2004) argued that language users prefer word orders that minimize the syntactic and semantic domains needed for recognizing the constituent structure – a principle called Minimize Domains. A domain is 'the smallest connected sequence of terminal elements and their associated syntactic and semantic properties that must be processed for the production and/or recognition of the combinatorial or dependency relation in question' (Hawkins 2004: 32). The domains in which immediate constituent (IC) relations can be processed are called constituent recognition domains. As an illustration, take the following sentence from Hawkins (2004: 23):

(10)   The old lady $_V$[counted] $_{PP1}$[on him] $_{PP2}$[in her retirement].

We can find many different domains, depending on what kind of information we are processing. If we focus on the VP and its three immediate constituents (V, PP_1, PP_2), the domain is *counted on him in*. We can already recognize the structure from this sequence. Alternatively, if we take the lexical meaning of the verb *count*, the sufficient domain is *counted on him*, or possibly just *counted on*.

The principle Minimize Domains is about making the domains as small as possible. For example, the domain for parsing the lexical combination and dependency between *count* and *on* is smaller if the preposition immediately follows the verb. Similarly, if we take the domain for the processing of the VP and its three immediate constituents, *counted on him in*, the domain is four words. If we change the order of the two prepositional phrases, as shown in (11), the domain necessary for recognizing the constituents will contain five words: *counted in her retirement on*. It will be longer. Therefore, the order in (11) is less efficient than the order in (10).

(11)   The old lady $_V$[counted] $_{PP2}$[in her retirement] $_{PP1}$[on him].

We can explain the preference in the example of heavy-NP shift, repeated below for convenience, by the same principle:

(12)   a. I've read $_{NP}$[the fascinating paper on nominal classifiers, which you sent me last week], $_{PP}$[with great interest].
        b. I've read $_{PP}$[with great interest] $_{NP}$[the fascinating paper on nominal classifiers, which you sent me last week].

In (12a), the domain is *read the fascinating paper on nominal classifiers, which you sent me last week, with*. It contains fourteen words. In (12b), it is *read with great interest the*, only five words. Thus, both Hawkins' constituent approach and the dependency distance approach predict that the word order in (12b) is more efficient and should therefore be preferred by language users.

The motivation for the principle Minimize Domains has to do with working memory and computation system (Hawkins 2014: 13). The smaller the recognition domain, the fewer additional phonological, morphological, syntactic and semantic decisions that need to be made simultaneously with the task of identifying the domain in question. There will be fewer competing structural decisions to resolve.

These theories nicely predict the behaviour of postverbal elements, which consistently follow the rule 'short before long'. There is also some evidence that preverbal constituents follow the rule 'long before short', as predicted by the processing principles above. In Japanese, for example, the order of objects and postpositional phrases, subjects and objects, and direct and indirect objects supports the theoretical expectations: long constituents are followed by short ones. This word order minimizes dependency distances and domains (Hawkins 1994; Yamashita and Chang 2001). But if we take two pre- or postpositional phrases depending on one verbal head, corpora of different languages reveal no clear preferences for long before short in the preverbal position (Liu 2020). The evidence for the dependency minimization account is thus not always clear.

Moreover, there are some arguments against the memory-based explanation of domain minimization. As Wasow (1997) argues, this account would require that both constituents are fully planned at the moment of speech, so that their weights can be compared. However, it is questionable if the speaker can do that. Instead, the actual formulation of the phrases takes place, at least, partly, after the order has been chosen. Wasow presents some corpus data to support his claim. He shows that collocations, e.g., *take into account/consideration* or *bring to an end/close*, more frequently participate in heavy-NP shift than non-collocations. The reason is that collocations are easier to produce for the speaker as one sequence before the more complex part that requires more planning. Note, however, that producing opaque collocations as one sequence can be more beneficial for the addressee, too, because it allows them to decide immediately on the lexical meaning of the verb (cf. Hawkins' example with *count on* in (10)). We need more research in order to understand how all these factors interact.

3.3.2 *Preferred Order of Elements within a Nominal Phrase*

Elements of a nominal phrase – Noun, Adjective, Determiner and Numeral – appear in a different order in languages of the world. For example, English has the order Determiner – Numeral – Adjective – Noun, as in *those three little kittens*, whereas in Basque, the order is Numeral – Noun – Adjective – Determiner, as in *three kittens little those*. At the same time, some orders are common, and some orders are extremely rare or even not attested, e.g., Adjective – Numeral – Determiner – Noun, as in *little three those kittens* (Culbertson, Schouwstra and Kirby 2020). In particular, in the preferred word orders, Adjective is placed closest to Noun, whereas Determiner is placed farthest away.

It seems that these preferences can be explained by the strength of association between objects and their different properties in the world. This account has been tested on corpus data by Culbertson et al. (2020), who used Pointwise Mutual Information as a measure of association. Associations are the strongest between Noun and Adjective. For example, wine is strongly associated with its colour (e.g., red or white), whereas skyscrapers are strongly associated with their height. Colour and height are inherent properties of wine and skyscrapers, respectively. Numerosity is less strongly associated with Nouns, although some objects usually come in pairs, e.g., shoes or socks, and some come in dozens or tens, e.g., eggs. Finally, Determiners, which usually specify the location and/or relation to the speech act participants, have the weakest association. This is not surprising, since individual Determiners are highly frequent and combine with very many diverse nouns.

Culbertson et al.'s findings can be explained by the principle of locality, which says that semantically and syntactically closely related elements should appear close to each other (see Section 3.2.1). This helps to maximize accessibility, decreasing memory load and expectation-based costs.

The principle of information locality can also explain the order of multiple adjectives in a nominal phrase, as demonstrated by Hahn et al. (2018) and Futrell (2019). For example, English allows the order *a large wooden table*, but not *a wooden large table*. The adjective with higher mutual information will be closer to the noun. Also, evaluative adjectives are placed further from the noun, e.g., *a beautiful red dress*, but not *a red beautiful dress*. This can be explained by the fact that evaluative adjectives do not restrict the set of referents but communicate the speaker's attitude. Their applicability to any given noun is determined by the speaker's subjective state rather than by the noun itself. Speaking simply, what is beautiful for one person can be ugly for another. This explains why evaluative adjectives are located on the periphery of a nominal phrase. The explanation is supported by diachronic evidence. According to Traugott (2010), as a linguistic unit develops more subjective meanings, its position also moves towards the periphery.

3.3.3 Cross-Linguistic Regularities in the Order of Morphemes

There are a few cross-linguistic generalizations concerning the order of elements within a word. Two of them are discussed in this section. The first one is the suffixing preference. The second one is the preference for a particular order of derivational and inflectional morphemes depending on the type of grammatical meaning they express.

It is well known that suffixing is more frequent cross-linguistically than prefixing, and both are more frequent than infixing (Greenberg 1963). Several explanations have been proposed. One theory belongs to Cutler, Hawkins and Gilligan (1985), who argue that suffixes are preferred to prefixes due to the fact that word onset is a particularly salient position serving as a strong cue for word recognition. Word endings are less salient than onsets, but more salient than middles. Moreover, according to Hupp, Sloutsky and Culcover (2009), beginnings are the most salient for any kind of sequences. If a word is distorted at its onset, the effects for processing are more disruptive than if the distortion happens at the end of the word. Therefore, by putting roots first, as the elements that carry the most important information, it is easier to avoid reanalysis or misunderstanding.

The causality can be also reversed, however. It may be that speakers of WEIRD languages (that is, spoken in western, educated, industrial, rich and democratic societies), which provide the main bulk of psycholinguistic evidence, learn to pay more attention to the onset because it is the most informative in those languages. Possibly, their experience with a suffixing language leads to perception of beginnings as the most salient position for determining similarity. In fact, Martin and Culbertson (2020) show that speakers of Kîîtharaka, a prefixing Bantu language, perceive endings as the most salient for determining similarity, contrary to Hupp et al. (2009).

Another explanation of the suffixing preference has to do with the tendency to provide disambiguating information early. As already mentioned (see Section 3.2.3), this tendency has been captured by Hawkins' (2004) principle Maximize On-line Processing, an efficient strategy in communication. A lexical root or stem is less predictable, or more informative than an affix because individual lexical roots are more diverse and less frequent in comparison with individual affixes. Therefore, affixes are less important for word recognition. By providing the maximum of information at the beginning, the speaker helps the addressee to make correct predictions about the word.

Yet another explanation was formulated by Himmelmann (2014), who argues that the suffixing preference is due to prosodic factors and grammaticalization processes. In general, affixes represent a result of greater grammaticalization and fusion of clitic function words with their lexical hosts. But if a function word precedes its lexical host, there can be a prosodic boundary between them, which impedes the fusion, as in the following example (Chafe 1980: 308, story 9):

(13)   And that's the end of the .. story.

The prosodic boundary separates the definite article from the head noun. In contrast, when a function word occurs after its lexical host, there are hardly any prosodic boundaries, and prosody does not impede the fusion. As a result, postpositional clitics become suffixes more frequently than clitics that precede their hosts.[5]

---

[5] Note that the cross-linguistic occurrence rates of preposed function words and postposed function words do not reveal this postposing preference (Bybee, Pagliuca and Perkins 1990: 5), which means that the initial position of the source function words expressing grammatical meanings (aspect, tense, mood, valency, etc.) that later become affixes is not a plausible explanation of the suffixing preference.

But why does the boundary occur more frequently when a function word occurs before its host than the other way round? According to Diessel (2019: Section 5.5), this can be explained by predictability. The conditional probability of a lexical unit (e.g., a noun) given a functional element (e.g., an article) is low. For example, the article *the* can be followed by thousands of different nouns. The conditional probability of a functional element given a notion word is higher. If we take a typical English noun, it is likely to be accompanied by *the*. Thus, function words are more predictable given content words than the other way round. If a function word occurs before its host, the order of production means that the host is not very predictable (e.g., *the girl/house/conference...*). Low predictability may trigger production difficulties, which can result in disfluencies like pauses and hesitations. In contrast, if a function word occurs after its host, the function word has a high degree of predictability. It is retrieved and produced more easily, which means that the chances of a prosodic boundary are lower. High predictability leads to fusion of the host and the postposed element, which explains why suffixing occurs more frequently in languages of the world. Therefore, the suffixing preference can be explained by the higher accessibility of postposed dependent units in comparison with preposed ones.

Notably, the suffixing preference is not monolithic. It is very strong in verb-final (OV) languages and in the grammatical markers expressing nominal number, case, as well as tense and aspect (Cysouw 2009). As for person marking, there is even a slight preference for prefixing.[6] Among potential explanations of this preference is word order (e.g., if Subject is before Verb, this can favour the emergence of subject prefixes), as well as the fact that the main participants of the situation often have high accessibility and are therefore produced earlier.

To finish this discussion, it is necessary to mention that the relative scarceness of infixing can be explained by the general tendency of keeping semantically related elements together (due to the information locality principle discussed in Section 3.2.1).

The second important cross-linguistic generalization related to the order of morphemes has to do with the relative distance of inflectional and derivational morphemes from the root. There are several well-known tendencies. Usually, derivational morphemes occur closer to the root than inflectional morphemes do. For example, in the wordform *teachers,* the derivational suffix *-er* is closer to the root *teach* than the plural marker *-s*. Inflectional morphemes also tend to be arranged in a particular order. For example, 'the expression of number

---

[6] The prefixing preference is observed in small paradigms with few person markers that are not syncretic with number. This may also be a 'founder' effect, however, because person prefixes are observed mostly in the Americas.

3.3 Examples of Efficient Word Order

almost always comes between the noun base and the expression of case' (Greenberg 1963: 112).

As for verbal derivational and inflectional morphemes, the order is usually as follows (Bybee 1985):

(14)   Valence > Voice > Aspect > Tense > Mood > Agreement (Person and Number)

Bybee argues that the position of a morpheme is determined by the effect that this morpheme has on the root meaning. Derivational morphemes are more relevant to the root meaning in the sense that they change it more dramatically. Similarly, number has 'a direct effect on the entity or entities referred to by the noun', while case has 'no effect on what entity is being referred to' (Bybee 1985: 34). Also, the categories on the left of the scale in (14) have higher relevance to the verb than the ones on the right. For example, valence changes the number and role of participants involved in the event. It is central to the semantics of the verb. The differences related to valence are often so striking that they are lexicalized, as in the causative–inchoative pairs *kill* and *die*. In contrast, mood has the whole proposition in its scope, so it is less relevant for the lexical meaning of the verb. Similarly, agreement markers, such as person and number inflections, refer to the participants and are therefore peripheral with regard to the meaning of the verb.[7]

We can explain these tendencies using the information locality principle. If we take aspect markers, which have a strong impact on the meaning of the verb, they would also be less freely applicable to different verbs than more peripheral markers. For example, an imperfective marker is more compatible with durative verbs than with punctual ones. Therefore, the mutual information of the root and the affix will be relatively high. In contrast, a person marker has fewer restrictions on the root. The mutual information would thus be lower. This reasoning is supported by a corpus study by Hahn, Degen and Futrell (2021), who investigated the order of morphemes in Japanese and Sesotho (a Southern Bantu language spoken in Lesotho and South Africa). Hahn et al. find that the order of morphemes correlates with mutual information, which represents the strength of association between neighbouring morphemes.

Similar reasoning can explain the order of case and number markers on nouns. According to Greenberg's Universal 39 (1963), number markers are usually located closer to the stem than case markers, as in Turkish *kitap-lar-ı*

---

[7] According to Bybee, the semantic relevance also determines the degree of fusion of morphemes. However, agreement markers are often strongly fused with the verb, although they are not highly relevant for the verb semantics. Ariel (1999) explains this paradox by the fact that agreement markers are the diachronic outcome of strongly reduced pronouns, which represent highly accessible referents in discourse.

'book-PL-ACC.DEF'. A series of experiments by Saldana, Oseki and Culbertson (2021) demonstrates that learners of a miniature artificial language consistently reproduce this order even in the absence of wordforms with both case and number markers in the input language. Their behaviour is independent of the learners' native language (English or Japanese), morpheme position with regard to the stem (prefixal or suffixal), degree of boundedness, frequency and other features. Importantly, this strong tendency can be reversed in the presence of case allomorphy. Since allomorphy increases the dependency between case markers and the stem, this serves as evidence for the principle of maximization of accessibility.

3.3.4 Subject-First Dominance

The dominance of the subject-first order in the world's languages is a well-known fact (Greenberg 1963; Dryer 2013). There are some grounds to believe that this preference is not a historical contingency. For example, experimental evidence reveals that even speakers of verb-initial languages (Irish, Tagalog) stick to subject-first order when communicating in gestures, while the 'native' verb-initial order is the third choice after SOV and SVO for those speakers (Futrell et al. 2015a). So, there is something deeply rooted in human cognition and communication that explains this dominance.

At the same time, the subject-first dominance is probably the champion if we count the number of explanations suggested in the literature. In fact, almost all the explanatory factors discussed in this chapter can play a role, potentially.

First of all, putting subject before object is efficient from the planning perspective because transitive subjects are usually highly accessible. That is, they are discourse-given, short, pronominal and animate (see Chapter 8). Therefore, it is efficient to place them first and use the remaining time to plan the less accessible elements (see Section 3.2.2).

A second explanation has to do with memory costs. If the subject comes first, the addressee will not expect an object because there is a chance that the sentence is intransitive. In contrast, if the first constituent is an object or adverbial phrase, there is still an expectation of the subject, which creates memory costs at this location (Gibson 1998). This theory, however, leaves unexplained the preference for subject-first order in ergative languages. If the subject with ergative marking appears first, it creates an expectation of an object because ergative marking signals that the sentence is transitive. It would be more efficient to place first the object marked with an absolutive case, which is similar formally to the intransitive subject, but this order is not very common among ergative languages.

The next potential explanation has to do with diagrammatic iconicity of order. In a prototypical transitive sentence, the action is transferred from Agent to Patient (Hopper and Thompson 1980). This means that the energy 'flows' from Agent to Patient, where the Agent is the initiator, and the Patient is the affected entity and endpoint. An example is the causative event in (15). The Agent (the woman) is the source of energy necessary for the change that occurs with the Patient (the door).

(15)   *The woman closed the door.*

The order of subject and object reflects iconically this flow of energy. Thus, there is a correspondence between the subject-first order and the conceptualization of a transitive event.

In addition, Fenk-Oczlon (1983) argues that subject-first basic orders are efficient because they produce a more uniform distribution of information for a randomly selected transitive clause. In contrast, the orders OSV and OVS are particularly inefficient. The logic behind this is as follows. According to Maurits' (2011: 117) data, there are fewer agents in the corpora than objects that the agents can manipulate. There are also multiple actions that the same agent can perform. In contrast, the number of objects is very high. This is why objects will have a very high surprisal value when they first appear. The information density will be more uniform, and surprisal peaks can be avoided, if there are some elements in front (subjects and/or verbs) which can help to reduce the surprisal of objects. Also, objects are highly predictive of verbs. For example, if 'pizza' is Object, then it is likely that the verb will be 'eat'. So, if an initial object is followed by Verb, e.g., *pizza eat*, there will be a peak in surprisal on the object, followed by a very low valley on the verb. This creates large fluctuations in information density, which is not efficient.

One problem with this approach is that the density is only evaluated at the sentence level, without previous context. Subjects are usually discourse-given and highly accessible from context. This is why their informativeness should be evaluated in discourse, rather than in an isolated sentence. Also, the empirical data provided by Maurits (2011) do not give consistent rankings of possible orders in terms of their information density profiles.

I propose that subject-first dominance can be explained by maximization of accessibility. Since subjects are usually given, putting them first reduces surprisal and minimizes memory costs. The iconic correspondence between word order and the conceptualization of energy flow from the agent to the patient arises because agents are usually humans. Since we usually speak about humans, they are often given and topical.

3.3.5 *Continuous Constituents and Rarity of Crossing Dependencies*

Cross-linguistically, syntactic trees with crossing dependencies are rare. In formal literature, such trees are called non-projective. They do not correspond

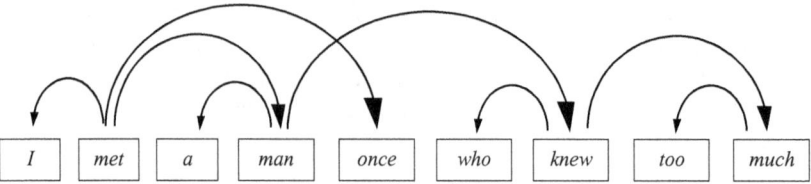

Figure 3.1 A sentence with crossing dependencies, according to the Universal Dependencies style

to structures generated by lexicalized context-free phrase-structure grammars (see an overview in Yadav, Husain and Futrell (2021)).

We often observe crossing dependencies if there is discontinuity between syntactically related constituents or their elements. Consider the sentence *I met a man once who knew too much*. An analysis of this sentence according to the Universal Dependencies style (Zeman et al. 2020) is presented in Figure 3.1.[8] The arcs that represent syntactic dependencies (from heads to dependents) cross because the adverb *once* separates the head noun from the relative clause.

There is corpus evidence that language users avoid crossing syntactic dependencies (Nivre and Nilsson 2005; Havelka 2007; Ferrer-i-Cancho et al. 2018). Yadav et al. (2021) demonstrate that the actual syntactic trees found in corpora have fewer crossing dependencies than random baselines. This means that language users have a bias against crossing dependencies.

A possible explanation of this fact lies in the tendency to keep semantically and grammatically related units close, in accordance with the principle of information locality, which, in its turn, is a manifestation of the principle of maximization of accessibility.

Discontinuities and crossed dependencies can arise due to planning issues in spontaneous language production and the tendency to put accessible information first, when these pressures override word order conventions. For example, discontinuities and crossing dependencies in Dutch are often motivated by the sentence bracket structure, which is similar to but looser than the German one, in the sense that diverse constituents are more often allowed to appear after the second (lexical) verb. The sentence in (16) contains a discontinuous nominal phrase with an extraposed prepositional phrase *een auto ... met zes deuren* 'a car ... with six doors', which is interrupted by the lexical verb *gekocht* 'bought'. Since the lexical verb is connected with the auxiliary 'have', and 'a car' is connected with the prepositional phrase, this sentence contains crossing dependencies.

---

[8] Note that a different analysis (e.g., if we treat 'man' as the head of 'who') would also lead to crossing dependencies.

(16) Dutch (De Smedt and Kempen 1996: 148)

Ik heb een auto gekocht met zes deuren.
I have a car bought with six doors
'I have bought a car with six doors.'

As De Smedt and Kempen (1996: 161) write, such discontinuities offer advantages for incremental sentence production. Right dislocations allow the speaker to produce the constituents that are ready and postpone the ones that are more complex and 'heavy' to a later stage. Therefore, discontinuities can help to save time. They can also help to minimize dependency lengths, and therefore save memory costs, both for the speaker and the addressee.

3.3.6 Greenbergian Word Order Correlations and Implications

Probably the most famous universals in typology are Greenbergian word order correlations and implications. For example, Greenberg's (1963) Universal 2 says, 'In languages with prepositions, the genitive almost always follows the governing noun, while in languages with postpositions it almost always precedes.' This is a bidirectional relationship. Notably, we find correlations between multiple features. For example, the order of Verb and Object correlates with the order of adposition and NP, copula verb and predicate, 'want'-verb and its complement, complementizer and complement clause, question particle and sentence, verb and adpositional phrase, noun and relative clause, adjective and standard of comparison, and some others (Dryer 1992).

Many discussions of these multiple correlations involve the notion of harmony. Word orders are harmonic if they co-occur in a language as predicted by the correlations. For example, the orders Preposition + Noun and Noun + Genitive are harmonic, as are the orders Noun + Postposition and Genitive + Noun, whereas, for example, Preposition + Noun and Genitive + Noun would be disharmonic.

There exist a plethora of explanations why harmonic orders are preferred. In particular, Dryer's (1992) Branching Direction Theory focuses on the relative order of phrasal (recursive, branching) and non-phrasal (non-recursive, non-branching) elements. It claims that languages tend to prefer only one order: either phrasal elements followed by non-phrasal ones, or non-phrasal elements followed by phrasal ones. For example, in a language with VO and Noun + Relative Clause orders, the branching elements (Object and Relative clause) follow the non-branching ones (Verb and Noun). In contrast, in a language with OV and Relative Clause + Noun, the branching elements precede the non-branching ones. Importantly, both languages would display harmonic orders.

Also, one often speaks of head-initial and head-final languages, depending on the order of the head (which is usually non-branching) and the dependent (which is usually branching), although Dryer (1992) showed that the criterion of branching direction is superior to that of head direction, in that the former predicts the cross-linguistic correlations more precisely. Moreover, the head status of some elements is controversial and depends on the theoretical framework.

Can efficiency explain these correlations? There is a possibility that they emerge due to the pressure to minimize processing costs. In particular, Hawkins (e.g., 1994, 2014) argues that head-initial, or right-branching, and head-final, or left-branching, languages satisfy the principle Minimize Domains, while mixed languages do not. For example, we can create four possible scenarios for a verb with an adpositional phrase (Hawkins 2014: 90, 99), where (17a) represents a right-branching and head-initial structure, (17b) represent a left-branching and head-final structure, and (17c) and (17d) are mixed.

(17) a. [$_{VP}$ went [$_{PP}$ to the movies]]
      b. [[the movies to $_{PP}$] went $_{VP}$]
      c. [$_{VP}$ went [the movies to $_{PP}$]]
      d. [[$_{PP}$ to the movies] went $_{VP}$]

The verb phrase recognition domains are underlined. According to Hawkins, the harmonic orders in (17a) and (17b) are efficient for processing because they result in smaller domains. This is why they are common cross-linguistically, unlike the non-harmonic variants in (17c) and (17d).

Using dependencies instead of constituents, Temperley (2008) argues that a 'same-branching' grammar will result in shorter dependencies. At the same time, in case of multiple dependents and one head, it can be advantageous when one-word constituents branch in the opposite direction. For example, it is efficient to put an adverb before the verb, as in (18a). Compare it with (18b), where the adverbial modifier is long, and it should not be placed before the verb.

(18) a. *She is **quickly** rising in the music industry.*
      b. *She is rising in the music industry **too quickly for her age**.*

Another relevant factor is analogy. This can be interpreted as a kind of priming due to structural or semantic similarity of the current structure to one experienced before. It was argued in Section 3.2.2 that priming occurs due to increased accessibility of a recent form or meaning, so analogy can be seen as a result of accessibility maximization. Analogy in the order of functionally similar units can be beneficial for processing because it allows us to reuse the same accessible schema (MacDonald 2013; see also Section 3.2.2). For example, the orders Verb + Object, Verb + Adverb and Auxiliary + Non-finite Verb can be generalized as the order of a finite verb followed by something else. Previous linguistic experience and immediate context with Verb + Object

3.3 Examples of Efficient Word Order

can prime the other two orders, making them more accessible, which makes production and comprehension easier.

The advantages of harmonic word orders may not be restricted to processing optimization only. They can also be easier to learn. For example, artificial language experiments reveal that adult and child language learners prefer harmonic word orders in the nominal phrase (e.g., either Adjective + Noun and Numeral + Noun, or Noun + Adjective and Noun + Numeral). This result does not depend on whether the learners' L1 is harmonic or not itself (Culbertson, Smolensky and Legendre 2012; Culbertson, Schouwstra and Kirby 2020).

Moreover, we should not underestimate the role of diachronic processes; for example, adpositions develop from verbs or nouns, which determines whether they become prepositions or postpositions (cf. Dryer 2019). This can explain some correlations (but not all, as shown in Section 5.6).

Let us now move to word order implications, which represent one-directional relationships between different word order patterns. Implications usually emerge as a result of competing motivations in language (cf. Croft 2003: Section 3.4). For illustration, consider Greenberg's Universal 25, 'If the pronominal object follows the verb, so does the nominal object' (Greenberg 1963). This is an implicational universal because it works only in one direction: if the nominal object follows the verb, the pronominal object may or may not do the same. This universal can be explained by two competing principles: the tendency to put accessible and short constituents first, and analogy, which means that functionally similar constituents should have the same position, due to the reasons explained above. In other words, the accessibility of specific words competes with accessibility of the abstract schema (cf. MacDonald's [2013] principles Easy First and Plan Reuse in Section 3.2.2).

Figure 3.2 shows how often nominal and pronominal objects occur after the lexical verb in the Universal Dependencies corpora (version 2.6, Zeman et al. 2020).[9] The numbers are proportions relative to the total number of objects of each type. The labels are the ISO 639-3 codes of the languages. In languages such as Hindi, Turkish, Japanese and others, which are located in the bottom left corner, both pronouns and nouns precede the verb, e.g., *I ice-cream love* and *I it love*. Here, the principle of analogy is fulfilled, but the maximization of accessibility of specific constituents is achieved only partially. The speaker can indeed produce accessible pronouns early, but there is no extra time for less accessible nouns. In the languages located in the top right corner (Arabic, English, Hebrew, Indonesian, Irish and others), pronominal and nominal objects follow the verb, e.g., *I love ice-cream* and *I love it*. Abstract analogy works here, too, whereas the planning of specific units is optimal only for

---

[9] Only corpora with at least 50 pronominal objects and 50 nominal objects were taken into account. The objects were counted in main clauses only.

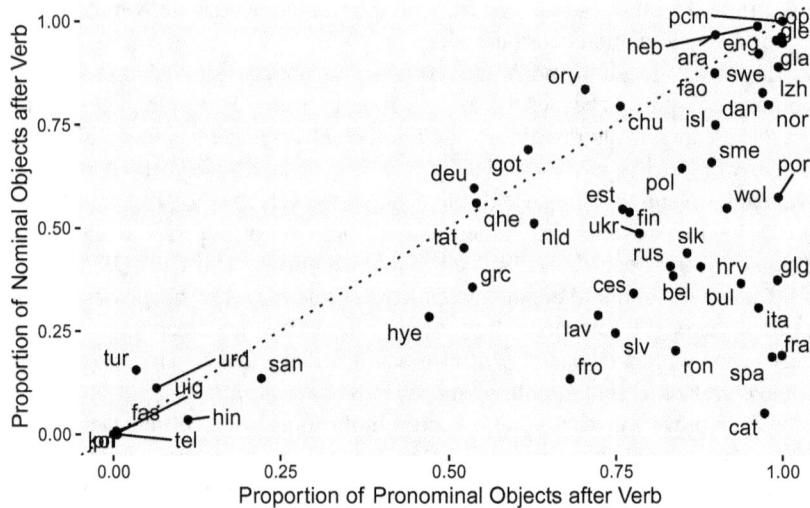

Figure 3.2 Proportions of nominal objects (horizontal axis) and pronominal objects (vertical axis) after verbs in the Universal Dependencies corpora

nouns because the speaker cannot produce accessible pronouns early. The Romance languages (French, Catalan, Spanish and others), which are located in the bottom right corner, have preverbal pronominal objects and postverbal nominal objects, e.g., *I love ice-cream*, but *I it love*. Here, the management of light and heavy objects is optimal, but the principle of analogy is not observed because the objects have different positions.

The top left corner is empty, in full accordance with Greenberg's Universal. There are no languages with preverbal nominal objects and postverbal pronominal objects, such that one could say *I ice-cream love*, but *I love it*. This order would violate both principles. While some of the attested languages correspond to this principle well (the Romance languages, in particular), and the others correspond to some extent (but are probably easier to learn, due to analogy), unattested languages would be very inefficient in terms of processing. They could also be more difficult to learn.

3.4 Star Wars and Violations of Conventional Word Order

In all above-mentioned examples, the speaker normally prefers a low-cost word order to a high-cost one. But in some cases an inefficient word order can be deliberately and ostensively chosen by the speaker in order to trigger certain cognitive effects in the addressee. This is accompanied by a violation of word order conventions. A famous example is the speech of Yoda, a powerful

3.4 Violations of Word Order Rules in Star Wars

Master Jedi from the Star Wars universe, who appeared in most of the films of the franchise (Episodes I, II, III, V and VI, as well as the sequels *The Force Awakens* and *The Last Jedi*, as a voice). Yoda belongs to an unknown species. One of his distinctive characteristics, in addition to large green ears, is the use of unusual word order patterns. Some examples are provided below:

(19)   a. *Friends you have there.* (Episode V)
        b. *Help you it will.* (Episode II)
        c. *The secret of the Ancient Order of the Whills, he studied.* (Episode III)

Yodish word order has been described by some linguists as OSV or XSV, where X stands for any complement that goes with the verb.[10] A more precise description would be as follows:

(20)   Non-finite part of predicate/Object/Oblique – Subject – Finite Verb/Auxiliary/Copula

The first part can be object, oblique, nominal part of the predicate or non-finite parts of the predicate, i.e., participle or infinitive with dependent elements. They are followed by the subject and the finite verb, auxiliary or copula. Below are some examples that support this generalization:

(21)   a. *Rest I need* (Episode VI)
        b. *To his family, send him.* (Episode III)
        c. *A certainty it is.* (Episode II)
        d. *Hard to see, the dark side is.* (Episode I)
        e. *Earned it, I have.* (Episode VI)

However, there are some exceptions, as in the examples below:

(22)   Copula/AUX – subject:

        a. *Not ready for the burden were you.* (Episode VI)
        b. *Heard from no one, have we.* (Episode III)

(23)   Object – subject – auxiliary – lexical verb:

        The outlying systems, you must sweep. (Episode III)

Importantly, some of Yoda's sentences have a standard word order:

(24)   a. *Master Obi-Wan has lost a planet.* (Episode II)
        b. *A Jedi's strength flows from the Force.* (Episode III)
        c. *That place is strong with the dark side of the force.* (Episode V)

---

[10] See a blog post by Geoffrey K. Pullum at http://itre.cis.upenn.edu/~myl/languagelog/archives/002173.html, a post by Mark Libermann at http://itre.cis.upenn.edu/~myl/languagelog/archives/002182.html, and an article in *The Atlantic* by Adrienne Lafrance www.theatlantic.com/entertainment/archive/2015/12/hmmmmm/420798/ (last access 16 October 2021).

Of course, the famous formula *May the Force be with you* is in standard English, too.

Remarkably, Yodish word order has longer dependency distances on average than its standardized version (Levshina 2019c). This conclusion is based on the Yodish data collected from the Internet Movie Scripts Database.[11] Data from five episodes were used: two episodes from the original trilogy (Episodes V and VI) and three episodes from the prequel trilogy (Episodes I, II and III).

The higher processing costs are to a large extent due to the fact that the auxiliaries and copulas are often separated from the non-finite and nominal parts of the predicates. Below is an example:

(25)   a. ***Failed*** *to stop the Sith Lord, I **have**.* (Episode III, original)
        b. *I **have failed** to stop the Sith Lord.* (standardized)

Thus, Yodish is less efficient than standard English due to the separation of non-finite, lexical parts from the auxiliaries and copulas. This pattern is not only inefficient, it is also quite unrealistic. The reason is that grammaticalized elements, such as auxiliary verbs, arise in highly predictable contexts (see Section 5.4). For instance, the future marker *going to* is reduced (cf. *gonna*) and semantically bleached in the contexts where it is followed by a verb. When the auxiliary is not accompanied by the lexical part, it is less predictable and therefore less likely to undergo formal reduction and semantic change. Frequent co-occurrence of the elements together is necessary for grammaticalization and also explains why auxiliaries usually lose their positional freedom (Lehmann 2015: 168). The existence of auxiliaries in Yodish that are often split from their lexical elements is then difficult to explain. This shows that Yodish is truly alien.

However, these additional processing costs are counterbalanced by additional cognitive effects. In particular, we can speak here of defamiliarization, a theoretic concept from Russian formalism:

> The technique of art is to make objects 'unfamiliar', to make forms difficult, to increase the difficulty and length of perception because the process of perception is an aesthetic end in itself and must be prolonged. (Shklovsky 2017: 16)

Such violations provide additional cognitive effects of 'strangeness', which are important for creation of a new fictional universe. George Lucas and other film creators responsible for Yoda's syntax seem to be exploiting the principle of positive correlation between benefits and costs. Extra efforts spent during the processing of Yoda's utterances promise the film audience extra benefits in the form of additional inferences. As Yoda says himself, 'You must unlearn what you have learned' (Episode V). Thus, although we can conclude that Yoda's

---

[11] See www.imsdb.com (last access 9 July 2022).

word order is not optimal by itself, it is perfectly efficient for the communication between the film creators and the audience.

3.5 Conclusions

This chapter discussed the main criteria of efficient order of meaningful elements, from morphemes to words and syntactic constituents. Examples of efficient and inefficient order were also given, with alternative theories and accounts explaining language users' preferences in production and difficulties in comprehension. It is not always easy to tell which explanatory factors are relevant and which are not.

Speaking very broadly, we can say that accessibility plays a crucial role in determining efficient order, similar to the coding length asymmetries discussed in Chapter 2. Many cross-linguistic generalizations – from relative position of morphemes and nominal phrase elements to the prevalence of subject-first orders and rarity of crossing dependencies – can be explained by the principle of maximization of accessibility. Accessibility has different aspects. One of them is the availability of a mental representation due to the semantic and discourse properties of a referent. For example, discourse-given referents are more accessible than new ones. Moreover, accessibility is also determined by the availability of a strong trace of an exemplar in the memory, due to its recency, as well as by surprisal of linguistic units.

Word order interacts with coding length. For example, if the position of an element is non-canonical, more articulatory effort can be necessary because the element will be less expected and therefore less accessible. In Section 3.2.4 it was mentioned that a non-iconic order of events in a sentence leads to the use of longer expressions (e.g., *I conquered after I came*). Consider a different example from Warlpiri discussed by Hawkins (2004: Ch. 6). When NP constituents are adjacent, as in (26a), the ergative case marking occurs just once in the NP and is not copied on all constituents. However, case copying occurs only if a noun and a dependent adjective are non-adjacent, as in (26b):

(26) Warlpiri: Pama-Nyungan (Hale 1973: 314)

    a. *tyarntu wiri-ngki+tyu yarlki-rnu*
        dog   big-ERG+me bite-PST

    b. *tyarntu-ngku+tyu yarlku-rnu wiri-ngki*
        dog-ERG+me bite-PST big-ERG
        'The big dog bit me.'

Another example is Korean, where object marking is probabilistic and depends on numerous parameters (see Chapter 8). All other things being equal, object marking is less likely to occur if the object is adjacent to the verb

(Kim 2008). These examples suggest that lower accessibility of the grammatical function due to word order can be compensated for by additional coding.

One caveat is that many of the existing processing theories are based on WEIRD languages, such as English and Dutch, which have many cross-linguistically rare features. However, recent typologically informed work (e.g., Martin and Culbertson 2020) suggests that the results based on such languages should not be extrapolated to all languages automatically. This means that some ideas presented here might be challenged later when more diverse languages are taken into account.

4 Other Ways of Saving Effort

4.1 Efficiency Beyond Coding Length and Word Order

In the previous two chapters we examined how language users save effort and time by using expressions of different length, or by rearranging meaningful elements. These strategies have received substantial attention in the literature. This chapter describes other methods of saving effort that are less frequently discussed but are equally important. These strategies include the following:

- the use of more accessible forms from a set of alternatives. Accessibility here stands for higher frequency (or expectedness) and greater transparency. The related strategies are discussed in Sections 4.2 and 4.3, respectively;
- *horror aequi*, or avoidance of identity, which helps to prevent similarity-based interference. This strategy is examined in Section 4.4;
- avoiding cognitive overload in the process of integrating new referents. This method is considered in Section 4.5.

These strategies are related to minimization of processing costs by maximizing accessibility, as will be shown below. They also interact with the other strategies of saving effort and time described in the previous chapters.

4.2 Preference for Accessible Units and Interpretations

As discussed in Chapter 3, word order plays an important role in increasing accessibility at a particular point in discourse. For example, minimization of dependency distances and syntactic domains can be regarded as strategies for maximizing accessibility. We can also increase accessibility by choosing the most accessible forms in production or the most accessible interpretation in comprehension. Unlike in the previous chapter, where we discussed syntagmatic choices, this is a paradigmatic choice. This tendency is probably so obvious that it is hardly noticed. But there is some theoretical support for this thinking. For example, Sperber and Wilson (1995) argue that addressees are very efficient information processors: they choose the interpretation that maximizes cognitive effects while minimizing cognitive costs. The latter component means that they choose the most accessible interpretation at the given moment. Section 5.4.1 argues that semantic bleaching, an important grammaticalization process, can be explained by the addressee's preference for the most accessible meaning of an expression. Similarly, we can say that speakers also minimize their processing costs, in particular by choosing the most accessible forms from a set of alternatives compatible with their communicative goals.

As in the previous chapters, several quantitative measures of accessibility can be relevant. It has been shown that objects are named faster in picture-naming experiments if their names are more frequent (Wingfield 1968). Moreover, disfluencies, which indicate difficulties in language production, are less likely to occur before frequent expressions (Schnadt and Corley 2006). As for comprehension, numerous studies demonstrate that it takes less time to recognize more frequent words in comparison with less frequent ones (e.g., Howes and Solomon 1951). Also, fixation time on infrequent words is longer than on frequent ones, as one can see from eye-tracking studies (e.g., Rayner and Duffy 1986).

Predictability from previous context plays an important role in production and comprehension, as well. Words that are highly predictable from context are produced faster (Cohen and Faulkner 1983). There is substantial evidence that units with high surprisal (that is, low conditional probability given previous words, as estimated from corpora) are more difficult for comprehension than units with low surprisal (i.e., high predictability) (Hale 2001; Levy 2008), as one can see from reading times (e.g., Smith and Levy 2013) and from brain activity patterns (Frank et al. 2015).

Accessibility is lower when there are interfering units with similar semantic or formal properties. During word retrieval, the lexical nodes of related words are activated. For example, if the speaker wants to produce the word 'cow', the lexical nodes of 'bull', 'goat', 'cattle', 'animal', etc. will be activated, as well. These nodes compete with each other. As a result, the more similar the activation levels of the nodes, the more difficult the decision (Schriefers, Meyer and Levelt 1990; Roelofs 1992). For example, an eye-tracking study (Rayner and Duffy 1986) revealed that participants spent a longer time fixating ambiguous words with two equally likely meanings than fixating ambiguous words with one highly likely meaning. In production, naming a pictured object (e.g., a shark) was slower when a competing word (e.g., *whale*) had been recently elicited by a definition (e.g., 'a very large mammal that lives in the sea'), which suggests a lexical interference effect (Wheeldon and Monsell 1994). The same holds for constructional variation. For example, when language users were forced to produce a prepositional dative in contexts where a double-object dative was more expected on the basis of available contextual features, or the other way round, they gestured more and were more likely to be disfluent than when they produced more preferred structures (Cook, Jaeger and Tanenhaus 2009). This indicates that production of more accessible constructional variants is less costly than production of less accessible ones.

We usually produce the most accessible forms, and choose the most accessible interpretation. But we also sometimes use less accessible ones in order to create desirable cognitive effects. Consider an illustration. Chapter 1 discussed Levinson's (2000) heuristics and implicatures (Section 1.4.2). Recall that I-implicatures contain the message that the meaning is ordinary, typical, expected, while M-implicatures suggest that the situation is non-stereotypical. In most cases, the contrasts also have length asymmetries, which means that they can be explained by the principle of negative correlation between accessibility and costs (see Chapter 2). For example, if we call someone's house a 'mansion', we can imply ironically that it is pretentious and immodest (Levinson 2000: 138). But in some cases, the length difference between available options is small or non-existent. Examples are some pairs of cross-register doublets, as in the following example from Levinson (2000: 139):

(1)   a. *He was reading a book.*
       (I-communicates → He was reading an ordinary book).
    b. *He was reading a tome.*
       (M-communicates → He was reading some massive, weighty volume).

How to interpret such contrasts? First of all, the stylistically marked words may be more difficult to extract from the memory and to comprehend. Their use signals to the addressee that the meaning is less accessible (a large heavy book). Moreover, we should recall the principle of positive correlation between benefits and costs: rare words are more costly for processing, but they can create additional cognitive effects as a compensation for more effort. The effects can be in the form of elevated style or irony, as in the case with *mansion* used to refer to someone's house. We can also expect that the ironic interpretation is supported by a special intonation and facial expression, which can help the addressee to infer the intended meaning.

The addressee's processing costs can also be reduced thanks to linguistic co-text and situational context. As an illustration, take the pair of stylistic synonyms *horse* and *steed* (Levinson 2000: 139). The accessibility of the word *steed* can be higher in actual language use than on its own because the word occurs mostly in fiction and with specific attributes, which make its surprisal low e.g., *his noble/trusty/mighty steed*.

4.3   Analytic Support

It has been claimed that a sentence can be easier to produce and comprehend, especially in cognitively demanding contexts, if the speaker uses analytic forms instead of synthetic ones. The choice can be made in the following cases, for example:

- English adjectival forms of comparison (e.g., *cleverer – more clever, fuller – more full*);
- the English genitive alternation (e.g., *the topic's relevance – the relevance of the topic*);
- English subjunctive alternation (*if he agree-Ø* vs. *if he agrees* vs. *if he should agree*);
- German past time alternation (*she brauchte – sie hat gebraucht* 'she needed');
- English future tense alternation (*will – going to*), since *will* is often contracted to *'ll*;
- Spanish future tense alternation (e.g., *comeré* vs. *voy a comer* 'will eat').

Although these forms differ in length (cf. Chapter 2), they also differ in the degree of autonomy of the grammatical elements. The choice between more and less bounded expressions can play an independent role for efficiency. In fact, Wilhelm von Humboldt claimed as early as 1836 that analyticity increases explicitness and transparency while decreasing comprehension difficulty (Humboldt 1836: 284–285).

Mondorf (2014) argues that the use of these forms can be explained in terms of processing demands. She supports her claims by showing that analytic forms are often used in situations that require more processing effort, while synthetic forms are used in easy-to-process environments. Complexity is multifactorial, and depends on many properties of contexts, from phonology to semantics and syntax. For example, analytic comparative and superlative forms are preferred when the word ends in a consonant cluster, as in *strict* or *apt*. Negation is also considered to add complexity to the context. This is why negated contexts generally increase the chances of the longer variant. This correlation has been found for the analytic and synthetic future in Mexican Spanish (Lastra and Butragueño 2010) and for the English subjunctive with zero-inflected verbs vs. *would*-subjunctive (Schlüter 2009). Syntactic complexity can also play a role. For example, as shown by Szmrecsanyi (2003), the more analytic future form with *going to* is more frequently used in structures that are more complex to process (longer sentences and dependent clauses) than the *will*-future (due to the frequent use of the contracted form *'ll*, it can be considered more synthetic).

Some examples of variation have to do with the accessibility of specific meanings and interpretations. For example, the analytic *more*-variant is chosen more often with adjectives that are infrequently used in the comparative (Mondorf 2003: 260–261). Also, the use of a synthetic comparative form is facilitated if a comparative form of any type has been previously activated in

4.3 Analytic Support

context (Mondorf 2003: 285–286), and the comparative meaning becomes more accessible. Moreover, abstract and figurative concepts are regarded as more complex than concrete and literal ones. Compare the figurative use of *bitter* in *the more bitter takeover battles of the past* with a literal use: *the beer is bitterer*.

Note that all the examples provided in this subsection display differences in length. Some of these can be explained by the principle of negative correlation between accessibility and costs. In particular, this motivates the user to choose more costly forms to signal that the information is less accessible due to the more complex environment.

But other explanations have been proposed, as well. For example, Szmrecsanyi (2003: 23) writes,

> Because BE GOING TO typically contains more material than WILL/SHALL, it provides a sort of redundancy that will ease online processing for hearers by making the predication more accessible.

Also, it may be advantageous for the speaker to use the longer form when they have planning problems. For example, by using the longer form *be going to*, speakers can 'stall' for planning time (Szmrecsanyi 2003: 23). This means that the longer forms can prevent cognitive overload both for the speaker and the addressee and avoid a breakdown in communication. However, this interpretation does not sound very plausible. There are more convenient devices for dealing with planning difficulties, most importantly, disfluency markers (e.g., *um* and *uh*), or word lengthening (e.g., *theeee*).

Another possible explanation of analytic support in complex environments has to do with transparency. The more transparent analytic forms can be easier to process, even if the length is the same. Why should that be the case? It is possible that at least some morphemes are weaker cues of the grammatical category than auxiliary words. For example, unlike the word *more*, the morpheme *-er* is ambiguous, being used to form both comparative forms and agentive nouns, e.g., *The boy is a little cleaner*. Also, suffixes can exhibit allomorphy due to phonological and other conditions, whereas auxiliary words are more formally stable. Analytic forms are also regular, while synthetic ones can be irregular. All these factors can create cognitive advantages for production and comprehension of analytic forms. Affixes and clitics are also more formally reduced and may be more difficult to identify in a noisy channel, even if they are highly frequent. For example, Hopper and Traugott (1993: 65) argue that the form *going to* is more substantive and therefore more accessible to hearers than *'ll* or even *will*. This means that different aspects of accessibility (in particular, in terms of memory retrieval and perception) can be in conflict.

In general, the preference for analytic expressions is stronger in spoken language than in writing. According to Szmrecsanyi (2009), who studied analytic and synthetic expressions in English, explicitness and transparency are particularly important for spoken communication. But the higher analyticity of speech can also be explained by the pressure for maximization of accessibility in situations when interlocutors have to compete for the floor. Analytic expressions consist of highly frequent function words, which are easy to access. Compare the highly accessible analytic expression *be happy* with the less accessible lexeme *rejoice*. More research is needed in order to disentangle these factors.

4.4 *Horror Aequi*, or Avoidance of Identity

The principle *horror aequi*, or avoidance of identity, says that language users tend to avoid production of formally or structurally similar units close to one another. In phonology, this principle is also known as the Obligatory Contour Principle (Leben 1973). For example, Rohdenburg (2003) points out that the bare infinitive after *help* is more likely if there is *to* before *help*. Consider an example:

(2)   a. *She corrected me because she wanted to help me improve my German.*
           b. *She corrected me because she wanted to help me to improve my German.*

Language users are likely to avoid the second *to* before *improve*. More information about this alternation is provided in Section 9.3.

The cognitive motivation of this avoidance is similarity-based interference (MacDonald 2013). For example, when two semantically related nouns are planned and uttered in close proximity, e.g., *the saw and the axe*, the production of utterances takes more time, and more errors are made than when the nouns were unrelated, e.g., *the saw and the cat* (Smith and Wheeldon 2004). When one word is chosen (e.g., *the saw*) for production, its semantic neighbours (e.g., *the axe*) need to be inhibited, which makes it more difficult to retrieve them again.

Interestingly, Gennari, Mirkovi and MacDonald (2012) show that participants produced active and passive relative structures about equally often if the head noun was inanimate, e.g., *the bag being punched by the woman – the bag the woman is punching*. But they used passives more often when the head noun was animate, e.g., *the man being punched by the woman*. Moreover, when participants used passive structures, they more frequently omitted the agent if the head noun was animate, *the man that's being punched*, than when the head noun was inanimate, e.g., *the bag that's being punched by a woman*. This can be regarded as avoidance of interference between semantically similar nouns (that is, *the man* and *the woman*).

Inhibitory effects of similarity can also affect comprehension. Evidence from different cognitive domains (including semantic visual and kinaesthetic

4.4 *Horror Aequi*, or Avoidance of Identity

information, tones and odours) reveals the same tendency: when some items are followed by stimuli that are similar to them along some dimensions, the original items are forgotten more quickly than in the absence of similarity (Lewis 1996; Van Dyke and McElree 2011).

Note that the interfering units need to be close to each other and be simultaneously present in working memory. If there is sufficient distance between them, formal and semantic similarity can in fact increase the accessibility of the target units, as evidence from structural priming shows (e.g., Bock et al. 1992).

Similarity-based interference also potentially explains the fact that sentences with double centre-embedded clauses are very difficult to process. Consider the following example, which was discussed in the previous chapter:

(3) *The administrator who the intern who the nurse supervised had bothered lost the medical reports.*

Many popular accounts are based on some ideas about the limited capacity of working memory (e.g., Gibson 1998, 2000; see Section 3.2.1). But the problems with (3) and similar sentences may also be due to the presence of too many structurally and semantically similar constituents with the same syntactic function (Lewis 1996). Remarkably, if we keep the same centre-embedded relative clause structure but make the forms more diverse, the sentence is easier to process:

(4) *The administrator everyone I supervised had bothered lost the medical reports.*

Another piece of evidence is V. Ferreira and Firato's (2002) experiment, in which two kinds of stimuli were presented. In the sentences like (5a), the target noun phrase was conceptually similar to three previous noun phrases in the same sentence, leading to greater similarity-based interference. In the sentences like (5b), the target phrase was conceptually dissimilar, leading to less interference. The use or omission of the complementizer *that* was distributed evenly between the semantic conditions.

(5) a. *The author, the poet, and the biographer recognized (that) <u>the writer</u> was boring.*
     b. *The author, the poet, and the biographer recognized (that) <u>the golfer</u> was boring.*

The task was to recall the sentences. Interestingly, speakers produced the complementizer more often before conceptually similar noun phrases like in (5a) than before dissimilar ones like in (5b). There were also more disfluencies. This means that similarity between elements indeed can cause additional processing costs (see also Walter and Jaeger 2008).

It is efficient therefore to avoid such interference. This can be seen as maximization of accessibility, or rather minimization of inaccessibility, because units that are highly similar to the ones used in the near context are temporarily less accessible.

4.5 Entry Place for New Referents

The last strategy discussed in this chapter has to do with the addressee's processing resources and the distribution of new and therefore less accessible referents in discourse. There are well-documented universal preferences in the organization of discourse, known as the Preferred Argument Structure (Du Bois 1987). One of these preferences is called 'Avoid more than one new core argument'. Another formulation is Chafe's (1987: 32) principle 'one new concept at a time'. It is believed that the introduction of new referents into the current discourse has high processing costs. This is why clauses with more than one new participant are avoided across different languages (Du Bois et al. 2003). For example, the sentence in (6) would have high processing costs:

(6)   *A German orders a martini.*

However, when the information is introduced in a piecemeal manner, the processing is easier, although the articulation costs are higher. Consider a joke in (7), where the story begins with the formula 'An X walks into a bar ...'. This makes the processing easier.

(7)   *A German walks into a bar and orders a martini. The bartender asks 'dry?' The German says 'Nein, just one.'*

There are different views about whether one needs special structures to facilitate the integration of new referents. Du Bois (1987) argues that intransitive subjects and direct objects are suitable entry points. Particularly useful are semantically bleached intransitive predicates like *come*, *arrive* and *appear*, which provide little conceptual information beyond the appearance of the new referent. Other useful structures can be presentational constructions (Lambrecht 1994), such as English *there is*. At the same time, Schnell, Schiborr and Haig (2021) do not find clear indications that syntactic argument structure is sensitive to newness. In their cross-linguistic spoken corpora, the only syntactic functions that show a consistently high proportion of new referents are direct objects and various oblique arguments. Schnell et al. argue that the specialized constructions are important only in very local discourse contexts, such as introductions of characters at the outset of a narrative (e.g., *Once upon a time there was a little girl* ...) or major scene transitions. Objects are convenient entry points because they allow the speaker/writer to anchor new referents to a state of affairs with an already established referent. This may be more efficient than isolating the referent in a special introductory clause, also because adding a new clause would be more costly. It is not clear yet whether word order (in particular, OSV or OVS) can affect this preference, though.

To summarize, language users avoid structures that require simultaneous integration of more than one new referent into discourse. This avoidance has several benefits. First, the preference for step-by-step introduction of new referents helps to avoid an overflow of inaccessible information. Moreover, when we have two or more new referents waiting for their integration, this can create competition and interference in the memory, similar to the effects discussed in the previous section. In addition, useful cognitive effects, which represent the main benefits of language communication (see Section 1.2.1), arise when we integrate old information with new, and make new relevant conclusions. If new information cannot be integrated with previous knowledge within a reasonable stretch of discourse, its relevance is questionable. As a result, benefits cannot be obtained, and the cooperation between the speaker and the addressee will be disrupted.

4.6 Conclusions

In this chapter we discussed types of efficiency beyond coding length asymmetries and word order. Language users have a preference for forms and meanings with higher accessibility, which can be understood broadly as ease of retrieval from long-term memory, transparency, or absence of interfering competitors. Higher accessibility facilitates processing. The examples of efficiency discussed here obviously require more research. In particular, we need to understand which aspects of accessibility facilitate processing, and how their preferences interact with other strategies, such as using longer forms for less accessible meanings, and providing additional cognitive benefits to compensate for higher costs.

Part II

Efficiency and Language Evolution

5 Emergence of Efficient Language Patterns

5.1 Changes Leading to Efficient Patterns

The previous chapters provided diverse examples of efficient language structures and usage preferences. Potential mechanisms that lead to them were mentioned, but not discussed systematically. This is the aim of the present chapter.

At this point, it is important to distinguish between efficiency as a descriptive parameter and as a factor that drives language change. The patterns discussed in the previous chapters help to save the speaker's effort without jeopardizing the transfer of a message. Therefore, we dealt with efficiency as a descriptive parameter. But are they all driven by the principles of efficient communication? Not necessarily. One can imagine spurious correlations between accessibility and effort, or correlations explained by other factors. In fact, some researchers argue that efficient grammatical asymmetries, e.g., unmarked singular and marked plural in many languages of the world, have nothing to do with the pressure for efficient communication (e.g., Cristofaro 2019; see also Section 5.3.4). It has also been argued that efficient patterns are a result of strengthening of representations of reduced forms in the speaker's mind rather than communicative concerns (cf. Bybee 2010; see also Section 5.4.3). These and some other alternative explanations are discussed in this chapter.

Changes leading to the emergence of efficient patterns in language can be formal, when the form adjusts to the function. They can also be semantic or pragmatic, when the function adjusts to the form. For example, when the meaning associated with a particular form becomes more accessible, the form will be reduced. This will be called efficient formal reduction. It may involve a phonologically or morphologically modified version of the original expression (e.g., *going to* > *gonna* or *mathematics* > *maths*) or come from some other source. The accessibility of meaning can increase due to cultural changes. For example, *car* replaced *automobile* (Zipf 1965 [1935]: 33), apparently due to the increasing popularity of this kind of transport. In German, the shorter variant *Auto* became the default, as opposed to the original form *Automobil*.

We can witness these changes with any kind of technological innovations that become popular, e.g., *app* instead of *application*, *phone* instead of *telephone*, and so on. All those are formal changes. At the same time, the longer variant of the German *Automobil* has changed its usage from neutral contexts to more pragmatically marked elevated or ironic contexts.[1] This semantic change is efficient because it helps to preserve the negative correlation between articulatory effort and accessibility of meaning.

Due to cultural changes or other factors, some meanings can become less accessible than previously. This often leads to formal enhancement. Some new phonological or morphological material may be added. Alternatively, a more costly and formally unrelated expression may be used. In speech, enhancement can also be achieved through hyperarticulation of the original features (as in *It's a **p**in, not a **b**in*).

Reduction and enhancement can go together. Consider an example from Tenejapa Tzeltal, a Mayan language spoken in Mexico (Witkowski and Brown 1983). Both reduction and enhancement are observed here. Before the conquest, the word *čih* designated deer. After the conquest, sheep were imported. The new and exotic animals were named by a longer expression, *tunim čih* 'cotton deer'. The form *čih* was formally enhanced to represent the new animals because they were categorized as a less accessible subcategory of deer. With time, sheep became popular, and the adjective 'cotton' was dropped, so that the word *čih* began to designate sheep. This is an instance of efficient formal reduction. The name for deer, which became less frequently mentioned than sheep, became *teʔtikil čih* 'wild sheep'. This is an example of efficient formal enhancement. Thus, we observe three stages, which are shown in (1).

(1) Tenejapa Tzeltal: Mayan (Witkowski and Brown 1983: 571)

	DEER	SHEEP
Stage 1 (pre-conquest)	*čih* 'deer'	-
Stage 2 (early post-conquest)	*čih* 'deer'	*tunim čih* 'cotton deer'
Stage 3 (contemporary)	*teʔtikil čih* 'wild sheep'	*čih* 'sheep'

Tenejapa Tzeltal is spoken in the Chiapas highlands, where sheep and the manufacture of woollen products are important. In contrast, in a closely related language, Bachajón Tzeltal, which is spoken in the lowlands, where sheep are uncommon, only the two first stages have happened. The name for sheep is still 'cotton deer'.

Formal and semantic changes often go together, as well. In this example, the shorter expression *čih* in Tenepaja Tzeltal conveyed first the originally more typical 'deer', but later, probably after a period of ambiguity, began to designate the increasingly popular concept 'sheep'. They can also develop in

---

[1] www.duden.de/rechtschreibung/Automobil (last access 12 July 2022).

parallel. For example, in the process of grammaticalization the meaning of a gram gravitates towards more general and therefore more probable functions, whereas the form often (but not always) undergoes gradual reduction (see Section 5.4).

Sometimes we cannot say for sure whether we are dealing with reduction, enhancement or both. Take the English complementizer *that*. Do English speakers omit it or add it (cf. Jaeger and Buz 2017)? Similarly, when discussing changes in word duration, it is often not clear whether we are seeing enhancement of less probable units or reduction of more probable ones (Vajrabhaya 2016).

Unfortunately, historical evidence about the development of grammatical constructions and lexemes is not always available. Moreover, in the absence of ancient texts for most languages, we can only estimate accessibility from contemporary corpora and extrapolate it to previous stages. The assumption is that the estimates of accessibility of most basic linguistic categories remain stable, both cross-linguistically and diachronically. An important tool for testing the general efficiency mechanisms is artificial language learning and communication.

The rest of this chapter is organized as follows. Sections 5.2 and 5.3 provide diachronic evidence of efficiency-driven reduction and enhancement, respectively. Alternative explanations are also discussed. Section 5.4 provides an overview of influential theories that specify the causal mechanisms of language change leading to efficient formal and semantic changes, including grammaticalization. Section 5.5 deals with different explanations of suppletive and compositional forms. In Section 5.6 I will discuss the emergence of efficient word order patterns. Finally, Section 5.7 addresses a more philosophical question about the role of teleology in explanations of language change.

5.2   Efficiency-Driven Formal Reduction

Formal reduction happens in situations when the speaker assumes that the addressee can easily recover the intended meaning even if the form is reduced. This leads to efficient formal asymmetries, for example, when the form that corresponds to the more frequent category undergoes formal erosion or loss of marking, while the form that corresponds to the less frequent category remains the same (Croft 2003: 116), or changes at a slower rate. This is called differential reduction (Bybee 2010: Section 3.3.3; Haspelmath 2008b, 2017).

As an illustration, consider the distinction between inalienable and alienable possessive constructions, which was mentioned in Section 2.3.3. Let us look at some additional examples. In Old Italian, the shorter inalienable pattern arose by formal reduction due to high frequency, whereas the longer alienable pattern did not undergo this process:

(2)   Old Italian < Latin (Rohlfs 1949–1954, cited from Haspelmath 2017: 222)
   a. *moglia-ma* < *mulier mea* 'my wife' (inalienable)
      fratel-to < *fratellus tuus* 'your brother' (inalienable)
   b. *terra mia* < *terra mea* 'my land' (alienable)

A similar contrast can be observed in English dialects:

(3)   Lancashire English (Hollmann and Siewierska 2007: 407, cited from Haspelmath 2017: 222)
   a. m[ɪ] brother (inalienable)
   b. m[aɪ] football shoes (alienable)

The basis for this reduction is the fact that inalienable objects are more typical in the role of possessees than alienable objects (Haspelmath 2017). In other words, their interpretation as possessees is more accessible. Therefore, this type of differential reduction is efficient.

Another example is the gradual loss of the final -*n* by English possessive determiners *mine* > *my* and *thine* > *thy* from Middle English to the eighteenth century (Hilpert 2012). Unlike the possessive determiners, their predicative counterparts (e.g., *This book is mine*) did not undergo reduction. The resulting formal asymmetry is efficient, since the dependent forms (i.e., the determiners) are used more frequently than the independent forms (i.e., the pronouns). Another example is Juba Arabic, a lingua franca spoken in Sudan, where the original form *bita-i* [POSS-1SG] 'my/mine' has been reanalysed as the dependent possessive and reduced to *tái* 'my', e.g., *ída tái* 'my hand', whereas the non-shortened form *bita-i* continues to be used as the independent possessive form, i.e., 'mine' (Michaelis 2019). The correlation between frequency and length of possessive constructions is supported by a large-scale cross-linguistic study in Ye (2020). It should be added here that the efficient asymmetries in possessives often emerge due to enhancement of existing forms by adding nominalizers, dummy nouns, case markers and other elements, rather than being due to differential reduction (Michaelis 2019). For example, the independent form *pa m nan* 'mine' in Haitian Creole is the result of lengthening of the dependent form *m (nan)* 'my', as in *se m* 'my sister' by the noun *pa* 'part'.

Differential reduction can also involve more subtle phonological contrasts. For example, Bybee and Scheibman (1999) investigate the reduction of the vowel of *don't*, which is natural in the highly frequent combination *I don't*. Compare (4a) and (4b). In (4a), the vowel is reduced, while in (4b) the reduction is blocked by the intervening adverb *really*. Since the reduced and less costly form is more frequent, it is more accessible than the full and more costly form.

(4)   a. *I don't even know where to find him.*
      b. *I really don't know where to find him.*

Many grammaticalization processes can also be explained by efficient formal reduction. See more on that in Section 5.4.1.

An example of differential reduction at the level of a phrase is provided by Ariel (2008: 184). In contemporary Hebrew, there is a tendency to delete the adjective *tov* 'good' from greetings, such as *Boker tov* 'Good morning' and *Laila tov* 'Good night'. However, this does not happen with *(axar ha) cohoraim* 'afternoon' and *erev* 'evening'. Ariel argues that the deletion in the first two greetings is possible because they are sufficiently frequent in discourse and are salient enough to license this omission.

There is some support of the idea of efficient differential reduction from artificial language learning experiments. In their study, Kanwal et al. (2017) used stimuli with two unfamiliar plant-like objects. Each of them was introduced under two names. One name was long and unique, and the other was short and ambiguous. For example, Plant A was called *zopekil* 50 per cent of the times it was mentioned and *zop* for the other 50 per cent. Similarly, Plant B was called either *zopudon* or *zop*. Note that the name *zop* was shared by both objects. In the experiment, one of the objects was presented more frequently than the other one. During online communication, which involved a director-matcher task in which one participant had to describe an object and the other had to guess which object it was, the participants used the shorter word (e.g., *zop*) increasingly more often to name the more frequent object. Importantly, this was observed only when two conditions were met. First, when the participants were motivated to achieve a maximum number of correct matches. Second, when the longer names took visibly longer to transmit than the shorter names. If either of these conditions was missing, the efficient form–meaning mapping did not emerge.

5.3 Efficiency-Driven Formal Enhancement

5.3.1 Reflexive Pronouns

As argued by Haspelmath (2008b), efficient coding often arises not because of differential reduction, but from the spread of a newly grammaticalized and longer form. I will call this differential enhancement. Enhancement is understood here very broadly, including both addition of some elements to the old form or use of a formally unrelated expression. We can expect the more probable meaning to be expressed by the old and shorter form, while the new and longer form takes over the less probable meaning. These changes arise for the purposes of overriding the default interpretation of linguistic cues.

An example is the rise of reflexive pronouns from emphatic forms (e.g., König and Vezzosi 2004; Ariel 2008: Chapter 6). As shown by Ariel, it is much more common to describe activities or situations in which a participant engages with other participants, rather than with him-/herself. For example, *John hit Peter/his enemy/his scientific opponent,* etc. is a more typical scenario than *John hit himself.* Coreferential arguments of the same predicate are a minority. This explains why in many languages reflexive pronouns are longer than non-reflexive ones, e.g., *John hit him – John hit himself* (see Section 2.2.3). Historically, they often originate from emphatic forms. For example, the emphatic *self* was added in Old English and then became a part of the reflexive pronouns. Ariel described this process as follows:

Old English speakers at some point started adjoining an independent emphatic form (self) to their pronouns in order to counteract the default pragmatic inference to disjointness. (Ariel 2008: 222)

Similar processes have taken place in other languages, where the origin of reflexive pronouns can be traced back to emphatic markers, e.g., in Turkic, Finno-Ugric, Caucasian, Persian, Japanese, Indic and Semitic languages (Ariel 2008: 223).

Importantly, König and Vezzosi (2004) point out that the onset contexts for the development of such reflexive anaphors are sentences with other-directed transitive verbs (e.g., *help* and *deliver*) and 3rd-person singular subjects. It is in these contexts, they argue, that the need for disambiguation and reinforcement is the greatest. If the action expressed by a verb is other-directed, the less probable coreferential objects need additional formal marking. Note that if the action is very likely to be self-directed, as in grooming verbs, e.g., *She washed and dressed herself*, it can be expressed without any pronoun, e.g., *She washed and dressed.*

As for the person-related grammaticalization asymmetry, this can be explained by the fact that a 3rd-person subject and a 3rd-person object can either be coreferential (in a pseudo-English without reflexives, that would be *she$_1$ sees her$_1$*) or have disjoint reference (*she$_1$ sees her$_2$*), while a 1st or 2nd-person subject and object (e.g., *I$_1$ see me$_1$*) are always coreferential. Therefore, the contexts where one needs to provide extra coding are those where the referent is more difficult to identify (that is, in the 3rd person) because there may be more than one candidate present in the discourse (see Section 2.2.1). This explains the cross-linguistic universal: if a language has a 1st-person reflexive pronoun, it also has a 3rd-person reflexive pronoun (Faltz 1985: 43, 120).

If the use of reflexives with other-directed verbs is conventionalized in coreferential contexts, this kind of differential enhancement will lead to a semantic change of the non-reflexive pronoun (e.g., *John chides him*), by virtue of an implicature based on the Q-heuristic 'What isn't said, isn't' (Levinson 2000: 287). In other words, the presence of the costly alternative expression triggers the inference that the low-cost expression is associated with the more accessible (that is, disjoint) interpretation. See also Section 5.3.2.

An alternative explanation, proposed by Newmeyer (2003: 694–695), is that the predominant tendency to grammaticalize the 3rd person distinction in languages of the world is due to the higher frequency of coreferential 3rd-person subjects and objects. He provides corpus data which show that reflexive pronouns in English are more common in the 3rd person than in the 1st and 2nd person. Since meanings that are more frequently mentioned are more likely to be lexicalized than those that are less frequently appealed to, the implicational relationship among reflexive pronouns follows automatically. There is no need to appeal to ambiguity-reducing 'usefulness' (Newmeyer 2003: 695).

Let us look closer at the frequency data reported by Newmeyer. He shows that the 3rd-person reflexive pronouns are predominant (*myself* – 169 occurrences, *yourself* – 94, *himself* – 511, *herself* – 203, *itself* – 272). These data come from the Lancaster - Oslo/Bergen Corpus (LOB), which represents written English (e.g., books and periodicals). No wonder that the 3rd-person pronouns are so frequent. It is well known that the frequencies of different person forms in a corpus depend on the genres and modalities it represents (e.g., Biber 1988). Written formal texts contain few references to the 1st and 2nd person, while spontaneous conversations contain plenty of them.

I took a subset of the spoken part of the Russian National Corpus with informal dialogues and conversations,[2] and searched for the full reflexive pronoun *sebja* as a direct object (this form is the same for all grammatical persons). After manual cleaning, I obtained 163 examples, where the object was coreferential with the subject.[3] The distribution of the person forms is very different from Newmeyer's: the reflexive pronoun coreferential with the 1st person is the most frequent (72 occurrences), followed by the 3rd person (54 occurrences) and the 2nd person (37 occurrences). Therefore, 3rd-person coreferential objects are not the most frequent in informal speech, which represents the primary mode of interaction between language users. From this we can conclude that the usage data do not provide evidence in favour of frequency-driven lexicalization. The principle of negative correlation between accessibility and costs involving the accessibility of disjoint and coreferential meanings for different persons remain the most plausible explanation.

---

[2] www.ruscorpora.ru/en/ (last access 29 April 2021).
[3] I only took examples where I could identify the coreference from the available context. I also discarded several expressions, e.g., *čuvstvovat' sebja* 'feel (oneself)' and *vesti sebja* 'behave (oneself)', where no non-coreferential substitutions of *sebja* are possible without a change in meaning.

5.3.2 Tense and Aspect

An important process in grammatical change is renewal. This is the tendency for periphrastic forms to replace morphological ones over time. This process can repeat again and again, in a kind of cycle (Meillet 1958; Hopper and Traugott 1993). I argue that it is constrained by the principle of negative correlation between accessibility and costs (although the other two principles of efficient communication can also play a role). The new costly form matches the less accessible meaning, while the old and less costly form covers the more accessible meaning. If the new form gains in frequency, it can undergo reduction and take over the functional range of the old form, and the process will repeat again.

In the domain of tense and aspect, many examples of renewal can be found in the development of future forms. The central function of the future tense is prediction (Bybee, Perkins and Pagliuca 1994: Chapter 7). New and longer future constructions often begin with peripheral functions, e.g., immediate future and intention, which are often related to motion and modal meanings (especially volition and obligation). After that, they can replace the old forms partly or completely. This has happened with the English future marker *will*, which has undergone a change from a full verb *willan* 'want' to the contracted form *'ll*, and can also be used to express pure predictions without traces of desire, willingness or intention on the part of the subject (e.g., *You'll regret your decision*). Although the modal meaning can still be discerned in uses like *I will never play with you again*, which express an intention, the prediction sense of *I'll* is highly accessible (Bybee and Pagliuca 1987).

Another example is English present tenses. In Old and Middle English, the present simple tense was used to designate both habitual and progressive meanings, i.e., *I walk* would mean 'I walk' and 'I'm walking'. In the Early Modern English period, a new and longer construction *be + Ving* became increasingly popular. Compare the examples below:

(5)   Early Modern English (Petré 2017: 236)
        a. *You are now poysoning your souls by sin...*
        b. *Thou pleasest thy throat, and poysonest thy soul.*

A possible reason for enhancement is the desire to be expressive and attract attention. Haspelmath (1999) calls it the principle of extravagance, 'speak in such a way that you are noticed'. Petré (2017) argues that the longer progressive forms are preferred due to the speaker's desire to make their expressions cognitively more salient, more noticeable in comparison with the neutral competitor, the simple present.

Although this may look like an alternative explanation at first glance, in fact, extravagance of this kind can also be regarded as a manifestation of efficiency. The additional cognitive effects achieved here with the help of enhanced forms

5.3 Efficiency-Driven Formal Enhancement

are emotional and interpersonal, rather than related to some objective information about the referential situation. These effects can be seen as extra benefits. The use of the longer form is then explained by the principle of positive correlation between benefits and costs. The progressive interpretation of *be* + *Ving* may be a by-product of such extravagance, since the ongoingness is usually associated with high speaker involvement, as argued by Petré.

Quite often, the older form keeps some semantic territory. If this happens, the older form is used to express the most accessible meaning, not allowing the new form to spread. This is called differential inhibition by Haspelmath (2008b, 2017). For example, the English progressive construction has never spread to designate the habitual aspect.[4] This is in fact common cross-linguistically (Bybee 1994: Section 6). Present progressive grams do not generalize their meanings to include habitual senses. While progressive grams may also cover imperfective in the past tense (e.g., in Turkish or Scots Gaelic), this is not observed in the present tense. As argued by Bybee, habitual is the default meaning of the present tense. Therefore, the new expressive present progressive construction started its grammatical 'career' by covering the less accessible meaning of ongoingness, while the old and less expressive construction has kept the most accessible present-tense function – i.e., the habitual meaning. This division of labour between the constructions can be considered efficient.

We cannot always be sure about how the existing tense and aspect systems emerged. The more valuable then are synchronic descriptions of variation and optionality, showing that the system is in flux. For example, this is happening in Nigerian Pidgin English, which has a zero past-tense form and several past forms with different additional markers. According to Poplack and Tagliamonte (1996), the zero form is the default form for neutral past-tense reference, which can be used to simply state what happened. This may be due to substrate influence, since the conceptual space marked by zero is very similar to what is covered by the unmarked past in some West African languages. The additional markers are used to divert from this neutral interpretation and express sequential, continuous, anterior remote or other readings. These constructions have not reached a high level of grammaticalization yet. At least, the lack of additional markers does not conventionally mean the lack of these more specific meanings. The exact interpretation is to be inferred from the context. If one or several of the additional markers with specific meanings become very frequent, we can expect these inferences to become conventionalized, and the meaning of the zero form will express non-sequential, non-continuous, etc. aspect.

---

[4] With the exception of so-called subjective progressives, e.g., *You're always losing your things!* or McDonald's advertising slogan *I'm lovin' it*. In such usages, the emphatic function is still alive.

According to Bybee (1994), the mechanism is as follows. When the longer construction designating the rare category becomes sufficiently frequent and obligatory for expressing the meaning associated with it (as the -*s* plural in English), the Q-heuristic comes into play. The shorter and simpler form becomes associated exclusively with the more frequent category. If the overt plural is always used when the plural meaning is intended, then by inference, the unmarked noun will be interpreted only as singular. The meaningful zero is 'parasitic' on the longer form (Garcia and van Putte 1989).

If the longer form is not obligatory for expression of a particular meaning, the shorter form will not trigger Q-implicatures. For example, consider the contrast between the simple past and habitual past constructions in English, e.g., *walked* vs. *used to walk*. The simple past tense in English can represent non-habitual, perfective events in the past, e.g., *On that day, she walked in the park, fed pigeons and went home*, but it can also represent habitual events, as in *She walked in the park every day*. As Bybee (1994: 239) argues, if the habitual past constructions, e.g., *She used to walk in the park*, had become obligatory, the aspectual meaning of the simple past, in the absence of *used to*, would be restricted to non-habitual meanings. See also similar reasoning in Section 7.2.1 on 'default' causatives.

From the efficiency perspective, we can say that the functional narrowing of the less costly forms is based on the principle of negative correlation between accessibility and costs, strengthened by the presence of a salient high-cost alternative expression with a less accessible meaning. The addressee infers that the interpretation of the less costly expression is highly accessible.

5.3.3 Alienable and Inalienable Possessive Constructions

The process of new and longer constructions taking over the territory of the older ones can be illustrated by some possessive constructions. Consider an example from Maltese (Koptjevskaja-Tamm 1996; Haspelmath 2017), which has a relatively novel construction with *ta'* 'of', which has different personal forms. The construction expresses alienable possession, as in (6b).

(6)   Maltese: Semitic (Haspelmath 2017: 224)

        a. Inalienable possession
           id 'hand' > *id-i* [hand-1SG.POSS] 'my hand'
        b. Alienable possession
           ktieb 'book' > **ktieb-i* [book-1SG.POSS]
                       il-ktieb tiegħ-i [ART-book of-1SG] 'my book'

The analytic construction is newer and has largely replaced the classical Arabic suffix *-i*, with the exception of body parts and kinship terms (with which both forms are possible), and a few fossilized expressions (Eksell Harning 1980; Koptjevskaja-Tamm 1996). It represents the longer alternative. At first, it was

5.3 Efficiency-Driven Formal Enhancement

used with rather untypical possessors, e.g., possession of an abstract noun or duration (e.g., a two hours' journey), as one can infer from the data from different Arabic dialects. As Koptjevskaja-Tamm (1996: 262) writes, 'it emerges first of all in those uses where the need for it is most acute, most pronounced'. This means that the longer construction is used when the accessibility of the possessive interpretation is lower. Later, however, the new analytic genitive took over a substantial part of the meaning of the initial synthetic genitive. At present, the synthetic genitive is restricted to relatively few classes, but it still has a relatively high relative frequency (Koptjevskaja-Tamm 1996), due to the central position of these nouns as possessees and their high individual token frequency. These stereotypical contexts are the stronghold of the older and shorter forms.

5.3.4 Number Marking

It was argued in Section 2.3 that global and local markedness in the domain of number distinctions is efficient. In particular, the meaning of singularity is more expected than the meaning of plurality. This is why singular nouns, e.g., *day*, are less likely to be marked for number than plural nouns, e.g., *day-s*, and dual ones (if available). Similarly, if a language has singulative forms, like Welsh, they will be applied to nouns that represent objects which are commonly talked about in plural (e.g., birds). Haspelmath and Karjus (2017) claim that these patterns arise due to the grammatical form–frequency correspondence principle, which can be regarded as a manifestation of efficiency.

There is no consensus about this explanation, however. Most prominently, Cristofaro (2019) emphasizes the role of source constructions in grammaticalization. For example, she shows that plural markers can develop from partitive forms, e.g., 'many of them', as in Bengali:

(7)   Bengali: Indo-Aryan (Chatterji 1926: 735–736, cited from Cristofaro 2019: 34)

    a.   *āmhā-rā*   *såbå*
          we-GEN   all
          'all of us'
    b.   *chēlē-rā*
          child-GEN
          'children'

Other source constructions for plural are distributive expressions ('house here and here') and expressions of multitude ('all'), as in Southern Paiute (Uto-Aztecan) and Maithili (Indo-Aryan). According to Cristofaro, '[t]hese various processes do not appear to be triggered by the higher need to disambiguate plural as opposed to singular' (2019: 34).

But this is not the whole story. With regard to the Bengali construction, Chatterji (1926: 726–727) points out that the addition of some noun of multitude (e.g., 'all') to the noun was a new device '[t]o indicate the plural, which had come to be indistinguishable from the singular' because of the loss of the original nominative plural affix – that is, exactly for the purpose of disambiguation. In other words, a more costly expression was provided in order to cancel the more accessible interpretation. The construction could be used to represent plural in New Bengali (from 1800 on), e.g., *rājārā-såbá* 'kings' (Chatterji 1926: 734), although the noun of multitude was already perceived as superfluous. Notably, it was first omitted with 1st and 2nd-person plural pronouns ('we', 'ye'), later with other pronouns and finally with nouns. The genitive marker thus became the nominative plural marker.

Generally speaking, the fact that original constructions performed different functions does not represent counter-evidence to the efficiency-based explanation. Language users create new form–meaning pairings by recruiting semantically suitable constructions for their needs, not by deciding that some new phonetic sequence will from now on represent the plural. This kind of recycling is the norm. What is crucial is that the opposite situation – i.e., when a morpheme or word becomes reanalysed as the singular marker, while the plural form has zero expression – is very rare. One such example is Imonda (a Papuan language), where the plural is unmarked, and some nouns take the singular marker that comes from the partitive construction (i.e., 'one from among the group of X'). However, this marker seems to be used only with five human nouns: women, men, girls, boys and enemies (Seiler 1984: 62–63). The fact that plural markers, regardless of their origin, propagate more frequently than singular markers, as in Imonda, suggests that the solution with marked plural and unmarked singular forms is more efficient than the one with unmarked plural and marked singular forms.

Experiments with artificial language learning by Kurumada and Grimm (2019) provide support for the efficiency explanation. Language learners were presented with two types of referents, some of which occurred more frequently as singletons, and others as multiples. Kurumada and Grimm found that language learners had a tendency to use plural marking more often on nouns that were less likely to occur with plural meaning. This shows that language learners tend to mark less accessible meanings.

5.4 Causal Models of Formal Reduction and Enhancement

5.4.1 *A Pragmatic Model Based on the Principle of Negative Correlation between Accessibility and Costs*

This section discusses several causal models of language change. The first one is a pragmatic model of language change which is based on the

5.4 Causal Models of Reduction and Enhancement

principle of negative correlation between accessibility and costs. I will focus only on three components, in order to make the model comparable with the other models:

- different types of frequency;
- accessibility of interpretation, which includes semantic and pragmatic functions ('meaning accessibility');
- articulation costs, which include length and level of articulatory detail. These can change due to formal reduction and enhancement.

A possible causal model that accounts for both grammatical and lexical changes, is displayed schematically in Figure 5.1.

Frequency is one of the factors that can increase or decrease the accessibility of an expression. Other factors include previous linguistic context, communicative situation and encyclopaedic information. They are represented by the small arrows on the left of 'Meaning accessibility'. I focus here only on frequency because it plays a crucial role in the other frameworks that the pragmatic model will be compared with.

If the meaning becomes more accessible, the speaker will reduce the form phonetically, following the principle of negative correlation between accessibility and costs. This process is obvious in grammaticalization, which is often (but not always) accompanied by loss of phonological substance (Lehmann 2015). As for the lexicon, articulation effort can be reduced with the help of clipping, abbreviation and lexical replacement.

Notably, grammaticalization can also happen without formal reduction. A large-scale study by Bisang, Malchukov and the Mainz Grammaticalization Project Team (2020) shows that formal reduction does not always accompany

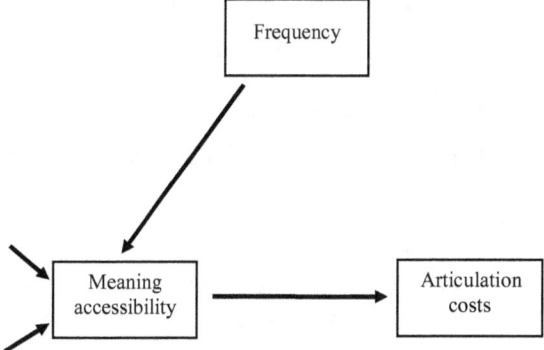

Figure 5.1 A pragmatic causal model of language change

semantic change.[5] For example, the Eastern and Mainland Southeast Asian languages (Bisang 2009) with near-isolating structure show little evidence of formal reduction. The grammaticalized meanings are simply layered on top of lexical meanings, without triggering differential reduction. There are several factors that can explain that lack of form–function correlation. One of them is the conservative effect of writing. Another is prosody: it is more natural to expect phonetic reduction in stress-based languages than in mora-based languages (see Bisang et al. 2020: 68–69). These factors can block the differential reduction of grammatical and lexical uses of the units.

If a meaning loses its accessibility, for example due to cultural factors (see Section 5.1), the speaker needs to provide additional coding, based on the principle of negative correlation between accessibility and costs. The addressee will then infer that the meaning is not very accessible. This is the case with renewal and other examples discussed in the previous section.

The unidirectionality of grammaticalization can be explained by the fact that the use of coding material necessary for formal enhancement should be somehow motivated. We cannot just append meaningless symbols to an expression if the meaning has become less accessible. Motivated additions usually come from new words or other meaningful units. This is why the principle of negative correlation between accessibility and costs does not mean adding some sounds to a grammaticalized word or morpheme, Instead, the principle manifests itself in renewal, which begins with the emergence of a new paraphrastic expression.

An important component of grammaticalization is the process of semantic bleaching. I argue here that semantic bleaching is accompanied by increased accessibility of meaning. Consider the example of *going to/gonna*, where the documented path of change is from directed motion to intention, and from intention to prediction of future events (cf. Bybee 2006). Consider the examples of these meanings below:

(8)   a. *Where are you going? – I'm going to see my aunt.* [Directed motion]
       b. *I'm going to write a letter.* [Intention]
       c. *I think I'm going to sneeze.* [Prediction]

Following Croft (2000: 162), directed motion with a human subject normally implies intention, as in (8a), while intention does not entail directed motion. Consider (8b), which expresses intention but does not convey directed motion. Similarly, intention often implies prediction, as in (8b), while prediction does not entail intention, as in (8c). Thus, intention is semantically broader than directed motion, and prediction is semantically broader than intention.

---

[5] Their results contradict the claims made in Bybee et al. (1994), who argue that formal reduction goes together with semantic change.

5.4 Causal Models of Reduction and Enhancement

Since broader meanings are applicable in more contexts, we can say that more abstract, semantically bleached meanings are also more accessible.

Semantic bleaching is likely to be driven by the addressee's cognitive processes. There is always a probability of mismatch between the speaker's implicatures and the addressee's inferences (Horn 2009). This can trigger a semantic change, which can later spread in the community and become conventionalized. An important condition is bridging context, like in *I'm going to see my aunt*, which allows for both interpretations (Heine 2002). The speaker may be providing information about their motion, whereas the addressee may infer that the speaker intends to see their aunt. Why would that happen? If there is some uncertainty, the addressee will prefer the interpretation that is the easiest to recover (cf. Detges and Waltereit 2002; Eckardt 2009) – that is, the most accessible one. By doing so, they follow the principle of maximization of accessibility (see Section 4.2).

Moreover, information about the cognitive states of other people, including intentions, is very important for humans. In most cases, information about other people's intentions will be more relevant for the addressee than information related to physical motion, creating more cognitive effects. This could explain why subjectification and intersubjectification phenomena are so pervasive in language change (Traugott 2010). Predictions of future events are also extremely valuable. They are crucial for our survival because they allow us to adjust our behaviour in advance. The general hypothesis is that cross-linguistically preferred paths of semantic change lead to those meanings that help to (a) maximize communicative benefits in the form of cognitive effects, and (b) have high accessibility.

Innovations, including the ones boosting efficiency, are more likely to occur in spontaneous conversations (although some occur in writing, cf. Biber and Gray 2011). First of all, shared common ground and the availability of instant repair create favourable circumstances for formal reduction. Second, spontaneous speech is produced under time pressure. One needs to be fast and efficient in order to claim and retain the floor. This is why reduced forms are often associated with informal speech, e.g., *gonna, wanna, hafta, gotta* (Krug 2000), *y'all, gimme, I'll, tryna* and other contractions.

5.4.2 Zipf's Model of the Rational Artisan

Zipf (1949) uses an elaborated analogy to explain human language. For him, words are tools that are used to convey meanings. A language user is a 'Rational Artisan', who has limited resources and should work in the most efficient way in order to survive. The words are tools on the artisan's bench. They are located in a particular order and have different sizes. Some are closer than others, and some are smaller and lighter than others. The total amount of work that the artisan has to perform can be represented by the equation below:

(9)   Work = Frequency * Mass * Distance

The task is to minimize the work performed by the artisan. This is the essence of the Principle of Least Effort.

If we think about language, the frequency of using a particular tool corresponds to the frequency of using a particular word. The mass of the tool is the word's length: 'under otherwise constant conditions, the work of uttering a longer word is greater than the work of uttering a shorter one' (Zipf 1949: 63). Finally, the distance on the working bench depends on the total number of tools. The shorter the working bench, the less the total effort. By minimizing Mass (length) and Distance (in particular, the number of words), one will minimize Work, which corresponds to the effort of using language. Language evolution is perceived as the constant development and rearrangement of tools:

> Some tools may have changed their form but preserved their usage; by definition this is a formal change. Some tools may have preserved their form and changed their usage; by definition this is a semantic change. And some may have done both and others may have done neither. Nevertheless, whatever alternations were, or were not, undertaken from moment to moment in the course of the shop's history, they were all undertaken, or not undertaken, as a response to the minimizing of the total work of the shop. (Zipf 1949: 63)

How exactly does that happen? The rational artisan will minimize effort by making sure that the most frequently used tools are easy to use (they have low 'mass'). The artisan can do so by making them smaller (with the help of truncation, e.g., *gasoline* > *gas*) or by changing their function (extending the meaning of short words in order to represent frequent meanings, e.g., using the word *car* instead of *automobile*). This is how the Law of Abbreviation works (see also Section 2.6). As Zipf puts it, 'the more frequently a tool is used the easier its use is made by abbreviation ... the easier the tool's use is made by abbreviation the more frequently it is used' (1949: 62). This means that there is a bidirectional relationship between the frequency of a word and its length (but see the discussion below).

A scheme of this model is shown in Figure 5.2. Note that Zipf was mainly interested in lexical forms and meanings. One can make interesting predictions about words judging from how well they fit this correlation: if a rare word is too short for its frequency range, its use may be declining. And the other way round, if a frequent word is too long, it may be on its way to becoming more popular.

Zipf's account leaves many questions open. As we saw in Section 2.6, the link between frequency and formal length is not entirely clear yet. Moreover,

5.4 Causal Models of Reduction and Enhancement

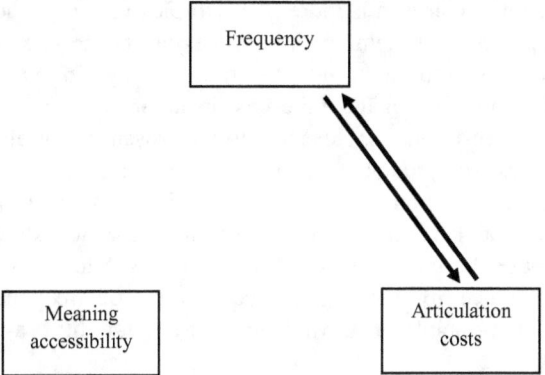

Figure 5.2 A causal model of language change based on Zipf's Rational Artisan

the causal relationship between frequency and length requires some clarification. In his earlier work, Zipf raises the question about the direction of causality: is the length of a word a cause or a result of its usage frequency? He writes,

> on the whole the comparative length or shortness of a word cannot be the cause of its relative frequency of occurrence because a speaker selects his words not according to their lengths, but solely according to the meanings of the words and the ideas he wishes to convey. (1965 [1935]: 29)

At the same time, the Rational Artisan analogy in his later work suggests that the relationship is bidirectional (see above). Interestingly, Baayen, Milin and Ramscar (2016) show in their data-driven causal model of the English lexicon that word length influences word frequency, whereas frequency does not affect word length directly. Apparently, this can be relevant when there are several near-synonymous expressions, and the shorter is preferred simply due to ease of articulation, when the semantic differences are less important.

Zipf also formulates several other principles describing efficient behaviour. It is also rational, for instance, to put the tools that are used more frequently closer to the working place. This saves effort because it minimizes the time that it takes to go from one place to another in order to bring the instruments. Since the more frequently used tools are also smaller, it will also help if the lighter tools are located closer than the heavier ones. In general, it is economical to make the tools that are close more versatile, and to get rid of the distant ones (the so-called Principle of Economical Versatility). If versatility in the lexicon is polysemy, this means that more frequent words should be more polysemous, and more polysemous words will be used more frequently.

According to Zipf, the artisan is more likely to pick up a more accessible tool that is located closer to them, even if it does not fit the task perfectly, than to fetch a more appropriate tool that is farther away. For example, we might use a knife to open a package if the scissors are in another room. Since accessibility in this sense (that is, closeness to the artisan) is correlated with frequency, we can expect frequent expressions to be preferred for expression of new meanings. This hypothesis was tested by Harmon and Kapatsinski (2017) in an artificial language learning experiment, which showed that speakers tend to use the more frequent forms for new categories. We can explain this preference by the higher accessibility of frequent words. Speakers follow the principle of maximization of accessibility, saving their processing effort.

Cross-linguistically, the source concepts for grammaticalization constitute the most basic human activities, movements or states, e.g., DO/MAKE, TAKE/HOLD, GIVE, SAY, GO, COME, STAND, LIVE (Heine, Claudi and Hünnemeyer 1991: 35). For example, the verb SAY is a common source of complementizers and quotatives, whereas DO and GIVE are common sources of causative grams (Bisang et al. 2020: 15). Thus, accessible words are preferred for new semantic extensions. Less frequent concepts like CRAWL or EXPLAIN are less commonly used for this purpose. Rare grammaticalization paths, however, can also provide evidence for the frequency account if they involve source concepts that are prominent in a particular culture. As Bisang et al. observe, this is particularly obvious in the development of nominal classifiers. For example, in some Uto-Aztecan languages a possessive classifier developed from the noun 'cattle' (Estrada-Fernándes 2020), while the Chinese general classifier *ge* is derived from *gè* 'bamboo tree' (Sun and Bisang 2020).

Also, in some cases it may be more efficient to use two or more near tools for performing a task instead of using one more appropriate tool that perfectly fits the task but is farther away. So, one can use composite expressions like *fear of heights* instead of *acrophobia*. Likewise, in contemporary Western culture with small nuclear families, languages lose different kinship terms related to extended family, e.g., *my father's sister* or *aunt on my father's side* instead of a special term, which would be used only very infrequently (cf. Kemp et al. 2018; see also Section 6.1). This preference is called by Zipf the Principle of Economical Permutation. However, when a combination of words becomes very frequent, it is helpful to adopt a single special tool for that purpose. This is called the Principle of Economical Specialization.

Zipf's model of the rational artisan makes many correct predictions and contains many insights. The relationships between frequency, form and function that he described are stable. Yet, the direction of these links and their cognitive and communicative motivation require some modification. It is very difficult to imagine that speakers choose more frequent words to express a new meaning by predicting how much it will help them to save effort in the long run, as the rational artisan would do. Language users' choices ultimately result in rational and efficient behaviour, but they are not based on a conscious process (see also Section 5.7). This is why I argue that frequency does not affect form directly. Its effect is mediated by the accessibility of the information the speaker wants to convey.

5.4.3 A Usage-Based Model by Joan Bybee

A highly influential theory of language change has been developed in detail in Joan Bybee's work (e.g., Bybee 1999, 2003, 2006, 2007, 2010). According to her theory, formal reduction happens as a result of automatization and routinization of articulation. For example, high-frequency words undergo formal reduction at a faster rate than low-frequency words. Crucially, what matters is frequency in reducing contexts. An example is negative auxiliaries in English, such as *don't, can't* and *aren't*. They have a high probability of final [t] deletion, not only in reducing contexts before consonants, but also before vowels. The lion's share of usage of these auxiliaries occurs before words beginning with consonants (that is, in a reducing context). These phonetic exemplars are stronger and therefore dominate, influencing their production across the board.

A very important condition that boosts formal reduction is chunking. If a compositional expression occurs frequently, it forms a chunk. This leads to formal reduction due to automatization and routinization. For example, *I don't know* becomes *I dunno*, *going to* becomes *gonna*, *I will* becomes *I'll*, Spanish preposition *a* 'to' and the article *el* become *al*. Note that frequency is not linearly related to chunking. It requires several repetitions, but the amount of improvement decreases as the frequency becomes higher. Similarly, repetition in discourse also has an effect; even low-frequency words are phonetically reduced if they are pronounced for the second time in discourse (Fowler and Housum 1987). Chunking makes production and comprehension more efficient, increasing fluency and ease (Bybee 2010: Section 3.2). It reduces all the linguistic costs discussed in this book: articulation, time and processing.

Chunking also has another important consequence. The more often a sequence of units (morphemes or words) is used together, the stronger it will become as a unit and, crucially, the less associated it will be with its components (Hay 2001). The sequence also becomes increasingly autonomous semantically (Bybee 2006). The more holistic processing leads to the assignment of meaning to the whole unit. An example is *in spite of*, e.g., *in spite of the difficulties*. Originally, the word *spite* meant 'defiance, contempt', and *in spite of* could be used only with a person, such as an enemy, as the object. Later, the meaning generalized, including any kind of obstacle – people, laws, cultural norms, diverse physical obstacles, etc. Note that formal changes are not always accompanied by semantic or pragmatic changes. Often, reduced chunks, e.g., *I'll*, *I don't feel* and *I don't like*, retain their meaning, while *I don't know* has undergone a semantic change, becoming a pragmatic marker (Bybee 2010: 48–49). Thus, there is no necessary parallelism between formal and semantic reduction. We have also seen examples where semantic generalization happens without formal changes (e.g., the grammaticalization layering in Southeast Asian languages discussed in Section 5.4.1).

But one may ask, why does the meaning of a highly frequent chunk become more abstract, as we see in grammaticalization? Certainly, the components' independence from the lexical meaning helps a change to take place, but why does it lead to semantic bleaching and generalization?

There are several ideas to mention here. One popular explanation of semantic bleaching has been habituation, by which a repeated stimulus loses some of its semantic force because people cease to respond to it at the same level (Haiman 1994; Bybee 2010). This happens, for example, to swear words, when they are used very frequently, ritual apologies and greetings, or Van Gogh's paintings when they are reproduced everywhere – on posters, dishes, scarves and umbrellas. Habituation may serve as a facilitating factor, which weakens the more specific aspects of a word's meaning (cf. Haspelmath 1999: 1062). So, the generalization process can be driven by frequency.

Bybee (2010: 109) also admits that the addressee may make inferences from more specific to more abstract interpretations. At the same time, she argues that in reality, there is no pressure for grammaticalized units and categories to have a very abstract meaning. Instead, very specific meanings can coexist with very abstract ones. Thus, instead of bleaching and generalization, we may have in fact an additive effect. The impression that grammatical elements have very abstract meaning can be due to the high relative frequencies of very abstract uses, in accordance with her exemplar model of language.

There is also a reverse effect of semantic generalizations on frequency. If an expression becomes semantically more general (and therefore accessible), its frequency will increase because it becomes applicable in more contexts.

As for the role of accessibility in determining the degree of formal reduction, Bybee seems to acknowledge that it plays a role:

The functioning of predictability in online processing depends upon the tendency for articulatory reduction to always be working while the speaker is controlling (largely unconsciously or automatically) the amount of reduction according to the listener's needs. (Bybee 2010: 40)

Thus, the accessibility of a unit to the addressee plays a role as a constraining factor for the speaker. At the same time, Bybee points out that reduction of a word is determined not only by online factors at the moment of speech, but

5.4 Causal Models of Reduction and Enhancement

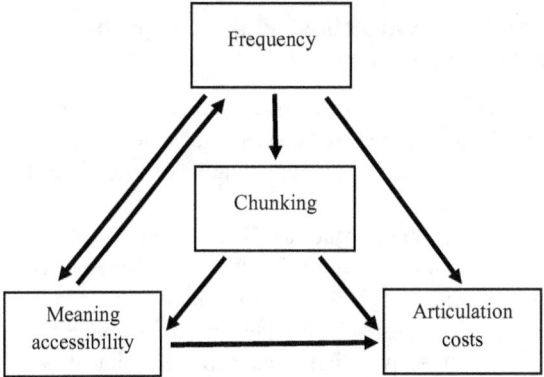

Figure 5.3 A causal model of language change based on Bybee's usage-based approach

also by the usage history of the word. Uses in reduction contexts strengthen the representations of the reduced forms, which make it more likely that the reduced forms will be used again in all contexts, also where reduction is less likely. This model is represented visually in Figure 5.3.

The fundamental role of frequency in determining formal reduction is not uncontroversial, as was discussed in Section 2.7. In particular, the phonological reduction of *be* and *have* in highly grammaticalized contexts has been explained by the high conditional probabilities of these words given their neighbours, rather than by their joint probabilities, as the frequency account would predict (Barth 2019). At the moment, there is not enough evidence for a final verdict. A complicating factor is that predictability measures and frequency are usually correlated because they are closely related mathematically.

5.4.4 Causal Models: A Conclusion

Of course, there are many factors and hypotheses that explain language change. Only a few of them have been discussed. But even this small overview, which involves only three nodes (frequency, meaning accessibility and articulation costs) reveals striking differences between the theories. We can only hope that future empirical research, including data-driven causal models (see Section 6.3), will shed light on the matter. I do not exclude the possibility that efficient patterns can emerge due to processes that are not directly related to communicative efficiency, such as the habituation effects in Bybee's model. This is why it can be useful to distinguish between efficiency as a descriptive phenomenon and efficiency as an explanatory principle, as was argued at the beginning of this chapter.

5.5 Suppletion, Compositionality and the Competition of Meanings for Forms

Why are some meanings expressed by simple forms, and others by compositional forms? For example, English has a lexical verb *kill*, but does not have a special word for making someone laugh. An analytic causative must be used instead. Why is this so?

Haspelmath (2008c: Section 6) argues that lexical causatives, which he calls suppletive, exist because they are highly frequent and therefore can be stored in the memory. For instance, English has unproductive morphological causatives *sadd-en* 'make sad', *wid-en* 'make wide', *hard-en* 'make hard', but it is only for high-frequency adjectives like *good* and *small* that it has suppletive causatives (*improve* 'make good', *reduce* 'make small').[6]

I will allow myself a literary intermezzo here. Jorge Luis Borges has a short story *Funes the Memorious*, which tells about a young man who, as a result of a head injury, could remember anything and forget nothing. He created his own system of enumeration, in which each number up to at least 24,000 was given an arbitrary name, and was thinking of a language that could give an arbitrary name to any object at any given point of time (similar ideas were expressed by John Locke). This came, however, at the cost of being unable to make generalizations and abstractions, that is, to ignore the subtle individual differences between objects and events.

In real life, a fully suppletive language of this type is impossible for many reasons. Even if we could store as much information as we wanted, there would be no mental categories, which come as a result of generalization, and therefore no linguistic ones. No grammar would be possible, either, because a grammar represents a result of generalization and abstraction.

But even if we had both a powerful memory like Funes and the ability to make generalizations, it would still be very impractical not to have productive constructions. New, unforeseen situations emerge every day. For example, during the COVID-19 pandemic the government ordered people to wear masks. It was a new type of causal event, which we did not have before (at least, the general public). Even if we all had very powerful memories, it would be impossible to negotiate every new lexical label. It would make language as a communicative tool prohibitively costly. With compositional expressions (e.g., 'make X wear a mask'), we are well prepared for new challenges.

---

[6] It is an open question whether one should take the absolute frequency of the base form or of the derived form in order to explain suppletion. There is evidence that it is the absolute frequency of the derived form that makes it resistant to analogical change (Bybee and Thompson 1997; Corbett et al. 2001).

5.5 Causes of Suppletion and Compositionality

Our experience is open-ended and requires productive compositional forms. As shown in a language evolution experiment by Selten and Warglien (2007), compositional grammars have communicative advantages in situations where language users need to express what has not been expressed before, whereas non-compositional grammars often break down in these circumstances.

But what about the fact that suppletive forms are usually frequent? Certainly, we cannot exclude that memory limitations play a role. Also, the conservative effect of frequency is an important factor that helps suppletive forms to persist (Bybee and Thompson 1997; Bybee 2010). But I believe that communicative efficiency also plays a role. Short, low-cost forms represented by roots are scarce. Different meanings will compete for them. According to the principle of negative correlation between accessibility and costs, the more accessible ones are likely to win.

Consider some examples from the causation domain. In a cross-linguistic study of causal–non-causal verb pairs (e.g., *raise* vs. *rise*, *kill* vs. *die*), Haspelmath et al. (2014) find that verb pairs in which the non-causal member is more frequent tend to be coded as anticausatives, while verb pairs in which the causal member is more frequent tend to be coded as causatives. Compare the expressions for the causal and non-causal 'break' and 'freeze' in Turkish:

(10) Turkish: Uralic (Haspelmath 1993: 119):
 a. *don-mak* 'freeze$_{INTR}$' > *don-dur-mak* 'freeze$_{TR}$'
 b. *kir-ıl-mak* 'break$_{INTR}$' < *kir-mak* 'break$_{TR}$'

The pair in (10a) illustrates the causative alternation. That is, the non-causal form is basic, and the causative form is derived. Verbs that tend to participate in causative alternations represent more spontaneous events like 'freeze$_{INTR}$', which occur more frequently in the non-causal sense. An even more radical case is agentive events, such as 'dance'. All languages seem to express the corresponding causative event compositionally, as 'make/cause X dance'.

The pair in (10b) is an example of the anticausative (inchoative) alternation. The causal form is basic, and the non-causal one is derived. Verbs that participate in the anticausative alternation are usually associated with events that involve an external agent, e.g., 'break$_{TR}$', which occur more frequently in the causal sense (see also Haspelmath 1993).

These data support the idea that different meanings (here, causal and non-causal) compete for the basic forms. Across different languages, the winners are the ones that are more accessible, such as the non-causal 'freeze', and the causal 'break'. They occupy the shorter basic forms. The losers are the less accessible ones, which are expressed with derived compositional forms. Similar claims were made by Fenk-Oczlon (2001) about Russian perfective and imperfective verbs, where the frequent aspect partner is usually the shorter and unproductive one.

Zipf (1949) argues that the frequency of concepts is crucial for the choice between basic and derived expressions (see Section 5.4.2). For example, the action of striking something with the chin is less common than striking with the foot. This is why English possesses a single word only for the second concept, i.e., *kick*. Another example is *brother* vs. *uncle's second wife's cousin's husband* (although languages with more complex family structure can have more special words for different relatives than English, cf. Sections 6.1 and 6.2.1). Similarly, Hawkins (2014: 17), who provides an example of *a teacher* and *a teacher who is late for class*, writes:

The more frequently selected properties are conventionalized in single lexemes or unique categories and constructions in all these examples. Less frequently used properties must then be expressed through word and phrase combinations and their meanings must be derived by semantic composition.

There are semantic and syntactic properties that frequently occur across languages and that have priority in grammatical and lexical conventions, such as causation, agenthood, patienthood, frequent speech acts (asserting, commanding, questioning). These functions usually have distinct formal expressions across grammars. Thus, more accessible meanings win the competition for less costly forms. Suppletion is only a special case of this general pragmatic mechanism.

5.6 Word Order Optimization

This chapter has focused on efficiency as minimization of articulation effort because the coevolution of form and meaning has been studied more extensively than the emergence of efficient order. However, some studies discuss possible scenarios of how some efficient word order patterns emerged.

Let us first consider word order correlations, which were discussed in Section 3.3.6. They are considered efficient for a number of reasons (harmony, minimization of domains, etc.). At least some of these correlations can be explained by the process of grammaticalization (Givón 1984). For example, the fact that VO languages tend to have prepositions, whereas OV languages tend to have postpositions is because adpositions commonly develop from verbs. The order of a verb and its object is retained in the order of the new adposition and noun phrase (Dryer 2019). Take two English prepositions *including* and *concerning*, which have developed from present participles followed by an object.

At the same time, there are correlations that cannot be easily explained by grammaticalization. For example, VO languages also tend to have the following orders: verb + adpositional phrase (*walk in the park*), verb + manner adverb (*walk slowly*), copula + predicate (*is a student*), complementizer + clause

5.6 Word Order Optimization

(*that she is arriving*) and some others. In contrast, OV languages have the opposite patterns (Dryer 2019). These correlations may be due to other factors, such as minimization of processing effort or maximization of learnability (cf. Section 3.3.6).

An important principle of efficient word order is minimization of dependency distances, which was discussed in Chapter 3. Some studies help us understand how this tendency manifests itself over time. In particular, Tily (2010: Ch. 3) analyses word order changes from Old to Middle English. He shows that there is a clear decrease in overall dependency distances with time. He compares the actual dependency distances with the optimal distances, produced by an algorithm that chose the order with the minimal sum distance. In the early manuscripts from the ninth century, the observed dependencies are on average about 1.5 times longer than the optimal values. By the end of the Middle English period, they are about 1.35 times the optimal lengths.

Gulordava and Merlo (2015) compare texts in Classical Latin (Caesar and Cicero) with the Late Latin of the fourth century AD (Vulgate and Peregrinatio). They also compare two Ancient Greek texts: Herodotus (fourth century BCE) and New Testament (fourth century CE). They compute the difference between the actual dependency lengths and the optimal lengths (controlled for sentence length). They find that the difference decreases from earlier texts to later texts, both in Latin and in Ancient Greek. Note that the modern Romance languages and modern Greek have dependency distances that are quite close to optimal (Futrell, Mahowald and Gibson 2015b).

One could ask, of course: if the system becomes more efficient, why were the earlier systems less optimal? Tily (2010) considers several factors, including the role of rich morphological cues in Old English, which might have mitigated the greater processing difficulties. Grammatical markers help the addressee in situations when accessibility is low, due to word order or other factors (see Chapter 2).

Often, some aspects of word order efficiency are lost, and some are gained. An example is the tendency to use more accessible forms first, which can be in conflict with the efficient reuse of abstract utterance schemas, which helps to decrease production effort (MacDonald 2013; see Section 3.2.2). Old English had substantial flexibility in the order of verb and object. Pronominal objects were normally used preverbally. With time, VO spread, but the tendency to keep pronouns before the verb survived well into the Middle English period. Heavier nominal objects were moved into the postverbal position (Tily 2010). This was efficient because pronominal objects are highly accessible and noun objects are less so. If pronouns are produced early, this saves time that can be spent on less accessible elements. Present-Day English is consistently VO, although some preverbal pronouns remain as fossilized expressions in Present-Day English, e.g., *I thee wed* and *until death do us part*. The order is now the same for functionally similar constituents, which can be beneficial for processing and learning.

5.7 A Note on Teleology

After discussing specific mechanisms and instances of language change, it is necessary to say a few words about the global causes of the emergence of efficient language systems. Different trends of functionalism have different views, as pointed out by Bybee (1999). For example, Dressler (1990: 76) argued that language development is teleological:

> Both linguistic universals and all language Systems have the teleology of overcoming substantial difficulties of language performances (including storage/memorization, retrieval, evaluation) for the purpose of the two basic functions of language: the communicative and the cognitive function.

In other words, languages change in order to become better systems for the purposes of communication and cognition.

There seems to be a lot of confusion around terms such as teleology, intentionality, and consciousness (cf. Keller 1994). One of these misconceptions is that functional explanations of language (such as the one developed in this book) are necessarily teleological, and therefore flawed, so it is important to clarify the main concepts.

The notion of teleology goes back to Aristotle and his theory of four causes. One of the causes is called final: the properties of an explanandum can be explained by what it is for. For example, Aristotle argues that animals have sharp front teeth for biting and flat molar teeth for grinding the food. Since this is a regularity, and not a coincidence, the shape of the teeth should be explained by their function.[7] Such explanations are called teleological.

Leaving aside the relevance of that pre-Darwinian explanation, one can speak about three possible types of teleological causes: some external benevolent force (intelligent aliens, magic, deities, etc.), smart self-optimization or intentional actions of language users. The first two are obviously not applicable. A language is not a sentient being that can adjust its behaviour, and there is no supernatural force that would cause it to become more efficient.

As for intentional actions of language users, the answer is less obvious. Users perform their communicative tasks intentionally, in order to meet their

---

[7] See Aristotle, *The Organon and Other Works*. Opensource collection. Translated under the editorship of W.D. Ross. https://archive.org/details/AristotleOrganon. Physics, Book II, Sections 8–9.

5.7 A Note on Teleology

practical needs. Their main concern is to get their message across, with all illocutionary and perlocutionary effects that they deem desirable (e.g., to influence others, to impress, to convince, to get important information). These conscious actions are made up of fully or partly unconscious sub-actions which determine the linguistic shape of an utterance, e.g., using the present continuous tense, choosing a word out of a set of synonyms, deleting final -*t* or -*d*, etc.

This hierarchical structure is typical of human actions: conscious goal-directed activities consist normally of automated unconscious sub-actions, such as pressing the keys when playing the piano, changing the gears when driving a car, or performing precise muscular movements when using a knife and fork. At the same time, unconscious sub-actions can be called intentional because they form part of intentional actions. The unconscious or conscious choices of individual users may propagate in the language system and become conventionalized as an unintended result of intentional actions in an 'invisible hand' process (Keller 1994).

The potential for conscious attention is also different for the different types of efficiency examined in this book. For example, creative M-implicatures (e.g., *Mary produced sounds that reminded us of Jingle Bells* → Mary's singing was terrible) are likely to be consciously produced, whereas the use of grammatical markers and function words or subtle reduction and enhancement of phonetic details in pronunciation are usually unconscious. However, even the use of such units can occasionally become conscious, e.g., when someone repeats a word with an emphasis on a segment in case of misunderstanding. Some abbreviations are often consciously introduced for the sake of efficiency. For example, after Annegret Kramp-Karrenbauer was nominated for the position of the Leader of the Christian Democratic Union in Germany, journalists began to refer to her as AKK because her full name was long and difficult to pronounce. This was a conscious choice, although later, after many months, it was probably no longer conscious. All these considerations are summarized in Table 5.1.

Table 5.1. *Different properties of language use and change*

Phenomenon	Driven by some external force or self-optimization	Intentional	Conscious
Individual use of language	No	Yes	Possible
Language change	No	No (except for language planning)	No (except for language planning)

Bybee has often argued against the view that language development has any long-term goal to aim at or any purposes to fulfil (e.g., Bybee et al. 1994: 297–298; Bybee 2010). She emphasizes the key role of fully unconscious cognitive processes within a language user's mind, such as entrenchment, schematization, routinization and chunking. For example, she wrote:

> The increase in efficiency in high-frequency words results from the way the general neuromotor system operates, and is neither restricted to language nor a conscious goal-directed process. (Bybee 2010: 146)

These processes are undoubtedly very important. But this does not contradict the fact that efficiency is driven by intentional (that is, goal-directed) actions of language users. Of course, this does not mean that they consciously pursue the goal of making language more efficient, although this can happen sometimes, as in the example with the abbreviation AKK. When we say that language users optimize their language, this is usually only a shortcut for a complex 'invisible hand' process.

5.8   Conclusions

The aim of this chapter was to discuss the basic principles and possible causal models of diachronic changes that lead to the emergence of efficient language structures. I argued that they are at least partly motivated by pragmatic principles discussed in the previous chapters. It is possible that there are other factors playing a role. For example, V. Ferreira (2008) hypothesizes that aspects of a language that are too ambiguous to use are likely too ambiguous to learn as well. Obviously, learnability for L1 and L2 users is an important factor in language evolution (cf. Levshina 2021b). We need to learn more about how these factors interact with communicative efficiency.

If pragmatic mechanisms shape language in the way described above, we can formulate several predictions for the evolution of linguistic units.

> Prediction 1. Two contrasting grammatical or lexical categories (e.g., singular and plural) that demonstrate asymmetries in their costs (most importantly, formal length) are likely to display differences in their probabilities in language use, so that the less costly form expresses the more accessible category, and the more costly form represents the less accessible category.
>
> Prediction 2. When a category exhibits a formal split – that is, if there are several different forms that perform the same grammatical function (cf. Haspelmath 2021b), as in differential object marking (see Chapter 8), the less costly form will specialize to a more accessible meaning, and the more costly one will express a less accessible meaning.

5.8 Conclusions

Prediction 3. If a new reduced and less costly form competes for some functional domain with an older and non-reduced one, the reduced form will first take over the more accessible functions or meanings in that domain. And conversely, if the new form is longer and more costly, it will first convey the less accessible meanings.

This chapter does not provide counterexamples to efficient change, but they do occur. For example, the German perfect tense with *haben* 'have', e.g., *hat gemacht* 'has made', has replaced the preterite form, e.g., *machte* 'made' in Upper German dialects and in colloquial speech, with the exception of highly frequent verbs with entrenched preterite forms, e.g., the verb *sein* 'be' and modal verbs. The perfect tense has developed into a general past. First it took over past events with current relevance, which was later reinterpreted as general past use (Fischer 2018).

Remarkably, the English present perfect also followed this path for some time. It was used to refer increasingly to events located wholly in the past in Early Modern English, with a peak in the eighteenth century. However, after that the development ebbed back. Nowadays, the English present perfect mostly performs traditional present perfect functions (Fischer 2020).

As a result, the division of labour between the present perfect and past-tense forms in English seems to be more efficient than that in German. The perfect form is longer than the preterite form, and therefore less efficient from the point of view of articulatory effort.[8] There have been many hypotheses that explain this development, from language contact to phonological reasons, such as apocope (see Fischer 2018), which require more research.

---

[8] Possibly with the exception of some clumsy preterite forms with consonant clusters and repetitive syllables, especially in the 2nd person (e.g., *du batst* 'you asked for' and *du meldedest* 'you reported'), where the perfect form can help to avoid articulatory difficulties (Fischer 2020).

6 From Trade-Offs to Causal Networks

6.1 Trade-Offs in Linguistics

The notion of a trade-off is used when spending the limited resources on gaining in one aspect leads to losing in other aspects. In linguistics, the idea of trade-offs has been present for a long time. Trade-offs are closely related to competing motivations in functional linguistics and typology (Du Bois 1985; MacWhinney, Malchukov and Moravcsik 2014). The behaviour of language users and learners is driven by different communicative and cognitive pressures. For example, analogy, or system pressure, forces human language users to organize linguistic forms into systems in which classes of forms behave similarly. In English, for instance, the overwhelming majority of nouns have an unmarked singular form and a plural form marked with -(e)s. This system is relatively easy to learn, in comparison with a system like in Welsh, where some nouns have plural marking, and some have singulative marking (see Section 2.3.2). System pressure can be in conflict with economic motivation (Haspelmath 2014). For example, if English had a singulative form for 'pea' (something like 'pea-one') and an unmarked plural form instead of 'peas', like in Welsh, this would lead to lower articulation costs because we usually speak of many peas, rather than one pea only (except for Hans Christian Andersen's fairy tale *The Princess and the Pea*). But this system would also be more complex – at least for learners. This can be thought of as a trade-off between articulatory costs and cognitive costs required for learning.

Another example of competing motivations is the interaction between phonological transparency and articulatory economy. Consider final devoicing of stems and affixes. For example, the noun *kod* 'code' in Russian has the Genitive singular form *kod-a* ['koda], while the Nominative singular form is *kod-Ø* [kot], which sounds like *kot* 'cat'. This and other phonological alternations make articulation easier but reduce transparency, which requires one-to-one mapping between form and meaning, and consequently diminish the learnability of a language (Hengeveld and Leufkens 2018).

6.1 Trade-Offs in Linguistics

All this suggests that a language cannot be ideal for all purposes. As put informally by Joseph Greenberg, '[a] speaker is like a lousy auto mechanic: every time [s]he fixes something in the language, [s]he screws up something else' (Croft 2002: 5).

The notion of trade-offs has been used to refer to negative correlations between linguistic variables representing different costs or linguistic cues for expressing a certain meaning. For example, one speaks of a trade-off between information conveyed by word-internal structure (morphology) and word order (Koplenig et al. 2017, see also below). More specifically, languages without case morphology tend to have rigid word order, while languages with morphology usually have flexible word order (see Section 6.3).

A negative correlation can also represent a Pareto frontier. Consider Figure 6.1. The axes represent two potential costs. The dots are observations from some imaginary data. The line corresponds to a Pareto frontier. The observations lying close to the Pareto frontier are optimal (or Pareto-efficient) because it is impossible to decrease one cost without increasing the other.

An example is the trade-off between cognitive complexity and communicative costs in kin naming systems (Kemp, Xu and Regier 2018). Cognitive complexity was defined by the number of rules needed in order to describe a kinship term in a language, such as mother(x, y) ↔ PARENT(x, y) ∧ FEMALE(x). For example, Northern Paiute has more complex rules than English (as well as more unique terms in total). The communicative costs are the divergence between the probabilities of different referents for the speaker

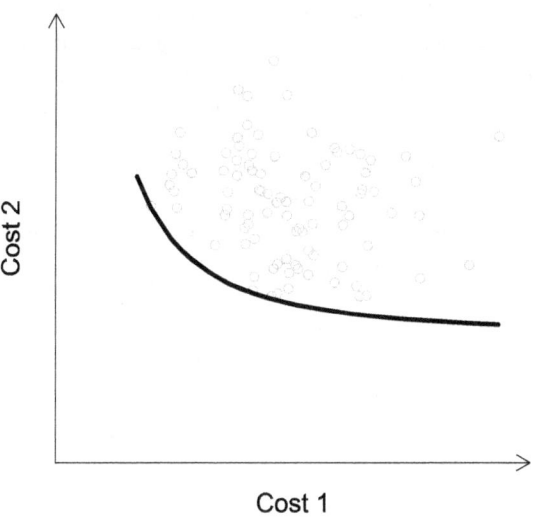

Figure 6.1 A Pareto frontier based on imaginary data with two different costs

and the hearer when the speaker uses a certain kinship term. For example, by using the word *aunt*, the speaker can mean the father's sister, but for the hearer the referent is vague: it can be either the father's or the mother's sister.[1] The greater this divergence, the higher the communicative costs. Kemp et al. used computer simulations to generate a large set of hypothetical kinship systems. This set of systems had a Pareto frontier, where the systems were efficient, such that a reduction in communicative costs led to an increase in the cognitive costs, and the other way round. Crucially, the kin naming systems observed in real languages were located close to the Pareto frontier. Languages like Northern Paiute have high cognitive complexity and low communicative costs, whereas languages like English have low cognitive complexity and high communicative costs.

The term 'trade-off' has been used to refer to implications, as well. For example, Cotterell et al. (2019) discovered a non-trivial relationship between paradigm size and irregularity (the paradigm entropy, or the average number of bits per distinct non-lemma form) in nouns and verbs in thirty-six diverse languages. That is, a language can mark a large number of morphosyntactic distinctions, as in Finnish, Turkish, and other agglutinative and polysynthetic languages; or it may exhibit high irregularity (unpredictability) of morphological forms, as in Russian nominal inflection. Some languages, importantly, have few irregular paradigms, and not many morphosyntactic distinctions. Examples are English and German. This means that the relationship is implicational rather than correlational: only systems with large paradigms and high irregularity are avoided, whereas all other combinations are possible. Yet, Cotterell et al. call this relationship a trade-off.

All this shows that the term 'trade-off' can describe different relationships, which can be confusing. It is advisable to be more specific about the nature of the relationship, namely, whether it is a correlation or an implication, and if one observes a Pareto frontier.

In addition to different interpretations of the term, there are numerous other problems which arise when one uses trade-offs as an explanation in functional linguistics. These problems have rarely been discussed, with the exception of Fenk-Oczlon and Fenk (2008) and Sinnemäki (2008, 2014). It may be very tempting to interpret any negative correlation as an efficient trade-off. In this chapter, I argue that many binary trade-offs related to efficiency are problematic. First of all, in most cases, the costs or benefits cannot be reduced to just a pair. Usually, there are other relevant factors that need to be taken into account. This means that we need a multivariate approach. Language is a very complex system, so it is unlikely that only two types of costs interact with each other,

---

[1] More technically, one extra bit of information needs to be added to the message in order to express precisely which referent the speaker has in mind.

without other factors intervening. Second, there can be different causal relationships between the variables, which we need to reflect in a model. Finally, different types of costs can work in synergy, rather than in competition. Language is not a zero-sum game. These points are illustrated in Section 6.2. Therefore, we should switch from binary correlational analyses to multivariate causal analyses (Blasi and Roberts 2017). This method will be demonstrated in a case study of Subject and Object cues based on corpora in thirty languages in Section 6.3.

6.2 Problems with Trade-Offs

6.2.1 Looking for 'the Third Man': The Role of Context

Most trade-offs discussed in the literature are binary (but see Fenk-Oczlon and Fenk 2008; Sinnemäki 2008). This can be seen as a simplification, which may be practically justified, but does not give due consideration to language as a complex system. Moreover, a relationship can change dramatically if other relevant factors are taken into account. A typical 'invisible' factor is context, understood here in a broad sense: linguistic co-text, encyclopaedic information, physical environment, common communicative experience and so on.

Let us take a trade-off from Piantadosi, Tily and Gibson (2012), which was used to explain why languages exhibit ambiguity. The trade-off is between two communicative pressures: clarity and ease. They write,

A clear communication system is one in which the intended meaning can be recovered from the signal with high probability. An easy communication system is one which signals are efficiently produced, communicated, and processed. There are many factors which likely determine ease for human language: for instance, words which are easy to process are likely short, frequent, and phonotactically well-formed. ... This means that in order to assign meanings unambiguously or clearly, one must also use words which are more difficult. (Piantadosi et al. 2012: 281)

However, the pressure for clarity does not necessarily mean that one has to use long and monosemous expressions, which are 'difficult'. If there is sufficient context, one can safely use 'easy' ambiguous words, which tend to be more frequent, accessible and well-formed (Piantadosi et al. 2012). There is plenty of evidence that ambiguity of linguistic expressions does not represent a serious problem in real communication, from Miller (1951) to Wasow (2015). In fact, Piantadosi et al. (2012) argue that all efficient communication systems should be ambiguous, provided that there is sufficient context that can help the addressee to infer the meaning.

Notably, Ariel (2014) shows that highly polysemous constructions, in which the meaning has to be inferred, have greater support from context (preceding discourse, non-linguistic information present in the common ground, etc.) than monosemous constructions. Consider an example of a polysemous construction *X or Y,* which can represent exclusive or inclusive disjunction, reformulation or a communicative repair, as in (1):

(1) (Ariel 2014: 337, from the Santa Barbara Corpus of Spoken American English)

> Mary: ... *Hand me that ashtray.*
> ... *Or your light,*
> *I mean.*

Here, *or* serves as a repair marker. The hearer has multiple cues for inferring the exact meaning. First, it is unlikely that Mary wanted to have either the ashtray or the light. Second, there is intonation of an afterthought. Third, *I mean* is a conventional marker of repair.

Two factors contribute to clarity for the addressee: coding effort and context richness. At the same time, these two components are negatively correlated for the speaker: the richer the context, the less coding effort is used. This relationship is directional: it is the availability of context that determines coding effort, not the other way round. The relationships between clarity, (coding) ease and context can be represented as shown in Figure 6.2. They cannot be reduced to a binary trade-off.

Similarly, the trade-off between communicative and cognitive costs in kinship terms reported by Kemp et al. (2018), which was discussed in Section 6.1, also depends on context. The question is, in particular, whether languages like English are really communicatively more costly than languages like Northern Paiute, given the cultural differences. In industrialized countries, people usually have nuclear families. As the society develops, complex kinship systems for different relatives fall out of use. For example, this has been happening in Russian, which went through industrialization in the twentieth century. Many terms are no longer understood and used, being replaced

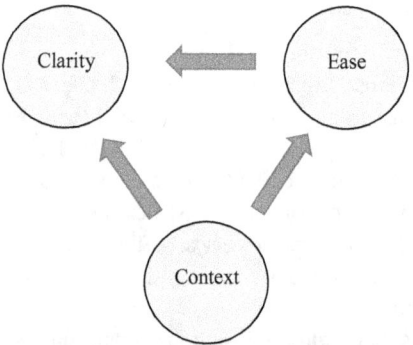

Figure 6.2 A causal graph showing relationships between clarity, ease and context in communication

6.2 Problems with Trade-Offs

by periphrastic expressions. For instance, the term *dever'* 'the husband's brother' is disappearing. If language users have different communicative needs due to different social circumstances, it may well be that the seemingly poorer and simpler systems are just as well adjusted to their circumstances of use as the richer and complex systems are to theirs. Obviously, this claim is extremely difficult to test, as one would need behavioural data from all languages in the sample in order to determine the communicative needs of speakers of those languages. We can hope that corpora will enable us to do this in the future.

Another example is a trade-off between simplicity and learnability from an iterative learning study by Kirby et al. (2015), who argue that compositionality in language is a result of two pressures. One is pressure for simplicity (compressibility) and learnability, and the other is pressure for expressivity, which arises from language use in communication. An open question is how much expressivity is needed when one has sufficient context.

As a more specific illustration, let us revisit the hypothesis that the subject is expressed only once, as argued by Berdicevskis, Schmidtke-Bode and Seržant (2020). This study was mentioned when we discussed the use and omission of referential expressions (Section 2.2.2). Using typological data, Berdicevskis et al. find that the overwhelming majority of languages in which familiar subjects are marked as bound elements attaching to the verb have predominantly optional independent subject pronouns. Languages without subject indexing have very variable chances of optional marking, but they are lower than in languages with subject indexing in most geographic macroareas. Eurasia is an exception. There are many languages which code the subject twice, e.g., German and Georgian, and many languages where the subject is not encoded obligatorily, e.g., Chinese and Japanese. At the same time, Berdicevskis et al. observe a tendency in many (but not all) Slavic corpora to use independent subject pronouns more often in the past forms without person agreement than in the present forms, which unambiguously specify the person. These findings are interpreted as evidence that languages tend to converge on optimizing the patterns by avoiding both redundancy (double encoding of person information, both as a subject NP and a verb index) and potential ambiguity (no encoding of person at all). In other words, we are dealing with an efficient trade-off.

One can ask why Eurasia and some Slavic languages do not follow this general pattern, of course. More importantly, this view considers the expression of subject in a sort of communicative vacuum. Many allegedly inefficient uses can be found to be perfectly efficient if we take into account the context. As discussed in Section 2.2, more accessible referents are expressed by shorter forms (e.g., zero or personal pronouns), while less accessible ones are expressed by longer forms (e.g., full NPs). Therefore, we can expect that lack of any encoding can be perfectly efficient with highly accessible subjects, and double encoding can be perfectly efficient with low-accessibility subjects.[2] There are contexts in which the accessibility of the subject is so high that it does not require any formal expression. An example is English imperative forms, e.g., *Come here!* with zero marking of the subject. Also, in informal spontaneous conversations, which are characterized by extensive common ground, the subject can be sometimes omitted when it is perfectly clear who the referent is:

(2)   *Wanna read it?* (BNC, Spoken, KB1)

Of course, we cannot exclude that there is a negative correlation between independent subject forms and verb marking in some contexts (e.g., declarative sentences, communication without rich common ground), but the claim that subjects should *always* be expressed once, and only once, requires a qualification.

6.2.2   Directionality of Relationships

Most researchers use the term 'trade-off' to describe a negative correlation (but see an example of an implicational relationship in Section 6.1). In principle, every negative correlation can be regarded as a trade-off in a very abstract sense: if one quantity decreases, then the other increases, and the other way round. But in order to speak of a real trade-off, the relationship should freely go in both directions. To give a simple example, one can indulge in instant gratification, spending all one's money now on pleasant things and having nothing tomorrow, or one can save money for a rainy day but have a less enjoyable life now.

Let us continue discussing the role of context, as in the previous section. There is ample evidence that common ground leads to shorter referential expressions used by interlocutors and shorter exchanges in general (e.g., Clark and Wilkes-Gibbs 1986). We can also interpret Ariel's (1990) Accessibility Theory as a correlation between context and coding length: there is a tendency for more accessible referents to be expressed by shorter forms (e.g., pronouns or zero expression) than less accessible ones, which are expressed by longer forms (e.g., noun phrases). Chapter 2 provided numerous examples of negative correlations between amount of linguistic encoding and accessibility of information from context. So, can we speak of a trade-off between context and articulation effort, in the strict sense specified above?

If we say 'yes', we lose important information about the directionality and freedom of choice: the ease of access is determined by common ground, which

---

[2] This observation was first formulated by Mira Ariel (p.c.). The ideas presented here form the basis of an ongoing project with Mira Ariel and John Du Bois.

6.2 Problems with Trade-Offs

is already given to the interlocutors. The speaker adjusts the amount of coding to the accessibility determined by the situation, but cannot adjust accessibility to the amount of coding they want to use.

It has already been mentioned that rigid word order and case morphology are negatively correlated. Languages tend to use either case marking (e.g., Latin or Lithuanian) or rigid word order (e.g., English or Mandarin Chinese).[3] Koplenig et al. (2017) speak about a general trade-off between information carried by word order and information carried by word-internal structure, measured with the help of information-theoretic concepts. The almost a thousand languages in their sample reveal a clear negative correlation. Isolating languages with high scores on information conveyed by word order, such as Mandarin Chinese, have low scores on information carried by word structure, while polysynthetic languages like Greenlandic Inuktitut or Ojibwa have low word order scores and high word structure scores. Koplenig et al. argue that this trade-off is efficient:

> If, for example, grammatical relationships in a sentence are fully determined by the ordering of words, it would constitute unnecessary cognitive effort to additionally encode this information with intra-lexical regularities. If, however, word ordering gives rise to some extent of grammatical ambiguity, we should expect this ambiguity to be cleared up with the help of word structure regularities in order to avoid unsuccessful transmission. (Koplenig et al. 2017: 4)

So, the causal effect seems to be from word order to morphology, rather than the other way round. This view has some support in diachronic studies. According to Kiparsky (1996), the shift to VO began in Old English. It happened before the case system collapsed, and also before the loss of subject–verb agreement. Also, Bauer (2009) demonstrates that the change to VO and rigid word order in Late and Vulgar Latin was before the loss of inflection, which happened later in Romance. Similarly, Fedzechkina, Newport and Jaeger (2016) had their participants learn a miniature artificial language with optional object marking. If the order was fixed, the case marking was used significantly less often than in the input language. This can be interpreted as an indication that rigid word order helps to lose distinct forms. The reverse (i.e., loss of word order rigidity) did not happen, although we could attribute that to an interference effect of the native language (English). To sum up, the existing evidence points in the direction of a one-way

---

[3] This correlation has been interpreted as a trade-off of different types of complexity (Sinnemäki 2014). It is believed that fixed word order makes a language more complex because it requires more rules that need to be learned (e.g., Sinnemäki 2008, but see Gell-Mann 1995 for a different definition of complexity). Yet, rigid word order can in fact save processing costs in comprehension because it helps to assign syntactic roles to sentence elements (Fenk-Oczlon and Fenk 2008).

relationship between word order and case marking. This directionality is not captured by the notion of a trade-off.

6.2.3 Synergy Effects

Encoding and interpreting visual and auditory information requires effort. It would be logical to expect that one modality of communication should be easier to process than several. In spoken languages, a message is transmitted via two major modalities: auditory message and visual signals, which are produced by the head, face, hands, arms and torso. Some of these signals may be relevant for comprehension, others may be irrelevant, which means that the addressee needs extra effort to distinguish between them, especially under the time constraints of spontaneous interaction with quick turn-taking. One would believe then that processing one modality should be at the cost of the other. However, this is not true – at least, for neurotypical speakers. There is evidence that interlocutors respond faster to questions that have an accompanying manual and/or head gesture than to questions without such visual components (Holler et al. 2019). In fact, Holler and Levinson (2019) argue that multimodal information is easier to process than unimodal (that is, only visual or only auditory) information because visual bodily signals may reduce uncertainty at the message level. Humans are good at creating multimodal Gestalts as a result of message unification. This means that different modalities have a synergetic effect. From this follows that the assumption of language as a zero-sum game, which is implicitly present in the idea of trade-offs, is too simplistic.

Notably, Silverman et al. (2010) carried out an experiment in which participants watched videos of a person describing one of four shapes shown on a computer screen, using speech-and-gesture or speech-only descriptions. Silverman et al. found that gestures facilitate comprehension only in neurotypical participants. In adults with high functioning autism, however, gestures hindered comprehension. This means that our assumptions about the relationships between different processing costs should be adjusted to different types of language users.

6.3 From the Trade-Off between Case Marking and Word Order to a Multivariate Causal Network

6.3.1 Research Questions

In this section I focus on the famous trade-off between case marking and word order, with particular attention to the expression of Subject and Object. This was discussed in Section 6.2.2. As early as 1921, Edward Sapir mentioned

6.3 From Trade-Off to Multivariate Causal Network

fixed word order as a compensatory strategy in languages without case marking, to help the addressee to understand who did what to whom (Sapir 1921). A more recent empirical study supports this claim, showing a negative correlation between argument marking and rigid word order (Sinnemäki 2014). This relationship is statistical, since there seem to exist languages that have relatively fixed word order and case marking (Kiparsky 1996). The questions are: if we take into account other cues, will this change the relationship? Also, is the relationship unidirectional (from word order to case marking) or is it bidirectional?

6.3.2 Types of Cues

Let us start with case marking. It is more complicated than it might seem. Some languages have consistent case marking on either the subject, the object, or both. For example, Lithuanian nouns, with the exception of some loanwords, have distinct Nominative and Accusative case forms in all declension types. Some languages have differential marking. This means that Subject and Object are marked in some situations and not marked in others. Differential marking is particularly common for objects. For example, in Hebrew, only definite objects are marked, whereas in Spanish and Hindi, the marking depends on definiteness/specificity and animacy (see more examples in Aissen 2003). Case syncretism can also be interpreted as differential marking. In some Indo-European languages, the distinctions between the Nominative and the Accusative forms are made only in some lexical classes, while the forms are identical in others, for example, in Latin neuter nouns, e.g., *bell-um* 'war-NOM/ACC', and Russian inanimate masculine nouns, e.g., *stol-Ø* 'table. NOM/ACC'. Some languages have probabilistic, or fluid marking, like Korean and Japanese. Differential marking is discussed in detail in Chapter 8. All this means that case marking can provide more or less information about the grammatical roles and therefore should be treated as a continuous variable.

Arguments can be also marked on the verb. This is called agreement, or indexing. Subject indexing is popular across languages, e.g., German *er komm-t* 'he come-3SG'. As for object agreement, it often remains at the stage of differential object indexing (Haig 2018).

Moreover, it is claimed that it is easier to assign the roles when the verb occurs between the subject and the object. Some evidence comes from experiments that involve gestural communication. It was found that participants usually prefer SOV when trying to convey a transitive event (Goldin-Meadow et al. 2008; Gibson et al. 2013; Hall, Mayberry and Ferreira 2013). However, SVO is used more often in the absence of any spatial marking (e.g., using different hands or space locations to designate Subject and Object) or when Subject and Object are interchangeable in the given context. According to Gibson et al. (2013), verb-medial order is more robust to the presence of noise when conveying the roles of Subject and Object – in particular, when one of the arguments is not discerned. If the argument that the addressee discerns is before the verb, e.g., *The mother hugs*, it can be identified as subject. If the noun is after the verb, e.g., *Hugs the boy*, then it should be Object. Note that this explanation presupposes that SVO order should be sufficiently rigid that language users can rely on the order of S and O with regard to the verb.

An interesting alternative explanation of these findings is proposed by Hall et al. (2015). They argue that SOV does not present problems for comprehenders, even when the events are reversible. The preference for SVO is in fact due to producers avoiding the sequence OV when the object is human. When representing a human subject or object, the producer takes on its role. Because action gestures are normally produced from the perspective of the agent, producers avoid OV when the object is human. But it is not clear how this account would explain the fact that some spoken languages prefer verb-medial order when the arguments are similar. For example, speakers of Tzeltal, a VOS Mayan language, choose SVO more frequently when the arguments share semantic features (e.g., two humans or two animals) (Norcliffe et al. 2015). We should also consider here the *horror aequi* principle, discussed in Section 4.4. The avoidance of interference between semantically similar units could explain the preference for the verb-medial structures reported in many experiments.

Finally, semantics can provide a strong cue for assigning the roles. For example, one can expect that it is a dog who bites a man, a hunter who kills a bear, a journalist who interviews a politician, and not the other way round. There are also strong associations between roles and more abstract referential features, such as animacy, definiteness, discourse status, etc. According to cross-linguistic spoken corpus data presented in Chapter 8, if an argument is human, 1st or 2nd person, definite or discourse-given, it is more likely to be Subject than Object. If an argument is non-human, 3rd person, indefinite or new, it is more likely to be Object than Subject.

Importantly, a language can have stronger or looser semantic restrictions on the referents that can play a certain grammatical role. For instance, Present-Day English has fewer semantic restrictions on the subject and object than Old English or German (Hawkins 1986, 2019). It is also said that English is a 'loose-fit' language, while German, as well as Russian, Korean and Turkish, are 'tight-fit' languages (Müller-Gotama 1994).

Previous studies show that some of these measures are correlated with either rigid word order or case marking. In particular, Greenberg's (1963) Universal 41 says: 'If in a language the verb follows both the nominal subject and nominal object as the dominant order, the language almost always has a case system.' This means that verb-final order is associated with case marking, while verb-medial order is associated with lack of case marking (cf. Sinnemäki 2010). Also, Hawkins (1986) wrote about the correlation between verb-finalness and semantic tightness, an observation that has been confirmed empirically on a sample of different languages (Levshina 2020b). Moreover, he predicted a positive correlation between case marking and semantic tightness. Verb-final languages should be semantically tight and have case marking because an early incorrect assignment of roles would result in reanalysis, which has high processing costs (see Section 3.2.2).

6.3.3 Corpus Data

In order to collect data about different cues, I used corpora from thirty languages:

- Indo-European family with the following genera: Baltic (Latvian and Lithuanian), Germanic (Danish, Dutch, English, German, Swedish), Romance (French, Italian, Portuguese, Romanian, Spanish), Slavic (Bulgarian, Croatian, Czech, Russian and Slovenian), Indic (Hindi), Iranian (Persian), and Modern Greek;
- Uralic family with two Finnic languages (Finnish and Estonian) and one Ugric language (Hungarian);
- Other families: Afro-Asiatic (Arabic), Austro-Asiatic (Vietnamese), Austronesian (Indonesian), Altaic (Turkish), Dravidian (Tamil), as well as Japanese and Korean (isolates).

The data were collected from online news corpora, freely downloadable from the Leipzig Corpora Collection (Goldhahn, Eckart and Quasthoff 2012). Each language was represented by one million sentences. The corpora were annotated in the Universal Dependencies style (Zeman et al. 2020), in order to extract transitive Subject and Object from the sentences.

The technical details are discussed in Levshina (2021b). Most importantly, I derived four different measures from the corpora:

- word order rigidity: first, I computed Shannon's entropy of order of Subject and Object, which is equal to 0 if only one order is observed (Subject is always followed by Object, or the other way round), and equal to 1 if both orders occur with equal probability (Levshina 2019b).[4] Second, the entropy scores were subtracted from 1 in order to represent the rigidity of word order;

---

[4] Entropy of two possible word orders is computed as follows: $H = -P(SO)*log\, P(SO) - P(OS) *log\, P(OS)$, where P is the proportion of a word order (SO or OS).

- informativeness of case marking, which is measured as Mutual Information of the roles and cases (expressed by bound morphemes, adpositions or case particles); a higher score means that the case forms help to differentiate between Subject and Object better;
- verb-medialness, as the proportion of verbs placed between Subject and Object in a sentence;
- semantic tightness, which is measured as Mutual Information of the grammatical roles and lexemes (Levshina 2020b), such that tight-fit languages have higher scores, and loose-fit languages have lower scores.

6.3.4 Correlational Analyses

Next, I performed a range of correlation analyses between these four measures, using resampling with permutation in order to account for the dependencies between the data points due to their shared genealogy. The technical details can be found in Levshina (2021b). Below I describe the main results.

As for case marking and word order rigidity, the correlation is negative and significant: Spearman's $\rho = -0.67, p = 0.004$. But will it change if we take the other two variables, verb-medialness and semantic tightness? We can answer this question with the help of partial correlations. The test shows that the correlation remains stable, $\rho = -0.66$, and statistically significant. Therefore, the correlation is not influenced by the presence of other variables. There is a stable relationship: rigid word order is accompanied by less 'helpful' case marking (or lack of any marking), and flexible word order is associated with more informative case marking. The previous accounts are therefore supported.

At the same time, case marking is correlated positively with tight semantics. The correlation coefficient is positive: 0.49 for 'normal' correlation and 0.44 if we compute partial correlation coefficients. That is, a language with case marking will tend to have more restrictions on what kind of lexemes can be Subject and Object.

As for case marking and the medial position of the verb, the relationship is negative. A language with informative case marking will tend to be verb-final, and a language without informative case marking will be verb-medial. The Spearman correlation between these variables Case Marking and Verb Middle is moderate ($\rho = -0.47$) if we do not control for other variables, but it becomes weak if we control for the other cues, computing partial correlations ($\rho = -0.22$).

6.3.5 A Causal Analysis

The data also allow us to test causal relationships between the cues. Recall that a true trade-off should not be one-directional, and should not involve more than two types of information. In order to test that, I used a causal analysis

6.3 From Trade-Off to Multivariate Causal Network

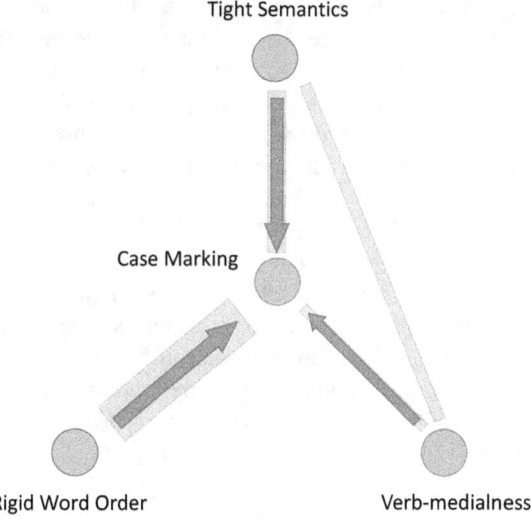

Figure 6.3 A graph displaying causal relationships between four types of cues

algorithm called FCI (Fast Causal Inference) (Spirtes, Glymour and Scheines 2000). A sampling procedure was used again to take into account the genealogical dependencies. In each sampling, the emergent causal links were logged. A graph showing the resulting network is shown in Figure 6.3.

We can see that not all possible links are present. There are only four edges. Case marking is in the middle. The thickness of the edges corresponds to their frequency in 1,000 simulations, during which languages were randomly sampled from the genera. The grey rectangles represent the total number of edges of different types. There was a causal link between rigid word order and case marking in 994 iterations. This means that the causal links between word order and case marking are strongly supported by the data, and the focus of researchers on this link is justified. Next follows the link between tight semantics and case marking. An edge between these two variables occurred in 320 simulations. The link between causal tight semantics and verb-medialness was observed only 59 times. Finally, the total number of edges from verb-medialness to case marking was only 30. No other edges were produced by the simulations.

The next question is, what about directionality? Most edges were unoriented, which means that no direction could be identified. Obviously, we need more data. But there were also many partially directional edges, which are represented by dark grey arrows on the graph. Partial directionality means that there is no certainty whether the relationship is $X \rightarrow Y$ or bidirectional, $X \leftrightarrow Y$.

Bidirectional edges usually indicate the presence of a common cause. Importantly, all of these edges are directed towards case marking. This means that case marking is more likely to change under the influence of the other variables than the other way round. The most frequent edge of this type is the one from rigid word order to case marking, with 344 occurrences in 1,000 simulations. This is followed by the edge from tight semantics to case marking, with 314 occurrences, and finally by the edge from verb-medialness to case marking, which occurred 30 times.

Therefore, word order rigidity or freedom affects case marking of the main arguments more than case marking affects word order. This supports the explanation provided by Koplenig et al. (2017) about the role of information expressed by word order and by morphology. Recall that they claimed that in the presence of word order information, complex morphology becomes redundant. This also agrees with the accounts by Kiparsky (1996) and Bauer (2009) discussed in Section 6.2.2.

6.3.6 Interpretation of the Results

The correlational and causal analyses have supported the previous claims from the literature. We found that the correlation between word order freedom and case marking is robust and cannot be reduced to the effect of other linguistic cues. Also, the causal analyses suggest that the causal direction is more likely to be from word order to case marking than the other way round. Notably, case marking seems to be the most malleable cue, which is affected by the other cues.

It is not surprising that one of the correlations was positive. The assumption of equal complexity of languages (that is, equal total costs) has been viewed critically for a long time (e.g., Shosted 2006). It has been shown that languages can accumulate new means of grammatical expression without shedding old ones, as happens in mature languages (Dahl 2004). Typological evidence suggests that all languages have some amount of redundancy (Hengeveld and Leufkens 2018).

The results of this case study should be tested on a larger number of languages. Moreover, we need to include more variables. In particular, sociolinguistic factors, such as the intensity of language contact, population size and the proportion of L2 speakers, can play an important role (Trudgill 2011). For example, McWhorter (2007) argues that languages that have served as a lingua franca with many L2 learners (e.g., English, Mandarin Chinese and Persian) are less grammatically complex then their close relatives. What is naturally easy for L1 children can be prohibitively difficult for adult learners. In addition, we should also take into account the amount of common ground that language users typically share. If it is large, then they may need fewer explicit means than if it is small, as argued in Section 6.2.1 about the role of context. There is a multitude of different factors in play, which are still waiting for their turn to be discovered and integrated into the causal network.

6.4 Conclusions

To conclude, negative correlations between pairs of linguistic cues or costs provide interesting hypotheses for empirical investigations. At the same time, there is a danger of oversimplification if one focuses only on correlations between two variables. It is time to move from these to causal (directional) networks with multiple factors. I tried to demonstrate how this can be done in the case study of semantic and morphosyntactic cues to the grammatical roles of Subject and Object.

Part III

Case Studies

7 Efficient Form–Meaning Mapping in Causative Constructions

7.1 The Causative Continuum

This chapter focuses on causative constructions in languages of the world. Causatives have received a lot of attention in the typological literature (e.g., Comrie 1989: Ch. 8; Song 1996; Dixon 2000; Shibatani and Pardeshi 2002; Haspelmath et al. 2014). Normally, they are classified into several types, which form the so-called causative continuum:

(1)   Lexical – Morphological – Analytic (or Periphrastic)

In lexical causatives, the cause and effect are expressed in one morpheme, e.g., *kill*, *break*, *give*. Morphological causatives contain a causative morpheme, e.g., Turkish *öl-dür-* 'kill' from *öl-* 'die'. Finally, analytic or periphrastic causatives are those in which the causative meaning is expressed by a combination of words, whereby the causing and caused events are expressed separately, e.g., *make* + NP + *dead*, *cause* + NP + *to die*.

These categories form a continuum because the boundaries between them are not clear-cut. In particular, one may argue about the class membership of non-productive morphological causatives, e.g., English *wid-en* and *solid-ify*, which may still exhibit morphological boundaries. Such causatives would be located between the prototypical lexical ones (e.g., *kill*) and the prototypical morphological ones (see the Turkish example above). Another example is formal variation within analytic causatives. For example, French causatives with *faire* 'make' are usually immediately followed by the infinitive, whereas constructions with *demander* 'ask, request' are followed by a nominal phrase, and then the infinitive, as in (2).

(2)   French (Comrie 1989: 169)

    a. *J'ai fait manger les pommes à Paul.*
       'I made Paul eat the apples.'
    b. *J'ai demandé à Paul de manger les pommes*
       'I asked Paul to eat the apples.'

In this case, the elements expressing cause and effect in the construction with *demander* will be less integrated than those in the construction with *faire*.

One can also mention here monoclausal and biclausal causatives, although this distinction is not clear-cut, either (Kulikov 2001: 887).

Probably the most famous cross-linguistic generalization about causatives is that the formal continuum in (1) corresponds to the semantic continuum of direct and indirect causation, as shown below:

(3)   Lexical – Morphological – Analytic
            more direct < – – – – – – – –> less direct

As Comrie (1989: 173) puts it, 'the kind of formal distinction found across languages is identical: the continuum from analytic via morphological to lexical causative correlates with the continuum from less direct to more direct causation'.

Although this idea has been very popular, it is somewhat surprising that empirical evidence for it has been equivocal (Escamilla 2012; Bellingham et al. 2020). The most important problem is probably that directness and indirectness of causation can be defined in different ways, which presents a challenge for studying causative constructions (cf. Bellingham et al. 2020). For example, one can speak about the spatiotemporal integration of events. Consider a famous example from Fodor (1970):

(4)   a. *John caused Bill to die (on Sunday by stabbing him on Saturday).*
          b. *John killed Bill (*on Sunday by stabbing him on Saturday).*

In (4a), the causing and caused events are not spatiotemporally integrated, and the causation is indirect. In contrast, in (4b) the events should occur in the same time and space, and the causation is direct. Formally, the periphrastic causative construction *cause to die* in (4a) represents the causing and caused events separately, whereas the lexical causative verb *kill* in (4b) contains both of them in one verbal root.

Another factor defining (in)directness is the presence or absence of physical contact between the participants (Haiman 1983). An illustration is provided in (5), taken from Haiman (1983: 784). In (5a), an instance of indirect causation, the Causer employs some unnatural force (e.g., magic or telekinesis) in order to cause the cup to rise without touching it. In contrast, in (5b) the Causer uses their own physical force to raise the cup and therefore has direct physical contact with the object.

(5)   a. *I caused the cup to rise to my lips.*
          b. *I raised the cup to my lips.*

Moreover, direct causation has been defined as causation in which the Causer is the main source of energy responsible for the caused event (cf. Verhagen and Kemmer 1997). When causation is indirect, there is some other source. For example, stabbing someone dead represents an instance of direct

7.1 The Causative Continuum

causation because the energy comes from the Causer. In contrast, imagine that someone tampers with another person's gun ammunition, so that the owner kills themselves. This would be an example of indirect causation.

The role of the Causee is crucial. Here, I use this term to refer to the participant immediately following the Causer in the causation chain, which performs an action or undergoes a change of state. If the Causee is animate, it can be the main source of energy. The Causer can make the causation indirect by giving directions to the Causee (so-called directive causation). However, this is only possible when the Causee is agentive and responds to the causing event (e.g., the Causer's command or request) by performing an action, as in (6a). When this agency is not present, e.g., when the Causee is asleep, as in (6b), the causation is direct despite the fact that the Causee is animate.

(6) a. *She made the children lie down.*
    b. *She laid the children down.*

This account also agrees with Givón's, who predicts that periphrastic causatives are more likely to code causation with a human-agentive 'manipulee' (i.e., Causee), whereas morphological and lexical ones are more likely to code causation with an inanimate manipulee (Givón 1990: 556).

Indirect causation is also associated with transitivity of the predicate that expresses the caused event, as in the next example, where the Causee (*the mechanic*) serves as an intermediary in bringing out the change in the Affectee (*my transmission*), or the end point of causation.

(7) *I had the mechanic fix my transmission.*

Since causation chains with transitive predicates are longer and involve more participants, the causation is considered indirect. Similarly, in Bellingham et al. (2020), indirectness is operationalized as the presence of a mediator (an agentive human or an instrument).

A special case of indirect causation is so-called curative causation, where the Causer has something done by the Causee. A typical example is when the action is a service provided by the Causee professionally:

(8) *I had my hair cut (by the hairdresser).*

The Causee is backgrounded and can be omitted, since it is not important who performs the action.

Moreover, one can also regard letting and permission as instances of indirect causation. In Talmy's Cognitive Semantics, letting is defined as non-impingement, or cessation of impingement. The Causee's intrinsic tendency towards rest or motion is not changed by the Causer (Talmy 2000: 417–421), which means that the Causer is not the source of energy for the caused event or state. Compare direct causation in (9a) with non-impingement in (9b) and cessation of impingement in (9c):

(9) a. *She rolled the stone up the hill* (i.e., using mostly her own energy).
b. *She let the rain cover her dry footprints* (i.e., by non-interference).
c. *The detective released the criminal's arm and let him fall from the roof* (i.e., by removing the obstacle to the force of gravity).

Directness and indirectness can manifest themselves differently, and should be thought of as prototypical categories with several features rather than semantic primitives. The above-mentioned features are summarized in (10). They are strongly correlated in language use (Levshina 2016). Note that this list includes the dimensions of (in)directness discussed in Bohnemeyer et al. (2010): mediation, contact and force dynamics.

(10) Semantic features relevant for (in)directness of causation:

	Direct causation	Indirect causation
a.	Spatiotemporal integration	Lack of spatiotemporal integration
b.	Physical contact	Lack of physical contact, causation by other means (e.g., communication)
c.	Causer is the main source of energy	Causee or another force (e.g., magic) is the main source of energy
d.	Causee is affected	Causee is an intermediary or agent
e.	Short causation chain (two participants, intransitive predicate expressing the effect)	Long causation chain (three participants, transitive predicate expressing the effect)
f.	Impingement ('making')	Lack or cessation of impingement ('letting')

It is possible to make other semantic distinctions, as well. One of them is whether the Causer is acting intentionally or accidentally. The sentence in (11a) is an example of intentional causation, whereas (11b) exemplifies accidental causation.

(11) a. *The thief opened the safe with a key.*
b. *Oops, I've just broken your Ming vase!*

This distinction may correlate with (in)directness, but it represents a dimension on its own. A Causer acting accidentally does not necessarily act indirectly, as in (12a), where the Causer has physical contact with the object, while acting intentionally does not mean acting directly, as in (12b), which represents an example of subtle manipulation by using communication.

(12) a. *Sorry, I've broken your iPad by sitting on it.*
b. *So how do you make it so that he does want to text you back?*[1]

---

[1] www.vixendaily.com/love/how-to-get-a-guy-to-text-you-back/ (last access 22 February 2021).

7.1 The Causative Continuum

Other semantic types include forceful and comitative causation, which are also difficult to interpret in terms of (in)directness, without making the latter distinction vacuous. These are discussed in the next sections.

The diverse interpretations of (in)directness often make it difficult to evaluate and compare the results of studies where the form–meaning correlation in (3) is tested. In what follows I will demonstrate that typological and corpus data support this correlation. See also Levshina (2016), where the use of analytic and lexical causatives in European languages is correlated with different parameters related to (in)directness, supporting the cross-linguistic generalization in (3).

The main focus of this chapter, however, is on the functional motivations for this generalization. It is traditionally explained by an iconic correspondence between form and function: '[t]he linguistic distance between expressions corresponds to the conceptual distance between them' (Haiman 1983: 782). The closer two events or objects are conceptually, the closer to each other the elements that express them will be. For example, in Fe'fe' Bamileke (Hyman 1971), two clauses can be separated by a coordinating conjunction *nī* 'and', as in (13a). The sentence conveys a strong implication that the events do not represent one unit. If the clauses are merely juxtaposed, there is a strong implication that the events take place at roughly the same time (Haiman 1983), as in (13b).

(13)　　Fe'fe' Bamileke (Haiman 1983: 788)

　a.　*à*　　*kà*　*gén*　*ntēe*　*nī*　*njwēn*　*lwà'*
　　　he　　PST　go　　market　and　buy　　yams
　　　'He went to the market and also (at some later date) bought yams.'

　b.　*à*　　*kà*　*gén*　*ntēe*　*njwēn*　*lwà'*
　　　he　　PST　go　　market　buy　　yams
　　　'He went to the market to buy yams.'

In this chapter, I will argue that efficiency provides a better explanation for cross-linguistic variation of causatives than iconicity of cohesion or distance, developing the line of argumentation in Haspelmath (2008c). My explanation involves asymmetries in the accessibility of the meanings expressed by different causative constructions. These asymmetries also explain the differences in the degree of conventionalization and grammaticalization of the constructions. I will argue that the principle of negative correlation between accessibility and costs, which involves the accessibility of different types of causative situations, plays a central role in such efficient form–meaning pairings. The meanings expressed by more compact causatives are more accessible (that is, direct causation and other frequent causation types), whereas the meanings expressed by less compact causatives are less accessible (indirect causation and other less frequent types). Less compact causatives normally have more costly forms in terms of articulation effort and time because they are usually longer. But one can also speak about asymmetries in processing effort (in particular, extraction from long-term memory and integration of parts of a periphrastic expression).

These ideas are compatible with a pragmatic account of causatives based on Levinson's (2000) I- and M-implicatures (see Section 1.4.2). It is argued that typical lexical causatives, as *stop* in (14a), trigger an I-implicature that the causation event is expected and typical. Analytic and periphrastic causatives, as *get to stop* in (14b), are 'marked' and therefore generate an M-implicature that the situation is untypical.

(14)   a. *Ann stopped the car.*
          (I-implicature → in the usual way, i.e., by putting her foot on the brake pedal)
       b. *Ann got the car to stop.*
          (M-implicature → in an unusual way, e.g., by using the emergency brake or crashing into a lamppost)

We can also interpret these expressions in terms of efficiency. Less costly expressions are matched with more accessible interpretations, while more costly expressions are matched with less accessible interpretations. The main difference is that we speak about the match between articulatory effort and accessibility, instead of a match between (un)typical forms and (un)typical meanings.

The arguments that support these ideas are the following.

1. The cross-linguistic variation of causative constructions with regard to their compactness is not restricted to (in)directness. There are other semantic parameters that are correlated with different degrees of formal compactness. This argument is developed in Section 7.2. I will argue that all these correlations, including the one related to (in)directness, can be explained by the accessibility of the corresponding causative meanings.
2. The cross-linguistic variation of causative constructions that express direct and indirect causation correlates more strongly with length differences than with the formal autonomy of the elements that express the cause and the effect, or the distance between them, as the iconicity account would predict. This is demonstrated in the typological study in Section 7.3.
3. Finally, one can model the development of efficient formal asymmetries in causatives without any iconic correlations. This is demonstrated in an artificial language learning experiment reported in Section 7.5. Artificial language learning is a valuable addition to the diachronic evidence showing how the efficient division of labour between causatives has emerged in some languages (see Section 7.4).

7.2 More than Just Direct and Indirect Causation

7.2.1 Causatives around the World

It was observed by Dixon (2000) that more and less compact causatives vary not only with regard to (in)directness of causation, but also with regard to other parameters, such as involvement of the Causer in the caused event and the Causer's intentions. If this is true, then the iconicity account presented in Section 7.1 is too narrow. At the same time, we will see that the principle of negative correlation between accessibility and costs can deal with the multi-factorial variation perfectly.

Let us begin with the scale of formal compactness in Dixon (2000), which decreases from lexical causatives (15a) to periphrastic causatives (15d):

(15) a. lexical causatives, e.g., $break_{TR}$ or $walk_{TR}$;
 b. morphological causatives, e.g., internal or tone change, reduplication, or affixation;
 c. complex predicates, e.g., serial verbs, French *faire* 'make' + V_{INF}, or causative particles;
 d. periphrastic causatives, which consist of verbs that belong to separate clauses, e.g., French *laisser* 'let' + NP + Infinitive or Portuguese *fazer* 'make' + (NP) + Infinitive.

According to Dixon, the degree of compactness is correlated with different semantic and syntactic features, as shown in Table 7.1 (Dixon 2000: 76). If a language has two different causative forms, a more compact and a less compact one, they will differ along one or more of the parameters.

Table 7.1. *Correlation between formal compactness and semantic and syntactic parameters according to Dixon (2000)*

	More compact forms	Less compact forms
1.	non-causal verb describing a state	non-causal verb describing an action
2.	intransitive (or intransitive and simple transitive) non-causal verb	transitive (or ditransitive) non-causal verb
3.	Causee lacking control	Causee having control
4.	Causee willing ('let')	Causee unwilling ('make')
5.	Causee partially affected	Causee fully affected
6.	direct causation	indirect causation
7.	intentional causation	accidental causation
8.	causation occurring naturally	causation occurring with effort

The ninth parameter discussed by Dixon is involvement of the Causer in the caused event. Yet Dixon did not find any correlations between this parameter and the degree of compactness. Note also that the fourth parameter in the table predicts more compact forms for willing Causees (letting), and less compact forms for unwilling Causees (making). It seems that two different distinctions are conflated here. The first distinction is whether the Causee resists the Causer's action or not. This is reflected in the eighth parameter, i.e., whether the causation occurs naturally or with effort. The second distinction is that between making and letting, or factitive and permissive causation. The typological data, which are presented below, as well as previous corpus-based research (Levshina 2016), show clearly that making is expressed by more compact forms than letting.

Unfortunately, Dixon does not provide a clear definition of direct and indirect causation. From the examples, however, one can infer that causation is direct when the Causer performs the caused event personally, by physically manipulating an object, while indirect causation means that the causation happens through someone or something else. The distinctive conceptual features are thus physical contact and mediation (see Section 7.1). Moreover, some of the other distinctions fit our broad definition of (in)directness based on the semantic features listed in (10). In particular, transitivity reflects the length of a causation chain. Transitive verbs will form causative constructions with three participants, which means that causation can be indirect. Also, controlling Causees are agentive, which can be interpreted as a sign of indirect causation. So, some of Dixon's parameters are closely related to (in)directness of causation in the maximally inclusive sense, which was discussed in the previous section.

But there are other parameters, as well. Let us have a look at intentional and accidental causation. In Section 7.1 it was argued that this distinction cannot be reduced to (in)directness. According to Dixon, if the Causer acts intentionally, the chances of a more compact form are higher than if the causation is accidental. An example can be found in Kammu, an Austro-Asiatic language spoken in Laos. In Kammu, the prefix *p(n)-* expresses intentional causation, whereas the particle *tòk* expresses accidental causation. Therefore, intentional causation is expressed by a more compact form than accidental causation.

(16) Kammu: Austro-Asiatic (Svantesson 1983: 103–111, cited from Dixon 2000: 70)

a. kə̀ə p-háan tráak
3SG+M CAUS-die buffalo
'He slaughtered the buffalo.'

b. kə̀ə tòk háan múuc
3SG+M CAUS die ant
'He happened to kill the ant (e.g., by accidentally treading on it).'

7.2 More Than Just Direct and Indirect Causation

Effortful vs. natural causation, as well as full vs. partial affectedness of the Causee, are also difficult to interpret in the sense of (in)directness, even if we use the broad definition proposed in Section 7.1.

The main question of this section is, do we find evidence of these correspondences between formal compactness and semantic features in languages of the world? We are particularly interested in the features beyond (in)directness of causation. Will Dixon's observations still hold if we obtain more data from diverse languages?

In order to answer this question, I took a sample of fifty-nine languages, each from a different language family, in which at least two causative constructions were described. The data come from reference grammars. Lexical causatives were excluded (usually grammars provide very little, if any, information about their shared functions), except for labile verb alternations. The list of languages and references is provided in Appendix 1.[2]

The causative constructions were then analysed semantically and formally, and all possible pairs of causatives were compared within each language. I found information about the semantic differences (which was either provided explicitly by the grammars or could be inferred from the examples) in the pairs from fifty-three languages (see more information in Appendix 1). Only these constructions are analysed in this section.

Compactness was determined according to Dixon's scale in (15). Labile verbs (e.g., *burn* or *melt*) were considered more compact than morphological causatives, whereas light verb constructions were considered more compact than serial verb constructions. Causatives with clitics were considered more compact than analytic causatives, but less compact than morphological causatives. Whether a causative was analytic, morphological, or something in-between, was determined according to the descriptions provided in the grammars. If two causatives belonged to the same type, their length was used as a criterion of compactness, following Dixon (2000: 75).

Table 7.2 presents the semantic features of the less compact form in a pair of causatives. This is done because in many cases only the less compact form has a special semantic description in a grammar, whereas the more compact form is treated merely as a valency-increasing device, or the 'default' causative. One example comes from Trumai, a language isolate from South America. In (17a), the default causative with the particle *ka* is used. In (17b), one can see the periphrastic causative with the verb *tao* 'order/give order', which means that the periphrastic construction represents causing someone to do something by order.

---

[2] The database is available on GitHub: https://github.com/levshina/TypoCaus.

Table 7.2. *Different types of causation in the typological sample, the meaning of the less compact form*

The less compact form expresses more/more often...	Languages in the sample	Number of languages
Indirect causation	Ma'di, Gumuz, Humburi Senni, Kayardild, Kusunda, Chimariko, Hebrew, Humburi Senni, Basque, Betta Kurumba, Yukaghir (Kolyma), Creek, Japanese, Urarina	15
Directive causation (as opposed to manipulative)	Diyari	1
Agentive or volitional Causee	Aguaruna, Cherokee, Lakhota, Motuna	4
Causation by communication (e.g., ordering)	Trumai, Great Andamanese	2
Mediated causation	Hindi	1
Factitive causation with a human intermediary	Noon	1
'Indefinite' causation (have something done) with a backgrounded Causee	Ainu	1
Weaker integration of events	Apinayé, Takelma	2
Distant causation (vs. contact causation)	Nivkh	1
'Mild' causation	Caddo	1
Causee as beneficiary	Tubu/Dazaga	1
Formed from dynamic verbs, actions (vs. states)	Wappo, Garrwa, Finnish	3
Letting, permissive (vs. making, factitive)	Ma'di, Kusunda, Finnish, Trumai, Hebrew, Teribe	6
Forceful causation	Basque, Wappo, Ik, Finnish	4
Non-volitional, not intentionally acting Causer	Tidore, Adang, Apinayé	3
Involved Causer	Cavineña	1
Distributive causation	Yukaghir (Kolyma)	1
Iterative causation	Yukaghir (Kolyma)	1
'Resultative' causation (keep X in a certain state)	Yukaghir (Kolyma)	1
Ballistic causation	Hup	1

Note that some languages are mentioned more than once because they have more than one pair of causatives that can be compared.

7.2 More Than Just Direct and Indirect Causation

(17) Trumai: isolate (Guirardello 1999: 302, 307)
  a. *hai-ts   Yakair-ø   sa   ka.*
     1-ERG   Yakairu-ABS   dance   CAUS
     'I made Yakairu dance.'
  b. *hai-ts   ka_in³   [Atawaka-ø   pa]   tao.*
     1-ERG   FOC/TNS   Atawaka-ABS   marry   order
     'I ordered Atawaka to marry.'

It is a difficult question whether the meaning of direct, intentional, non-forceful, factitive, etc. causation, which is not expressed by the more semantically specialized constructions, is encoded in the default causatives, or if it should be pragmatically inferred on the basis of Q-implicatures (Levinson 2000, see also Sections 1.4.2 and 5.3.2). The addressee can reason, 'The speaker has not used a more semantically specific construction, therefore this meaning is not implied here.' If the more specific construction becomes sufficiently frequent, Q-implicatures of this kind will become conventionalized (Bybee 1994). That is, the more compact causative will become conventionally associated with direct, intentional, etc. causation. To what extent this conventionalization has taken place is difficult to judge from the available descriptions, but this does not prevent us from assigning the more accessible meanings to the default causatives.

Moreover, I have encountered several combinations of features of the less compact form:

- making/letting/compelling (Khoekhoe: Khoe-Kwadi);
- permissive and not implicative (Waimiri-Atroarí: Cariban);
- permission or coercion (Lahu: Sino-Tibetan, Slave: Na-Dene);
- indirect and/or non-implicative (Korean: isolate);
- indirect and/or unintentional (Indonesian: Austronesian, Motuna: East Bougainville, Filomeno: Totonacan);
- 'weak' causation with the semantics of motion, i.e., 'send' (Yagua: Peba-Yaguan).

The distinction between direct and indirect causation is the most popular one, especially if we also consider the features that can be interpreted as indirect causation using the list in (10): directive, mediated or distant causation, causation with agentive or volitional Causee, letting, and some others. So, it is not by chance that the distinction between direct and indirect causation plays a special role in the typology of causatives. Of course, we cannot exclude that this distinction is reported more frequently because it was introduced in the famous works.

---

[3] The combination of morphemes *ka_in* in Trumai represents a lexicalized unit, which signals that the information is new and should get special attention. It is also a tense marker, showing that the event occurs in the present or has occurred in the recent past. The morphemes can be separated by an adverb, hence the underscore sign (Guirardello 1999: 169).

And yet, we also observe features, such as forceful, non-intentional, distributive and iterative causation, which are more difficult to interpret in terms of (in)directness. Note that Dixon's observations about the major types are mostly supported by the data, with the exception of letting, which is clearly expressed by less compact forms (see also Levshina 2016). There are also two problematic cases: Kayardild (Tangkic, Australia) and Mutsun (Penutian, North America). In Kayardild, the causative suffix expressing direct causation is actually longer and therefore less compact than the one expressing indirect causation, as shown in (18). However, the indirect causative suffix {-lu-tha} is also used in the factitive function, which means 'cause to be in a state' (Evans 1995: 355). This functional overlap makes it difficult to say which of the constructions in general is more direct and which is less direct, since causing a state is usually associated with less agentive Causees.

(18)　　Kayardild: Tangkic (Evans 1995: 355)

    a. direct causation: suffix *-THarrma-tha*
      thulatha 'descend' > *thulatharrmatha* 'take down'
      dalija 'come' > *dalijarrmatha* 'bring'
    b. indirect causation: suffix {-lu-tha}
      dulbatha 'sink (intr)' > *dulbalutha* 'cause to sink, drown' (e.g., by shooting and not allowing to get out of water)

The other problematic case is found in Mutsun, where the mediopassive-causative suffix *-mpi* (causing a change of state) is actually longer than the active causative *-si* (making someone do something). An example is provided in (19), where (19a) illustrates the causative with *-mpi* and (19b) the causative with *-si*.

(19)　　Mutsun: Penutian (Okrand 1977: 216, 219)

    a. *mala-n* 'to get wet' > *mala-**mpi**-* 'to cause (someone) to get wet'
    b. ka·n-was   lolle-**si**-Ø   sinnise
      I-him   babble-CAUS-NPST   baby.OBJ
      'I made the baby babble.'

This exception can be explained historically: the suffix *-mpi* in fact represents a fusion of the mediopassive suffix *-n* and the suffix *-pi*, which no longer occurs autonomously (Okrand 1977: 215–216).

And yet, we see that Dixon's predictions are overall supported. Remarkably, we find one language in which involvement of the Causer in the activity (in addition to the Causee) is expressed by a less compact form (Cavineña, a Tacanan language), although Dixon did not find any formal asymmetries in his data (Dixon 2000: 75). We also find some features that were not mentioned, such as iterative, distributive, resultative causation (Yukaghir Kolyma), ballistic causation (Hup: Nadahup) or causation with a beneficiary Causee (Tubu/Dazaga: Saharan). In addition, in Manambu, a Sepik language, verbal cause–effect

7.2 More Than Just Direct and Indirect Causation

compounds express the specific type of causing event, e.g., *vya-puti-* (hit-fall. off) 'shake something off by hitting, e.g., dust from a mat or a sheet'. Compare those with caused motion constructions and resultative constructions in English, e.g., *throw the ball into the street* or *paint the door green* (e.g., Hampe 2011).

Since many of the distinctions go beyond (in)directness, the iconicity account is problematic. It is more natural to explain the findings in Dixon (2000) and in my typological survey by the principle of negative correlation between accessibility and costs. Less compact forms are more costly, and they are associated with less accessible functions, such as indirect, accidental, and other rare types, including the 'exotic' ones mentioned in the paragraph above. Note that the Manambu case fits this explanation well because specific types of causation should be less frequent and therefore less compact than non-specific, generic causation types. I expect that as we study more and more languages, the number of possible semantic distinctions will grow asymptotically, never exhausting all possible semantic shades. At the same time, all of them will have one thing in common: the rare types of causation will be expressed by less compact forms.

But how do we know that the features expressed by the more costly forms are less accessible? This will be shown in the next section, where we will look at corpus frequencies of different causation features.

7.2.2 How Accessible Are Different Causative Meanings?

This section presents spoken corpus data from three languages (English, Lao and Russian), which show very clearly that the features that are expressed cross-linguistically by more compact forms are more accessible than the ones that are expressed by less compact forms. From this follows that the formal differences between different causatives are related to the accessibility of the causative meanings they express, such that the forms and the meanings are paired in an efficient way.

In order to obtain the frequencies, I took different spoken corpora in three languages: English, Lao and Russian. For English, I took samples of text from fourteen spontaneous informal conversations in the Santa Barbara Corpus of Spoken American English (Du Bois et al. 2000–2005). I searched manually for all kinds of causative meanings, where one could distinguish the Causer, the Causee and the causing and caused effects, at least potentially. The constructions were transitive verbs (lexical causatives, such as *break* and *kill*), analytic causatives (e.g., *make/let/force/order/help* + (to) Infinitive), and resultative constructions (e.g., *keep* X in a certain state). In total, I obtained 205 causative situations.

For Lao, I took the transcripts of Enfield's (2007) dialogues from the appendix of his grammar of Lao. These are five dialogues about family, agriculture, fishing and work. I found only sixty instances in the entire corpus.

For Russian, I took one large text from Zemskaja and Kapanadze (1978), which contained the transcripts (with additional contextual information) of one day in a Soviet family. It includes all interactions between the wife, the husband, their son and the husband's mother during one day. It gives an idea of typical linguistic behaviour of educated Russian speakers in the 1970s. The family members speak about food, health, childcare and home-making. The total number of causative examples was ninety.

The examples from the corpora were coded for several variables, which represent different types of causation expressed cross-linguistically by the less compact form. First, there is a block of variables representing different shades of (in)directness known in the literature. They are not orthogonal to one another, or mutually exclusive. They are followed by several other features, which I was able to code in the corpora.

1. 'No Overlap': There is no temporal or spatial overlap between the Causer's actions (or non-interference) and the event or state that corresponds to what happened with the Causee. Example: *The professor had her students keep a diary.*
2. 'Human Causee': The Causee is human. Examples: *She laid the children down; She made the children lie down.*
3. 'Controlling Causee': The Causee is in control of the caused event. In other words, the Causee can choose, in principle, whether to perform what the Causer causes or allows the Causee to do. Example: *The professor had her students write long term papers,* where the students can choose, in principle, whether they comply or not.
4. 'Caused Action': The Causee performs an action (rather than gets into or keeps being in a certain state). Example: *The general had her troops run 10 miles.* The caused situation should be dynamic and the Causee should be in control (see Parameter 3).
5. 'Communication': The Causer uses only communication in order to achieve the outcome. Example: *John talked his grandparents into sponsoring his album.*
6. 'Human Intermediary': The situation implies a human intermediary, who participates so that the caused event takes place. Example: *She made him dig a hole in the ground.*
7. 'Letting': The causing event is permissive. Example: *He let the child play in the yard.*
8. 'Forceful': Forceful causation, as opposed to natural. Causation requires more effort from the Causer than usual. It is also possible to paraphrase the Causer's action with 'force'. Example: *Ann forced Peter to sign the agreement.*
9. 'Non-intentional': The Causer affects the Causee unintentionally, or is incapable of intentional actions (e.g., inanimate). Example: *John broke the window when he was playing football.*

7.2 More Than Just Direct and Indirect Causation

10. 'Involved Causer': The Causer is involved in the caused event. In other words, the Causee performs the caused action or is in the caused state together with the Causee. Example: *Susan brought her friends to the party* (and came herself).
11. 'Causee Benefits': The Causee benefits from the caused event. Example: *John fed the child*.
12. 'Non-implicative': There is a possibility that the caused event does not actually happen. Example: *John ordered Bill to surrender* (but Bill did not do it).
13. 'Distributive': The caused event occurs several times, each time with a different Causee. Example: *John baked a cake on Wednesday and brownies on Thursday*.
14. 'Keeping': The event can be paraphrased as 'keep X in a certain state or location'. Example: *Ann kept all her savings under the mattress*.
15. 'Iterative': The causation repeats several times (with the same Causee). Example: *The gamer had to kill the villain again and again, until the villain had no more lives left*.
16. 'Assistive': The Causer helps the Causee to perform the caused event. Example: *John walked the child into the room*.

In a few cases, it was difficult to determine the value due to lack of additional context, but the proportion of missing values was never greater than 4 per cent of the total number of examples in each of the three languages.

Figure 7.1 presents the proportions of the functions that are cross-linguistically expressed by less compact forms. One can see that none of them accounts for more than a third of all instances of causation in any of the corpora. This means that compact forms express more frequent functions. Interestingly, the Causee is more frequently human, controlling, performing a caused action and serving as an intermediary in Lao than in the other two languages. This can be explained by the fact that the longest of the dialogues contains a discussion of employment, in particular, situations when the boss has the servant do something. Still, these types of causation are not frequent. The frequency of beneficiary Causees in the Russian data is relatively high because the language users often speak about childcare (feeding, dressing, putting to sleep, etc.). Assistive causation is not present in the data.

To summarize, the data from informal spontaneous spoken dialogues demonstrate that the features of causative situations expressed by less compact forms across languages are less frequent than the features represented by more compact forms. I argue that this pattern arises due to the principle of negative correlation between accessibility and costs. Since iconicity relies on (in)directness as the core semantic parameter correlating with formal distance between the elements expressing causing and caused events, it fails to explain the full range of cross-linguistic variation.

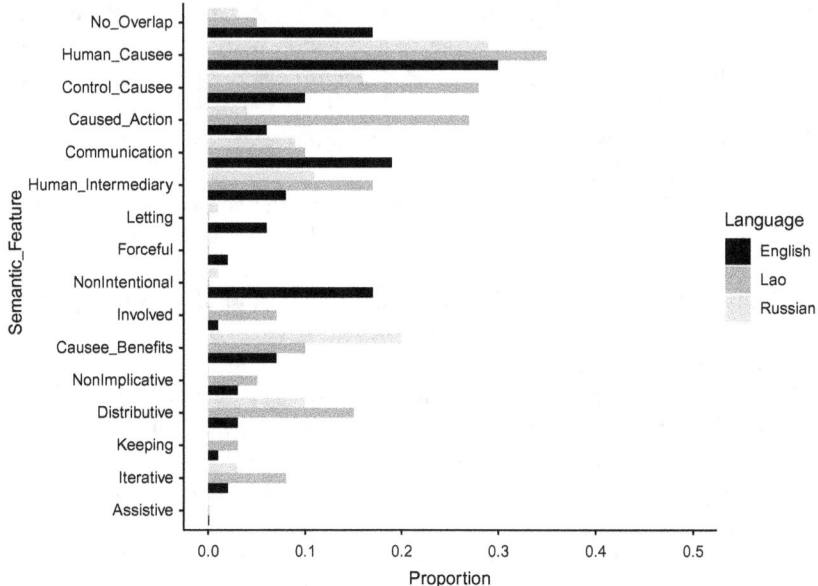

Figure 7.1 Percentage of the total number of causative situations in corpora of three languages

7.2.3 Taking a Multifactorial Approach: Evidence from a Parallel Corpus

In Section 7.2.1, we looked at the distribution of individual semantic features. But they co-occur in real language use. Take the sentence, *The burglar broke the window in order to get in.* We can say that the causation is direct, intentional, physical, factitive, and so on. Will we see the same correlations between meaning and form if we test each semantic parameter while controlling for the others? A positive answer to this question is given in Levshina (2016), where lexical and analytic causatives from fifteen European languages were compared. The goal of this section is to test the hypothesis on a sample of more diverse languages and constructions.

For this purpose, I found 387 causative situations in the English segment of the ParTy corpus of film and TED Talks subtitles.[4] The situations were coded manually for the variables representing Dixon's parameters of semantic and syntactic variation (see Table 7.3). In addition, I coded animacy of the Causer

---

[4] The aligned film subtitles are available at https://github.com/levshina/ParTy-1.0.

7.2 More Than Just Direct and Indirect Causation

Table 7.3. *Semantic variables used in the study based on the parallel corpus*

Variable	Abbreviation	Values	Examples
Semantics of the caused event	CausedEvent	'Action' 'NonAction'	The teacher had the students ask questions. Sue broke the vase.
Number of main participants	NoPart	'2' '3'	Sue broke the vase. Ann made Bill steal the money.
Controlling Causee	CeControl	'Yes' 'No'	The teacher had the students ask questions. Sue broke the vase.
Causee acting willingly	CeVol	'Yes' 'No'	The teacher let the students leave earlier. The minister made the journalists wait for him.
Making or letting	MakeLet	'Make' 'Let'	Sue broke the vase. The teacher let the students leave earlier.
Causer acting directly	CrDirect	'Yes' 'No'	John broke Bill's arm during the fight. The teacher had the students ask questions.
Causer acting intentionally	CrIntent	'Yes' 'No'	The thieves broke the window to get in. Oops, I've broken your Ming vase.
Causer acting effortfully	CrForce	'Yes' 'No'	Ann forced Bill to steal the money. The teacher had students ask questions.
Causer involved in caused event	CrInvolved	'Yes' 'No'	Bring your friends! Sue broke the vase.

and Causee. Next, I coded the translations of the English causatives in ten languages (Chinese, Finnish, French, Hebrew, Indonesian, Japanese, Russian, Thai, Turkish and Vietnamese), classifying them into three types: lexical, morphological and analytic (including periphrastic ones). Consider an example in (20) from the film *Avatar* and its translations into French, Turkish and Vietnamese. The French version contains a lexical causative, the Turkish one has a morphological one, and the Vietnamese translation has an analytic causative with the verb *làm* 'make, do'.

(20)   *Avatar: (Don't shoot), you'll piss him off.*

    a.   French
        Vous   *allez*   *l'*   *énerver.*
        2PL   go.2PL   him   make.nervous
    b.   Turkish
        Onu   *kız-dır-acak-sın.*
        3.ACC   get.angry-CAUS-FUT-2SG
    c.   Vietnamese
        Câu   *sẽ*   *làm*   *nó*   *nổi*   *điên*   *đó.*
        2SG   FUT   make   3SG   get   mad   PART

Translations that were too different semantically from the original were excluded from the analysis. Next, the associations between the forms and the

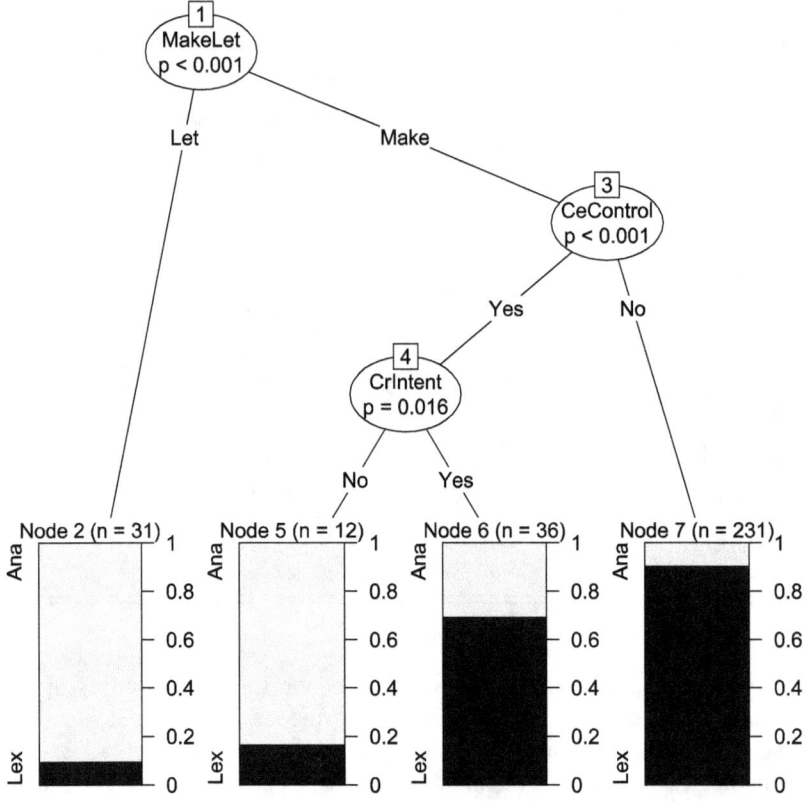

Figure 7.2 A conditional inference tree for French

semantic features were tested with the help of conditional inference trees (Tagliamonte and Baayen 2012; Levshina 2020a). This was done separately for each language. Figure 7.2 shows the conditional inference tree for analytic and lexical causatives in French. The interpretation is as follows. First, the algorithm looks for the semantic variable that is most strongly associated with the form (that is, analytical or lexical causative). This variable is making or letting (see Node 1). The algorithm makes a binary split in that variable, separating the observations with letting (the branch on the left) from the ones with making (the branch on the right). Next, it tries to find another variable that is significantly associated with the form (with $p < 0.05$). In the case of letting, no such variable is found. The bar plot in the node leaf (Node 2) shows that cases of letting are expressed predominantly by analytic causatives. In the case of making, the next split is made in the variable 'Controlling Causee' (*CeControl*), see Node 3. If the Causee has no control, lexical causatives are

7.2 More Than Just Direct and Indirect Causation

predominantly chosen (Node 7), and no further splits are made. If the Causee is in control, there is another binary split in Node 4, which is done in the variable 'Causer acting intentionally' (*CrIntent*). If the Causer acts intentionally, lexical causatives are preferred (Node 6). If not, analytic ones are more frequently chosen (Node 5). All this suggests that the variation is multifactorial and cannot be reduced to direct or indirect causation, in either narrow or broad sense. We can also conclude that Dixon's parameters predict correctly the use of more and less compact forms, even when the variables are tested simultaneously. Moreover, we see that the variables interact with each other.

This procedure was repeated for the other languages. Where available, I tested the contrasts between analytic, morphological and lexical causatives. For Japanese, only the contrast between lexical and morphological causatives was possible, due to the fact that analytic causatives were missing. Table 7.4 shows which variables participate in the splits in the trees when the models compared analytic and lexical causatives. Table 7.5 displays the splits in the models which compared morphological and lexical causatives. Finally, Table 7.6 contains the splits relevant for the comparison of analytic and morphological causatives.

Table 7.4. *Variables participating in splits that separate analytic from lexical causatives*

Model	CausedEvent	NoPart	CeControl	CeVol	MakeLet	CrDirect	CrIntent	CrForce	CrInvolved
Chinese	+	+		+	+		+		
Finnish	+				+		+		
French			+		+		+		
Hebrew	+	+		+	+				
Indonesian	+				+	+	+		
Russian	+	+	+	+	+				
Thai	+		+		+		+		
Turkish		+			+	+			
Vietnamese	+	+			+		+		

Table 7.5. *Variables participating in splits that separate morphological from lexical causatives*

Model	CausedEvent	NoPart	CeControl	CeVol	MakeLet	CrDirect	CrIntent	CrForce	CrInvolved
Finnish						+			
Hebrew									+
Indonesian									
Japanese				+					
Turkish							+		

Table 7.6. *Variables participating in splits that separate analytic from morphological causatives*

Model	CausedEvent	NoPart	CeControl	CeVol	MakeLet	CrDirect	CrIntent	CrForce	CrInvolved
Finnish		+			+				
Hebrew	+	+			+				
Indonesian	+								
Turkish		+			+				

Recall that Dixon (2000) did not find any formal asymmetries that correspond to the Causer's involvement in the caused event (action). The conditional inference tree of lexical and morphological causatives in Hebrew shows that the proportion of morphological causatives is significantly higher in contexts with the Causer's involvement than in the other cases. This supports the finding reported in the typological case study above.

It is notable that the variable 'making or letting' (*MakeLet*) is particularly strongly associated with analytic causatives, separating them from the other types. It participates in a split in every language. This may be due to the fact that English subtitles have many instances of letting, which can be explained culturally. According to Wierzbicka (2006: Section 6.2.3), letting is an important category in Anglo-Saxon culture because it is associated with non-interference, non-imposition and personal freedom. Also, actions as caused events and longer causation chains (more than two participants) are strong cues for analytic causatives. The contrasts between lexical and analytic causatives are particularly strong and involve many different variables. This is not surprising, since these constructions represent two ends of the causative continuum, so the differences between them must be particularly striking. Lexical and morphological causatives are the least distinguishable (with no significant differences in Indonesian), and their differences are the least systematic across the languages. Forceful (effortful) causation is rare in the parallel corpus data, which probably explains why it is not relevant.

Obviously, we need to perform similar analyses on other data sources and text types. It is reassuring, though, that the text source (i.e., the film or TED Talk where the causation situations are mentioned) appeared only in one Finnish tree. This means that the form–meaning associations reported here do not depend on the translator's whim. But even if the prominence of some situations (in particular, letting) in the English source texts has an effect on the results, what we see here is enough to conclude that the formal variation depends on multiple factors. Although the variables that can be interpreted in terms of direct and indirect causation do play a central role, we see that intentional and accidental causation is also quite powerful across the languages. Importantly, all associations between form and meaning are in line with the efficiency predictions based on accessibility of the semantic features. Finally, it is notable that the data support the correlation between semantic directness and formal integration. In the next section, we will zoom in on this correlation and discuss its multiple explanations.

7.3 Competition between Formal Parameters

This section focuses on the formal parameters of causatives associated with direct and indirect causation. The goal is to demonstrate that the principle of negative correlation between accessibility and costs explains the associations better than iconicity does. I will also discuss productivity, which has been proposed as a factor correlated with (in)directness.

When speaking about the formal variation of causatives, it is convenient to use Haiman's (1985: 105) scale of linguistic distance, which is shown in (21).

(21)   a.   X # A # B # Y
           b.   X # A # Y
           c.   X + A # Y
           d.   X # Y
           e.   X + Y
           f.   Z

In this cline, X and Y are the linguistic expressions of interest that express the cause and the effect in a causative construction, A and B are other intervening units, # represents a word boundary, + stands for a morpheme boundary, and Z is a morpheme where X and Y are fused. It is important to note that Haiman's scale incorporates two related but distinct formal distinctions: formal distance and autonomy of X and Y. In some contrasts, they overlap. Take the types (21e) X + Y and (21f) Z, which differ both in distance and autonomy. But this is not always the case. For example, the types (21a) X # A # B # Y and (21b) X # A # Y differ only in the distance between X and Y, but not in their autonomy. In contrast, (21d) X # Y and (21e) X + Y differ only in autonomy, but not in distance. The difference between autonomy and distance will be important later in this section.

To give a simple illustration, lexical causatives like *kill* have both zero autonomy and zero distance, because X and Y are perfectly fused in one morpheme. Compare that with an example of an analytic causative. The causing and caused event in the sentence *John caused Bill to die* are represented by two relatively autonomous units, i.e., the words *cause* and *die*, and are separated by the past-tense morpheme *-ed*, the proper name *Bill* and the particle *to*. Under the iconicity account, greater autonomy and longer distance are associated with less direct causation, while dependent and closely located X and Y will convey more direct causation.

There exists yet another formal parameter, which was discussed by Shibatani and Pardeshi (2002: Section 5), who argue that indirectness of causation correlates with the degree of productivity of constructions: productive forms tend to express indirect causation, whereas lexically restricted forms are more associated with direct causation. Japanese morphological causatives provide a good illustration. For instance, the verb *oros-* 'bring down' from *ori-* 'come down', which expresses direct causation, is a non-productive causative. In contrast, the form *ori-sase-* 'cause to come down', which is formed with a productive suffix *-(s)ase*, is productive and expresses indirect causation. Shibatani and Pardeshi claim that (in)directness is more strongly correlated with productivity than with the traditional formal distinction between lexical, morphological and analytic causatives.

Another piece of evidence comes from Amharic. It has causative prefixes *a-* and *as-* (Amberber 2000). The prefix *a-* is not productive. It only applies to intransitive unaccusative verbs, e.g., verbs of motion and (change of) state, e.g., 'exist', 'melt', 'grow', 'enter', and to transitive verbs of ingestion (e.g., 'eat' and 'drink'). It cannot be used with unergative verbs (e.g., 'dance' or 'laugh'). The prefix *a-* is used to express situations when the Causer is directly involved in the causation. This is illustrated in (22b), where the Causer transports the Causee. In contrast, the causative prefix *as-* is productive. It can be added to transitive and intransitive verbs of all classes. It is used to express indirect causation, as in (22c), where the Causer is not directly involved and can simply issue an order or permission. Thus, indirectness correlates with productivity.

(22)　　Amharic: Afro-Asiatic (Amberber 2000: 320)

    a. *aster*　　*wət't'a-čč*
       A.　　　　exit+PERF-3F
       'Aster exited.'
    b. *ləmma*　*aster-in*　***a**-wət't'a-t*
       L.　　　　A.-ACC　　CAUS-exit+PERF+3M-3F.OBJ
       'Lemma took Aster out (as in 'out of the house').'
    c. *ləmma*　*aster-in*　***as**-wət't'a-t*
       L.　　　　A.-ACC　　CAUS-exit+PERF+3M-3F.OBJ
       'Lemma made/let Aster exit.'

These and other examples (cf. Shibatani and Pardeshi 2002: Section 5) demonstrate that more productive morphological causatives often express indirect causation, and less productive ones express direct causation. At the same time, they belong to the same class of morphological causatives. From this follows that productivity may be more directly aligned with the (in)directness distinction than autonomy or formal distance.

The associations between these formal parameters and (in)directness were tested in Levshina (2018 [2016]) on the same typological data set as the one

7.3 Competition between Formal Parameters

discussed in Section 7.2. In forty-six languages, (in)directness or similar semantic distinctions were mentioned as a distinctive semantic parameter of two or more different causative constructions. Consider an example from the Amur dialect of Nivkh (a Paleosiberian isolate) in (23). One of the constructions consists of a non-productive causative suffix *-u* and expresses contact factitive causation, as in (23b). The other morphological causative, shown in (23c), contains a productive suffix *-ku/-γu/-gu/-xu* and usually expresses distant factitive or permissive causation (Nedjalkov and Otaina 2013: 133).

(23) Nivkh: isolate (Nedjalkov and Otaina 2013: 234)

  a. *Lep   ṭʻe-ḍ.*
     bread   be.dry-IND
     'The bread dried up.'
  b. *If   lep+se-**u**-ḍ.*
     s/he   bread+be.dry-CAUS-IND
     'He dried up the bread' (for dried crusts).
  c. *If   lep+ətu-doχ   qʻau-r   ṭʻe-**gu**-ḍ.*
     s/he   bread+cover-SUP   not.be-CONV:NAR:3SG   be.dry-CAUS-IND
     'Not covering the bread, he let (it) dry up.'

It is crucial to discuss how (in)directness was operationalized. Grammars vary greatly in the semantic distinctions they mention. The full list of the distinctions used in the data sources which were interpreted as direct vs. indirect is as follows (see Table 7.2 for examples of languages):

- direct vs. indirect causation;
- strong vs. weak integration of the causing and caused events, separability of events;
- manipulative vs. directive causation;
- contact vs. distant causation;
- direct vs. mediated causation;
- the Causee as non-controlling undergoer vs. controlling agent (and therefore the main source of energy);
- default vs. ballistic causation;
- factitive vs. permissive causation;
- caused state (or change of state) vs. caused activity;
- default causation vs. causation with human intermediary;
- default vs. curative or 'indefinite' causation;
- general vs. 'mild' or 'weak' causation;
- default vs. caused by ordering X to do Y;
- implicative vs. non-implicative causal relationships.

This inclusive approach allows us to test the different shades of (in)directness that were mentioned in Section 7.1. It also includes the main dimensions of (in)directness mentioned by Bohnemeyer et al. (2010): mediation, contact and force dynamics. At the same time, it does not include the intentions of the Causer and some other parameters that are difficult to interpret in terms of conceptual distance and integration (see Sections 7.1 and 7.2).

Note that implicative vs. non-implicative relationships are included because they reflect integration of events, which is important for the iconicity account (Givón 1980). Example (24) from a Cariban language Waimiri-Atroarí illustrates a combination of the factitive/permissive distinction and implicativity. The causative suffix *py* in (24a) expresses factitive causation, whereas the periphrastic construction with *injaky* 'let/permit' and particle *tre'me* shown in (24b) expresses permission. In addition, causation in (24b) is non-implicative, which means that we cannot say for sure whether the caused event actually happened or not.

(24) Waimiri-Atroarí: Cariban (Bruno 2003: 100, 103)

  a. *Ka   k-yeepitxah-**py**-pia.*
     3PRO 1+2OBJ-laugh-CAUS-IM.P
     'She/he made us laugh.'
  b. *A   ka m-**injaky**-piany   wyty   ipy-na   **tre'me**.*
     1PRO ?[5] 2OBJ-permit/let-REC.P meat   look.for-?   PART
     'I permitted you to/let you leave to hunt.'

As was already discussed in Section 7.2.1, the authors of grammars often treat the causative simply as a tool for increasing valency, or speak about 'default' or 'general' causatives. For example, one can find such distinctions as default vs. permissive, or default vs. curative causation. As was argued in the previous section, in such cases, the addressee is likely to derive a Q-implicature which precludes the non-default interpretation of the default construction. This is why pairs of causative constructions, where one construction is described as the default causative, are also counted here as instances of the (in)directness distinction.

In total, I found seventy-four contrasts related to (in)directness in forty-six languages. Other semantic distinctions involve forceful, unintentional, distributive, iterative causation and other types. These were discussed in the previous section and are not considered here. In each pair of constructions, the construction that expresses (more) direct causation is referred to as the direct causative, and the construction that represents (more) indirect causation is represented here as the indirect causative. The pairs of constructions were compared with regard to the four formal parameters mentioned above: distance, autonomy, productivity and length. That is, I asked if the direct causative was shorter, less productive, and consisted of less autonomous and distant elements than its indirect counterpart. The formal criterion for distance was the

---

[5] The author of the cited grammar used question marks to gloss some units, as in this example.

7.3 Competition between Formal Parameters

number of phonological segments (i.e., phones or phonemes) in the in-between elements, including affixes, clitics and autonomous words, which are obligatorily used between the elements representing the cause and effect. Autonomy, which is similar to bondedness of a sign, or 'the degree to which it depends on, or attaches to ... other signs' (Lehmann 2015: 131), was determined by using the following cline:

(25)   one morpheme < morphemes in a word < clitic + host < parts of one verbal phrase (monoclausal) < clauses in a sentence (biclausal)[6]

Lexical causatives, such as *kill* or *break$_{TR}$*, display no autonomy, while analytic causatives, such as *cause X to die*, have the greatest autonomy. Morphological causatives are in-between. Productivity is the ability of a unit to freely combine with other units. Commonly, a language has a causative construction that can be used with all verbs, and another with only intransitives or stative verbs (Dixon 2000). Finally, length comparisons were based on the number of segments in grammatically equivalent forms of the same verb. See Levshina (2018 [2016]) for more details about the coding procedure.

To illustrate the approach, let us take two morphological causatives from Urarina, a language isolate in Peru. The causative which usually expresses direct causation is formed with the help of the suffix *-a* (26a). The indirect causative contains the suffix *-erate* (26b). The first causative is shorter and less productive than the second. In addition, it can be attached only to intransitives (Olawsky 2006: 609–621). Judging from the description, the causatives differ neither in terms of the distance between the suffixes and the non-causal root, nor in terms of their autonomy.

(26)   Urarina: isolate (Olawsky 2006: 610–611, 616)

   a.   *eno-a* 'enter' > *eno-a-a* 'make enter'
        nalɨ-a 'fall' > *nalɨ-a-a* 'drop'
   b.   *sau-a* 'cut' > *sa-eratia* 'make cut'
        hjani-a 'leave' > *hjane-ratia* 'make leave'

Table 7.7 displays the counts for the individual contrasts between direct and indirect causatives. The numbers in parentheses show the number of languages in which these contrasts were found. Note that the number of contrasting constructions is higher than the number of languages because some languages have more than one contrasting pair. For example, compare the bottom cell in the column 'Direct causative < Indirect causative'. The numbers tell us that the data contain 59 contrasts where the direct causative is shorter than the

---

[6] This cline was used for comparisons within a specific language, so the categories do not represent comparative concepts in the sense of Haspelmath (2010).

Table 7.7. *Formal parameters associated with (in)directness of causation: number of contrasting pairs*

Parameter	Direct causative < Indirect causative	Direct causative = Indirect causative	Direct causative > Indirect causative
Distance	44 (27)	30 (26)	0 (0)
Autonomy	41 (24)	33 (28)	0 (0)
Productivity	40 (24)	33 (28)	1 (1)
Length	59 (39)	13 (10)	2 (2)

indirect causative with respect to length. The number 39 in parentheses means that these 59 contrasts occurred in 39 languages.

The numbers reveal that the parameter most strongly associated with (in)directness is formal length. It gives correct predictions for more than 75 per cent of contrasts and languages. Direct causatives are as long as the indirect causatives in only 13 contrasts from 10 languages. There are two exceptions, when the direct causative is longer than its indirect counterpart (see examples from Kayardild and Mutsun, which were discussed in Section 7.2.1). Length is followed by distance: direct causatives are less distant than indirect causatives in 44 contrasts from 27 languages, whereas in 30 contrasts from 26 languages there is no difference. Next follows autonomy, with 24 languages and 41 contrasts, where autonomy is less in the direct causative. The parameter that is least strongly associated with (in)directness is productivity (24 languages and 40 contrasts, plus one exception from the predicted direction).

A series of binomial exact tests with random sampling of contrasts from individual languages show that the biases towards direct causatives having smaller length, distance, autonomy and productivity than indirect causatives are statistically significant (see Levshina 2018 [2016] for details). The null hypothesis is that there is no difference with regard to the direction of the asymmetry. In other words, we can have either a direct causative with a shorter form, less autonomy, smaller distance and lower productivity than an indirect causative, or the other way round. The null hypothesis could be safely rejected ($p < 0.0001$).

I also performed comparisons between direct and indirect causatives in situations when both are morphological – that is, they represent affixal derivations, root changes, augmentations, reduplications or tonal changes (cf. Dixon 2000). I found that formal length is again the most strongly associated with (in)directness, followed by productivity. However, only length asymmetry was statistically significant ($p = 0.01$).

If one takes all contrasts where both direct and indirect causatives are analytic, including monoclausal verbal compounds, serial verbs, light verbs

7.3 Competition between Formal Parameters

and biclausal periphrastic causatives, we see again that length is the most prominent parameter, closely followed by distance. The biases, however, do not reach statistical significance, probably due to the small sample size. Only twelve contrasts between syntactic causatives were found in the data.

Finally, if we take only the contrasts where one of the causatives is morphological and the other is analytic, we see that length is again in the leading role, followed by distance. Productivity is the least strongly associated parameter. All biases are in the expected direction and statistically significant (all $p < 0.001$).

The results of these analyses show that in general, all previous accounts have some grain of truth in them. The indirect causation constructions are either more distant/autonomous/productive/longer than the direct causation constructions, or at least as distant/autonomous/productive/long as those. The exceptions are very scarce. Therefore, the typological data overall support the correlation between conceptual and formal integration or distance. This contradicts the results reported by Escamilla (2012) and Bellingham et al. (2020), who did not find significant correlations between (in)directness and formal integration or compactness. This may be due to some methodological choices, such as the use of a more restrictive definition of (in)directness than in the present study. In particular, Bellingham et al. (2020) used ratings of linguistic descriptions of videos with different causation events. The descriptions contained causatives of different degrees of formal compactness. Indirectness of causation was operationalized mainly as the presence of mediation. An example of a mediated scenario from their stimuli is as follows: a woman sneaks up behind a man and yells loudly, startling him, and causing him to knock over a tower of cups. Spatiotemporal integration was not taken into account. Their ordinal regression analysis showed that mediation did not have a significant effect on the ratings of causative constructions with different degrees of formal integration. However, there was a significant effect of the presence or absence of physical contact, which can also be interpreted as a manifestation of (in)directness.

Escamilla (2012) used grammar descriptions of fifty genealogically diverse languages. A binomial test showed that the association between formal compactness in Dixon's (2000) sense and (in)directness was not significant. Unfortunately, it is unclear which criteria were used for defining (in)directness, and how one derives this information from reference grammars for different constructions. Also, Escamilla seems to compare the number of languages where (in)directness leads to correct predictions with the total number of languages where this distinction is mentioned, not with the number of violations (although this is not entirely clear from the description, either). This is different from the current study. Here, we test if the number of pairs supporting the generalization is greater or smaller than the number of pairs going against it. All this demonstrates very vividly how much our claims about validity of cross-linguistic generalizations depend on the choice of comparative concepts (c.f. Haspelmath 2010) and methodology.

Importantly, one can see that relative length is the parameter which is the most strongly associated with the (in)directness distinction, both in the whole data set and in each constructional type. The results thus favour the explanation based on the principle of negative correlation between accessibility and costs. Indirect causation forms are longer than direct causation forms because the indirect causation scenarios are less accessible than direct causation scenarios, which results in efficient formal asymmetries. It cannot be excluded that other factors may be relevant, too, but the efficiency account is supported by the strongest evidence.

7.4 Diachronic Evidence

Unfortunately, there is not much historical evidence of how causatives have emerged and developed in different languages, especially as far as more compact forms are concerned. Sometimes one can infer information about the diachronic sources of causative auxiliaries and morphemes from their colexifications with non-causative expressions. The known sources of causative markers and auxiliaries include the following:

- 'make' and 'do', e.g., suffix *-(i)fy* in English, which comes from Latin *ficāre* 'to do, make'; Dutch analytic causative with *doen* 'do';
- verbs of communication, e.g., 'order' (Trumai: isolate), 'say' (Skou: Skou) and 'ask' (Great Andamanese family);
- verbs of possession: 'have' and 'get' (English), 'take' (Hup: Nadahup), 'give' (Finnish: Uralic), 'hold, grasp' (Kayardild: Tangkic);
- motion verbs, e.g., 'send' (Yagua: Peba-Yaguan);
- position verbs, e.g., 'stand' (Hup: Nadahup);
- verbs of caused motion: 'bring' (Humburi Senni: Songhay), 'put' (Kayardild: Tangkic), 'pull' (Tubu/Dazaga: Saharan), 'push' (South Eastern Huastec: Mayan);
- abstract verbs, e.g., 'cause' (English), 'affect' (Adang: Timor-Alor-Pantar), 'force' (Ik: Eastern Sudanic) or 'treat in a certain way' (Yuracaré: isolate);
- verbs of physical contact: 'hit', 'step on' and 'bite' (Manambu: Sepik);
- instrumental and manner affixes, e.g., 'by hand' (Northern Paiute: Uto-Aztecan) or 'using a sawing action' (Nishnaabemwin: Algic).

One can see that the sources are extremely diverse and come from different domains of human experience. At the same time, some are more popular than others. In particular, the evolution of verbs with the meaning 'do' and 'make' into causative markers is among the most common grammaticalization paths cross-linguistically (Bisang et al. 2020: 15).

7.4 Diachronic Evidence

In addition, causative morphemes can coincide with the following grammatical markers:

- transitivizers and verbalizers (Yapese: Austronesian);
- directional (allative) case markers, e.g., 'towards' (Ijo/Izon: Niger-Congo);
- intensifying affixes (Chichewa: Niger-Congo);
- aspectual affixes, e.g., punctual action (Mari: Uralic);
- passive markers (Southern Min: Sino-Tibetan);
- applicatives (Uto-Aztecan languages);
- benefactive affixes (Khasi: Austro-Asiatic);
- complementizers (Thai: Tai-Kadai).

In most cases, it is very difficult or even impossible to determine the path of historical development. There are some arguments, however, that causative constructions often undergo the process of formal reduction and semantic shift from less syntactically and semantically integrated constructions, such as purposive and subjunctive constructions, to more semantically and formally integrated ones (Song 1996). An example is 'X made such that Y should happen' or 'X ordered that Y does Z'.

Let us consider the development of the English causative with *make*. In Old English, it was followed by finite *that*-clauses, as in the following example:

(27)   Old English, Heptateuch (Exodus 96: 14; cited from Lowrey 2012)[7]

   Ge habbaþ us gedon laþe Pharaone and eallum his folce and **gemacod** *þæt hig wyllað us mid hyra sweordum ofslean*

   'You have made us hateful to Pharaoh and to all his people, and made them want (lit. that they want) to slay us with their swords'.

In Middle English and Early Modern English the *to*-infinitive was predominant, but the bare infinitive occurred as well (Hollmann 2003: 166–167; Moriya 2017). Consider two examples from the King James Bible (1611):

(28)   Early Modern English, King James Bible (Moriya 2017: 44)

   a. *And wherefore haue ye made vs to come vp out of Egypt, to bring vs in vnto this euil place?* (Numb. 20.5)
   b. *And hee doeth great wonders, so that hee maketh fire come downe from heauen on the earth in the sight of men* (Rev. 13.13)

Moriya (2017) argues that the preference for the bare or *to*-infinitive was guided by various factors. One is *horror aequi*, or avoidance of identity, which was discussed in Section 4.4. In the presence of *to* before *make*, the bare form was more likely. Another is the linguistic distance between *make* and the

---

[7] Heptateuch: Marsden, R., ed., *The Old English Heptateuch and Ælfric's Libellus de Veteri Testamento et Novo* (vol. I), EETS 330. Oxford University Press, 2008.

second verb (in particular, the length of the nominal phrase in-between). The marker is used when the environment is complex, according to Rohdenburg's principle of cognitive complexity (see Section 2.4.2). One can also say that long linguistic distance makes the interpretation of the infinitival complement as belonging to *make* less accessible, which triggers the use of the more costly variant. Although the evidence for the semantic differences between the two variants is not conclusive and a lot of variation looks random, there are also some instances of the *to*-infinitive being preferred in contexts with willing Causees, which represent a less typical kind of causation, as one can judge from the low frequencies of human (and potentially willing) Causees discussed in Section 7.2.2. This suggests that the marker was preferred in contexts where the interpretation was less accessible, while the bare infinitive first spread in stereotypical causative situations and subschemata of the construction. At the moment, the causative *make* is used with the bare infinitive (e.g., *This makes me laugh*), with the exception of the passive form (e.g., *He was made to sit on an uncomfortable stool*). Due to its low frequency, the passive causative has low accessibility, and therefore remains the last bastion of the marked infinitive. Notably, the passive form of either the matrix verb or the infinitive was associated with the *to*-form in Late Middle English infinitival complements in general (Fischer 1995).

Importantly, the gradual disappearance of *to* after *make* has not happened in the other factitive causatives (*cause, force, get, persuade*, etc.). This can be regarded as an example of differential formal reduction (see Section 5.2). Hollmann (2003: 151–158) finds that the *make*-construction scores higher on semantic boundedness (which is operationalized as a weighted score based on directness, intentionality, punctuality, etc.) than the other constructions. I assume that the features which are associated with greater semantic boundedness by Hollmann and others are simply more accessible due to their higher frequency in discourse (see Section 7.2.2). Unfortunately, there is too little data about the development of the causative with *have*, which is used with the bare infinitive, although it has relatively low frequency.

Another example of formal reduction is provided by Song (1996: 88). In Ijo (Izon), a Niger-Congo language, there is a causative suffix *-mọ*, which is also identical with the directive case marker. In some cases, a separate lexical element *mie* is added, which expresses the causing event. Compare (29a) and (29b):

(29)   Ijo [Izon]: Niger-Congo (Song 1996: 88)

    a. *àràú*   *tobóu*   *mìe*   *búnu-mo-mi*
          she   child   make   sleep-CAUS-ASP
          'She soothed the child to sleep.'
    b. *àràú*   *tobóu*   *búnu-mo-mi*
          she   child   sleep-CAUS-ASP
          'She laid the child down to sleep.'

7.4 Diachronic Evidence

Song argues that the original purposive construction with two predicates (*mie* and the verb expressing the caused event) and the originally purposive marker *mo-* is giving way in this language to the morphological causative. The first predicate is normally omitted. The shorter causative in (29b) expresses more direct causation than the longer one in (29a). This can be explained by efficiency considerations, too: shorter forms represent more accessible causation scenarios.

Mithun (2002) shows that causative morphemes can emerge as a result of semantic generalization and reanalysis of more specific, concrete meanings. For example, in diverse Northern American languages, there are numerous prefixes of manner and means, e.g., doing things with hands, feet, teeth, a knife, by pressure, etc. For instance, the manner prefixes *yu-*, *pa-* and *ka-* described different hand motions in Lakhota, e.g., *bláya* 'be level, plain' – *yubláya* 'open, spread out, unfold, make level'. They are highly frequent, since language users do many things with hands. In the long run, they were reanalysed as general causative prefixes, and the more specific meaning of a hand movement has disappeared, as in the pair *bléza* 'clear' – *yubléza* 'make clear'.

The general grammaticalization path of causatives seems to be the following: from less accessible functions (including indirect causation) and analytic forms to more accessible functions (including direct causation) and more compact forms. The general pragmatic mechanism based on the principle of negative correlation between accessibility and costs was proposed in Section 5.4.1. As a construction becomes more frequent, the causativizing element becomes more predictable, and its meaning becomes more accessible, which leads to its shortening. A construction that formerly expressed only indirect causation can be used in a reduced form to represent more direct causation. The link of the expression with the more typical meaning leads to a further increase in frequency and greater reduction, and so on.

As for the increasing bondedness of causative markers, this has been explained by the fact that short elements do not have enough bulk to stand on their own and need a host (Haspelmath 2008c: Section 6). However, it is also possible that a strong association between the units in a construction leads both to their formal integration and reduction. As a result of its high accessibility, the causativizing element becomes reduced.

An efficient formal asymmetry is created when a new causative emerges with a longer form and less accessible meaning than the old one. Consider Old Dutch. After the Germanic morphological causatives with the suffix *-ja* stopped being productive (possibly due to the loss of transparency in umlaut), there remained many lexical (ex-morphological) causatives. In the twelfth to the thirteenth centuries, analytic causatives with *doen* 'do' and *laten* 'let' emerged (van der Horst 1998). The earliest instances of the *doen*-causative expressed curative causation (i.e., having someone do something), which implied an agentive Causee, as in the following example:

(30) Middle Dutch (van der Horst 1998: 56)

si	sullen	sin	hus	doen	breken
they	want	his	house	do	burst

'They will have his house broken down.'

The first attestations of the construction with *laten* had a permissive sense:

(31) Middle Dutch (van der Horst 1998: 64)

lat	dise	arme	kinde	leuen
let	these	poor	children	live

'Let these poor children live.'

These constructions were used for the relatively infrequent functions, while the more frequent ones were performed by lexical causatives (e.g., *breken* 'break, burst', *weuen* 'weave', *spreiden* 'spread' or *leggen* 'lay'). Nowadays the causative construction with *doen* occupies the niche of affective causation (e.g., to make someone cry, think, believe), especially in Netherlandic Dutch, while the construction with *laten* expresses very diverse types of indirect causation, including permission, similar to German *lassen* (Verhagen and Kemmer 1997; Levshina 2011). Both constructions represent less accessible types of semantics in comparison to lexical causatives, which are the default way of expressing a variety of direct causation scenarios.

Thus, if there is a novel causative expression, it is likely to begin with indirect causation or other non-stereotypical functions. If a costly expression is used, one is tempted to attribute to it less accessible meanings. For example, the speaker and the addressee know that there are some typical and untypical ways of making someone dead. They also know that the costs of the new longer form are higher for the speaker (and the addressee) than the costs of the default short form. The more costly expression signals that the interpretation is not trivial.

If the innovation spreads in the community and becomes conventional, this may cause the more compact form to trigger a Q-implicature (see Section 1.4.2). In particular, this will mean that the causation expressed by the compact form is not indirect, not non-intentional, etc., because otherwise the speaker would have chosen the less compact form. Compare Russian and German. In Russian, lexical causatives can still be used to express indirect curative causation:

(32) Šnur vstavil zuby za 250000$.[8]
Sh. inserted teeth for 250000$

'Shnur (a celebrity) had his teeth replaced (lit. replaced his teeth) for $250,000.'

---

[8] From a YouTube video, which is unfortunately no longer available in Germany.

The exact meaning is inferred from the context. In some cases, one can name the actual Causee (e.g., say 'at the dentist's') or the price, as in this example, to indicate that this was a service provided by a professional, but this information is not obligatory. This use of lexical causatives is possible because Russian does not have a special construction to express non-forceful and non-permissive curative causation that would correspond to the English 'have something done by someone'.

In contrast, German has more frequent analytic causatives, in particular, the causative with *lassen* 'let' (cf. Levshina 2015). In the example below, the analytic auxiliary *lassen* cannot be omitted if one is referring to the standard procedure performed by a dentist:

(33)   *Wollen Sie sich während Ihres Aufenthalts in Rumänien dritte Zähne einsetzen *(lassen)?*[9]
        'Would you like to have your dentures (lit. third teeth) done during your stay in Romania?'

The lexical causative *einsetzen* 'set in, insert' cannot be used to express indirect curative causation because it would trigger the Q-implicature that the subject would do the dentures oneself. Speakers of German are aware of the conventional alternative with *lassen*. This blocks the use of a lexical causative in this context.

7.5 An Artificial Language Learning Experiment

The previous section provided indirect evidence that the form and function of causatives evolve according to the principle of negative correlation between accessibility and costs. The aim of this section is to demonstrate that language users indeed have a bias towards efficient form–meaning mappings of causatives. That is, they tend to express a more accessible meaning by a shorter construction, and a less accessible one by a longer form. This bias is demonstrated with the help an artificial language learning experiment in Levshina (2019a). One can observe in real time how linguistic systems undergo change, revealing the cognitive and communicative biases of language users (Kirby, Cornish and Smith 2008; Hudson Kam and Newport 2009; Smith and Wonnacott 2010; Caldwell and Smith 2012; Verhoef 2012; Kirby, Griffiths and Smith 2014; Tamariz 2016; Little, Eryılmaz and de Boer 2017, and many others). The assumption is that those linguistic features that are easier to learn and to use in communication will spread at the expense of less 'fit' alternatives (Smith et al. 2017). Also, using artificial languages can help us to control for

---

[9] www.siebenbuerger.de/zeitung/pdfarchiv/suche/erhard%20gillich/ (last access 14 July 2022).

different semantic and functional properties of causatives, which are usually highly correlated in real languages, as we saw above.

In this case study, I focus on the claim that more frequent situations are expressed by means of less coding material than less frequent ones. Such differences are predicted by the efficiency account. In the previous sections, it was shown that more expected causative situations are usually expressed by shorter causatives, whereas less typical ones are expressed by longer constructions. But will artificial language users use such a system spontaneously when learning and using an artificial language? This is the main question that motivates the experiment.

The experiment was performed online, using Google Forms with built-in YouTube videos. The procedure was as follows. The participants of the experiment had to learn an artificial language. The instruction was as follows:

In this experiment you will learn the lingua franca of a highly developed civilization that exists on a planet in a galaxy far, far away... The planet is called Atruur. Its only vegetation form is called 'grok'. It is similar to a cactus and is used by the Atruurians for food, as fuel for their flying vehicles and for entertainment. Because the Atruurians traditionally detest any form of physical activity, they have developed a technology for teleportation and telekinesis.

The word order in Atruurian was SV (for intransitives) or SOV (for transitives), as in the example below:

(34) *Grok   babum.*
      cactus   grow
      'A grok (cactus) grows.'

(35) *Sia   grok   hum.*
      Atruurian   cactus   see
      'An Atruurian sees a grok (cactus).'

In the training part, the participants learned the language by copying sentences that described thirty-two situations shown in video clips. In each of them, there was a UFO which hovered above the plant and flashed a yellow or blue light. After that, the plant either appeared, disappeared, grew or shrank. Different types of UFOs were shown. Figure 7.3 demonstrates four fragments from one video clip.

Crucially, the causing events were of two types. A UFO could flash either a yellow light above the plant or a blue light from the left-hand side of the plant. There was no reason to assume that one type of causation was more or less direct than the other. The yellow-light causing event was three times as frequent as the blue-light causing event. This means that the yellow-light causative event was more accessible.

7.5 An Artificial Language Learning Experiment

Figure 7.3 Fragments of a video clip used in the experiment

In the artificial language, each of the causing events was represented by two allomorphs. One of them was expressed by the forms *tere-* or *te-*, as in (36), and the other was described using the forms *gara-/ga-*. The association between the pair and the event varied for different subjects. Most importantly, the short and long prefixes were evenly distributed among different events, such that the use of the longer and shorter forms did not depend on the type of caused events or other conditions.

(36)   a. *Sia   grok   te-babum.*
            Atruurian plant CAUS-grow
            'The Atruurian caused the plant to grow (by flashing with yellow light from above).'

       b. *Sia   grok   tere-babum.*
            Atruurian plant CAUS-grow
            'The Atruurian caused the plant to grow (by flashing with yellow light from above).'

The prediction was that the participants would regularize the free variation, such that the output language is more efficient than the input language. More precisely, I expected them to choose the short allomorphs more frequently to

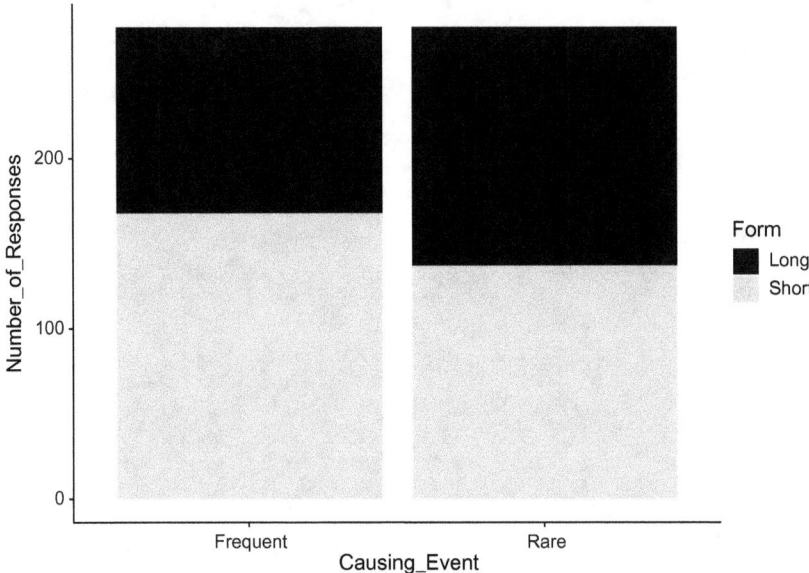

Figure 7.4 Counts of short and long causative forms in the responses

convey the frequent causing events, using the long allomorph to express the rare causing events.

In the testing part, the task was to describe what was going on in video clips. The stimuli represented a selection from the previous stimuli: each of the caused events was presented with causing event A and causing event B.

The participants were recruited via my personal network and LinguistList. Overall, I obtained 554 valid data points from 70 participants with different L1 backgrounds. None of the participants guessed the purpose of the experiment judging by their responses to a control question at the end.

Figure 7.4 displays the counts of the long and short forms produced by the participants. Overall, the short forms are more preferred than the long ones, but the stimuli with the more frequent causing event are more likely to be described by a short form in comparison with the stimuli with the rare causing event. In the latter case, the proportions of the short and long forms are almost equal. These results are supported by a generalized linear mixed-effects model with individual participants as random effects (intercepts). If the causing event is rare, the odds of the longer form being chosen are 1.66 times greater than when the event is frequent (log-odds ratio $b = 0.501$, $p = 0.006$).

To summarize, the results demonstrate that frequent causative situations become more commonly expressed by shorter forms, whereas subjects are more tolerant of longer forms when expressing rare causative situations. As a result, a more efficient system emerges. The fact that the effect was detected in a non-iterative experiment with only one 'generation' of language learners suggests that the bias is strong. This provides evidence in favour of the efficiency-based account of functionally similar expressions. Since both forms were originally available to the learners, we can witness competition between the existing forms and how they become specialized in different causative situations.

7.6 Conclusions

This chapter presented evidence based on typological data, corpora and an artificial language learning experiment which supports the claim that the form–meaning correspondences in causative constructions are best explained by the principle of negative correlation between accessibility and costs. The other accounts, which involve iconicity and productivity as explanatory factors, are less successful in predicting and explaining the famous correlation between formal and semantic integration of events in causative constructions. Moreover, the efficiency account explains other form–meaning correspondences beyond event integration and the distinction between direct and indirect causation, such as intentional vs. accidental causation. Finally, this account predicts correctly the emergence of efficient formal asymmetries in an artificial language experiment which do not involve an iconic correspondence between form and meaning.

Arguing for efficiency, I do not want to exclude iconicity completely. It may be that iconicity matters at early stages, when a new causative expression is coined. For example, the temporal or spatial distance between the causing and caused events may be emphasized by presenting the cause and effect using two independent clauses, as in the following example:

(37)   *He pressed the button and down in the control room all the screens suddenly came to life.*[10]

However, when a novel expression becomes popular, efficiency considerations become more important.

This chapter did not include semantic distinctions based on marking of arguments (most importantly, the Causee). Consider an example from Dutch in (38):

(38)   Dutch (Kemmer and Verhagen 1994: 136)

    a. *Hij liet haar de brief lezen.*
       he let her the letter read
       'He let/had her read the letter.'

---

[10] Anders de la Motte, *Bubble*. Atria Books, 2014.

b. *Hij liet de brief door iemand lezen.*
   he let the letter by   someone read
   'He had the letter read by somebody.'
c. *Hij liet de brief aan iedereen lezen.*
   he let the letter to everyone read
   'He let/had everybody read the letter.'

In (38a), the Causee *haar* 'her' is not case-marked. The meaning is that the Causee reads the letter for content. This is the stereotypical interpretation. The use of the preposition *door* 'by' in (38b) implies that the Causee is conceptualized as an instrument. Here, the Causer may be interested in having the letter checked for spelling and grammar, for instance. In (38c), the Causee is marked with a preposition *aan* 'to'. The meaning is similar to (38a), in that the Causee reads for content. The difference is that the Causee in (38c) is less accessible than in (38a). Dative-marked Causees in Dutch are likely to be full noun phrases, which are often indefinite and non-topical (Kemmer and Verhagen 1994: 137). Such Causees are postponed, which makes the planning and production more efficient (see Section 3.2.2).

In contrasts like this one, we can predict that the participants that are more accessible will have zero or shorter marking than less accessible ones. This prediction needs to be tested.

8 Differential Case Marking and Efficiency

8.1 Differential Case Marking

This chapter discusses differential marking of transitive subject and object. In the typological literature, they are often represented as comparative concepts A and P, which correspond to the agent-like and patient-like arguments of a two-place transitive clause. This chapter addresses only differential case marking, or flagging. Case markers include both affixes and adpositions. Differential case marking is defined here in a very broad sense. I speak about differential marking when subjects, objects or other arguments are sometimes marked, and sometimes unmarked, depending on their own semantic, pragmatic and other properties and/or on the properties of other arguments, or other parameters, including gender, number, tense, aspect, word order, distance from the predicate, and so on. In this regard, my approach is different from some earlier ones (e.g., Bossong 1985; Sinnemäki 2014). The reason for this is that efficiency is likely to manifest itself in many of these phenomena, not only in those traditionally discussed in the literature.

An example of differential subject marking can be found in Qiang, where the inanimate A is marked, and the animate A is unmarked:

(1) Qiang: Sino-Tibetan (LaPolla and Huang 2003: 79–80)

    a.   Animate A: unmarked
         The: qa dʐete.
         3SG 1SG hit
         'He is hitting me.'
    b.   Inanimate A: marked
         *Moʁu-**wu*** *qa da-tuə-ʐ.*
         wind-**AGT** 1SG DIR-fall.over-CAUS
         'The wind knocked me over.'

The example of differential object marking in (2) is from Spanish, where animate objects tend to be formally marked, while inanimate objects are unmarked, although definiteness and individual verbs also play a role (von Heusinger and Kaiser 2007):

(2)   Spanish (García García 2018: 211)
    a. Inanimate P: unmarked
       Pepe   ve   la   película.
       Pepe   see.3SG   DEF   film
       'Pepe sees the film.'
    b. Animate P: marked
       Pepe   ve   a   la   actriz.
       Pepe   see.3SG   **OBJ**   DEF   actress
       'Pepe sees the actress.'

Differential marking has been widely discussed in the typological literature (e.g., Silverstein 1976; Comrie 1978; Dixon 1979, 1994; Bossong 1985; Aissen 1999, 2003; de Hoop and de Swart 2008; see also a comprehensive overview in Witzlack-Makarevich and Seržant 2018).

There are many intriguing questions about differential marking. One of these is to what extent it is constrained by different hierarchies, or scales, of semantic, discursive and other features, such as the animacy hierarchy. For example, there is a popular claim that languages with differential object marking are more likely to mark animate objects than inanimate objects. The example from Spanish illustrates that tendency. There are different opinions about to what extent these constraints are universal. This topic is addressed in Section 8.2, where I also present typological data that support at least some cross-linguistic generalizations.

Another question is how to explain the observed common patterns. There are quite a few different theories, which involve frequency, iconicity, disambiguation, identification, topicality and other notions, which are discussed in Section 8.3. I argue for the efficiency account of these patterns, which is similar in spirit to Haspelmath (2021b). In a language with differential case marking, a referential expression is more likely to be formally marked if there are no reliable cues that can help the addressee to infer its thematic role, and less likely to be marked if there are strong cues. For example, animacy can serve as a cue that the expression is more likely to be A than P. In other words, animacy makes the interpretation of an argument as a P more accessible. Corpus evidence for this claim is presented in Section 8.4. Similar reasoning can be applied to other features, such as definiteness, pronominality, givenness, and so on. Cues increasing accessibility can also come from other sources: the other arguments, the predicate, word order or extralinguistic context. In Section 8.5 I will discuss the use of object marking depending on the presence or absence of visual cues, and present some experimental evidence in support of the efficiency account.

8.2 Cross-Linguistic Generalizations Related to Differential Case Marking

There is a widespread opinion that the use or absence of markers is constrained by universal referential scales, such as the ones presented by Croft (2003: 130–132) and Haspelmath (2021b) (see also Haude and Witzlack-Makarevich 2016):

(3)   a. Person: 1 and 2 > 3
      b. Nominality: pronoun > noun[1]
      c. Animacy: human > animal > inanimate
      d. Definiteness/specificity: definite > specific > non-specific
      e. Givenness: discourse-given > discourse-new
      f. Focus: background (topic) > focus

Each of the scales may be more or less relevant to the use of differential marking in an individual language. However, there is a remarkable cross-linguistic tendency, which has fascinated linguists for many years. If a language has a coding split, more prominent P arguments (i.e., the ones on the left) are usually formally marked, while less prominent ones (i.e., the ones on the right) are unmarked. The example (2) from Spanish shows the effect of the animacy scale, where animate objects are marked and inanimate ones are unmarked. It has also been claimed that the reverse holds for A arguments. The Qiang example in (1), where animate subjects are unmarked and inanimate ones are marked, supports this view.

In general, differential object marking is more frequent typologically (also see below). In fact, typological data show that differential case marking is the attractor state for object marking (Sinnemäki 2014). That is, if a language has object marking, it is more likely to be differential than to be consistently used on all objects. The most relevant features for differential object marking cross-linguistically are animacy and definiteness. For example, the definiteness hierarchy plays a role in Biblical Hebrew, where the marker *ʔet* is only used with definite nouns:

(4)   a. (Gen. 1:26)
      naase   adam   be-tzalme-nu
      create man   in-image-our
      'Let's create a man in our image...'

---

[1] This scale sometimes includes kinship terms and proper names. As for the former, their position is different depending on the usage of these terms in the language. In some languages, kinship terms are used very broadly, having a pronominal-like status, while in others they are closer to common nouns. As for proper names, Helmbrecht et al. (2018) have recently demonstrated that they do not play an important role in typological generalizations based on the animacy hierarchy.

b. (Gen. 1:27)
va-yivra Elohim *ʔet* ha-adam *b'-tzalm-o*
and-created Almighty **OBJ** DEF-man in-image-his
'So God created the man in his image...'

Animacy is important in Dhargari, a Pama-Nyungan language spoken in Australia, in which all animate objects are case-marked. Also, in Sinhalese, an Indo-Aryan language, inanimate objects are never marked, whereas animate objects may receive case marking optionally (Aissen 2003).

Very commonly, animacy and definiteness/specificity interact. An example is Hindi, where case marking is obligatory with human objects, as well as with definite and specific inanimates. It is optional with non-specific human-referring objects. Finally, it is not used with indefinite inanimate objects (Aissen 2003). The Romanian object marker *pe*, mostly combined with clitic doubling, applies to human objects only if they are definite, specific or topicalized (von Heusinger and Onea Gáspár 2008).

Differential subject marking is less common and also less regular (de Hoop and Malchukov 2008). Moreover, systems that involve the animacy hierarchy, as in the Qiang example (1), are rare (Fauconnier 2011). There seems also to be little consistent evidence (due to many exceptions) that indefinite or non-specific subjects are marked. Instead, languages use alternative strategies, e.g., passives or presentative constructions similar to the English construction *there is...* (Comrie 1989:130; Malchukov 2008).

There have been some critical voices, claiming that the scale effects are not supported enough by cross-linguistic data. In particular, personal pronouns are the greatest offenders (Filimonova 2005). This can be explained by the conserving effect of frequency (Bybee and Thompson 1997), since personal pronouns are typically very frequent in discourse. As a result, they are stored and accessed as independent units, rather than as members of a morphological paradigm. This is why distinct pronominal case forms in English, e.g., *I* and *me*, *she* and *her*) persist, while the nominal case distinctions have been lost. In this case, the fact that some pronouns can be case-marked fits the nominality scale: some pronouns are object-marked (although the forms can be suppletive), while all nouns are unmarked. However, this mechanism can also cause unexpected patterns. For example, in some Indo-Aryan and Iranian languages, pronominal subjects are marked, and nominal ones are unmarked, contrary to what one might expect. This can be explained by the fact that these languages are undergoing a change from ergative to tripartite and then to Accusative case marking. Due to their resistance to change, personal pronouns retain the old ergative forms in the subject position, while nouns, which have undergone a sweeping change, have lost their marking. This can explain why the scale-based predictions are violated.

A critical view has also been expressed by Bickel, Witzlack-Makarevich and Zakharko (2015b), who argue that universal scale effects in differential case marking do not exist. A quantitative analysis of large-scale cross-linguistic data shows that there are no significant effects that would hold in all parts of the world. How should we evaluate their claim? As argued by Schmidtke-Bode and Levshina (2018), at least some of the scale effects in object marking can still be considered universal if one uses an alternative statistical method (mixed-effects regression analysis instead of the Family Bias method used by Bickel et al.) and applies a different definition of universal effects. We find significant differences in the chances of marking in pronominality and high/low prominence of nouns, which represents a conflation of animacy, definiteness and other features in Bickel et al.'s data (see more information below). Pronominality and nominal prominence are not equally important for differential object marking in different geographic macroareas. For example, pronominal objects are substantially more likely to be marked than nominal objects in Africa, Australia and Papua New Guinea. High-prominence nouns are much more likely to be marked than low-prominence nouns in Eurasia and both Americas. Crucially, we find no significant violations of the scale effects, e.g., a macroarea where high-prominence objects are unmarked, and low-prominence objects are marked.

I believe that statistical evidence of the relevance of each scale in every possible area of the world is not required for the efficiency account. If there is a marking split, we should evaluate the general principle: it is efficient to mark an expression which is unlikely to function as A or P, given the available cues, and not to mark an expression with a high probability of performing that role. Exactly what those cues are may vary cross-linguistically. The main reason for this variation lies in the strong correlations between the features of individual roles. For example, a transitive subject is usually animate, non-lexical, discourse-given and definite (see below). It is extremely difficult to predict which of these features will become distinctive in a grammar. But if they do, we can predict the direction. If we take a particular scale, for example animacy, one would expect to find more languages with unmarked inanimate objects than with unmarked animate objects, and not the other way round (see Section 8.4 for corpus data showing why this should be the case).

This situation is similar to what we saw in Chapter 7 on causative constructions. When we discussed the semantics of the less compact causatives, we saw that the directionality of the formal asymmetries is universal: less accessible causative meanings are expressed by more costly forms than more accessible ones. This fact should not be obscured by the richness of the semantic distinctions and causation types that we find in the world's languages.

Still, it is instructive to look at the cross-linguistic data, as we did in Chapter 7, in order to see which features and scales are relevant for differential marking. Below I present frequencies from the AUTOTYP database (Bickel et al. 2017), version 0.1.0, which show which of the scales are more and less relevant for A and P cross-linguistically. Languages have many possible ways of combining the scales. Imagine Language X, which marks animate nominal and pronominal P arguments, and Language Y, which marks only animate nominal ones. In this case, Language X has a split on the animacy scale, whereas Language Y has a split on both the nominality scale (noun vs. pronoun), and on the animacy scale within nouns (inanimate vs. animate).

One feature of AUTOTYP is that it uses the labels 'high' and 'low' to indicate high or low prominence in discourse (DP). High-DP means that an argument is either given, definite, animate, topical, etc., or a combination of these features. Low-DP indicates the absence of these features (or some of them). This is why it is impossible to separate definiteness from animacy precisely. Instead, we have a very syncretic discourse prominence hierarchy:

(5) Discourse prominence hierarchy:

High-DP (human/animate, definite/specific, given, topical) > Low-DP (non-human/inanimate, indefinite/non-specific, non-topical, new)

The frequencies of the splits found in AUTOTYP are presented in Tables 8.1 and 8.2. I excluded those that also involve splits between different language-specific lexical classes of nouns, the 1st and 2nd-person, singular and plural forms, or inclusive and exclusive pronouns. Splits in number and person are particularly frequent in pronouns (see more information in Schmidtke-Bode and Levshina 2018), which is probably explained by the conserving frequency effects causing the idiosyncratic patterns described by Filimonova (2005). I also excluded cases where one could interpret the data as both a fit and a violation. For example, Menya (an Angan language spoken in Papua New Guinea) has differential object marking, where pronouns and nouns with low discourse prominence are unmarked, while nouns with high discourse prominence are marked. This means that the system fits the DP prominence scale within nouns (high-DP nouns are marked, while low-DP nouns are unmarked), but violates the nominal scale, according to which pronouns should be marked if (some) nouns are marked.

Let us consider the results for transitive subjects presented in Table 8.1. The double vertical bar '||' represents a split. The features on the left of the sign are unmarked, and the features on the right are marked. Importantly, the marking is understood by the authors in the Silversteinian sense (see Bickel et al. 2015b): an argument is unmarked if it has the same expression as S (intransitive subject). In practice, it usually means zero expression. The parentheses contain the language family and the geographic macroarea.

Table 8.1. *Cross-linguistic distribution of differential transitive subject marking in AUTOTYP 0.1*

Distinction	Scale(s)	No. languages	No. families	No. areas	Examples
Pronouns ‖ Nouns	Nominality	20	7	3	Djapu (Pama-Nyungan, Pacific), Kryz (Nakh-Daghestanian, Eurasia), Cashinahua (Pano-Tacanan, Americas)
1st & 2nd Person ‖ 3rd Person (incl. Nouns)	Person	11	4	2	Kham (Sino-Tibetan, Eurasia), Yidiny (Pama-Nyungan, Pacific)
Animates ‖ Inanimates (both pronouns and nouns)	Animacy	2	2	2	Mayali (Gunwinyguan, Pacific), Northern Qiang (Sino-Tibetan, Eurasia)
Pronouns, Animate Nouns ‖ Inanimate Nouns	Nominality, Animacy	1	1	1	Hittite (Indo-European, Eurasia)
Pronouns, Personal Proper Names ‖ Other Nouns	Nominality, Animacy	1	1	1	Djinang (Pama-Nyungan, Pacific)
Pronouns, DP Animate Nouns ‖ Other Nouns	Nominality, Animacy, DP	1	1	1	Mangarrayi (Mangarrayi-Maran, Pacific)
Pronouns, Proper Nouns, Kinship terms ‖ Other Nouns	Nominality	1	1	1	Central Pomo (Pomoan, Americas)
The most DP Pronouns and Nouns ‖ Other	DP	1	1	1	Tukang Besi (Austronesian, Pacific)
Pronouns, Proper nouns, Kinship terms ‖ Non-kin common nouns	Nominality	1	1	1	Eastern Pomo (Pomoan, Americas)
Common Nouns ‖ Pronouns, Proper Nouns	Nominality	1	1	1	Gitksan (Tsimshianic, Americas)

Table 8.2. Cross-linguistic distribution of differential object marking in AUTOTYP 0.1

Distinction	Scale(s)	No. languages	No. families	No. areas	Examples
Nouns ‖ Pronouns	Nominality	65	33	4	Logba (Kwa, Africa), Khanty (Uralic, Eurasia), Garrwa (Garrwan, Pacific), Rama (Chibchan, Americas)
Low-DP nouns ‖ Pronouns, high-DP nouns	Nominality, DP	59	21	4	Dizi (Omotic, Africa), Awa Pit (Barbacoan, Americas), Tamil (Dravidian, Eurasia), Akoye (Angan, Pacific)
Indefinite nouns ‖ Pronouns, definite nouns	Definiteness, Nominality	14	8	3	Amharic (Semitic, Africa), Chuvash (Turkic, Eurasia), Barasano (Tucanoan, Americas)
Nouns, 3rd person pronouns ‖ 1st & 2nd person pronouns	Person, Nominality	7	6	4	Dyirbal (Pama-Nyungan, Pacific), Kutenai (isolate, Americas), Waskia (Madang, Pacific), Tsova-Tush (Nakh-Daghestanian, Eurasia)
Inanimate nouns ‖ Pronouns, animate nouns	Animacy, Nominality	7	4	2	Hittite (Indo-European, Eurasia), Anamuxra (Madang, Pacific)
Inanimate and low-DP animate nouns ‖ Pronouns and high-DP animate nouns	Nominality, DP	6	3	2	Hup (Nadahup, Americas), Djapu (Pama-Nyungan, Pacific)
Low-DP pronouns and nouns ‖ High-DP pronouns and nouns	DP	5	5	3	Tariana (Arawakan, Americas), Kharia (Austro-Asiatic, Eurasia), Tainae (Angan, Pacific)
Inanimate nouns and pronouns ‖ Animate nouns and pronouns	Animacy	2	2	1	Imonda (Border, Pacific)

Split	Features			Language (family, macroarea)
Common, non-kin nouns ‖ All other	Nominality	2	2	Eastern Pomo (Pomoan, Americas), Sardinian (Indo-European, Eurasia)
Non-specific nouns ‖ All other	Definiteness, Nominality	2	2	Persian (Indo-European, Eurasia)
Nouns and low-DP 3rd person pronouns ‖ All other pronouns	Nominality, DP	1	1	Yidiny (Pama-Nyungan, Pacific)
Non-kin nouns, low-DP 3rd person pronouns ‖ All other	Nominality, DP	1	1	Central Pomo (Pomoan, Americas)
Low-DP nouns, inanimate pronouns ‖ All other	DP, animacy	1	1	Afrikaans (Indo-European, Africa)
Pronouns, high-DP nouns ‖ low-DP nouns	Nominality, DP	1	1	Maithili only in dependent clauses with converbs (Indo-European, Eurasia)
1st & 2nd person pronouns ‖ 3rd person pronouns, nouns	Person, Nominality	1	1	Osage (Siouan, Americas)
Highest-DP pronouns and nouns ‖ All other	DP	1	1	Tukang Besi (Austronesian, Pacific)

Table 8.3. *Number of languages that fit (violate) the scales in the cross-linguistic differential and optional marking database*

Argument	Animacy scale	Definiteness scale	Nominality scale	Person scale
A	3 (0)	0 (0)	4 (1)	4 (0)
P	8 (0)	11 (0)	9 (0)	4 (0)

The predominant category for subject marking is clearly nominality (cf. de Hoop and Malchukov 2008: 567), followed by person. Animacy and discourse prominence only rarely play a role on their own. This supports the previous observations. There is a violation of the nominality scale (see the shaded row): in Gitksan (a Tsimshianic language spoken in Canada) subjects expressed by common nouns are unmarked, but subjects expressed by proper nouns and pronouns are marked.

The splits in object marking are shown in Table 8.2. The results partly support the previous claims. Inanimate, indefinite and low-DP nouns are overwhelmingly unmarked. However, the most frequent distinction is between nouns and pronouns. Person seems to produce the lowest number of splits. Again, there are a few exceptions (see the shaded rows), but they are not numerous.

To summarize, subjects tend to be marked if they are nominal and, less frequently, if they are 3rd person. The evidence for the other scales is rather weak. Objects tend to be marked if they are pronominal, high-DP (including animacy and definiteness) and 1st or 2nd person. The evidence for the person scale is the weakest.

One problem with this database is that the category DP hides many scales, so that we cannot directly test different scales. Also, there is no information about the presence or absence of case markers. Table 8.3 displays some frequencies from the cross-linguistic differential and optional marking database (Sommer and Levshina 2021), which currently includes detailed descriptions of differential A and P marking in twenty-five languages from diverse families and all parts of the world. The counts are the number of languages in which a particular scale effect is found. Only productive patterns with segmental case markers are taken into account. Importantly, almost all these languages fit the scales. We find only one violation of the predictions. This provides additional support of the universal directionality of the scale effects described above. The evidence for objects is more convincing than the evidence for subjects, in accordance with the previous observations. More data will tell us if these observations are correct.

The next question is, how do we know that the coding asymmetries are indeed due to efficiency? And why is it more efficient to mark definite objects, for example? The next section addresses these questions.

8.3 Explanations of Differential Case Marking

8.3.1 Disambiguation and Economy

There exist many theories and accounts that explain the observed scale effects in differential case marking. Probably the most popular explanation has to do with disambiguation, or distinguishing between the arguments. It is often argued that two nominal phrases, when they are simultaneously present in the transitive clause, should be distinguished (Comrie 1978: 379–380, 1989: 124–127; Dixon 1979; Givón 1984: 184; Aissen 2003, among others). It is assumed that disambiguation interacts with economy. If a context is not ambiguous, or the argument in question has typical properties, it does not require formal marking. Only situations that may lead to misunderstanding require marking.

This principle is very clear in the systems in which the marking of the subject depends on the properties of the object, and the other way round (cf. de Hoop and Malchukov 2008). Such marking is called global, in contrast to local marking, which depends only on the properties of the argument itself (Witzlack-Makarevich and Seržant 2018). For example, Malayalam (a Dravidian language) marks animate objects and usually does not mark inanimate objects. However, when the sentence is potentially ambiguous, the object marker can also be used on inanimate objects, as in (6).

(6)   Malayalam: Dravidian (Asher and Kumari 1997:204, cited from de Swart 2007: 88)

    a.   *Kappal   tiramaalakaí-e   bheediccu.*
          ship.NOM   waves-ACC   split.PST
          'The ship broke through the waves.'
    b.   *Tiramaalakaí   kappal-ine   bheediccu.*
          waves. NOM   ship-ACC   split.PST
          'The waves split the ship.'

More examples can be found in de Swart (2007: Section 3.2).

Also, mood, tense and aspect can play a role. For example, object marking is less likely in imperative sentences in Udihe (Altaic) and Mutsun (Penutian) (Sommer and Levshina 2021). This may have to do with the fact that imperatives usually do not contain subjects, so there is no competing nominal. Interestingly, Rapanui (Austronesian) has higher chances of object marking in imperative sentences with explicit subject than without it, which supports this explanation.

Yet, global marking systems like in (6) are less frequent than systems with local marking, as we can judge from the cross-linguistic data. A possible explanation is that local differential marking provides a convenient shortcut, which works in most situations, is easier to learn and probably helps to save processing effort during language production and comprehension. It can be easier to process a sentence incrementally, constituent after constituent, than to monitor it as a whole for potential ambiguity in language production (Seržant 2019: 169), or run the risk of incorrect role assignment and reanalysis in comprehension. Moreover, if animate objects, for example, are often marked in order to avoid ambiguity with subjects in a global marking system, this marking can become entrenched and be triggered automatically by animacy. For example, speakers of Spanish know that *la actriz* 'the actress', when it functions as a direct object, is used with the marker *a*, while *la película* 'the film' is used without any marker (Diessel 2019: 238). No further considerations are required. It may be that both processing optimization and learning mechanisms contribute to the fact that global marking is less frequent cross-linguistically than local marking, and when it does occur, it usually plays a subordinate role with regard to other constraints (Seržant 2019).

Different referential features (and other contextual information) serve as cues that help the addressee to infer the grammatical role immediately. As Comrie writes (1978: 385–386),

there seems to be a general supposition in human discourse that certain entities are inherently more agentive than others, and as such inherently more likely to appear as A of a transitive verb and less likely to appear as P of a transitive verb.

For example, animacy is a strong cue for subjecthood, as opposed to objecthood. If a referent is animate, it is more likely to be a subject than an object. The addressee does not need much help in assigning the role. An inanimate entity is much more likely to be an object than a subject. Thus, inanimacy is a strong cue for objecthood. As Royen (1929: 590) observed, 'Eine Person ist vor allem agens, ein Impersonale vor allem patiens [A person is mainly Agent, a non-person is mainly Patient]' (1929: 590). If this is true, then additional marking on a human P or on non-human A would help the hearer to identify the role easier. In fact, this idea had already been proposed by Bishop Robert Caldwell (1856: 271, cited from Filimonova 2005: 78):

The principle that it is more natural for rational beings to act than to be acted upon; and hence when they do happen to be acted upon – when the nouns by which they are denoted are to be taken objectively – it becomes necessary, in order to avoid misapprehension, to suffix to them the objective case-sign.

An example is Korean, which has probabilistic marking. In particular, Subject is marked more frequently in colloquial speech when it is 3rd person, a non-human participant and a common noun, than when it refers to speech act participants and other human referents expressed by pronouns or proper nouns. For Object, the tendencies are mostly reversed (Lee 2009). Consider an example of a pronominal object in (7).

8.3 Explanations

(7) Korean (Kwon and Zribi-Hertz 2008: 263)

yeongmi-ga   uli-leul   moim-e   chodae ha-ess-eo
yeongmi-SBJ us-OBJ   meeting-LOC invitation do-PST-DEC/INF
'Yeongmi invited us to the meeting.'

As will be shown in Section 8.4, the features with higher chances of marking are weaker cues to the grammatical roles.

There are many cases that cannot be easily explained by disambiguation at the sentence level. Consider the following example from Japanese:

(8) Japanese (Kurumada and Jaeger 2015: 156)

Sensei-ga   seito-o   ekimae-de   mi-ta-yo.
teacher-SBJ   student-OBJ station-LOC   see-PST-SFP
'The teacher saw the student at the station.'

The subject marker *-ga* makes the sentence unambiguous. Still, Kurumada and Jaeger (2015) show that the chances of the object marker are higher for animate nouns than for inanimate ones in sentences like this. In addition, they find that the participants tend to mark the object when it occurs in a less plausible configuration of A and P, as in (9a). In contrast, in more stereotypical contexts, such as the one in (9b), the marker is often omitted:

(9) a. *The police officer attacked the criminal in the middle of the night.*
     b. *The criminal attacked the police officer in the middle of the night.*

The accessibility of the object interpretation in (9a) is lower than in (9b) because it is criminals who usually attack police officers. By using the object marker, the speaker signals that the situation does not correspond to the stereotypical situation. Importantly, the subject marking is always present in their stimuli. There is thus no ambiguity. The object marker helps to override the more accessible interpretation.

According to Haspelmath (2019), differential marking is motivated by expectation management rather than by ambiguity avoidance. Another argument is the fact that coding asymmetries in some languages involve a shorter and a longer marker. The longer marker is preferred in less predictable role–reference associations. This tendency cannot be explained by ambiguity avoidance because there is no ambiguity in the first place. But it can be explained by the principle of negative correlation between accessibility and costs (see also Section 1.4.2).

Differential marking is influenced not only by the referential properties of one or both arguments, but also by other factors, such as word order, tense and aspect, etc. An example is Gurindji Kriol, a mixed language spoken in Australia, which has SVO as the dominant word order. The ergative marker is used on subjects in about 66 per cent of all cases. However, in rare cases when the subject follows the verb, more than 90 per cent of such subjects have an ergative marker (Meakins 2008: 283). Another important variable is the distance from the verb. For example, in conversational Korean, the chances that an object will remain bare gradually decrease as the number of words between the object and the verb increases (Kim 2008). This does not necessarily mean that the order must be untypical. For example, there can be an adverb intervening between the object and the verb while the word order remains canonical (i.e., SOV). These cases can also be interpreted as providing additional formal cues in more challenging contexts, where the addressee may have problems with accessing the intended interpretation.

At the same time, it should be said that the facilitation of local role assignment and ambiguity avoidance at the more general sentence level are two sides of the same coin. In both cases, the use of marking depends on the accessibility of the intended interpretation to the addressee. It is necessary to repeat here that the importance of ambiguity for explaining language structure and use is overrated (Ferreira 2008; Wasow 2015; see also Section 6.2.1). In most cases, language users have enough contextual cues to understand each other. Note that even languages with a high level of grammatical ambiguity and underspecification, like those in east and mainland Southeast Asia (Bisang 2009), are still communicatively effective. At the same time, many languages are vastly redundant (see Section 6.3.6). However, if a language develops a coding split, it is likely to be efficient in the sense that more formal cues are provided to express a less accessible meaning. Accessibility is evaluated either globally, at the level of the entire clause, or – more often – locally, depending on the properties of the argument.

8.3.2   Iconicity of Markedness and Economy

Iconicity of markedness means that semantically (or cognitively) marked members of grammatical categories are usually marked formally, while semantically unmarked ones are also formally unmarked. The relationship between semantic and formal marking is iconic. This idea, also labelled by Givón (1995) as the meta-iconic markedness principle, has been used as an explanation of differential marking (cf. Dalrymple and Nikolaeva 2011: 3). As noted by Aissen (2003), iconicity of markedness interacts with the principle of economy because semantically unmarked arguments are left formally unmarked. Semantically and formally unmarked subjects are prominent (animate or human, definite and specific), while marked subjects are non-prominent. For objects, the reverse is claimed to be the case (Aissen 2003).

A problem with this account is that markedness is a slippery concept, which has very many interpretations (Fenk-Oczlon 1991; Haspelmath 2006). There is a danger of using it in a circular way (e.g., this form has no marking because it is semantically/conceptually unmarked, and it is semantically/conceptually unmarked because it has no marking, and so infinitely). Following Fenk-Oczlon (1991) and Haspelmath (2006), I assume that many, if not all, aspects of markedness relevant for grammar can be explained by frequency asymmetries between different categories.

8.3.3 Indexing Function and High Transitivity

Another explanatory principle suggested in the literature is the identifying, or indexing, function of differential marking. As de Hoop and Malchukov (2008) argue, both prominent subjects and prominent objects will be marked because they make for better and more individuated participants. Animate subjects, are, for instance, volitional and agentive, which is why they make good subjects. Animate objects are considered to be more (obviously) affected than others and therefore make for better objects. This is why, it is argued, differential object marking is more common than differential subject marking. In differential object marking, the distinguishing and identifying functions overlap: animate or definite objects are both prominent and similar to subjects (and therefore need to be distinguished from the latter). For subjects, however, these principles are in conflict because animate subjects are prominent but they do not require disambiguation, while inanimate subjects are not prominent but require disambiguation (Malchukov 2008).

This approach is related to the one taken by Hopper and Thompson (1980), who say that the situations where differential object marking is observed indicate high transitivity. The latter is argued to be associated with the foregrounding function in discourse. Highly transitive events involve highly individuated subjects and objects, and the object is highly affected. Presumably, definite and animate subjects and objects satisfy these conditions and therefore lead to high transitivity.

Note that high transitivity is different from typical transitivity. For instance, Næss (2007) claims that the prototypical transitive clause is one where the subject and the object are maximally semantically distinct. Similarly, Comrie (1989: 128) speaks of 'natural transitive constructions', in which the subject is high on animacy and definiteness, and the object is low on animacy and definiteness.

Certainly, de Hoop and Malchukov's account is very elegant and nicely explains the relative scarceness of evidence for scale effects in differential subject marking. However, attempts by some researchers to use affectedness in order to explain differential case marking have not brought conclusive results so far (see García García 2018). Animacy and definiteness, as we have seen, play a very important role in differential object marking, but there are far fewer cases where affectedness would play a role per se.[2] Finally, it is not quite clear what kind of cognitive or pragmatic mechanism is responsible for marking the more salient, more representative, etc. participants, while leaving the others unmarked.

How to explain the rarity of scale effects in differential subject marking then? First of all, ergative languages, where differential subject marking is found, are relatively infrequent, which leaves us with fewer opportunities for variation. A possible reason is a cognitive bias towards processing the unmarked first nominal phrase as the subject (Bickel et al. 2015a). This bias, which can be explained by general processing principles (see Section 3.3.4), exists in ergative languages, as well. This may account for the fact that ergativity is disfavoured cross-linguistically. Other reasons may be the infrequent use of full lexical forms of subjects in discourse (see Section 8.4) and frequent omission of pronominal subjects due to their high accessibility (see Section 2.2), which do not allow the marking to grammaticalize.

8.4 Reverse Engineering: Cross-Linguistic Generalizations and Corpus Data

8.4.1 *A Reverse-Engineering Approach to Differential Case Marking*

This section focuses on the previous functional-adaptive accounts that involve the notions of disambiguation and iconicity of markedness. Which of them fits the cross-linguistic data the best? In order to compare the explanations, we can perform a kind of reverse engineering. We will use the cross-linguistic tendencies discussed in Section 8.2 to predict how the features of Subject and Object would need to be distributed in discourse for the observed patterns to arise, according to each of the strategies. In order to compare the predictions with the discourse data, I analyse corpora in diverse languages.

Let us begin with the distinguishing account. There are at least two strategies that language users may employ. According to one strategy, language users will tend to mark Subjects that look like typical Objects, and Objects that look like typical Subjects. As Aissen puts it (2003: 437), 'it is those direct objects which most resemble typical subjects that get overtly case-marked'. In other words, those Subjects that have properties of typical Objects get extra marking, and the other way round. I will call this strategy **'Mark Impostors, Don't Mark the Authentic'**.

---

[2] For example, in Yuki, a Wappo-Yukian language in North America, affectedness can be a potential factor for differential marking of animal objects, but its role is not totally clear (Balodis 2011: 251).

8.4 Reverse Engineering

Formally, this can be expressed with the help of conditional probabilities. Let $\mathbb{P}$ (Feature|A) stand for the conditional probability of a certain Feature (i.e., animacy, definiteness, etc.) given the A role. For brevity, we will use conventional labels A and P to represent transitive subject and object, respectively. The symbol $\mathbb{P}$ stands for probability, which can be approximated by the proportion of A's with this feature in the total number of A's in a reasonably large sample of discourse. The symbol $\mathbb{P}$ should not be confused with P, which represents a grammatical role. The predictions are then as follows:

(10) Reverse-engineering predictions based on the distinguishing account and the strategy 'Mark Impostors, Don't Mark the Authentic'

Prediction for A:
If A with $Feature_i$ tends to be formally marked in languages of the world, then the probability $\mathbb{P}$ ($Feature_i$ |P) in discourse should be high. If A tends to be unmarked, then $\mathbb{P}$ ($Feature_i$ |P) should be low.[3]

Prediction for P:
If P with $Feature_j$ tends to be formally marked in languages of the world, then the probability $\mathbb{P}$ ($Feature_j$ |A) in discourse should be high. If P tends to be unmarked, then $\mathbb{P}$ ($Feature_j$ |A) should be low.

If this approach is correct, one would expect that a typical P in discourse is nominal and 3rd person, since A's with these features are marked cross-linguistically, as was shown in Section 8.2. An untypical P is then pronominal and 1st or 2nd person, because these features are not marked on A. As for A's, their most common properties should be pronominality, high discourse prominence (givenness and definiteness, including humanness/animacy), and 1st or 2nd person, because P's with these features are usually marked in the typological data. From this follows that A's should rarely be nominal, low-DP, including inanimacy, or 3rd person.

The other interpretation of distinguishability involves interpreting the features as strong or weak cues for assigning a grammatical role. This disambiguation strategy can be labelled as **'Mark Weak Cues, Don't Mark Strong Cues'**.

(11) Reverse-engineering predictions based on the distinguishing account and the strategy 'Mark Weak Cues, Don't Mark Strong Cues'

Prediction for A:
If A with $Feature_i$ tends to be formally marked in languages of the world, then $\mathbb{P}$ (A| $Feature_i$) should be low. If A tends to be unmarked, then $\mathbb{P}$ (A| $Feature_i$) should be high.

---

[3] Here and below, 'high' stands for greater than 0.5, or 50 per cent, and 'low' stands for less than 0.5.

Prediction for P:
If P with Feature$_j$ tends to be formally marked in languages of the world, then $\mathbb{P}$ (P| Feature$_j$) should be low. If P tends to be unmarked, then $\mathbb{P}$ (P| Feature$_i$) should be high.

The notation $\mathbb{P}$ (A| Feature$_i$) represents the conditional probability of A given a certain feature. It can be computed as the proportion of A's among all core arguments with this feature (in our case, A and P). $\mathbb{P}$ (P| Feature$_i$) stands for the conditional probability of P given a feature and can be estimated as the proportion of P's relative to all A's and P's with this feature. The cross-linguistic distribution of the features, which was discussed in Section 8.2, suggests that one could expect to find few A's among nominal core arguments (i.e., A and P taken together) and possibly among 3rd-person referents because A's with these features tend to be marked cross-linguistically. We can also expect low proportions of P's in pronominal, high-DP, animate or definite and possibly 1st and 2nd-person arguments, because P's with these features tend to be marked.

As for iconicity of markedness, this has to do with the typicality of different A's and P's, regardless of the other argument. This principle can be called **'Mark Weirdos, Don't Mark Normals'**. Since markedness is associated with the relative frequency of two or more members within one category, e.g., singular and plural within the category of number (Greenberg 1966), we need to compute the proportions of particular referents (animate, definite, etc.) in the total number of A's or P's, and take the least probable ones. One can formulate the predictions as follows:

(12) Reverse-engineering predictions based on the markedness principle and the strategy 'Mark Weirdos, Don't Mark Normals'

Prediction for A:
If A with Feature$_i$ tends to be formally marked in languages of the world, then $\mathbb{P}$ (Feature$_i$ |A) should be low. If A tends to be unmarked, then $\mathbb{P}$ (Feature$_i$ |A) should be high.

Prediction for P:
If P with Feature$_j$ tends to be formally marked in languages of the world, then $\mathbb{P}$ (Feature$_j$ |P) should be low. If P tends to be unmarked, then $\mathbb{P}$ (Feature$_i$ |P) should be high.

As explained above, the quantities $\mathbb{P}$ (Feature$_i$ |A) and $\mathbb{P}$ (Feature$_i$ |P) represent conditional probabilities of a given feature given the role (A or P, respectively). If this principle is relevant, A should have a low proportion of nouns and possibly 3rd-person referents, while P should have a particularly low number of pronouns, high-DP, animate and possibly 1st and 2nd-person referents, since all these are the formally marked features of A and P in the cross-linguistic data. The predictions for the three marking strategies are

8.4 Reverse Engineering

Table 8.4. *Reverse-engineered predictions for the distribution of features of A and P in discourse*

Marking strategy	Prediction for A distribution	Prediction for P distribution	Conditional probability
Mark Impostors	A is usually pronominal, high-DP/animate (1&2 person).	P is usually nominal and 3rd person.	ℙ (Feature|Role), the other role
Don't Mark the Authentic	A is rarely nominal, low-DP/animate (3rd person)	P is rarely pronominal and 1st & 2nd person.	
Mark Weak Cues	Nominal and 3rd person arguments are rarely A.	High-DP/animate, pronominal arguments (and 1st & 2nd person) are rarely P.	ℙ (Role|Feature), the same role
Don't Mark Strong Cues	Pronominal and 1st & 2nd person arguments are usually A.	Low-DP/inanimate, nominal arguments (and 3rd person) are usually P.	
Mark Weirdos	A is rarely nominal and rarely 3rd person.	P is rarely pronominal, high-DP/animate (and 1st & 2nd person).	ℙ (Feature|Role), the same role
Don't Mark Normals	A is usually pronominal and 1st and 2nd person.	P is usually nominal, low-DP/inanimate (and 3rd person).	

summarized in Table 8.4. The features in brackets are less clearly supported cross-linguistically.

As for the identifying explanation, I leave it out from testing. In order to test this hypothesis, we need independent evidence that the degree of individuation, affectedness, salience, etc., influences the probability of marking for any role. It seems that such evidence can only be provided experimentally, which is why this hypothesis is beyond the scope of the present corpus-based study.

8.4.2 Recycling Old Data

If any of the functional-adaptive accounts presented here is correct, we can expect to find a correspondence between corpus-based conditional probabilities ℙ (Role\|Feature) or ℙ (Feature\|Role) and the cross-linguistic distribution. In fact, some statistical evidence was provided by Thomson

(1909), who looked at transitive verbs in contemporary Russian and found that almost three-quarters of them had exclusively a person as the subject. Only 14 per cent of transitive verbs had a human being as the object (e.g., the Russian verbs denoting 'undress' and 'hug'), and more than half could be used with a human object (e.g., 'see' and 'steal a child'). In contrast, inanimate things were normally subjects for 10 per cent of all transitive verbs. About 45 per cent of the verbs always had an inanimate thing as a patient, and three-quarters of the verbs could take an inanimate object. Thomson (1909) did not provide the exact frequencies, unfortunately, nor did he describe his sampling method.

After a long period when language in use was not the main focus of most theorists, the end of the twentieth century witnessed a strong interest in discourse-based explanations of grammatical patterns. There was a fruitful discussion of the Preferred Argument Structure as the basis for ergativity, as well as quite a few studies of animacy effects in grammar (e.g., Du Bois 1987; Dahl and Fraurud 1996; Dahl 2000; Du Bois et al. 2003; Haig and Schnell 2016). As a useful product of these studies and debates, one can find a considerable amount of available data showing the distributional properties of A and P in different types of corpora and languages. This section examines these data as evidence for or against the predictions formulated in Section 8.4.2. I chose those studies in which it was possible to find the original frequencies for the parameters of interest and a description of data sources. L2 learner corpora and language impairment data were not considered because I could not find comparable data in many languages for these varieties.

When recycling data from different studies by different authors, one has to make some compromises. First of all, the definitions of transitivity varied somewhat from one study to another. For example, Dahl and Fraurud (1996) only include those clauses in Swedish in which both the subjects and the objects are overt noun phrases. However, since Swedish is not a subject pro-drop language, the results can still be comparable with the other studies, where non-overt arguments are also counted (e.g., the Multi-CAST data). When pro-drop languages were considered, I only included those studies where both overt and covert A's and P's were counted. This was done for the sake of comparability of the results. Moreover, there were some discrepancies in the features. For example, most studies coded humanness, but some described the animacy of A and P. This difference was tolerated, since in my own experience, animals are infrequently mentioned in contemporary corpora. Also, most studies counted the 1st and the 2nd-person reference based on the grammatical properties of the arguments, but Dahl (2000) uses the notion 'egophoric', which includes reference to the speech act participants, generic and logophoric reference, like *he* in *Peter says that he is sick*. Still, I hope that these differences lead to relatively small imprecisions.

8.4 Reverse Engineering

The results that are directly relevant for our research question are summarized in Tables 8.5–8.7. The tables display the percentages which represent different conditional probabilities of the features of A and P. The original corpus counts are provided in Appendix 2. The features presented here were chosen because they were available in numerous studies. They are the following:

- lexical, i.e., full nominal phrase vs. pronouns, affixes or zero;
- human or animate (when specified) vs. all other semantic types;
- 1st and 2nd person (or egophoric reference in Dahl's approach) vs. the 3rd person;
- new vs. given or inferable from context.

Note that I did not aggregate the frequencies of pronouns because there was a lot of variation with regard to the acceptability of zero anaphora in a language. For instance, English allows pronouns to be omitted only in a few cases (most typically, the subject of an imperative sentence), while in Lao zero anaphora is a very common reference-management device for both subjects and objects (see Chapter 2, Section 2.2.1). This is why I make a distinction between lexical and non-lexical expressions here. Definiteness is absent from this list because this feature is very rarely reported, unfortunately. However, the study based on new data in Section 8.4.3 shows that the frequencies of definite A's and P's are similar to those of discourse-given arguments.

The total number of corpora is nineteen. They represent fourteen languages from seven families and different parts of the world: Indo-European (English, French, Northern Kurdish, Persian, Portuguese, Spanish, Swedish), Austronesian (Teop and Vera'a), Afro-Asiatic (Hebrew), Araucanian (Mapudungun), Eskimo-Aleut (Inuktitut), Mayan (Sakapultek) and Sino-Tibetan (Chinese). Different registers and types of discourse are included: spontaneous conversations, transcribed talk shows, narratives retelling films, autobiographical and traditional narratives, stimulus-based monologues in sociolinguistic interviews, child language use and miscellaneous written texts.

Table 8.5 shows the distribution of the above-mentioned features within the A role. In other words, the numbers show the proportion of lexical, human, 1st or 2nd person or new A's in the total number of A's. The data show that typical A's are human/animate, not new and not lexical. Therefore, untypical A's are new, non-human/inanimate and lexical. The person varies a lot. The highest proportion of 1st and 2nd-person arguments is observed in Inuktitut child language (97.4%), followed by the English autobiographical narratives and Swedish spontaneous conversations. The lowest is observed in the Persian stimulus-based narratives (3.6%).

Do these results support any of the predictions based on the conditional probabilities of a feature given the grammatical role A? Recall that these

Table 8.5. *Distribution of features of A (transitive subjects) within the role (%)*

Study	Corpus	Lexical	Human	1st & 2nd	New
Du Bois 1987	*Pear Story* narratives in Sakapultek	6.1	100	NA	3.2
Chui 1992	*Ghost* narratives in Chinese	38.1	NA	NA	2.9
Ashby & Bentivoglio 1993	interviews (monologues) in French	6.7	NA	NA	0
	interviews (monologues) in Spanish	6.1	NA	NA	0.4
Dahl & Fraurud 1996	written Swedish	NA	56	NA	NA
Sutherland-Smith 1996	Several oral narratives in modern Hebrew	6.7	NA	NA	2.2
Dahl 2000	spontaneous conversations in Swedish	NA	93.2 (animate)	60.7 (ego)	NA
Allen & Schröder 2003	Inuktitut child language	1.1	99 (animate)	97.4	0.7
Arnold 2003	Mapudungun narrative texts	14.9	NA	NA	1.2
Everett 2009	English talk shows	9.7	91.8	NA	NA
	Portuguese talk shows	17.1	87.1	NA	NA
Lin 2009	Chinese conversations	20	NA	NA	15
	Chinese narratives	18.8	NA	NA	12.5
	Chinese written texts	15.9	NA	NA	20.5
Schiborr 2016	English autobiographical narratives	8.2	92.8	59	NA
Haig & Thiele 2016	Northern Kurdish traditional narratives	13	96.7	32.5	NA
Abidifar 2016	Persian stimulus-based narratives	13.6	96.2	3.6	NA
Mosel & Schnell 2016	Teop traditional narratives	9.7	95.4	25.6	NA
Schnell 2016	Vera'a traditional narratives	7.4	94.7	15.4	NA

probabilities are relevant for two marking strategies, namely, 'Mark Impostors, Don't Mark the Authentic' and 'Mark Weirdos, Don't Mark Normals'. As for the strategy 'Mark Impostors, Don't Mark the Authentic', we expected A's to be predominantly pronominal and high-DP/animate (and 1st and 2nd person). The A arguments in the corpora are overwhelmingly non-lexical, non-new and human/ animate. There is no preference for the 1st and 2nd person, but this feature does not play a very important role in the differential case marking of P. Therefore, we can say that the predictions are mostly supported by the corpus data. Since the proportions of different values of the same feature (e.g., human and non-human)

8.4 Reverse Engineering

are mirror images of each other, the conclusion for the second part of the strategy, 'Don't Mark the Authentic' is the same.

As for the strategy 'Mark Weirdos, Don't Mark Normals', we expected A's to be infrequently nominal and frequently pronominal, and also rarely have 3rd-person reference, and frequently 1st and 2nd-person reference. Indeed, we find relatively few lexical A's. However, the 3rd person predominates in the data. Overall, the distribution of the person values is very scattered. The 3rd person seems to be frequent in traditional narratives, and the 1st and the 2nd person in autobiographic narratives, child speech and spontaneous dialogues. We can conclude that the predictions are only partly met. In addition, non-human/inanimate and new A's are also rare, but these features are rarely marked formally by languages, as was shown above. It has already been mentioned that languages avoid indefinite and non-specific subjects, which are usually new, using passives or other strategies.

Table 8.6 shows the proportions of the features within the P role. The most typical properties of P are 3rd-person reference and non-humanness/inanimacy. The other features display substantial variation. The proportion of lexical P's varies from 6% in Inuktitut child language to 94% in Chinese narratives. The fraction of new arguments also fluctuates from 24.7% in Sakapultek to 72.5% in Chinese narratives.

Are our predictions borne out? As for the strategy 'Mark Impostors, Don't Mark the Authentic', we expected to find predominantly nominal or lexical P's, and 3rd-person referents, and rarely non-lexical and 1st and 2nd-person referents. Most of the P's are indeed lexical, although there are a few exceptions. The 3rd-person P's are predominant. Thus, we can say that this strategy is mostly supported.

The other relevant strategy, 'Mark Weirdos, Don't Mark Normals', is partly supported by the data. We expected P's to be rarely pronominal, animate/ high-DP, and 1st and 2nd person, and frequently nominal, inanimate, low-DP and 3rd person. These features should be infrequent in discourse. P's in the corpora are indeed rarely animate/human and 1st and 2nd person, but they are neither overwhelmingly lexical, nor new. Therefore, these predictions are only partly supported.

Table 8.7 displays the distribution of the roles (only A) within each feature. The percentages stand for the proportions of A's and P's among all arguments in the sample with a given feature. To obtain the corresponding proportions for P, one can simply subtract these numbers from 100%. With the exception of the 3rd person, the distributions are quite compact and mostly contain values less than 50% or greater than 50%. This makes them good candidates for explaining cross-linguistic generalizations. Overall, if an argument (A or P) is non-lexical, human, 1st or 2nd person, and not new, it is more likely to be A; if it is lexical, non-human and new, it is more likely to be P. As for the 3rd-person arguments, they tend to be P rather than A, but there are exceptions in the data.

Table 8.6. *Distribution of features of P within the role (%)*

Study	Corpus	Lexical	Human	1st & 2nd	New
Du Bois 1987	*Pear Story* narratives in Sakapultek	45.8	10	NA	24.7
Chui 1992	*Ghost* narratives in Chinese	84.3	NA	NA	33.6
Ashby & Bentivoglio 1993	interviews (monologues) in French	67.4	NA	NA	29.7
	interviews (monologues) in Spanish	59.7	NA	NA	24.9
Dahl & Fraurud 1996	written Swedish	NA	13	NA	NA
Sutherland-Smith 1996	Several narratives in modern Hebrew	56.3	NA	NA	23.9
Dahl 2000	spontaneous conversations in Swedish	NA	16.4 (animate)	4.3	NA
Allen & Schröder 2003	Inuktitut child language	6	21.1 (animate)	14.3	27
Arnold 2003	Mapudungun narrative texts	85.1	NA	NA	47.8
Everett 2009	English talk shows	59.7	12.6	NA	NA
	Portuguese talk shows	84.7	6.1	NA	NA
Lin 2009	Chinese conversations	80	NA	NA	55.6
	Chinese narratives	94	NA	NA	72.5
	Chinese written texts	81.8	NA	NA	70.1
Schiborr 2016	English autobiographical narratives	47.8	12.4	4.8	NA
Haig & Thiele 2016	Northern Kurdish traditional narratives	54.7	25.9	6.8	NA
Abidifar 2016	Persian stimulus-based narratives	52.7	18	0	NA
Mosel & Schnell 2016	Teop traditional narratives	43	43.3	4.7	NA
Schnell 2016	Vera'a traditional narratives	56.1	35.3	8.6	NA

Do the results in Table 8.7 support the predictions of the strategy 'Mark Weak Cues, Don't Mark Strong Cues'? Let us first have a look at the weak cues and the predictions for the first part, 'Mark Weak Cues'. We expected nominal (lexical) and 3rd-person arguments to be A only infrequently. This is supported by the corpus data mostly, although two out of seven data points of

Table 8.7. Distribution of the roles within the features (only A shown) (%)

Study	Corpus	Lexical A	Non-lexical A	Human A	Non-Human A	1st & 2nd A	3rd A	New A	Non-new A
Du Bois 1987	*Pear Story* narratives in Sakapultek	11.9	63.8	91.7	0	NA	NA	12.5	58.6
Chui 1992	*Ghost* narratives in Chinese	33.6	81.6	NA	NA	NA	NA	9	62.1
Ashby & Bentivoglio 1993	interviews (monologues) in French	9	74.1	NA	NA	NA	NA	0	58.7
	interviews (monologues) in Spanish	9.3	70	NA	NA	NA	NA	1.4	57
Dahl & Fraurud 1996	written Swedish	NA	NA	75.3	25.9	NA	NA	NA	NA
Sutherland-Smith 1996	Several narratives in modern Hebrew	14	74.6	NA	NA	NA	NA	11.3	63.8
Dahl 2000	spontaneous conversations in Swedish	NA	NA	88.8 (animate)	6.9	92.9 (ego)	27.5	NA	NA
Allen & Schröder 2003	Inuktitut child language	15.9	51.3	82.7 (animate)	1.4	87.2	2.9	2.4	58.1
Arnold 2003	Mapudungun narrative texts	14.9	85.1	NA	NA	NA	NA	2.5	65.4
Everett 2009	English talk shows	13.8	68.9	87.8	8.4	NA	NA	NA	NA
	Portuguese talk shows	16.4	83.7	93.1	11.6	NA	NA	NA	NA
Lin 2009	Chinese conversations	20	80	NA	NA	NA	NA	21.7	66.4
	Chinese narratives	16.1	92.9	NA	NA	NA	NA	14.7	76.1
	Chinese written texts	16.3	82.2	NA	NA	NA	NA	22.8	72.9
Schiborr 2016	English autobiographical narratives	13.9	62.3	87.6	7.1	92	28.8	NA	NA
Haig & Thiele 2016	Northern Kurdish traditional narratives	19	65.4	78.6	4.2	82.5	41.7	NA	NA
Abidifar 2016	Persian stimulus-based narratives	19.9	63.7	83.7	4.3	100	48.1	NA	NA
Mosel & Schnell 2016	Teop traditional narratives	22.5	67.2	74	9.6	87.6	50.3	NA	NA
Schnell 2016	Vera'a traditional narratives	16.4	75.8	79.9	10.8	72.7	57.8	NA	NA

the 3rd person are slightly greater than 50 per cent. Also, we expected pronominal, high-DP/animate and 1st and 2nd-person arguments to be P's only rarely. This is also what we find in the corpora: non-lexical, non-new and human/animate arguments are unlikely to be P's, as well as the 1st and 2nd-person arguments. Therefore, the predictions are supported. The cues that are marked formally are indeed weak in terms of their frequencies. Still, there are a few features with low probability of A (i.e., non-human A and new A) that do not lead to widely attested marking in the cross-linguistic data. Therefore, the strategy overgenerates predictions.

If we focus on the second part of the strategy, 'Don't Mark Strong Cues' and examine the features with particularly high median probabilities $\mathbb{P}$ (Role| Feature), we will see that the predictions are met both for A (non-lexical and 1st & 2nd person) and for P (lexical, non-human, new, animate and predominantly 3rd person).

8.4.3 Data from Informal Conversations

In order to control for the register and add the proportions of definite and discourse-given arguments, I also took data from informal spoken conversations in five languages: English and Russian (Indo-European), Lao (Tai-Kadai), N||ng (Tuu) and Ruuli (Bantu). The annotation for English, Lao and Russian was performed by myself. The annotation for N||ng and Ruuli was performed by Alena Witzlack-Makarevich (the database is available upon request). More details about the data and method can be found in Levshina (2021a).

The A and P arguments in transitive clauses were coded for the following variables:

- lexicality: lexical (common and proper nouns, adjectival or other nominalizations) or non-lexical (diverse pronouns and implicit arguments);
- person: 1st, 2nd or 3rd;
- semantic class: animate (human, animal, kinship term, organization) or inanimate (physical object, abstract entity, event);
- definiteness (identifiability): definite, indefinite (specific or non-specific);
- givenness (discourse accessibility): given (mentioned previously or inferable from context) or new.

The probabilities of features given A and P are displayed in Figures 8.1 and 8.2, respectively. The proportions that represent complementary features (e.g., Non-lexical vs. Lexical, Animate vs. Inanimate) are a mirror image of each other. Figure 8.1 shows that A's are nearly exclusively non-lexical, animate, definite and discourse-given. As for the person, we do not see consistent results. In Russian, English and N||ng, the A's are predominantly 1st and

8.4 Reverse Engineering

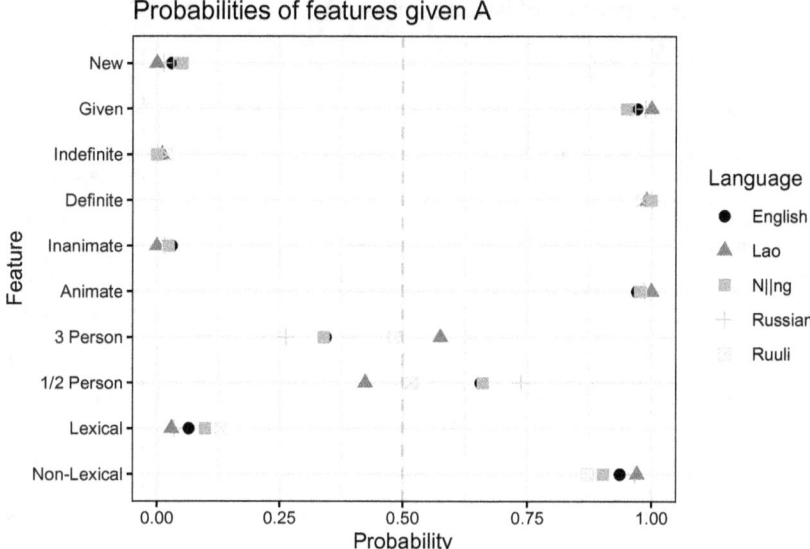

Figure 8.1 Probabilities of different features of A based on corpora of spontaneous conversations in five languages

2nd person, but this is not the case in Lao, which has more 3rd person A's than 1st/2nd-person ones. This may have to do with the fact that the largest text in the Lao corpus can be characterized as gossip about other people. Also, in Ruuli, the probabilities of 1st/2nd-person and 3rd-person A's are nearly equal. This type of probability is highly sensitive to the topic of conversations. When gossiping, for example, people use more 3rd-person subjects than 1st or 2nd-person subjects. These descriptive observations are supported by mixed-effects Poisson regression models (see Levshina 2021a).

Figure 8.2 shows the probabilities of the features given P. Many P's are non-lexical. The 1st and 2nd-person P's are very unlikely, while 3rd-person P's are extremely likely. P also tends to be inanimate. It is also more frequently definite and given than indefinite and new. Again, all these effects are statistically significant.

How do these results relate to the predictions? As for the strategy 'Mark Impostors, Don't Mark the Authentic', the prediction was that A's will be predominantly pronominal, animate and high-DP, which means in this context given and definite. This is what we observe. As for the weaker prediction that A's are usually 1st and 2nd person, it is not supported. There is a lot of variation. If we go back to our predictions for P's, we will recall that we expected to find predominantly nominal, or lexical arguments and the

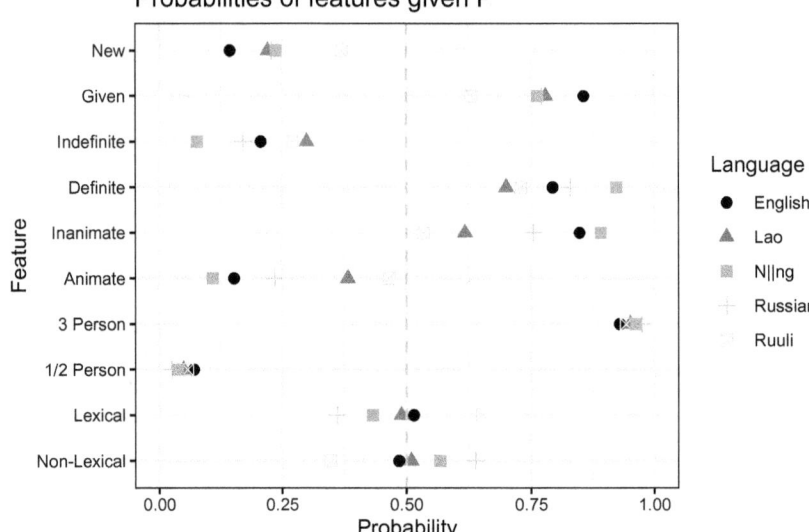

Figure 8.2 Probabilities of different features of P based on corpora of spontaneous conversations in five languages

3rd-person referents among P's. The first prediction is not borne out, while the second one is very clearly supported.

As for the strategy 'Mark Weirdos, Don't Mark Normals', we predicted that A will be frequently pronominal and infrequently nominal. This prediction is supported. Lexical A's are very rare. They should also usually have 1st or 2nd-person reference and rarely 3rd-person reference. This prediction is confirmed only partly in some languages. If we look at P arguments, we expected them to be frequently nominal, inanimate/low-DP and 3rd person and rarely pronominal, animate/high-DP, and 1st and 2nd person. These predictions hold only for animacy and person. Nominality displays a lot of variation, whereas definiteness and givenness have the opposite results from what was expected: definite and given P's are in fact predominant.

Now let us consider the third strategy, 'Mark the Weak Cues, Don't Mark Strong Cues'. This is connected with the probabilities of roles given features. The plot displaying the probabilities of A given the ten features is shown in Figure 8.3. The plot with the same probabilities for P is a mirror image of this one, and is not displayed.

We expected nominal (lexical), and 3rd-person arguments to be A only infrequently, because this would support the sub-strategy 'Mark Weak Cues'. This is supported by the corpus data. Also, the prediction was to find fewer

8.4 Reverse Engineering

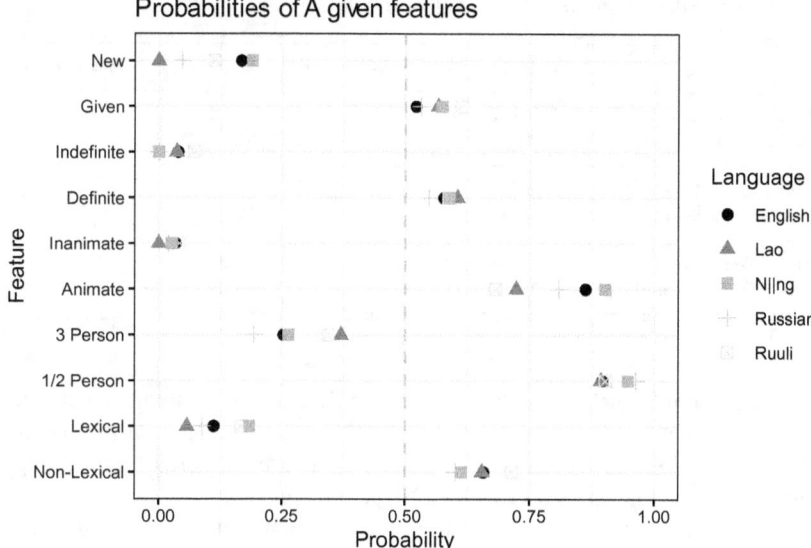

Figure 8.3 Probabilities of the role A given different features based on corpora of spontaneous conversations in five languages

pronominal, high-DP/animate and 1st and 2nd-person P's than A's. These expectations are supported by the data. The arguments that are case-marked are indeed weak cues. As for 'Don't Mark Strong Cues', the predictions are met both for A, which has a high probability given non-lexical and 1st & 2nd-person referents, and for P, which has a high probability given lexical, 3rd-person, inanimate, indefinite and new referents.

8.4.4 Summary of Findings

In this section I have tested reverse-engineered predictions based on the cross-linguistic patterns in differential case marking. These predictions were formulated for three marking strategies, which are based on the available explanations of the typological data involving disambiguation pressure and iconicity of markedness. We expected to find relative frequencies of different A and P that would account for the typological data. A summary of the results for the three strategies is shown in Table 8.8. If one cell contains two words, e.g., 'Mostly/Partly', the former refers to the data recycled from the previous studies (Section 8.4.2), and the latter refers to the new data from spontaneous conversations (Section 8.4.3).

The weakest support is found for the strategy based on iconicity of markedness, 'Mark Weirdos, Don't Mark Normals'. Its predictions are

Table 8.8. *Reverse-engineered predictions and the data*

Marking strategy	Prediction for A distribution	Prediction for P distribution
Mark Impostors	Mostly	Mostly/Partly
Don't Mark the Authentic	Mostly	Mostly/Partly
Mark Weak Cues	Mostly/Yes	Yes
Don't Mark Strong Cues	Yes	Yes
Mark Weirdos	Partly	Partly
Don't Mark Normals	Partly	Partly

supported only partly. The first strategy based on ideas about the distinguishing function of differential marking, 'Mark Impostors, Don't Mark the Authentic', does better. Most of its predictions are supported. The exceptions concern the person for A's, which displays more variation than predicted, and nominality (lexicality) for P's. Especially in the conversations, there are fewer nominal objects than expected. The strategy 'Mark Weak Cues, Don't Mark Strong Cues' provides the best account of the observed cross-linguistic tendencies, especially the second part 'Don't Mark Strong Cues'. This strategy is also related to the distinguishing function of marking. From the efficiency perspective, this strategy has a straightforward interpretation in terms of the principle of negative correlation between accessibility and costs. For example, in the case of differential object marking where animate objects are marked and inanimate ones are unmarked, this principle guides the addressee who is processing an inanimate argument that the most probable interpretation (i.e., the P role) should be taken. This reasoning is similar to Haspelmath's hypothesis about differential object marking and animacy:

Since more inanimate nominals have P-function than animate nominals, hearers are less surprised when they encounter an inanimate P-argument and therefore have less need for special coding. (Haspelmath 2021a: 12)

Importantly, the conditional probabilities of A and P given specific features of the arguments, i.e., $\mathbb{P}$ (Role|Feature), which are associated with the winning strategy, are distributed quite uniformly across different registers and languages. It is logical to assume that cross-linguistic universals should correspond to similar distributions across and within languages. Therefore, the homogeneous distributions of $\mathbb{P}$ (Role|Feature) are good candidates for explaining the universal scale effects.

Some of the strategies overgenerate predictions. This means that there are discourse tendencies that do not have correspondences in the cross-linguistic distribution of differential case marking. This is relevant for subjects in particular. We still need to account for this fact.

These results support the more general principle formulated by Haspelmath (2021b: 125): 'Deviations from usual associations of role rank and referential prominence tend to be coded by longer grammatical forms if the coding is asymmetric.' Note that by role rank it is meant that the A argument is ranked higher than the P argument, whereas referential prominence is associated with the values on the left in the animacy, definiteness and other scales in (3). Based on the findings presented above, we are able to formulate this principle in a more precise manner. Namely, Haspelmath's 'deviations from usual associations' correspond to low conditional probabilities of roles given referential features. Moreover, we have identified the functional pressure responsible for this. It has to do with weak and strong cues that are supposed to help the addressee infer who did what to whom.

Note that we formulated the predictions for A and P without considering the properties of the other argument. In other words, we did not consider different scenarios, e.g., a 'downstream scenario', where A is more prominent than P, an 'upstream scenario', where P is more prominent than A, and a 'balanced scenario', where A and P have equal prominence (Haspelmath 2021b). The reason for this is that the synchronic evidence for co-argument sensitivity of the Malayalam type, or global marking, is rare in comparison with local differential marking of the Spanish or Turkish type, which depends (at least, in the majority of cases) on the properties of the argument that is marked or unmarked.

8.5 Development of Differential Case Marking

Differential case marking emerges as a result of differential reduction and differential enhancement of case forms. The former is described less often than the latter. However, there are a few examples. In particular, Harari, a Semitic language, case-marks only definite objects, while in Old Harari the Accusative suffix also marked indefinite nouns (Tosco 1994).

As for differential enhancement, Old Russian represents a particularly interesting case (Seržant 2019). The emergent differential object marking comes from Proto-Slavic. Due to the overall loss of all word-final consonants, in most Proto-Slavic declensions, the singular Accusative and Nominative markers were phonetically indistinguishable. Over time, these turned into zero markers. The Genitive case marker then replaced the old zero Accusative on some pronouns and on animate nouns in some declension classes. The historical data suggest that the emergence of differential object marking was explained by the fact that subject and object forms were indistinguishable.

We know from the corpus data that pronouns and animate nouns are less likely to be objects than inanimate nouns. Therefore, this development can be regarded as a case of efficient formal enhancement.

When a marker emerges, it often expands from one context to new types of referents. In Spanish, the marker *a* was first used on strong personal pronouns referring to humans. Now it is used with animate (or at least human) definite and specific objects (at least in Standard Spanish), whose interpretation as direct objects is also not very accessible. As for indefinite animate objects, there is variation. Inanimate objects are usually unmarked (von Heusinger and Kaiser 2007). They represent the last bastion of zero marking, although instances of marked inanimate objects were attested even in Old Spanish (García García 2018), which means that there has been sufficient time to develop marking for them, too. As shown in Section 8.4, inanimate and indefinite arguments have higher probability of being objects than subjects, so the lack of case marking is efficient.

A similar development happened in Persian. The object marker *râ* first appeared on the 1st and 2nd-person pronouns, then spread to definite animate objects, then definite objects, but was still optional. In Modern Persian, it became obligatory on all definite objects and topical indefinite objects (Dalrymple and Nikolaeva 2011: 203). Focal indefinite objects thus remain the last bastion of zero marking.

Similarly, in Hindi the use of object marking started from the pronouns representing speech act participants. In the fourteenth century, the marking of those pronouns was obligatory. In other situations, it was optional. Later, the frequency of marking increased in human nouns. In modern Hindi, they are always marked. If we take only small clauses (complements of main verbs), the marking was first optional on human and inanimate nouns. In modern Hindi, it is obligatory with human nouns and very frequent with inanimate nouns (Montaut 2018).

These examples demonstrate that marking expands depending on the accessibility of the interpretation of an argument as A or P. Notably, languages choose different cut-off points and levels of optionality. How to explain this fact is an intriguing question.

Not all researchers agree that differential marking is actually explained by communicative pressures, however. In particular, Cristofaro (2019) argues that the distributional restrictions on the use of an additional subject or object marker in marking splits (e.g., only with animate objects or nominal subjects) originate from the reinterpretation of an element of a pre-existing construction with similar distributional restrictions. For instance, some object markers come from topical markers. Since topics are usually definite, animate and pronominal (e.g., *As for me*, . . .), the marking has spread to objects with all or some of these features, as in Kanuri:

(13)   Kanuri: Nilo-Saharan (Cyffer 1998: 52, cited from Cristofaro 2019: 28)
   a.   *Músa   shí-ga   cúro.*
        Musa   3SG-ACC   saw
        'Musa saw him.'
   b.   *wú-ga*
        1SG-as.for
        'as for me'

Topicality also plays a prominent role in Iemmolo's (2010) account. He observes that dislocated topical objects are case-marked in many Romance varieties. See also Dalrymple and Nikolaeva (2011).

The idea that differential object marking originates from topic markers does not exclude the efficiency explanation, in fact. Subjects tend to be the topic par excellence, while objects can be both topics and foci. In particular, Maslova (2003) reports that transitive sentences in Kolyma Yukaghir (a Yukaghir language spoken in the Russian Far East) have mostly topical subjects and topical objects (65 per cent), while topical subjects and focal objects are responsible only for approximately 35 per cent, and less than 1 per cent of all clauses have focal subjects and topical subjects. These numbers suggest that the probability that a focal nominal is an object is much higher than the probability that it is a subject. Focalness therefore serves as a perfect cue for objecthood, while topical objects may need some extra help to be distinguished from subjects, the primary topics. This can be interpreted as a manifestation of efficiency.

One can also say that the marking of topical objects is motivated by the need to attract the addressee's attention to a new topic (Diessel 2019: Section 11.6). The tendency to mark topical objects represents 'a hearer-oriented strategy to mark an atypical P argument that deviates from listener's linguistic expectations' (Diessel 2019: 244), especially in an unusual position. Therefore, there are good reasons to believe that topical objects are marked due to the principle of negative correlation between accessibility and costs.

While object markers can develop from topical markers, ergative markers can originate from focalizing constructions involving appositional pronominals and demonstratives, as in 'The farmer he/this killed the duckling' (McGregor 2008). These examples can also be explained by efficiency: new and focal agents are very untypical and therefore need extra marking.

In addition, markers participating in differential marking can develop from other case markers. Ergatives often emerge from ablatives, instrumentals, locatives and genitives. Object markers can also develop from various oblique markers, such as the dative marker *a* in Spanish, the genitive case marker *-a* in Russian, the comitative marker *saṇī* (*haṇī*) 'with' in Garhwali and Kumaoni, Indo-Aryan languages spoken in India (Montaut 2018: 308). Another source is different verbs, e.g., *bǎ* 'hold, take' in Chinese (Yang 1995: 165), the verbal root *lag* 'touch, be stuck to' > *lā* in Marathi (Montaut 2018: 307) or a copula or presentative verb *(-)(ʔ)à* in the Khoe languages (McGregor 2018).

I believe that reanalysis of other source constructions and markers does not constitute sufficient evidence against the efficiency account. Language users create new constructions from semantically compatible material at hand. What is important is that all these different scenarios lead to similar outcomes: a highly grammaticalized marker for subjects or objects, used in a similar fashion in diverse languages of the world. It is unlikely that such convergence can be explained by the lasting impact of the source constructions alone.

8.6 Experimental Evidence from Artificial Languages

This section discusses recent experimental work on differential argument marking. The experimental study of optional marking in Japanese by Kurumada and Jaeger (2015) was mentioned in Section 8.3.1. Other experiments involve an artificial miniature language. In a pioneering study, Fedzechkina, Jaeger and Newport (2012) used a language with optional object case marking that was not conditioned on the typicality of objects. The learners watched videos of transitive events and had to repeat the sentences in the artificial language. The subjects were always human, while 50 per cent of the objects were human and 50 per cent were inanimate. The participants also had a comprehension task and a production task in which they had to describe a novel transitive event. This procedure was repeated on several days. The experiment showed that the learners used significantly more case markers on atypical (animate) objects than on typical (inanimate) objects.

In the second experiment, the objects were always inanimate, while 50 per cent of the subjects were animate and 50 per cent were inanimate. In the production task, there was an increase in the use of marking with time, but there was no consistent direct effect of animacy on its own.

In a follow-up study, Fedzechkina, Newport and Jaeger (2016) used a language with either flexible or fixed word order, and optional marking. They found that learners dropped the case marker more often in the fixed-order language, while retaining it in the flexible-order language. Therefore, their behaviour mirrored the negative correlation between case marking and rigid word order observed across languages (see Section 6.3). There were also indications that untypical OSV order, which was used less often in the training phase, resulted in more case marking than the more typical SOV order.

A more recent study by Smith and Culbertson (2020) could not replicate the results in Fedzechkina et al. (2012). Importantly, the latter only involved language learning and no communication. However, when Smith and Culbertson (2020) carried out an interactive experiment that involved a director-matching task between a participant and Smeeble, a monster presented

8.6 Experimental Evidence from Artificial Languages

to the participants as the tutor in the artificial language,[4] the sentences produced by the participants exhibited the expected differential marking. Thus, language users make their languages efficient due to communicative pressures. The results found in learning-only experiments (see also Section 7.5) can be explained by a spillover from communication. Similar to D. Slobin's 'thinking for speaking', participants engage in 'learning for communicating'.

I have tested the distinguishing account in an online communication game, where two participants first learned an 'alien' language with optional case marking. The stimuli introducing the language showed two different aliens. Sometimes one of them was the agent, and the other the patient, and sometimes it was the other way round. Half of the objects in the alien language were case-marked, and half were unmarked. The dominant word order (75%) was SOV, but OSV was also used (25%).

In the communication game, one participant had to describe one of two pictures in the alien language so that the other participant could guess which picture was meant. They did it in turns. The goal was to earn as many points (correct matches) as possible. The pictures were of three types:

- 'Different Roles': Both pictures showed the same actions but had different Agent and Patient. I expected the participants to use the object marker the most frequently because there were no other cues to infer this information from.
- 'Different Actions': The two pictures showed different actions with the same Agent and Patient. In that case, I expected the participants to use the object marker the least frequently because it was clear from the visual context who did what to whom.
- 'All Different': The pictures showed different actions with different Agent and Patient. I expected the frequency of marking to be less frequent than in the first condition but more frequent than in the second condition because one could use the verb as a reliable cue for helping to choose between the pictures.

The proportions of marked object forms produced by twenty-eight pairs of participants are shown in Figure 8.4. On average, the chances of marking are low. Some of the pairs do not use marking in any situation. The participants probably rely on word order. Yet, the condition 'Different Roles' has on average the highest proportions of marked objects, as predicted. We do not find that 'Different Actions' has the lowest probability. Its mean and median values are in fact slightly higher than those of 'All Different', but the difference is not statistically significant. These results show that the availability of

---

[4] Smeeble's behaviour was based on a computational algorithm which approximated the behaviour of a rational user.

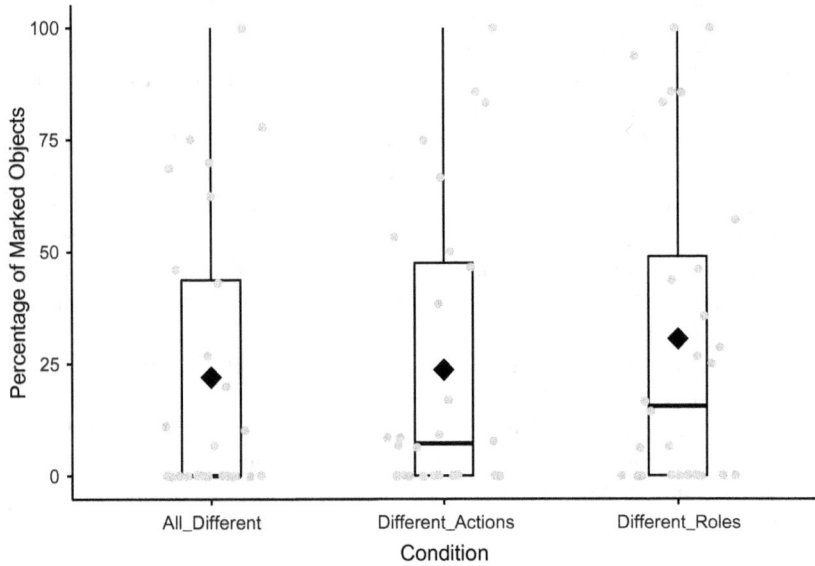

Figure 8.4 Proportions of marked object forms produced by different pairs of participants in the online communication game. The black diamonds show the mean proportions. The black lines in the boxes are the median values.

cues helping to choose between the referents can be responsible for differential marking, as predicted by the efficiency account developed here. If the information is present visually and fully accessible, there is no need to use case marking.

Finally, I should also mention here the study by Tal et al. (2022), who tested the hypothesis that given objects would be more frequently case-marked than new ones. This is related to the popular view that emergence of differential marking is driven by topicality (see Section 8.5). This prediction was not borne out. At the same time, it is possible that the relationship may be indirect: they do find that object marking is more frequent in OSV sentences, which are produced more frequently when the object is topicalized. As argued above, this is a manifestation of efficient behaviour.

8.7 Conclusions

This chapter discussed diverse typological, corpus-based and experimental evidence related to differential argument marking of subject and object. The different types of evidence converge, supporting the efficiency-based interpretation of differential marking based on the principle of negative correlation

8.7 Conclusions

between accessibility and costs. This chapter provides a novel contribution to this well-explored topic because the intuitions about the causes that lead to the emergence of cross-linguistic patterns are captured in the form of measurable probabilities that can be found in corpus data. Of particular importance here are the conditional probabilities of the role given the referential features of arguments that determine the accessibility of the intended role interpretation. Also, this chapter demonstrates that we can disentangle some competing explanations of differential marking using experiments with artificial language learning and communication.

9 Efficient Use of Function Words in English Alternations

9.1 Construction–Filler Predictability and Efficiency

Chapter 2 discussed examples of efficient language use where a function word can be used or omitted depending on the accessibility of the intended semantic and syntactic interpretation. This chapter provides some additional illustrations of constructional variation of this kind. I will discuss the following alternations:

- stative verb + (*at*) *home*, as in *More and more young fathers stay (at) home;*
- *help* + (*to*) Infinitive, as in *I helped him (to) install the software;*
- *go (and)* Verb, as in *Go (and) bring me a beer.*

The main focus will be on the relationships between the constructions and the lexemes that fill in their slots. For example, *give, show* and *send* are frequent slot fillers in the Verb slot of the double-object dative construction, e.g., *She gave/showed/sent him a letter*. The construction *help* + (*to*) Infinitive has slot fillers in the Infinitive slot, such as *install, make, understand, get*. There is overwhelming evidence that language users learn and store information about the probabilistic relationships between constructions and their slot fillers (e.g., Goldberg, Casenhiser and Sethuraman 2004, 2005; Gries, Hampe and Schönefeld 2005; Ellis and Ferreira-Junior 2009; Taylor 2012). This is why it is logical to assume that the associations between a lexical slot filler and the construction influence the probability of using optional function words.

Based on the principle of negative correlation between accessibility and costs, we can formulate the following hypothesis:

(1)   Hypothesis of Construction–Lexeme Accessibility and Formal Length

   The less accessible (probable) a lexeme given a construction or a construction given a lexeme, the greater the chances of the longer constructional alternative; conversely, the more accessible (probable) the lexeme given the construction, the greater the chances of the shorter variant.

In order to measure the accessibility of a construction and its lexeme, we can compute two measures. The first measure is the probability of the lexeme given the construction. More exactly, I will use informativity, which represents a log-transformed inverse of the corresponding conditional probability, as shown in (2):

(2) $\quad InfoLex = -\log_2 P(L|C) = -\log_2 \dfrac{P(L,C)}{P(C)} = -\log_2 \dfrac{f(L,C)}{f(C)}$

where $P(L, C)$ stands for the probability of the filler in the slot, and $P(C)$ represents the probability of the construction. In practice, $P(L, C)/P(C)$ is measured as the token frequency of the lexeme in the construction divided by the token frequency of the construction in a corpus. Because of the negative log-transformation, high probabilities correspond to low informativity, whereas low probabilities correspond to high informativity. The logarithm base 2 is commonly used in information theory to measure information in bits. This measure reflects how unexpected the lexeme is if we encounter the construction.

The second probabilistic measure is informativity of the construction given a particular lexeme. It is shown in (3):

(3) $\quad InfoCxn = -\log_2 P(C|L) = -\log_2 \dfrac{P(L,C)}{P(L)} = -\log_2 \dfrac{f(L,C)}{f(L)}$

where $P(L, C)/P(L)$, again, can be obtained from the token frequency of the lexeme in the construction, divided by the token frequency of the lexeme in a corpus. This measure reflects how unlikely the lexeme is to be found in this construction.

These two measures have analogues in usage-based Construction Grammar, which are known as *Attraction*, i.e., the conditional probability of a lexeme given a construction, and *Reliance*, i.e., the conditional probability of a construction given a lexeme (Schmid 2000), or *Faith* (Gries et al. 2005). Due to the negative log-transformation, the higher informativity, the smaller *Attraction* or *Reliance (Faith)*. Although many corpus linguists find it useful to compute one bidirectional measure that represents the association between a construction and one of its collexemes (e.g., Stefanowitsch and Gries 2003 and later work), Schmid has argued that *Attraction* and *Reliance* represent two different types of information, each valuable on its own (e.g., Schmid and Küchenhoff 2013). This approach is pursued here, as well.

Accessibility is then associated with high predictability and low informativity of a lexeme given the construction, or the other way round. A series of quantitative analyses presented below provide statistical evidence that accessibility allows us to predict the use or omission of function words (the particle *to*, preposition *at* and conjunction *and*), such that higher accessibility is associated with the shorter forms without the function words, and lower accessibility is associated with the longer variants with the function words, in accordance with the Hypothesis of Construction–Lexeme Accessibility and Formal Length in (1). Section 9.2 discusses the use of *(at) home*. Section 9.3 focuses on the construction *help + (to)* Infinitive, followed by the discussion of *go (and)* Verb in Section 9.4.

9.2 Stay *(at)* *Home*, Save Lives!

The present section discusses the use of locative adverbials *home* and *at home* in US English. When the meaning is directional, e.g., *go/return/bring (someone) home* or *a long way home*, no preposition is used. The forms *home* and *at home* can only be interchangeable when the meaning is locative, as in (4):

(4)   a. *Dads who stay **at home*** (COCA, Magazines)
       b. *Stories abound of men **staying home** to look after newborns* (COCA, Magazines)

One of the few mentions of this alternation can be found in Huddleston and Pullum (2002: 683). They claim that *home* marks location only as a subject-oriented complement, as in *Are you home? We stayed home*, but not in other contexts, e.g., **I kept my computer home* or **Home, the children were playing cricket*.

At the same time, the use of these expressions attracts language learners' attention, judging from numerous discussions on internet fora.[1] Moreover, in the period of the COVID-19 pandemic, there are many slogans advising people to stay home or at home, e.g., *Keep calm and stay at home* or *Stay Home, Protect the NHS* [UK National Health Service], *Save Lives*. I will focus on US English, where this variation seems to be more common, as one can conclude from language users' intuitions and experts' comments.[2]

As shown in Levshina (2018a), the use of *at* depends on many diverse factors. The data from the Corpus of Contemporary American English suggest that the bare form is strongly preferred when *(at) home* is preceded by *back*:

(5)   *It's good to be back home again.*

The short form is also strongly preferred when someone has returned home:

(6)   a. *Darling, I'm **home**!*
       b. *I was **home** from college for the summer, and I said I'd do it.* (NPR Weekend)

In contrast, the long form *at home* is nearly always preferred in a figurative sense, when the construction expresses one's feeling of being comfortable and at ease in a particular situation:

(7)   *And he's probably more comfortable and **at home** with his stage makeup every day.* (Ind Geraldo)

---

[1] E.g., https://english.stackexchange.com/questions/21286/im-home-or-im-at-home, www.usingenglish.com/forum/threads/68883-Correct-Usage-home-or-at-home and numerous others (last access 18 July 2022).

[2] E.g., www.bbc.co.uk/worldservice/learningenglish/grammar/learnit/learnitv240.shtml (last access 18 July 2022).

9.2 Stay (at) Home, Save Lives!

Another case is a semantic generalization, when *(at) home* is used to refer to the city or country where one lives. Here, the longer form is preferred, as well:

(8) But for all his achievements on the international scene, the problems he faces ***at home*** *seem insurmountable.* (ABC Nightline)

This can be seen as a manifestation of the principle of negative correlation between accessibility and costs because the semantic extensions are less accessible than the literal meaning.

The long form is also much more likely with transitive verbs (*I build furniture at home*), as sentence adjuncts (*At home, I drink only tea*), attributes (*Their stores at home are even emptier than here*), in existential constructions (*There is too much stress at home*), and as part of an elliptic structure (*Finally, at home!*).

In all these cases, there are quite strong preferences for one or the other form. The only type of context that exhibits substantial variation is when *(at) home* is an adjunct of an intransitive predicate (e.g., *I'm home*), the meaning is literal, there is no semantics of arrival and the adjunct is not preceded by *back*. The variants *home* and *at home* are almost equally distributed in these contexts.

In order to test the Hypothesis of Construction–Lexeme Accessibility and Formal Length formulated in (1), I extracted all occurrences of the alternation from the spoken component of COCA, focusing only on these contexts. Set expressions (e.g., *charity begins at home, be home free, romp home*) were excluded. After manual cleaning, there were 4,032 occurrences with 71 different verbs. The bare variant was used 2,623 times (65%), while the prepositional form occurred 1,409 times (35%). The frequencies of each verb with *(at) home* and the total frequencies of the verb in the spoken subcorpus were obtained. Based on that information, the informativity scores were computed for each verb, using the approach described in Section 9.1.

The data are distributed in a rather straightforward way. Most verbs are followed by *at home* only. Only seven verbs are followed both by the prepositional and bare variants in the sample: *be, stay, belong, sit, remain, wait* and *live*. Six of those verbs (with the exception of *belong*, which occurs only once with *home* and once with *at home*) are among the top twelve verbs that have the highest frequency with *(at) home*. They are displayed in Table 9.1. In particular, the verbs *be, stay* and *sit* have the highest proportions of the bare variant. Notably, they are also the top most frequent verbs that occur with both variants. This means that they have the lowest informativity of the lexeme given the construction. Moreover, the verbs *stay* and *sit* also have very low informativity of the construction given the lexeme in comparison with the other verbs. All this supports the Hypothesis of Construction–Lexeme Accessibility and Formal Length.

Table 9.1. *Frequency and informativity of the top twelve verbs most frequently used with locative* (at) home

Verb	Bare variant	Prepositional variant	Total frequency with *(at) home*	InfoLex	InfoCxn
be	1796 (77.1%)	505 (22.9%)	2301	0.81	11.06
stay	760 (76.9%)	229 (23.1%)	989	2.03	4.83
sit	62 (24%)	196 (76%)	258	3.97	6.67
live	2 (1.5%)	135 (98.5%)	137	4.88	8.38
work	0 (0%)	66 (100%)	66	5.93	10.28
watch	0 (0%)	54 (100%)	54	6.22	9.22
die	0 (0%)	21 (100%)	21	7.58	10.15
start	0 (0%)	17 (100%)	17	7.89	11.79
wait	1 (5.9%)	16 (94.1%)	17	7.89	10.57
play	0 (0%)	15 (100%)	15	8.07	11.35
happen	0 (0%)	14 (100%)	14	8.17	12.64
remain	1 (7.1%)	13 (92.9%)	14	8.17	9.57

To summarize, we observe here accessibility effects. If a verb is highly expected to occur before *(at) home*, the bare form is preferred or permitted. With most verbs, the full form is the norm, although we observe occasional uses of the bare form. The effect of a verb as a strong or weak cue to the following *(at) home* is less clear, because the verb *be*, which occurs with the bare variant the most frequently, is multifunctional and does not serve as a strong cue for *(at) home*. The corpus annotation, however, does not allow me to distinguish between the auxiliary and lexical uses of *be*, which may have different representations in the mental lexicon, so which direction of predictability is more important remains an open question. We could also interpret some of the other features, such as figurative semantics and syntactic function different from the intransitive use, as indicators of lower accessibility of the construction. It is not surprising, then, that they are usually associated with the full form.

9.3 Efficient Use of *Help (to)* Infinitive

This section discusses the English construction with *help* followed by the infinitive with or without *to*, as in the examples below:

(9) a. *If this book does not* **help** *you* **to survive** *the Zombie Apocalypse, a full refund may be obtained from the author.*[3]

---

[3] www.amazon.co.uk/Z-Day-UK-surviving-Apocalypse-Britain/dp/1490389873 (last access 18 July 2022).

9.3 Efficient Use of *Help (to)* Infinitive

b. *Just to be on the safe side you might want to start doing these 8 exercises that will **help** you **survive** the zombie apocalypse.*[4]

The construction *help* + (*to*) Infinitive is a rare case where the choice between the bare and the *to*-infinitive is possible in Present-Day English. This choice depends on many factors. For instance, it has been argued that the variant with the bare infinitive designates a more active involvement of the Helper in carrying out the event expressed by the infinitival complement (Dixon 1991: 199). Consider the following examples:

(10)   (Dixon 1991: 199)

   a. *John **helped** Mary **eat** the pudding (he ate half).*
   b. *John **helped** Mary **to eat** the pudding (by guiding the spoon to her mouth, since she was still an invalid).*

When *to* is omitted, as in (10a), the sentence is likely to describe a cooperative effort where Mary and John ate the pudding together; when *to* is included, as in (10b), the sentence means that John acted as a facilitator for Mary, who actually ate the pudding herself (Dixon 1991: 199, 230). Similarly, Duffley (1992: Section 2.3) suggests that the use of the *to*-infinitive evokes help as a condition that enables the Helpee to bring about the event denoted by the infinitive. It has also been argued that animate Helpers have a potentially greater involvement in the event (Lind 1983). Indeed, Lohmann (2011) finds that animate Helpers have higher odds of the bare infinitive than inanimate Helpers, although the effect is not very strong. These tendencies might be explained by the higher accessibility of the cooperative interpretation, although more evidence is needed to defend this claim. Also, many researchers have questioned the relevance of this semantic distinction. For example, Huddleston and Pullum (2002: 1244) argue that there are numerous contexts and examples where this distinction cannot be traced. Similar claims were made by McEnery and Xiao (2005).

Another relevant factor is the principle of avoidance of identity, or *horror aequi*. *Horror aequi* is a widespread tendency to avoid repetition of identical elements (Rohdenburg 2003), which was discussed in Section 4.4. Avoidance of identity helps to avoid similarity-based interference. When the verb *help* is itself preceded by *to*, the following infinitive is usually without *to* (Biber et al. 1999: 737), as in the following example:

(11)   *Sorry, but how is this supposed **to help** answer the question? (GloWbE, GB)*[5]

---

[4] http://steadystrength.com/8-exercises-that-will-help-you-survive-the-zombie-apocalypse/ (last access 18 July 2022).
[5] This annotation means that the sentence is taken from the GloWbE corpus, a subcorpus from Great Britain www.english-corpora.org/glowbe (last access 4 August 2022).

The next factor has to do with the principle of reduction of cognitive complexity (Rohdenburg 1996), which was discussed in Section 2.4.2. Cognitive complexity here depends on the number of words between *help* and the infinitive. Consider an example of a complex environment below, where the distance between *help* and the infinitive is six words.

(12)   ...*it's a way for me to make a contribution, to **help** the country in a small way **to get back** on its feet.* (GloWbE, GB)

The longer the distance, the more likely it is that the infinitive will be marked by the particle *to*. This effect has already been explained from the efficiency perspective in Section 2.4.2. The greater the distance between the matrix verb and the infinitive, the less accessible the mental representation of the matrix verb. Low accessibility leads to more formal coding. Moreover, there is an interaction between distance and *horror aequi*: the more words there are between *help* and the infinitive, the weaker the influence of *horror aequi* (Lohmann 2011; Levshina 2018b).

It has also been shown that the inflectional forms of the verb *help* have individual preferences for the bare or *to*-infinitive. In particular, Lohmann (2011) observes that the form *helping* tends to be more frequently used with the *to*-infinitive in British English than the other inflectional forms of *help* (see also Levshina 2018b). According to Rohdenburg (2009: 317), the effect of *helping* has an analogy with *daring* and *needing*, which differ from all forms of *dare* and *need* by being virtually always associated with marked infinitives. In addition to that, there is a weakly significant preference of the 3rd-person singular form *helps* for the *to*-infinitive in comparison with the base form (Lohmann 2011). As we will see, *helping* is the least frequent inflected form that occurs in this construction, so the principle of negative correlation between accessibility and costs may play a role here, as well.

The presence or absence of the Helpee is another relevant factor. Biber et al. (1999: 735) show that the bare infinitive is particularly dominant in the pattern *help* + NP + infinitive clause. This observation is also supported by Lohmann (2011). Similarly, it matters whether the form of *help* is passive or active: According to McEnery and Xiao (2005), the passive form should always take a *to*-infinitive. One could again think about the low accessibility of such constructions as a reason for preferring the longer form. As for the complement, one can find examples of both the bare and *to*-forms of passive infinitives, as shown below.

(13)   a. *If rural voices are important – the bread basket, our farmers, our miners – then an electoral approach, not a pure popular vote, **helps** them **to be heard**.* (GloWbE, USA, general, 288902)
       b. *Thank you so much for sharing and **helping** our Vets **be heard**!* (GloWbE, USA, blog, 3177307)

Moreover, the shorter variant with the bare infinitive is considered to be less formal than the one with the marked infinitive (e.g., Rohdenburg 1996: 159; see also Biber et al. 1999: 736–737). This may be due to the fact that formal expressions are used in situations with less common ground between the participants. Lower accessibility of information can lead to more costly expressions. Across cultures, the association between formality and verbosity becomes conventionalized, with speech registers and styles as a result.

In addition, previous studies show that the bare infinitive has been gradually replacing the *to*-infinitive after *help* over the last two centuries. A corpus study by Rohdenburg (2009: 318–319) shows that the infinitive marker *to* was dropped very rarely in British and American English with authors born before the end of the eighteenth century, but there was a significant increase in the dropping of the marker by the end of the nineteenth century. This tendency continued in US English also in the twentieth century. British English speakers followed suit with some delay. Similarly, McEnery and Xiao (2005) find that the bare infinitive is used more frequently in the British and American corpora from 1991 than in the data from 1961, and that the American variant of *help* is more frequently used with the bare infinitive (see also Mair 2002). Therefore, we are dealing with regional variation in differential formal reduction.

Finally, it is necessary to mention phonological factors. There is some evidence that the use of *to* in different constructions depends on prosody. Wasow et al. (2015), in particular, found an effect of prosody on the use of the bare or *to*-infinitive in their investigation of the DO-BE construction, e.g., *All we want to do is (to) celebrate*. Namely, they discovered that *to* was used to eliminate stress clash when both the copula and the first syllable of the infinitive after *be* were stressed (see also Schlüter 2003). Lohmann (2011) tested two other phonetic variables, namely, whether the infinitive begins with a vowel, and whether the first syllable of the infinitive is stressed. Neither of the variables had a significant effect on the choice between the forms of the infinitive. In Levshina (2022a) I investigated the potential impact of stress clash and stress lapse more directly, but found no effect either.

In the remaining part of this section, I will test the Hypothesis of Construction–Lexeme Accessibility and Formal Length in order to see if the probability of the infinitive given the construction, or the other way round, plays a role in the formal variation. Since the construction with *help* is not very frequent, and the distribution is skewed in favour of the bare infinitive, especially in US English and in informal registers, I used the British data set of Google Books Ngrams, which is based on books published in Great Britain.[6]

---

[6] http://storage.googleapis.com/books/ngrams/books/datasetsv2.html (last access 18 July). I used Version 2 (marked as 20120701), which provides part-of-speech tags and is based on improved OCR methods and more accurate metadata than Version 1.

For my analyses, I used 1-grams, 2-grams, 3-grams and 4-grams with part-of-speech (POS) tags. For Modern English, Google promises the accuracy of the POS tags to be around 95 per cent, and likely above 90 per cent for older English texts.[7] The data represent mostly formal registers (e.g., academic publications).

Only a fraction of this huge data set was used, representing the years from 2001 to 2009. Instances of the construction were extracted from the data sets with 2-grams, 3-grams and 4-grams. More exactly, I extracted the following patterns, where X stands for any string, Y denotes the object personal pronoun *me*, *you*, *him*, *her*, *it*, *us* and *them*, and * represents any ending, including zero:

- help*_VERB X_VERB
  e.g., *helps_VERB make_VERB*
- help*_VERB Y_PRON X_VERB
  e.g., *helped_VERB me_PRON build_VERB*
- help*_VERB to_PRT X_VERB
  e.g., *helping_VERB to_PRT achieve_VERB*
- help*_VERB Y_PRON to_PRT X_VERB
  e.g., *help_VERB her_PRON to_PRT understand_VERB*

By making this contextual restriction, it was possible to control for some of the relevant factors that influence the use of one or the other variant: linguistic distance (zero or one word), the Helpee (explicit or implicit) and the morphological form of *help*. The restrictions of the Helpees to personal pronouns are explained by the size of *n*-grams and by concerns about possible spurious hits. Previous corpus work (Levshina 2018b) suggests that zero and pronominal Helpees account for approximately 80 per cent of all uses of the construction in the corpora. I assume, therefore, that the extracted *n*-grams can be used as a testing ground.

Both upper-case and lower-case characters were allowed. The verbs in the open slot were later manually checked, and the finite forms, participles and misspellings were excluded. The verbs were normalized with regard to the spelling variant (e.g., *organise* and *organize* were treated as one lemma). The total number of occurrences of the construction was 2,471,027, and the total number of individual verbs was 1,672. The relative frequencies of the *to*-infinitive and bare infinitive were very similar: 47.1 and 52.9 per cent, respectively.

The frequencies for separate combinations of the forms of *help* and the presence or absence of the Helpee are displayed in Table 9.2. Notably, we observe a correlation between the relative frequency of the bare form and the total frequency of the form of *help* followed by the (*to*) Infinitive with and without the Helpee. The higher the total frequency, the higher the relative

---

[7] https://books.google.com/ngrams/info, last access 18 July 2022.

9.3 Efficient Use of *Help (to)* Infinitive

Table 9.2. *Frequencies of different subschemata of the construction with* help

Context	Total frequency	Frequency of the *to*-infinitive	Frequency of the bare infinitive	Number of verb types
help + Inf	897,120 (100%)	328,329 (36.6%)	568,791 (63.4%)	1,329
helped + Inf	459,042 (100%)	273,218 (59.5%)	185,824 (40.5%)	1,354
helps + Inf	295,028 (100%)	193,759 (65.7%)	101,269 (34.3%)	873
helping + Inf	120,815 (100%)	106,905 (88.5%)	13,910 (11.5%)	750
help + Helpee + Inf	497,241 (100%)	155,565 (31.3%)	341,676 (68.7%)	688
helped + Helpee + Inf	87,622 (100%)	41,619 (47.5%)	46,003 (52.5%)	321
helps + Helpee + Inf	73,982 (100%)	41,687 (56.3%)	32,295 (43.7%)	236
helping + Helpee + Inf	40,177 (100%)	22,782 (56.7%)	17,395 (43.3%)	210

frequency of the bare form. This can be regarded as a manifestation of efficiency.

The total frequencies of the individual verbs were obtained from the file with 1-gram frequencies in the entire British English data set for the period from 2001 to 2009. Also, the frequencies of use with both variants were summed for each individual verb. Based on these frequencies, the two informativity measures were computed as described in Section 9.1.

Consider an example. The verb *understand* occurs in the construction with *help* 85,815 times. The total frequency of the construction is 2,471,027. Therefore, the informativity score of *understand* given the construction is $-log_2 (85,815/2,471,027) \approx 4.85$. The verb occurs 3,239,809 times in the entire data set. From this follows that the informativity value of the construction given the verb is $-log_2 (85,815/3,239,809) \approx 5.24$.

In order to test the correlation between information context and the use or omission of *to*, I computed Spearman's partial correlations between the proportions of the *to*-infinitives and each informativity measure. Partial correlations allow us to measure the correlation between two variables while controlling for the other(s). The correlations are displayed in Table 9.3.

In accordance with the Hypothesis of Construction–Lexeme Accessibility and Formal Length, we expect positive correlations between the proportion of *to* vs. zero and the informativity measures. This expectation is supported. At least one of the informativity measures is positive and significant for each

Table 9.3. *Spearman's coefficients representing partial correlations between the proportions of* to-*infinitives and the informativity measures*

Context	InfoLex	InfoCxn
help + Inf	0.066 ($p = 0.002$)	0.169 ($p < 0.0001$)
helped + Inf	0.431 ($p < 0.0001$)	0.225 ($p < 0.0001$)
helps + Inf	0.547 ($p < 0.0001$)	0.147 ($p < 0.0001$)
helping + Inf	0.552 ($p < 0.0001$)	-0.055 ($p = 0.134$), n.s.
help + Helpee + Inf	0.007 ($p = 0.857$), n.s.	0.122 ($p < 0.0001$)
helped + Helpee + Inf	0.204 ($p = 0.0002$)	0.123 ($p = 0.027$)
helps + Helpee + Inf	0.512 ($p < 0.0001$)	-0.05 ($p = 0.447$), n.s.
helping + Helpee + Inf	0.407 ($p < 0.0001$)	0.115 ($p = 0.099$), n.s.

individual context. The correlations for *help* + Infinitive and *help* + Helpee + Infinitive are quite low; only the former is significant. This may be an artefact of the data, since it is very difficult to control for possible *horror aequi* effects in *n*-gram data due to the lack of left context (e.g., *?This is an opportunity to help to protect millions of lives*). Notably, the subschemata with individual inflectional forms display different behavioural properties, which is typical of so-called inflectional islands (Newman and Rice 2006).

To summarize, we find that the accessibility of constructions and lexemes correlates positively with the chances of the less costly variant, in accordance with the principle of negative correlation between accessibility and costs. Moreover, the total frequency of the subschemata with different forms of *help* with and without the Helpee correlates with the relative frequencies of the bare infinitive in these subschemata, which can also be considered efficient. The variation of *help (to)* Infinitive involves very many factors, but it seems that most of them can be interpreted in terms of accessibility related to the meaning, familiarity of inflected forms, memory decay, common ground and other factors.

9.4 Alternation *Go (and)* Verb

The third and final alternation discussed in this chapter is *go (and)* Verb, which is illustrated by the following example:

(14)   *Let's go (and) get some pizza!*

This alternation has been widely discussed in the generativist literature. The main question of these studies is how the shorter variant is derived by formal operations from the construction with *and* (see, e.g., Pullum 1990 and Wulff 2006 for an overview). Some semantic differences have been observed, as well. In particular, Carden and Pesetsky (1979: 81) point out that *go and* Verb,

9.4 Alternation *Go (and)* Verb

unlike *go* Verb, can express unexpected events. They provide the following examples:

(15) a. *??As we had arranged, the President went and addressed the graduating class.*
 b. *To our amazement, instead of addressing the graduating class, the President went and harangued the janitors.*

The use of *go and* Verb is more suitable when the action is surprising, as in (15b), than when it is planned, as in (15a). This can be seen as a direct manifestation of efficiency. The more costly form is used when the information is surprising and therefore less accessible.

In addition, Shopen (1971) argued that *go* Verb implies volitionality, which is not always observed with *go and* Verb. The shorter variant is also associated with motion away from the viewpoint location. This is why it is possible to say, *Go and come back to our house,* but not **Go come back to our house.*

More recently, Wulff (2006) found that the lexical overlap between the constructions is not very large. Her distinctive collexeme analysis also suggests that the verbs most distinctive of the *go* Verb construction are process verbs (e.g., *run*, *work*, *walk* and *fly*).

Another relevant usage-based study is Flach (2017), where data about the syntactic environment of the constructions are provided. Her corpus frequencies suggest that *go* Verb is more frequently used after adhortative *let's* and in the imperative mood, whereas *go and* Verb is preferred after modals and as a *to*-complement.

According to the Hypothesis of Construction–Lexeme Accessibility and Formal Length, we can expect the longer variant to be preferred if a verb is highly informative given the construction *go (and)* Verb, or if the construction is highly informative given the verb.

In order to test this prediction, I extracted all instances of *go* followed by a verb in the base form, with or without *and* between them, from the spoken component of COCA. This data source was chosen because *go* Verb seems to be more popular in American English (e.g., Pullum 1990).[8] These strings could be followed by any word, with the exception of function words, adverbials (e.g., *go there*), adjectives (e.g., *go crazy*) and participles (e.g., *go unnoticed* and *go shopping*). After that, it was necessary to check the data manually because some of the verbs were annotated incorrectly (e.g., the second verb in *go figure* was tagged as a noun). The result was 6,540 instances of the alternation with 627 individual verbs. The *go* + Verb construction

---

[8] In British English, the distribution is heavily skewed in favour of *go and* Verb. Wulff (2006) finds only 454 instances of *go* Verb in the entire British National Corpus, and 5,320 instances of *go and* Verb.

occurred more frequently than *go and* + Verb: 4,618 occurrences against 1,922 occurrences. I also extracted the token frequencies of individual verbs from the spoken component of COCA. Using this information, I computed the informativity measures as described in Section 9.1.

The relationships between the variants and the informativity measures were tested with the help of Generalized Additive Models (GAMs).[9] The main distinctive characteristic of GAMs is that they allow for straightforward and convenient modelling of non-linear relationships between the predictors and the response variable. This is done with the help of smooth terms, which can be of various types and degrees of 'wiggliness'. In order not to oversmooth or undersmooth the data, various regression diagnostics were performed, based on the goodness-of-fit measures provided in the model summary, AIC (the measure that combines the goodness of fit with parsimony), visualization tools and built-in tests. More information about the basic concepts and modelling strategies of GAMs can be found in Wood (2006), Sóskuthy (2017) and Wieling (2018).

The response was based on the frequencies of *go and* Verb and *go* Verb for every individual verb. The predictors were again the informativity variables with a bivariate tensor product smooth, which turned out to provide a better fit than individual univariate smooths, since the former produced smaller deviance than the latter.[10]

The effect of both informativity variables on the chances of the longer variant is shown in Figure 9.1. The lighter regions represent the values where the chances of *go and* Verb are higher. They are observed at the top, where the informativity of the construction given a verb is higher, and the accessibility is lower. Many of those verbs are highly frequent, such as *be, become, come, give* and *join*, e.g., *Do you want to go and be in a coma?* and are used in many different constructions. Because of their 'promiscuity', they do not provide a strong cue to the construction and its meaning. The darker regions show the values where the chances of *go and* Verb are lower. They are observed in the bottom part of the plot, where the informativity value of a verb given *go (and)* Verb is lower. Some of the verbs with the lowest values are *pee, hunt, check, rent, visit* and *golf*, e.g., *Why did you decide to go visit Saddam Hussein?*

---

[9] The models presented in this study were fitted with the help of the package *mgcv* (Wood 2006) in R, open-source statistical software (R Core Team 2020). The modelling revealed some overdispersion due to excess zero proportions. To fix that, a quasi-binomial model was fitted. The smooth with 7.11 effective degrees of freedom was significant ($p < 0.0001$). The settings were as follows: binomial (logit) family, tensor product smooths, thin plate regression splines as the basis, wiggliness parameter gamma = 1.4, the scaling parameter was 1.25. The intercept was $b_0 = -0.26^{***}$ (the log-odds of the longer form). The explanatory power of the model was moderate (adjusted R^2: 0.25; explained deviance: 29.3%).

[10] For all other purposes, the default fast Restricted Maximum Likelihood estimation was used, which enables computationally efficient calculations. The settings of the models were the following: binomial (logit) family, tensor product smooths, thin plate regression splines as the basis, the wiggliness parameter gamma set at 1.4.

9.4 Alternation *Go (and)* Verb

Go AND Verb vs. Go Verb

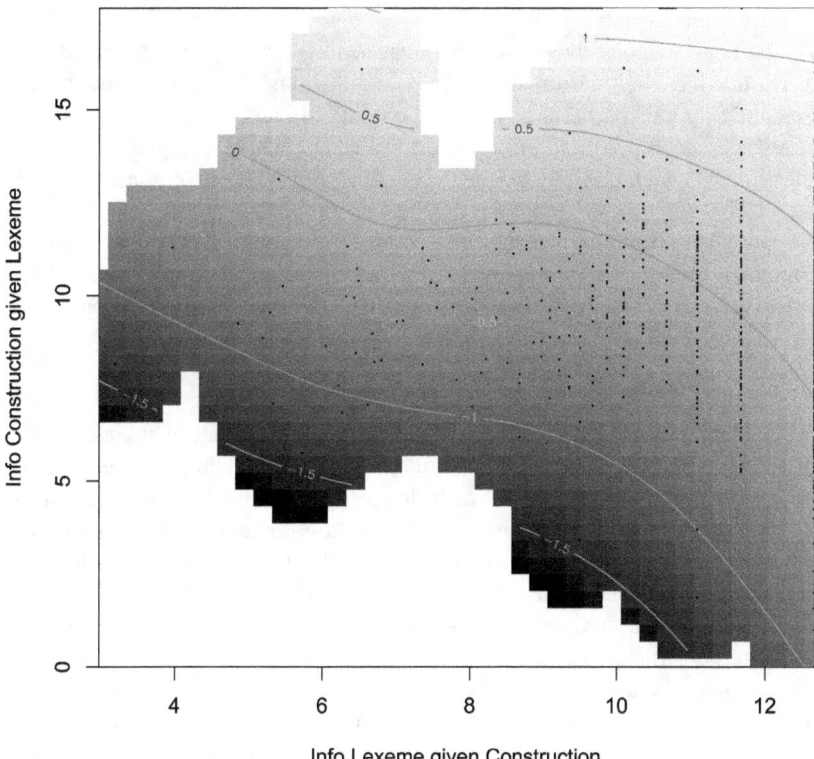

Figure 9.1 Effect of informativity on the chances of *go and* Verb vs. *go* Verb, based on a Generalized Additive Model

These verbs provide strong cues to the construction. Therefore, the shorter variant is preferred when the construction is more expected given the verb, and the longer variant is preferred in contexts when the construction is less expected. This is exactly what is predicted by the Hypothesis of Construction–Lexeme Accessibility and Formal Length.

As for informativity of the verb given the construction, represented by the horizontal axis in Figure 9.1, we can see that the regions of high informativity on the right are somewhat lighter than the regions of low informativity, which is also according to the expectations. There is some non-additivity in the effect of both informativity measures, as one can see from the curvy isolines, which is why the tensor products are preferred to individual univariate smooths.

Additional partial correlation analyses show that both informativity measures are positively correlated with the chances of the longer form, as predicted.

Spearman's correlation coefficients are 0.087 ($p = 0.03$) for informativity of the verb given the construction, and 0.186 ($p < 0.0001$) for informativity of the construction given the verb.

The analyses thus show that the longer form *go and* Verb is preferred with verbs that have high informativity (in both directions). It is noteworthy that the semantics of unexpectedness, which, according to Carden and Pesetsky (1979), is associated with *go and* Verb, is accompanied by relative unexpectedness of its slot fillers, which can be measured quantitatively. Of course, these variables should be tested in the presence of other factors that influence the use of the variants, but preliminary analyses of *go (and)* Verb with additional contextual variables (in collaboration with Susanne Flach, in preparation) reveal similar effects of informativity, which means that the observed effects are robust.

9.5 Conclusions

This chapter presented three case studies that demonstrate that accessibility based on associations between constructional slots and their fillers plays a role in constructional alternations with longer and shorter alternative forms. I formulated the Hypothesis of Construction–Lexeme Accessibility and Formal Length, which predicts that longer forms will be used when the associations are weaker, and shorter forms when the associations are stronger.

Based on these findings, we can formulate a prediction for the evolution of existing constructions and emergence of new ones. When a construction has two or more variants with closely related functions, the less costly variant will be used when the association between the constructions and their slot fillers is higher, and the more costly variant will be used when the mutual predictability between the constructions and the fillers is lower.

These results have consequences for the study of the associations between constructions and collexemes. Construction Grammar has traditionally focused on semantic compatibility (e.g., Goldberg 1995; Stefanowitsch and Gries 2003). The present study demonstrates that the probabilistic relationships between constructions and collexemes can explain the choice between the shorter and longer constructional variants. This needs to be integrated into the constructionist theory.

We also see many other manifestations of high and low accessibility that determine the use of longer and shorter variants. This shows that language users adjust their output to the individual situation in many very subtle ways, depending on semantic features, inflectional forms, distances between constructional components, and many other factors. There is a multitude of soft probabilistic constraints in which communicative efficiency manifests itself in language use. This should have important consequences for probabilistic grammar and lexicology (cf. Grafmiller et al. 2018). We may need to rethink many of the discovered factors in terms of accessibility.

10 Conclusions and Perspectives

This book has argued that language users have a bias towards efficient communication. They tend to minimize the cost-to-benefit ratio, where the benefits are desirable cognitive effects in the addressee, and the costs are related to articulation, processing and time. If we have several ways of formulating something, the most efficient expression will be the one with minimal costs, under the condition that the same cognitive effects are achieved.

A central role is played by accessibility. If intended meanings, interpretations, syntactic parses and so on are highly accessible, they can be expressed by less costly forms in terms of articulation effort and time, and also produced as soon as possible. Low accessibility means that more effort and time needs to be spent in order to get the message across.

Examples of efficient choices include forms of different length related to various generalized implicatures, more and less explicit anaphoric expressions, asymmetric grammatical categories, e.g., singular and plural, the use and omission of function words and grammatical morphemes, reduced or hyperarticulated phonetic variants of the same word, and many others. These examples were discussed in Chapter 2. Examples of efficient word order, which were provided in Chapter 3, include the subject-first bias in languages of the world, cross-linguistic preferences in the order of morphemes, Greenbergian correlations and implications, and the preference for structures that minimize syntactic domains and dependency distances. It can also be useful to choose more accessible forms and meanings and avoid less accessible ones, as argued in Chapter 4. Chapters 5 and 6 discussed different diachronic paths and causal scenarios that can explain how these efficient language patterns emerge and survive in language use. Although I do not exclude that some efficient patterns can emerge due to factors other than the pressure for efficiency, it was argued that efficiency may be a more successful explanatory factor in many cases.

Chapters 7 to 9 zoomed in on a set of diverse grammatical phenomena: causative constructions and differential case marking in languages of the world, as well as variation in the use or omission of function words in some

English alternations. In all these cases, the amount of coding material negatively correlates with the accessibility of an intended interpretation. These diverse case studies and numerous other examples allow us to conclude that we are dealing with a universal phenomenon that is observed in different unrelated languages, across different levels of language structure and in the form of categorical and probabilistic rules. This book provides a unified framework for discussing these examples, bringing together insights from diverse accounts and theories: Neo-Gricean pragmatics, audience design, Ariel's (1990, 2008) Accessibility Theory, Zipf's Principle of Least Effort, some aspects of markedness theory (cf. Fenk-Oczlon 1991, 2001; Haspelmath 2006) and Optimality Theory (e.g., de Hoop and Malchukov 2008), and many other ideas.

There remain many open questions and tasks for future research. First of all, the framework presented here needs to be tested on a wider range of linguistic phenomena in the future. I expect many more instances of efficient formal asymmetries to be found in languages of the world. There is a certain danger of being selective, picking up the phenomena that provide support to the account presented here, and ignoring the violations. We need to find out how we can sample the grammatical functions and the corresponding forms, and to reject the null hypothesis of no correlation between benefits and costs in a more systematic way.

The main challenge for efficiency research is how to integrate different types of costs in one metric. Ideally, we would need to compute total metabolic costs in calories or other units. But we do not know how to measure these yet. Until we find a solution, efficiency research is likely to remain a patchwork of different cost types.

There are many open issues in the debate about the role of audience design, mind reading and cognitive control. According to Croft (2000: 163), 'it is clear that the speaker chooses degree of reduction of a constructional form with the hearer in mind'. But the extent to which the hearer is present in the speaker's mind can be different. This study has argued that the choice of forms should be driven by simple heuristics, which work automatically and do not require conscious control and theory of mind. However, we can imagine that mentalizing mechanisms and cognitive control can be involved to different extents, depending on the specific case. My expectation is that they may be involved more if there are alternative ways of saying the same thing which are highly entrenched and conventionalized. Examples are particularized Gricean implicatures and Yoda's word order (see Section 3.4).

Crucially, the connection between production efficiency and learning should be explored. A system that is easy to use may be difficult to acquire, and the other way round. One can hypothesize that there could be a negative correlation between articulatory ease and learnability. For example, formal reduction leads to ease of articulation but may obscure the identity of units. Automatization of articulation due to chunking is efficient for production but makes it more difficult to retrieve the individual components. At the same time, there may be a positive correlation between some aspects of processing ease and learnability. In particular, more accessible production plans (MacDonald 2013) can also be easier to learn. Also, transparency may be a factor where these two motivations converge. For example, analytic constructions may be easier both to learn and to process than synthetic forms, although they are often more costly in terms of articulation (cf. Section 4.3).

Another important and understudied aspect of efficient behaviour is individual variability. In particular, we need more research on the correlation between theory of mind and efficiency (cf. Turnbull 2019), in particular, on the differences between neurotypical and autistic individuals. We can also expect differences between speakers of different ages.

There is some evidence that men and women may have different strategies in some aspects of language processing. Namely, in one experiment Wang et al. (2010: 820) found that

> females process information in an exhaustive way, and that they rely on all available information before rendering judgment. In contrast, male information processing is usually partial and incomplete, relying on a subset of highly available and salient cues instead of detailed message elaboration.

Wang et al. (2010) show that men are sensitive only to semantic anomalies that happen in the focus position, as in (1a), while women are sensitive to semantic violations regardless of the information structure, both in (1a) and (1b).

(1)   a. What kind of vegetables did mum buy for dinner today? – Today mum bought BEEF for dinner.
          b. Who bought the vegetables for dinner today? – Today MUM bought beef for dinner.

This finding suggests that men prefer to minimize the costs, at the same time risking losing some benefits, while women maximize the benefits, at the same time increasing the costs. It is an open question which strategy is optimal.

Finally, the ideas about efficiency presented in this book should be formalized in the framework of probabilistic pragmatics (Franke and Jäger 2016), as in Rational Speech Act Theory (Frank and Goodman 2012), for example. The general principles should be spelled out formally and tested empirically, for instance, in communication games. At the same time, it is a matter of ongoing debate to what extent these sophisticated models can capture real communication. Recent empirical evidence shows that the rational models do not predict addressees' communicative behaviour better than a baseline model driven solely by literal word meaning and a prior reflecting the contextual salience of referents (Sikos et al. 2021).

Communicative efficiency is more relevant for society than one might think. Everything that has to do with distribution of resources, including time and metabolic energy, is a question of power. In ideal communication, both the speaker and the addressee should benefit from their efforts. However, there are some examples where this ratio is different for different communicators. For example, when a boss gives an employee a task in a cryptic message without detail, they save their own effort while exploiting the cognitive resources of the employee. Additionally, they may avoid the social costs of taking responsibility if the task does not bring the expected results. They can say, 'This is not what I meant!' Another example is when the addressee has no interest in processing the speaker's message because there are no cognitive benefits for them, but keeps doing so out of politeness or fear. One can think about women's and men's communication, where men take the floor more often, while women listen patiently. This is a consequence of a long tradition of institutionalized misogyny, when religious and social authorities told women to keep silent in public (and in many places of the world still do).[1] This asymmetry in benefits and costs may not be obvious, but it cements further the existing inequality, especially as it permeates daily interaction. This is why communication efficiency is a political issue. We may not always have enough power or self-confidence to avoid disbalance, but we should be aware of how much each participant invests and gains from communication. How to transform communicative practices, taking into account the interests of underprivileged individuals and groups, remains an important question.

Language is an efficient tool that has helped us to become what we are as a species. It allows us to achieve great things collaboratively. With the development of new communication technologies, the costs and benefits change. For example, nowadays predictive text technology (T9) helps us to minimize writing effort. It is highly successful, despite all the anecdotes about awkward mistakes (and sometimes high social costs). On Twitter, the maximal length of a message is restricted to 280 characters. As a result, Twitter users are very aware of the space costs of different expressions, which has a strong effect on their linguistic choices. Communication via online conference software, such as Skype or Zoom, helps to connect people from all parts of the world, opening new opportunities, but at the same time it is more demanding for the brain than face-to-face communication.[2] The number of visual signals about body language is restricted, and it is more difficult to connect emotionally. Communication between multiple participants in the gallery view in Zoom, for example, is difficult, as well, because one has to monitor too many cues

---

[1] Cf. 'Women are to be silent in the churches. They are not permitted to speak, but must be in submission, as the law says' (New Testament, Corinthians 14:34).
[2] www.mpi-talkling.mpi.nl/?p=46&lang=en (last access 18 July 2022).

simultaneously. These are all additional costs of communication that we need to accommodate to.

Where are we heading? Elon Musk's start-up Neuralink has been working on a brain implant that could communicate with a computer or mobile phone. In addition to helping people with injuries and disabilities, it could also allow people to communicate with each other without using language.[3] This kind of telepathy would be extremely efficient. No time and effort would be spent on encoding a message in words and decoding them. Yet I do not think that language will become obsolete in the foreseeable future. Even if one disregards the privacy and ethical issues,[4] the sheer complexity and diversity of the human brain does not allow anyone to decipher a brain signal and turn it into concepts, and all the way back. Linguists have nothing to worry about at the moment. But surely this line of research will lead to new and more efficient communication tools and gadgets, in ways that no one can predict now.

---

[3] www.independent.co.uk/life-style/gadgets-and-tech/news/elon-musk-joe-rogan-podcast-language-neuralink-grimes-baby-a9506451.html (last access 18 July 2022).

[4] See an enlightening article by Mark Dingemanse at https://aeon.co/essays/why-language-remains-the-most-flexible-brain-to-brain-interface (last access 18 July 2022).

Appendices

Appendix 1: List of Languages in the Typological Sample Used in Chapter 7

1. List of languages (families) that have pairs of causatives with an (in)directness distinction (in a broad sense), used for the case studies in Chapter 7. The genetic classification is provided according to the World Atlas of Language Structures (WALS, Dryer and Haspelmath 2013).

   Africa (5):
   : Gumuz (isolate), Humburi Senni (Songhay), Khoekhoe/Nama (Khoe-Kwadi), Ma'di (Central Sudanic), Noon (Niger-Congo)

   Australia (3):
   : Diyari (Pama-Nyungan), Garrwa (Garrwan), Kayardild (Tangkic)

   Eurasia (13):
   : Ainu (isolate), Basque (isolate), Betta Kurumba (Dravidian), Finnish (Uralic), Great Andamanese (isolate), Hebrew (Afro-Asiatic), Hindi (Indo-European), Japanese (isolate), Korean (isolate), Kusunda (isolate), Lahu (Sino-Tibetan), Nivkh (isolate), Yukaghir Kolyma (Yukaghir)

   North America (12):
   : Caddo (Caddoan), Cherokee (Iroquoian), Chimariko (Hokan), Creek (Muskogean), Filomeno (Totonacan), Lakhota (Siouan), Mutsun (Penutian), Northern Paiute (Uto-Aztecan), Slave (Na-Dene), Takelma (unclear), Teribe (Chibchan), Wappo (Wappo-Yukian)

   Papua and Austronesia (4):
   : Indonesian (Austronesian), Motuna (South Bougainville), Skou (Skou), Yimas (Lower Sepik-Ramu)

   South America (9):
   : Aguaruna (Jivaroan), Apinayé (Macro-Ge), Hup (Nadahup), Mocoví (Guaicuruan), Mosetén (Mosetenan), Trumai (isolate), Urarina (isolate), Waimiri-Atroarí (Cariban), Yagua (Peba-Yaguan)

2. Additional languages with other distinctions related to compactness
   Africa (2):
   Ik (Eastern Sudanic), Tubu/Dazaga (Saharan)
   Papua and Austronesia (3):
   Adang (Greater West Bomberai), Manambu (Sepik), Tidore (North Halmaheran)
   South America (2):
   Cavineña (Pano-Tacanan), Karó (Tupian)
3. Languages where no semantic distinctions between causative constructions have been found:
   Africa (1):
   Sandawe (isolate)
   Eurasia (1):
   Udihe (Altaic)
   Papua and Austronesia (1):
   Meninggo/Moskona (East Bird's Head)
   South America (3):
   Mapuche (Araucanian), Paresi-Haliti (Arawakan), Yuracaré (isolate)

Appendix 2: Corpus Frequencies of Different A and P from Previous Studies Used in Chapter 8

Corpus	Study	Role	Total	Lexical	Human	1st & 2nd person	New	Notes
Sakapultek Pear Story	Du Bois 1987	A	187 or 180	11/180 (6.1%)	187/187 (100%)	NA	6/187 (3.2%)	
		P	177 or 170	81/177 (45.8%)	17/170 (10%)	NA	42/170 (24.7%)	
Chinese narratives (retelling the film *Ghost*)	Chui 1992	A	407	155 (38.1%)	NA	NA	12 (2.9%)	
		P	363	306 (84.3%)	NA	NA	122 (33.6%)	
French monologic speech	Ashby & Bentivoglio 1993	A	481	32 (6.7%)	NA	NA	0 (0%)	
		P	481	324 (67.4%)	NA	NA	143 (29.7%)	
Spanish monologic speech	Ashby & Bentivoglio 1993	A	571	35 (6.1%)	NA	NA	2 (0.4%)	
		P	571	341 (59.7%)	NA	NA	142 (24.9%)	
Written Swedish	Dahl & Fraurud 1996	A	3127	NA	1766 (56.5%)	NA	NA	Only clauses with overt subject and object
		P	4476	NA	580 (13%)	NA	NA	
Four oral narratives in Modern Hebrew	Sutherland-Smith 1996	A	270	18 (6.7%)	NA	NA	6 (2.2%)	Syntactic transitives + semantic transitives
		P	197	111 (56.3%)	NA	NA	47 (23.9%)	
Spoken Swedish	Dahl 2000	A	2991	NA	Animate 2789 (93.2%)	Egophoric 1815 (60.7%)	NA	
		P	3244	NA	Animate 531 (16.4%)	Egophoric 139 (4.3%)	NA	
Inuktitut child language	Allen & Schröder 2003	A	617, 613 or 616	7/617 (1.1%)	Animate 610/616 (99%)	601/617 (97.4%)	4/613 (0.7%)	Mostly affixal referring expressions
		P	617 or 603	37/617 (6%)	Animate 128/606 (21.1%)	88/617 (14.3%)	163/603 (27%)	

							Only main clauses
Mapudungun narrative texts	Arnold 2003	A	161	24 (14.9%)	NA	NA	2 (1.2%)
		P	161	137 (85.1%)	NA	NA	77 (47.8%)
English talk shows	Everett 2009	A	392	38 (9.7%)	360 (91.8%)	NA	NA
		P	397	237 (59.7%)	50 (12.6%)	NA	NA
Portuguese talk shows	Everett 2009	A	155	27 (17.4%)	135 (87.1%)	NA	NA
		P	163	138 (84.7%)	10 (6.1%)	NA	NA
Chinese conversations	Lin 2009	A	100	20 (20%)	NA	NA	15 (15%)
		P	100 or 97	80/100 (80%)	NA	NA	54/97 (55.6%)
Chinese spoken narratives	Lin 2009	A	80	15 (18.8%)	NA	NA	10 (12.5%)
		P	83 or 80	78/83 (94%)	NA	NA	58/80 (72.5%)
Chinese written texts	Lin 2009	A	88	14 (15.9%)	NA	NA	18 (20.5%)
		P	88 or 87	72/88 (81.8%)	NA	NA	61/87 (70.1%)
English autobiographical narratives	Schiborr 2016	A	1046	86 (8.2%)	971 (92.8%)	617 (59%)	NA
		P	1114	532 (47.8%)	138 (12.4%)	54 (4.8%)	NA
Northern Kurdish traditional narratives	Haig & Thiele 2016	A	422	55 (13%)	408 (96.7%)	137 (32.5%)	NA
		P	428	234 (54.7%)	111 (25.9%)	29 (6.8%)	NA
Persian stimulus-based narratives	Abidifar 2016	A	603	82 (13.6%)	580 (96.2%)	22 (3.6%)	NA
		P	628	331 (52.7%)	113 (18%)	0 (0%)	NA
Teop traditional narratives	Mosel & Schnell 2016	A	797	77 (9.7%)	760 (95.4%)	204 (25.6%)	NA
		P	616	265 (43%)	267 (43.3%)	29 (4.7%)	NA
Vera'a traditional narratives	Schnell 2016	A	1360	101 (7.4%)	1288 (94.7%)	210 (15.4%)	NA
		P	917	514 (56.1%)	324 (35.3%)	79 (8.6%)	NA

References

Adibifar, Shirin. 2016. Persian. In Geoffrey Haig and Stefan Schnell (eds.), *Multi-CAST: Multilingual Corpus of Annotated Spoken Texts*, Version 2108. https://multicast.aspra.uni-bamberg.de/, accessed 5 April 2022.

Aissen, Judith. 1999. Markedness and subject choice in optimality theory. *Natural Language and Linguistic Theory* 17: 673–711.

2003. Differential object marking: Iconicity vs. economy. *Natural Language and Linguistic Theory* 21: 435–483.

Allen, Shanley E.M., and Heike Schröder. 2003. Preferred Argument Structure in early Inuktitut spontaneous speech data. In John W. Du Bois, Lorraine E. Kumpf and William J. Ashby (eds.), *Preferred Argument Structure: Grammar as Architecture for Function*, 301–338. Amsterdam: John Benjamins.

Amberber, Mengistu. 2000. Valency-changing and valency-encoding devices in Amharic. In R.M.W. Dixon and Alexandra Y. Aikhenvald (eds.), *Changing Valency: Case Studies in Transitivity*, 312–332. Cambridge: Cambridge University Press.

Anderson, Frank C., and Marcus G. Pandy. 2001. Dynamic optimization of human walking. *Journal of Biomechanical Engineering* 123: 381–390.

Ariel, Mira. 1990. *Accessing Noun-Phrase Antecedents*. London: Routledge.

1999. The development of person agreement markers: from pronouns to higher accessibility markers. In Michael Barlow and Suzanne Kemmer (eds.), *Usage-Based Models of Language*, 197–260. Stanford, CA: CSLI Publications.

2001. Accessibility theory: An overview. In Ted Sanders, Joost Schliperoord and Wilbert Spooren (eds.), *Text Representation*, 29–87. Amsterdam: John Benjamins.

2008. *Pragmatics and Grammar*. Cambridge: Cambridge University Press.

2014. *Or* Constructions: Monosemy versus polysemy. In Brian MacWhinney, Andrej Malchukov and Edith Moravcsik (eds.), *Competing Motivations in Grammar and Usage*, 333–347. Oxford: Oxford University Press.

Arnold, Jennifer E. 2001. The effects of thematic roles on pronoun use and frequency of reference. *Discourse Processes* 31: 137–162.

2003. Multiple constraints on reference form: Null, pronominal, and full reference in Mapudungun. In John W. Du Bois, Lorraine E. Kumpf and William J. Ashby (eds.), *Preferred Argument Structure: Grammar as Architecture for Function*, 225–245. Amsterdam: John Benjamins.

2010. How speakers refer: The role of accessibility. *Language and Linguistics Compass* 4(4): 187–203. DOI https://doi.org/10.1111/j.1749-818x.2010.00193.x.

References

Arnold, Jennifer E., and Zenzi M. Griffin. 2007. The effect of additional characters on choice of referring expression: Everyone counts. *Journal of Memory and Language* 56(4): 521–536. DOI https://doi.org/10.1016/j.jml.2006.09.007.

Arnold, Jennifer E., Anthony Losongco, Thomas Wasow and Ryan Ginstrom. 2000. Heaviness vs. newness: The effects of structural complexity and discourse status on constituent ordering. *Language* 76(1): 28–55. DOI https://doi.org/10.1353/lan.2000.0045.

Ashby, William B., and Paola Bentivoglio. 1993. Preferred argument structure in spoken French and Spanish. *Language Variation and Change* 5(1): 61–76.

Asr, Fatemeh Torabi, and Vera Demberg. 2012. Implicitness of discourse relations. In *Proceedings of COLING 2012: Technical Papers*, 2669–2684. COLING 2012, Mumbai, December 2012.

Aylett, Matthew, and Alice Turk. 2004. The smooth signal redundancy hypothesis: A functional explanation for relationships between redundancy, prosodic prominence, and duration in spontaneous speech. *Language and Speech* 47(1): 31–56.

2006. Language redundancy predicts syllabic duration and the spectral characteristics of vocalic syllable nuclei. *Journal of Acoustical Society of America* 119(5): 3048–3058.

Baayen, R. Harald, Petar Milin and Michael Ramscar. 2016. Frequency in lexical processing. *Aphasiology* 30(11): 1174–1220. DOI https://doi.org/10.1080/02687038.2016.1147767.

Baese-Berk, Melissa, and Matthew Goldrick. 2009. Mechanisms of interaction in speech production. *Language and Cognitive Processes* 24(4): 527–554.

Baggio, Giosuè, and Peter Hagoort. 2011. The balance between memory and unification in semantics: A dynamic account of the N400. *Language and Cognitive Processes* 26(9): 1338–1367.

Balodis, Uldis Ivars Jānis. 2011. *Yuki Grammar in Its Areal Context with Sketches of Huchnom and Coast Yuki*. PhD dissertation. Santa Barbara, CA: University of California.

Bartek, Brian, Richard L. Lewis, Shravan Vasishth and Mason R. Smith. 2011. In search of on-line locality effects in sentence comprehension. *Journal of Experimental Psychology: Learning, Memory, and Cognition* 37(5): 1178–1198.

Barth, Danielle. 2019. Effects of average and specific context probability on reduction of function words *BE* and *HAVE*. *Linguistics Vanguard* 5(1): 20180055. DOI https://doi.org/10.1515/lingvan-2018-0055.

Bašnáková, Jana, Kirsten Weber, Karl Magnus Petersson, Jos van Berkum and Peter Hagoort. 2014. Beyond the language given: The neural correlates of inferring speaker meaning. *Cerebral Cortex* 24: 2572–2578. DOI: https://doi.org/10.1093/cercor/bht112.

Bauer, Brigitte M. 2009. Word order. In Philip Baldi and Pierluigi Cuzzolin (eds.), *New Perspectives on Historical Latin Syntax*: Vol 1: Syntax of the Sentence, 241–316. Berlin: Mouton de Gruyter.

Beattie, Geoffrey W., and B.L. Butterworth. 1979. Contextual probability and word frequency as determinants of pauses and errors in spontaneous speech. *Language and Speech* 22(3): 201–221. DOI https://doi.org/10.1177/002383097902200301.

Behaghel, Otto. 1909. Beziehungen zwischen Umfang und Reihenfolge von Satzgliedern. *Indogermanische Forschungen* 25: 110–142.

Bell, Alan, Daniel Jurafsky, Eric Fosler-Lussier, Cynthia Girand and Daniel Gildea. 2003. Effects of disfluencies, predictability, and utterance position on word form variation in English conversation. *Journal of the Acoustical Society of America* 113(2): 1001–1024.

Bell, Alan, Jason Brenier, Michelle Gregory, Cynthia Girand, and Dan Jurafsky. 2009. Predictability effects on durations of content and function words in conversational English. *Journal of Memory and Language* 60(1): 92–111.

Bell, Allan. 1984. Language style as audience design. *Language in Society* 13: 145–204.

Bellingham, Erika, Stephanie Evers, Kazuhiro Kawachi, Alice Mitchell, Sang-Hee Park, Anastasia Stepanova and Jürgen Bohnemeyer. 2020. Exploring the representation of causality across languages: Integrating production, comprehension and conceptualization perspectives. In Elitzur Bar-Asher Siegal and Nora Boneh (eds.), *Perspectives on Causation. Selected Papers from the Jerusalem 2017 Workshop*, 75–119, Cham: Springer. DOI https://doi.org/10.1007/978-3-030-34308-8_3.

Benor, Sarah, and Roger Levy. 2006. The chicken or the egg? A probabilistic analysis of English binomials. *Language* 82(2): 233–278.

Bentz, Christian, and Ramon Ferrer-i-Cancho. 2016. Zipf's law of abbreviation as a language universal. Capturing phylogenetic algorithms for linguistics. In Christian Bentz, Gerhard Jäger and Igor Yanovich (eds.), *Proceedings of the Leiden Workshop on Capturing Phylogenetic Algorithms for Linguistics*. University of Tübingen. https://publikationen.uni-tuebingen.de/xmlui/handle/10900/68558.

Berdicevskis, Alexandrs, Karsten Schmidtke-Bode and Ilja Seržant. 2020. Subjects tend to be coded only once: Corpus-based and grammar-based evidence for an efficiency-driven trade-off. In *Proceedings of the 19th International Workshop on Treebanks and Linguistic Theories*, October 2020, Düsseldorf, Germany. Düsseldorf: ACL. www.aclweb.org/anthology/2020.tlt-1.8.pdf.

Biber, Douglas. 1988. *Variation across Speech and Writing*. Cambridge: Cambridge University Press.

Biber, Douglas, and Bethany Gray. 2011. Grammar emerging in the noun phrase: The influence of written language use. *English Language and Linguistics* 15: 223–250.

Biber, Douglas, Stig Johansson, Geoffrey Leech, Susan Conrad and Edward Finegan. 1999. *Longman Grammar of Spoken and Written English*. Harlow: Longman.

Bickel, Balthasar, Alena Witzlack-Makarevich, Kamal K. Choudhary, Matthias Schlesewsky and Ina Bornkessel-Schlesewsky. 2015a. The Neurophysiology of language processing shapes the evolution of grammar: Evidence from case marking. *PLoS ONE* 10(8): e0132819. DOI https://doi.org/10.1371/journal.pone.0132819.

Bickel, Balthasar, Alena Witzlack-Makarevich and Taras Zakharko. 2015b. Typological evidence against universal effects of referential scales on case alignment. In Ina Bornkessel-Schlesewsky, Andrej L. Malchukov and Marc Richards (eds.), *Scales*, 7–43. Berlin: de Gruyter Mouton.

Bickel, Balthasar, Johanna Nichols, Taras Zakharko, Alena Witzlack-Makarevich, Kristine Hildebrandt, Michael Rießler, Lennart Bierkandt, Fernando Zúñiga and

John B. Lowe. 2017. *The AUTOTYP Typological Databases.* Version 0.1.0. https://github.com/autotyp/autotyp-data/tree/0.1.0.

Bisang, Walter. 2009. On the evolution of complexity: Sometimes less is more in East and mainland Southeast Asia. In Geoffrey Sampson, David Gil and Peter Trudgill (eds.), *Language Complexity as an Evolving Variable*, 34–49. Oxford: Oxford University Press.

Bisang, Walter, Andrej Malchukov and the Mainz Grammaticalization Project Team. 2020. Position paper: Universal and areal patterns in grammaticalization. In Walter Bisang and Andrej Malchukov (eds.), *Grammaticalization Scenarios: Cross-Linguistic Variation and Universal Tendencies*, Vol. 1, 1–87. Berlin: De Gruyter Mouton.

Blakemore, Diane. 1987. *Semantic Constraints on Relevance.* Oxford: Blackwell.

Blasi, Damián E., and Seán G. Roberts. 2017. Beyond binary dependencies in language structure. In Nick J. Enfield (ed.), *Dependencies in Language*, 117–128. Berlin: Language Science Press. DOI https://doi.org/10.5281/zenodo.573774.

Blumenthal-Dramé, Alice, and Bernd Kortmann. 2017. Causal and concessive relations: Typology meets cognition. Paper presented at the 39th Annual Conference of the German Linguistic Society, March 8–10 2017, Saarbrücken.

Bock, J. Kathryn. 1982. Toward a cognitive psychology of syntax: Information processing contributions to sentence formulation. *Psychological Review* 89(1): 1–47.

1986. Syntactic persistence in language production. *Cognitive Psychology* 18: 355–387.

Bock, J. Kathryn, and David E. Irwin. 1980. Syntactic effects of information availability in sentence production. *Journal of Verbal Learning and Verbal Behavior* 19(4): 467–484. DOI https://doi.org/10.1016/S0022-5371(80)90321-7.

Bock, J. Kathryn, and Richard K. Warren. 1985. Conceptual accessibility and syntactic structure in sentence formulation. *Cognition* 21(1): 47–67. DOI https://doi.org/10.1016/0010-0277(85)90023-X.

Bock, Kathryn, Helga Loebell and Randal Morey. 1992. From conceptual roles to structural relations: bridging the syntactic cleft. *Psychological Review* 99(1): 150–171. DOI https://doi.org/10.1037/0033-295x.99.1.150.

Bohnemeyer, Jürgen, Nicholas J. Enfield, James Essegbey and Sotaro Kita. 2010. The Macro-Event Property: The segmentation of causal chains. In Jürgen Bohnemeyer and Eric Pederson (eds.), *Event Representation in Language: Encoding Events at the Language-Cognition Interface*, 43–67. Cambridge: Cambridge University Press.

Bolinger, Dwight. 1963. Length, vowel, juncture. *Linguistics* 1: 5–29.

Bornkessel, Ina, Matthias Schlesewsky and Angela D. Friederici. 2003. Eliciting thematic reanalysis effects: The role of syntax-independent information during parsing. *Language and Cognitive Processes* 18(3): 269–298. DOI https://doi.org/10.1080/01690960244000018.

Bossong, Georg. 1985. *Empirische Universalienforschung: Differentielle Objektmarkierung in den neuiranischen Sprachen.* Tübingen: Narr.

Bouma, Gosse. 2016. Om-omission. In Martijn Wieling, Martin Kroon, Gertjan van Noord and Gosse Bouma (eds.), *From Semantics to Dialectometry: Festschrift in honor of John Nerbonne*, 65–74. London: College Publications.

Bresnan, Joan, Anna Cueni, Tatiana Nikitina and Harald Baayen. 2007. Predicting the dative alternation. In Gerlof Bouma, Irene Krämer and Joost Zwarts (eds.),

Cognitive Foundations of Interpretation, 69–94. Amsterdam: Royal Netherlands Academy of Science.

Britt, Allison E., Casey Ferrara and Daniel Mirman. 2016. Distinct effects of lexical and semantic competition during picture naming in younger adults, older adults, and people with aphasia. *Frontiers in Psychology* 7: 813. DOI https://doi.org/10.3389/fpsyg.2016.00813.

Bruno, Ana Carla. 2003. *Waimiri Atroarí Grammar: Some Phonological, Morphological, and Syntactic Aspects*. PhD dissertation. Tucson, AZ: University of Arizona.

Buz, Esteban, Michael K. Tanenhaus and T. Florian Jaeger. 2016. Dynamically adapted context-specific hyper-articulation: Feedback from interlocutors affects speakers' subsequent pronunciations. *Journal of Memory and Language* 89: 68–86.

Bybee, Joan L. 1985. *Morphology: A Study of the Relation Between Meaning and Form*. Amsterdam: John Benjamins.

   1994. The grammaticization of zero: Asymmetries in tense and aspect systems. In William Pagliuca (ed.), *Perspectives on Grammaticalization*, 235–254. Amsterdam: John Benjamins.

   1999. Usage-based phonology. In Michael Darnell, Edith A. Moravcsik, Frederic J. Newmeyer, Michael Noonan and Kathleen Wheatley (eds.), *Functionalism and Formalism in Linguistics*. Volume I: General papers, 211–242. Amsterdam: John Benjamins.

   2003. Cognitive processes in grammaticalization. In Michael Tomasello (ed.), *The New Psychology of Language: Cognitive and Functional Approaches to Language Structure*, Vol. 2, 145–167. Mahwah, NJ: Erlbaum.

   2006. From usage to grammar: The mind's response to repetition. *Language* 82(4): 711–733.

   2007. *Frequency of Use and the Organization of Language*. Oxford: Oxford University Press.

   2010. *Language, Usage, and Cognition*. Cambridge: Cambridge University Press.

Bybee, Joan L., and William Pagliuca. 1987. The evolution of future meaning. In Anna Giacalone Ramat, Onofrio Carruba and Giuliano Bernini (eds.), *Papers from the 7th International Conference on Historical Linguistics*, 109–122. Amsterdam: John Benjamins.

Bybee, Joan, and Joanne Scheibman. 1999. The effect of usage on degrees of constituency: The reduction of *don't* in English. *Linguistics* 37(4): 575–596.

Bybee, Joan, and Sandra A. Thompson. 1997. Three frequency effects in syntax. *Berkeley Linguistics Society* 23: 378–388.

Bybee, Joan L., William Pagliuca and Revere Perkins. 1990. On the asymmetries in the affixation of grammatical material. In William Croft, Keith Denning and Kemmer, Suzanne (eds.), *Studies in Typology and Diachrony: Papers Presented to Joseph H. Greenberg on his 75th Birthday*, 1–42. Amsterdam: John Benjamins.

Bybee, Joan L., Revere Perkins and William Pagliuca. 1994. *The Evolution of Grammar: Tense, Aspect, and Modality in the Languages of the World*. Chicago, IL: The University of Chicago Press.

Caldwell, Christine A., and Kenny Smith. 2012. Cultural evolution and perpetuation of arbitrary communicative conventions in experimental microsocieties. *PLoS ONE* 7 (8): e43807. DOI https://doi.org/10.1371/journal.pone.0043807.

Carden, Guy, and David Pesetsky. 1979. Double-verb constructions, markedness, and a fake co-ordination. In *Papers from the Thirteenth Regional Meeting of the Chicago Linguistic Society* 13, 82–92. Chicago, IL: Chicago Linguistic Society.

Chafe, Wallace L. (ed.). 1980. *The Pear Stories: Cognitive, Cultural, and Linguistic Aspects of Narrative Production*. Norwood, NJ: Ablex.

  1987. Cognitive constraints on information flow. In Russell S. Tomlin (ed.), *Coherence and Grounding in Discourse*, 21–51. Amsterdam: John Benjamins.

Chatterji, Suniti Kumar. 1926. *The Origin and Development of the Bengali Language*. Calcutta: Calcutta University Press.

Chui, Ka-Wai. 1992. Preferred argument structure for discourse understanding. In *Proceedings of COLING-92*, Nantes, August 23–28 1992, 1142–1146.

Clark, Herbert H. 1996. *Using Language*. Cambridge: Cambridge University Press.

Clark, Herbert H., and William G. Chase. 1974. Perceptual coding strategies in the formation and verification of descriptions. *Memory and Cognition* 2: 101–111.

Clark, Herbert H., and Catherine R. Marshall. 1981. Definite reference and mutual knowledge. In Aravind K. Joshi, Bonnie L. Webber and Ivan A. Sag (eds.), *Elements of Discourse Understanding*, 10–63. Cambridge: Cambridge University Press.

Clark, Herbert H., and Edward F. Schaefer. 1989. Contributing to discourse. *Cognition* 13: 259–294.

Clark, Herbert H., and Deanna Wilkes-Gibbs. 1986. Referring as a collaborative process. *Cognition* 22: 1–39.

Cohen, Gillian, and Dorothy Faulkner. 1983. Word recognition: Age differences in contextual facilitation effects. *British Journal of Psychology* 74(2): 239–251. DOI https://doi.org/10.1111/j.2044-8295.1983.tb01860.x.

Cohen Priva, Uriel. 2008. Using information content to predict phone deletion. In Natasha Abner and Jason Bishop (eds.), *Proceedings of the 27th West Coast Conference on Formal Linguistics*, 90–98. Somerville, MA: Cascadilla Proceedings Project.

Comrie, Bernard. 1978. Ergativity. In W.P. Lehmann (ed.), *Syntactic Typology. Studies in the Phenomenology of Language*, 329–394. Austin, TX: The University of Texas Press.

  1986. Markedness, grammar, people, and the world. In Fred R. Eckman, Fred R., Edith A. Moravcsik and Jessica R. Wirth (eds.), *Markedness*, 85–106. New York: Plenum Press.

  1989. *Language Universals and Linguistic Typology*, 2nd edn. Oxford: Blackwell.

Cook, Susan W., T. Florian Jaeger and Michael K. Tanenhaus. 2009. Producing less preferred structures: More gestures, less fluency. In *Proceedings of the 31st Annual Meeting of the Cognitive Science Society (CogSci09)*, 62–67. Amsterdam: Cognitive Science Society.

Corbett, Grevile, Andrew R. Hippisley, Dunstan Brown and Paul Marriott. 2001. Frequency, regularity, and the paradigm: A perspective from Russian on a complex relation. In Joan L. Bybee and Paul J. Hopper (eds.), *Frequency and the Emergence of Linguistic Structure*, 201–226. Amsterdam: John Benjamins.

Cotterell, Ryan D., Christo Kirov, Mans Hulden and Jason Eisner. 2019. On the complexity and typology of inflectional morphological systems. *Transactions of the Association for Computational Linguistics* 7: 327–342. DOI https://doi.org/10.1162/tacl_a_00271.

Coupé, Christophe, Yoon Mi Oh, Dan Dediu and François Pellegrino. 2019. Different languages, similar encoding efficiency: Comparable information rates across the human communication niche. *Science Advances* 5(9): eeaw2594. DOI: https://doi.org/10.1126/sciadv.aaw2594.

Cristofaro, Sonia. 2003. *Subordination*. Oxford: Oxford University Press.

2019. Taking diachronic evidence seriously: Result-oriented vs. source-oriented explanations of typological universals. In Karsten Schmidtke-Bode, Natalia Levshina, Susanne M. Michaelis and Ilja Seržant (eds.), *Explanation in Typology: Diachronic Sources, Functional Motivations and the Nature of the Evidence*, 25–46. Berlin: Language Science Press.

Croft, William. 2000. *Explaining Language Change: An Evolutionary Approach*. Harlow, Essex: Longman.

2002. On being a student of Joe Greenberg. *Linguistic Typology* 6(1): 3–8. DOI https://doi.org/10.1515/lity.2002.001.

2003. *Typology and Universals*, 2nd edn. Cambridge: Cambridge University Press.

Culbertson, Jennifer, Paul Smolensky and Géraldine Legendre. 2012. Learning biases predict a word order universal. *Cognition* 122(3): 306–329. DOI https://doi.org/10.1016/j.cognition.2011.10.017.

Culbertson, Jennifer, Marieke Schouwstra and Simon Kirby. 2020. From the world to word order: Deriving biases in noun phrase order from statistical properties of the world. *Language* 96(3): 696-717. DOI https://doi.org/10.1353/lan.2020.0045.

Cutler, Anne, John A. Hawkins and Gary Gilligan. 1985. The suffixing preference: A processing explanation. *Linguistics* 23: 723–758.

Cysouw, Michael. 2009. The asymmetry of affixation. *Snippets* (Special issue in honor of Manfred Krifka, ed. by Sigrid Beck and Hans-Martin Gärtner) 20: 10–14. www.ledonline.it/snippets/.

Dahl, Östen. 2000. Egophoricity in discourse and syntax. *Functions of Language* 7(1): 37–77.

2004. *The Growth and Maintenance of Linguistic Complexity*. Amsterdam: John Benjamins.

Dahl, Östen, and Kari Fraurud. 1996. Animacy in grammar and discourse. In Thorstein Fretheim and Jeannette Gundel (eds.), *Reference and Referent Accessibility*, 47–64. Amsterdam: John Benjamins.

Dalrymple, Mary, and Irina Nikolaeva. 2011. *Objects and Information Structure*. Cambridge: Cambridge University Press.

Davies, Mark. 2008–. *The Corpus of Contemporary American English (COCA): 560 million words, 1990–present*. https://corpus.byu.edu/coca/.

de Hoop, Helen, and Andrej L. Malchukov. 2008. Case-marking strategies. *Linguistic Inquiry* 39(4): 565–587. DOI https://doi.org/10.1162/ling.2008.39.4.565.

de Hoop, Helen, and Peter de Swart (eds.). 2008. *Differential Subject Marking*. Dordrecht: Springer.

De Smedt, Koenraad. 1994. Parallelism in incremental sentence generation. In Geert Adriaens and Udo Hahn (eds.), *Parallel Natural Language Processing*, 421–447. Norwood, NJ: Ablex.

De Smedt, Koenraad, and Gerard Kempen. 1996. Discontinuous constituency in Segment Grammar. In Harry Bunt and Arthur van Horck (eds.), *Discontinuous Constituency*, 141–164. Berlin: Mouton de Gruyter.

De Swart, Peter. 2007. *Cross-Linguistic Variation in Object Marking*. PhD dissertation. Nijmegen: LOT Publications.

Degen, Judith, Robert D. Hawkins, Caroline Graf, Elisa Kreiss and Noah D. Goodman. 2020. When redundancy is useful: A Bayesian approach to 'overinformative' referring expressions. *Psychological Review* 127(4): 591–621. DOI https://doi.org/10.1037/rev0000186.

Delbrück, Berthold. 1919. *Einleitung in das Studium der indogermanischen Sprachen*, 5th edn. Leipzig: Breitkopf & Härtel. https://archive.org/details/einleitungindas00delbgoog.

Demberg, Vera and Frank Keller. 2008. Data from eye-tracking corpora as evidence for theories of syntactic processing complexity. *Cognition* 109: 193–210. DOI https://doi.org/10.1016/j.cognition.2008.07.008.

Detges, Ulrich, and Richard Waltereit. 2002. Grammaticalization vs. reanalysis: A semantic-pragmatic account of functional change in grammar. *Zeitschrift für Sprachwissenschaft* 21(2): 151–195. DOI https://doi.org/10.1515/zfsw.2002.21.2.151.

Diessel, Holger. 2019. *The Grammar Network: How Linguistic Structure Is Shaped by Language Use*. Cambridge: Cambridge University Press.

Dixon, Robert M.W. 1979. Ergativity. *Language* 55: 59–138.

1991. *A New Approach to English Grammar, on Semantic Principles*. Oxford: Clarendon Press.

1994. *Ergativity*. Cambridge: Cambridge University Press.

2000. A typology of causatives: Form, syntax and meaning. In R.M.W. Dixon and Alexandra Y. Aikhenvald (eds.), *Changing Valency: Case Studies in Transitivity*, 30–83. Cambridge: Cambridge University Press.

Dressler, Wolfgang U. 1990. The cognitive perspective of 'naturalist' linguistic models. *Cognitive Linguistics* 1: 75–98.

Dryer, Matthew S. 1992. The Greenbergian word order correlations. *Language* 68: 81–138.

2013. Order of Subject, Object and Verb. In Matthew S. Dryer and Martin Haspelmath (eds.), *The World Atlas of Language Structures Online*. Leipzig: Max Planck Institute for Evolutionary Anthropology. http://wals.info/chapter/81.

2019. Grammaticalization accounts of word order correlations. In Karsten Schmidtke-Bode, Natalia Levshina, Susanne Maria Michaelis and Ilja A. Seržant (eds.), *Explanation in Typology: Diachronic Sources, Functional Motivations and the Nature of the Evidence*, 63–95. Berlin: Language Science Press.

Dryer, Matthew S., and Martin Haspelmath (eds.). 2013. *The World Atlas of Language Structures Online*. Leipzig: Max Planck Institute for Evolutionary Anthropology. http://wals.info.

Du Bois, John W. 1985. Competing motivations. In John Haiman (ed.), *Iconicity in Syntax*, 343–365. Amsterdam: John Benjamins.

1987. The discourse basis of ergativity. *Language* 63: 805–855.

Du Bois, John W., Lorraine E. Kumpf and William J. Ashby (eds.). 2003. *Preferred Argument Structure: Grammar as Architecture for Function* (Studies in Discourse and Grammar 14). Amsterdam: John Benjamins.

Du Bois, John W., Wallace L. Chafe, Charles Meyer, Sandra A. Thompson, Robert Englebretson and Nii Martey. 2000–2005. *Santa Barbara Corpus of Spoken American English, Parts 1–4.* Philadelphia, PA: Linguistic Data Consortium.

Duffley, Patrick J. 1992. *The English Infinitive.* London: Longman.

Eckardt, Regine. 2009. APO: Avoid Pragmatic Overload. In Maj-Britt Mosegaard Hansen and Jacqueline Visconti (eds.), *Current Trends in Diachronic Semantics and Pragmatics*, 21–41. Bingley: Emerald. DOI https://dx.doi.org/10.1163/9789004253216_003.

Eksell Harning, K. 1980. *The Analytical Genitive in Modern Arabic Dialects.* PhD dissertation, Orientalia Gothoburgensia 5. Gothenburg: University of Gothenburg Press.

Ellis, Nick C., and Fernando Ferreira-Junior. 2009. Construction learning as a function of frequency, frequency distribution, and function. *The Modern Language Journal* 93(3): 370–385. DOI https://doi.org/10.1111/j.1540-4781.2009.00896.x.

Enfield, N.J. 2007. *A Grammar of Lao.* Berlin: Mouton de Gruyter.

Engelhardt, Paul E., Ş. Bariş Demiral and Fernanda Ferreira. 2011. Over-specified referring expressions impair comprehension. *Brain and Cognition* 77: 304–314.

Ernestus, Mirjam. 2014. Acoustic reduction and the roles of abstractions and exemplars in speech processing. *Lingua* 142: 27–41. DOI http://dx.doi.org/10.1016/j.lingua.2012.12.006.

Escamilla, Ramón M. Jr. 2012. *An Updated Typology of Causative Constructions: Form–Function Mappings in Hupa (Californian Athabaskan), Chungli Ao (Tibeto-Burman) and Beyond.* PhD dissertation. Berkeley, CA: University of California.

Estrada-Fernández, Zarina. 2020. Grammaticalization in Uto-Aztecan languages from northwestern Mexico. In Walter Bisang and Andrej Malchukov (eds.), *Grammaticalization Scenarios: Cross-Linguistic Variation and Universal Tendencies*, Vol. 2, 853–902. Berlin: De Gruyter Mouton.

Evans, Nicholas D. 1995. *A Grammar of Kayardild: With Historical-Comparative Notes on Tangkic* (Mouton Grammar Library 15). Berlin: Mouton de Gruyter.

Everett, Caleb. 2009. A reconsideration of the motivation for preferred argument structure. *Studies in Language* 33(1): 1–24. DOI https://doi.org/10.1075/sl.33.1.02eve.

Faltz, Leonard M. 1985. *Reflexivization: A study in Universal Syntax.* New York: Garland.

Fauconnier, Stefanie. 2011. Differential agent marking and animacy. *Lingua* 121(3): 533– 547. DOI https://doi.org/10.1016/j.lingua.2010.10.014.

Fedzechkina, Maryia, T. Florian Jaeger and Elissa L. Newport. 2012. Language learners restructure their input to facilitate efficient communication. *PNAS* 109(44): 17897–17902. DOI https://doi.org/10.1073/pnas.1215776109.

Fedzechkina, Maryia, Elissa L. Newport and T. Florian Jaeger. 2016. Balancing effort and information transmission during language acquisition: Evidence from word order and case marking. *Cognitive Science* 41(2): 416–446. DOI https://doi.org/10.1111/cogs.12346.

Fenk, August, and Gertraud Fenk. 1980. Konstanz im Kurzzeitgedächtnis - Konstanz im sprachlichen Informationsfluß. *Zeitschrift für experimentelle und angewandte Pshychologie* XXVII(3): 400–414.

Fenk-Oczlon, Gertraud. 1983. Ist die SVO-Wordfolge die 'Natürlichste'? *Papiere zur Linguistik* 29(2): 23–32.

1989. Word frequency and word order in freezes. *Linguistics* 27: 517–556.

1991. Frequenz und Kognition – Frequenz und Markiertheit. *Folia Linguistica* 25: 361–394.

2001. Familiarity, information flow, and linguistic form. In Joan L. Bybee and Paul J. Hopper (eds.), *Frequency and the Emergence of Linguistic Structure*, 431–448. Amsterdam: John Benjamins.

Fenk-Oczlon, Gertraud, and August Fenk. 2008. Complexity trade-offs between the subsystems of language. In Matti Miestamo, Kaius Sinnemäki and Fred Karlsson (eds.), *Language Complexity: Typology, Contact, Change*, 43–65. Amsterdam: John Benjamins.

Ferreira, Fernanda. 1991. Effects of length and syntactic complexity on initiation times for prepared utterances. *Journal of Memory and Language* 30: 210–233.

2003. The misinterpretation of noncanonical sentences. *Cognitive Psychology* 47: 164–203. DOI https://doi.org/10.1016/S0010-0285(03)00005-7.

Ferreira, Victor S. 2008. Ambiguity, accessibility, and a division of labor for communicative success. *Psychology of Learning and Motivation: Advances in Research and Theory* 49: 209–246. DOI https://doi.org/10.1016/S0079-7421(08)00006-6.

Ferreira, Victor S., and Gary S. Dell. 2000. Effect of ambiguity and lexical availability on syntactic and lexical production. *Cognitive Psychology* 40(4): 296–340. DOI https://doi.org/10.1006/cogp.1999.0730.

Ferreira, Victor S, and Carla E. Firato. 2002. Proactive interference effects on sentence production. *Psychonomic Bulletin and Review* 9(4): 795–800. DOI https://doi.org/10.3758/BF03196337.

Ferreira, Victor S., and Hiromi Yoshita. 2003. Given–new ordering effects on the production of scrambled sentences in Japanese. *Journal of Psycholinguistic Research* 32: 669–692. DOI https://doi.org/10.1023/A:1026146332132.

Ferrer-i-Cancho, Ramon. 2006. Why do syntactic links not cross? *Europhysics Letters* 76(6): 1228.

2017. The placement of the head that maximizes predictability: An information theoretic approach. *Glottometrics* 39: 38–71.

Ferrer-i-Cancho, Ramon, Carlos Gómez-Rodríguez and J.L. Esteban. 2018. Are crossing dependencies really scarce? *Physica A: Statistical Mechanics and Its Applications* 493: 311–329. DOI https://doi.org/10.1016/j.physa.2017.10.048.

Ferrer-i-Cancho, Ramon, Christian Bentz and Caio Seguin. 2020. Optimal coding and the origin of Zipfian laws. *Journal of Quantitative Linguistics* 29(2): 165–194. DOI https://doi.org/10.1080/09296174.2020.1778387.

Filimonova, Elena. 2005. The noun phrase hierarchy and relational marking: Problems and counterevidence. *Linguistic Typology* 9(1): 77–113. DOI https://doi.org/10.1515/lity.2005.9.1.77.

Fillmore, Charles J. 1986. Pragmatically controlled zero anaphora. *Proceedings of the Berkeley Linguistics Society* 12: 95–107.

Fischer, Hanna. 2018. *Präteritumschwund im Deutschen: Dokumentation und Erklärung eines Verdrängungsprozesses*. Berlin: Walter de Gruyter.

2020. The development of the perfect in selected Middle and New Germanic languages. In Thomas Jügel and Robert Crellin (eds), *Perfects in Indo-European Languages and Beyond*, 96–122. Amsterdam: Benjamins. DOI https://doi.org/10.1075/cilt.352.04fis.

Fischer, Olga. 1995. The distinction between bare and to-infinitival complements in late Middle English. *Diachronica* 12: 1–30.

Flach, Susanne K. 2017. *Serial Verb Constructions in English: A Usage-Based Approach*. PhD dissertation. Berlin: Freie Universität Berlin.

Fodor, Jerry A. 1970. Three reasons for not deriving 'kill' from 'cause to die'. *Linguistic Inquiry* 1(4): 429–438.

Fowler, Carol A., and Jonathan Housum. 1987. Talkers' signaling of 'new' and 'old' words in speech and listeners' perception and use of the distinction. *Journal of Memory and Language* 25: 489–504.

Fox, Barbara A. 1987. The Noun Phrase Accessibility Hierarchy reinterpreted: Subject primacy or the Absolutive Hypothesis? *Language* 63(4): 856–870.

Frank, Michael C., and Noah D. Goodman. 2012. Predicting pragmatic reasoning in language games. *Science* 336(6084): 998. DOI https://doi.org/10.1126/science.1218633.

Frank, Stefan L., and Rens Bod. 2011. Insensitivity of the human sentence-processing system to hierarchical structure. *Psychological Science* 22(6): 829–834. DOI https://doi.org/10.1177/0956797611409589.

Frank, Stefan L., Leun J. Otten, Giulia Galli and Gabriella Vigliocco. 2015. The ERP response to the amount of information conveyed by words in sentences. *Brain & Language* 140: 1–11. DOI https://doi.org/10.1016/j.bandl.2014.10.006.

Franke, Michael, and Gerhard Jäger. 2015. Probabilistic pragmatics, or why Bayes' rule is probably important for pragmatics. *Zeitschrift für Sprachwissenschaft* 35(1): 3–44. DOI https://doi.org/10.1515/zfs-2016-0002.

Frazier, Lyn, and Keith Rayner. 1990. Taking on semantic commitments: Processing multiple meanings vs. multiple senses. *Journal of Memory and Language* 29(2): 181–200. DOI https://doi.org/10.1016/0749-596X(90)90071-7.

Fromkin, Victoria A. 1973. The non-anomalous nature of anomalous utterances. In Victoria A. Fromkin (ed.), *Speech Errors as Linguistic Evidence*, 215–242. The Hague: Mouton.

Fukumura, Kumiko, and Roger P.G. van Gompel. 2012. Producing pronouns and definite noun phrases: Do speakers use the addressee's discourse model? *Cognitive Science* 36: 1289–1311. DOI https://doi.org/10.1111/j.1551-6709.2012.01255.x.

Futrell, Richard. 2019. Information-theoretic locality properties of natural language. In *Proceedings of the First Workshop on Quantitative Syntax (Quasy, SyntaxFest 2019, Paris)*, 2–15. Paris: ACL. www.aclweb.org/anthology/W19-7902.pdf.

Futrell, Richard, and Roger Levy. 2017. Noisy-context surprisal as a human sentence processing cost model. In Mirella Lapata, Phil Blunsom and Alexander Koller (eds.), *Proceedings of the 15th Conference of the European Chapter of the Association for Computational Linguistics: Volume 1, Long Papers*, 688–698. Valencia: EACL. www.aclweb.org/anthology/E17-1065.

Futrell, Richard, Roger Levy and Edward Gibson. 2020. Dependency locality as an explanatory principle for word order. *Language* 96(2): 371–413.

Futrell, Richard, Tina Hickey, Aldrin Lee, Eunice Lim, Elena Luchkina and Edward Gibson. 2015a. Cross-linguistic gestures reflect typological universals: A subject-initial, verb-final bias in speakers of diverse languages. *Cognition* 136: 215–221. DOI https://doi.org/10.1016/j.cognition.2014.11.022.

Futrell, Richard, Kyle Mahowald and Edward Gibson. 2015b. Large-scale evidence of dependency length minimization in 37 languages. *Proceedings of the National*

Academy of Sciences 112(33): 10336–10341. DOI https://doi.org/10.1073/pnas
.1502134112.
Garcia, Erica C., and Florimon van Putte. 1989. Forms are silver, nothing is gold. *Folia Linguistica Historica VIII* (1–2): 365–384.
García García, Marco. 2018. Nominal and verbal parameters in the diachrony of differential object marking in Spanish. In Ilja Seržant and Alena Witzlack-Makarevich (eds.), *Diachrony of Differential Argument Marking*, 209–242. Berlin: Language Science Press.
Gast, Volker. 2007. I gave it him – on the motivation of the 'alternative double object construction' in varieties of British English. *Functions of Language* 14(1): 31–56. DOI https://doi.org/10.1075/fol.14.1.04gas.
Gell-Mann, Murray. 1995. What is complexity? *Complexity* 1(1): 16–19. DOI https://doi.org/10.1002/cplx.6130010105.
Gennari, Silvia P., Jelena Mirkovi and Maryellen C. MacDonald. 2012. Animacy and competition in relative clause production: A cross-linguistic investigation. *Cognitive Psychology* 65(2): 141–176. DOI https://doi.org/10.1016/j.cogpsych.2012.03.002.
Gibson, Edward. 1998. Linguistic complexity: locality of syntactic dependencies. *Cognition* 68: 1–76.
  2000. The dependency locality theory: A distance-based theory of linguistic complexity. In Alec Marantz, Yasushi Miyashita and Wayne O'Neil (eds.), *Image, Language, Brain: Papers from the First Mind Articulation Project Symposium*, 94–126. Cambridge, MA: MIT Press.
Gibson, Edward, and Tessa Warren. 2004. Reading-time evidence for intermediate linguistic structure in long-distance dependencies. *Syntax* 7(1): 55–78. DOI https://doi.org/10.1111/j.1368-0005.2004.00065.x.
Gibson, Edward, Steven T. Piantadosi, Kimberly Brink, Leon Bergen, Eunice Lim and Rebecca Saxe. 2013. A noisy-channel account of crosslinguistic word-order variation. *Psychological Science* 24(7): 1079–1088. DOI https://doi.org/10.1177/0956797612463705.
Gibson, Edward, Richard Futrell, Steven Piantadosi, Isabelle Dautriche, Kyle Mahowald, Leon Bergen and Roger Levy, 2019. How efficiency shapes human language. *Trends in Cognitive Science* 23(5): 389-407. DOI https://doi.org/10.1016/j.tics.2019.02.003.
Gildea, Daniel, and David Temperley. 2010. Do grammars minimize dependency length? *Cognitive Science* 34(2): 286–310. DOI https://doi.org/10.1111/j.1551-6709.2009.01073.x.
Gilligan, Gary Martin. 1987. *A Cross-Linguistic Approach to the Pro-Drop-Parameter*. PhD dissertation. Los Angeles: University of Southern California.
Giora, Rachel, Shir Givoni and Ofer Fein. 2015. Defaultness reigns: The case of sarcasm. *Metaphor and Symbol* 30(4): 290–313. DOI: http://dx.doi.org/10.1080/10926488.2015.1074804.
Givón, Talmy. 1980. The binding hierarchy and the typology of complements. *Studies in Language* 4(3): 333–377.
  (ed.). 1983. *Topic Continuity in Discourse: A Quantitative Cross-Language Study*. Amsterdam: John Benjamins.
  1984. *Syntax: A Functional-Typological Introduction*, Vol. I. Amsterdam: John Benjamins.

1990. *Syntax. A Functional-Typological Introduction*, Vol. II. Amsterdam: John Benjamins.

1995. Markedness as meta-iconicity: Distributional and cognitive correlates of syntactic structure. In Talmy Givón, *Functionalism and Grammar*, 25–69. Amsterdam: John Benjamins.

2017. *The Story of Zero*. Amsterdam: John Benjamins.

Glass, Lelia. 2020. Verbs describing routines facilitate object omission in English. In Patrick Farrell (ed.), *Proceedings of the Linguistic Society of America* 5(1), 44–58. DOI https://doi.org/10.3765/plsa.v5i1.4663.

Goldberg, Adele E. 1995. *Constructions: A Construction Grammar Approach to Argument Structure*. Chicago: University of Chicago Press.

2005. Argument realization: The role of constructions, lexical semantics and discourse factors. In Jan-Ola Östman and Mirjam Fried (eds.), *Construction Grammars: Cognitive Grounding and Theoretical Extensions*, 17– 44. Amsterdam: John Benjamins.

Goldberg, Adele E., Devin Casenhiser and Nitya Sethuraman. 2004. Learning argument structure generalizations. *Cognitive Linguistics* 15: 289–316. DOI https://doi.org/10.1515/cogl.2004.011.

2005. The role of prediction in construction learning. *Journal of Child Language* 32: 407–426. DOI https://doi.org/10.1017/S0305000904006798.

Goldhahn, Dirk, Thomas Eckart and Uwe Quasthoff. 2012. Building large monolingual dictionaries at the Leipzig Corpora Collection: From 100 to 200 languages. In Nicoletta Calzolari, Khalid Choukri, Thierry Declerck et al. (eds.), *Proceedings of the Eighth International Conference on Language Resources and Evaluation*, 759–765. Istanbul: ELRA. www.lrec-conf.org/proceedings/lrec2012/pdf/327_Paper.pdf.

Goldin-Meadow, Susan, Howard Nusbaum, Spencer D. Kelly and Susan Wagner. 2001. Explaining math: Gesturing lightens the load. *Psychological Science* 12(6): 516–522.

Goldin-Meadow, Susan, Wing Chee So, Aslı Özyürek and Carolyn Mylander. 2008. The natural order of events: How speakers of different languages represent events nonverbally. *PNAS* 105(27): 9163–9168. DOI https://doi.org/10.1073/pnas.0710060105.

Gordon, Peter C., and Davina Chan. 1995. Pronouns, passives, and discourse coherence. *Journal of Memory and Language* 34: 216–231.

Grafmiller, Jason, Benedikt Szmrecsanyi, Melanie Röthlisberger and Benedikt Heller. 2018. General introduction: A comparative perspective on probabilistic variation in grammar. *Glossa: A Journal of General Linguistics* 3(1): 94. DOI http://doi.org/10.5334/gjgl.690.

Greenberg, Joseph H. 1963. Some universals of grammar with particular reference to the order of meaningful elements. In Joseph H. Greenberg (ed.), *Universals of Human Language*, 73–113. Cambridge, MA: MIT Press.

1966. *Language Universals, with Special Reference to Feature Hierarchies* (Janua Linguarum, Series Minor, 59). The Hague: Mouton.

Gregory, Michelle, William D. Raymond, Alan Bell, Eric Fosler-Lussier and Daniel Jurafsky. 1999. The effects of collocational strength and contextual predictability in lexical production. *Proceedings of the Chicago Linguistic Society* 35: 151–166.

Grice, H. Paul. 1975. Logic and conversation. In Peter Cole and Jerry L. Morgan (eds.), *Syntax and Semantics*, Vol.3. Speech Acts, 41–58. New York: Academic Press.

Gries, Stefan Th. 2003. *Multifactorial Analysis in Corpus Linguistics: A Study of Particle Placement*. New York: Continuum Press.
Gries, Stefan Th., and Anatol Stefanowitsch. 2004. Extending collostructional analysis: A corpus-based perspective on 'alternations'. *International Journal of Corpus Linguistics* 9(1): 97–129. DOI https://doi.org/10.1075/ijcl.9.1.06gri.
Gries, Stefan Th., Beate Hampe and Doris Schönefeld. 2005. Converging evidence: Bringing together experimental and corpus data on the association of verbs and constructions. *Cognitive Linguistics* 16(4): 635–676. DOI https://doi.org/10.1515/cogl.2005.16.4.635.
Griffin, Timothy M., and Rodger Kram. 2000. Penguin waddling is not wasteful. *Nature* 408: 929.
Grodner, Daniel J., and Edward Gibson. 2005. Consequences of the serial nature of linguistic input for sentential complexity. *Cognitive Science* 29: 261–291. DOI https://doi.org/10.1207/s15516709cog0000_7.
Guirardello, Raquel. 1999. *A Reference Grammar of Trumai*. PhD dissertation. Houston, TX: Rice University.
Gulordava, Kristina, and Paola Merlo. 2015. Diachronic trends in word order freedom and dependency length in dependency-annotated corpora of Latin and Ancient Greek. In *Proceedings of the Third International Conference on Dependency Linguistics (Depling 2015)*, 121–130. Uppsala, Sweden: ACL.
Ha, Renee R. 2010. Cost–benefit analysis. In Michael D. Breed and Janice Moore (eds.), *Encyclopedia of Animal Behavior*, Vol. 1, 402–405. Oxford: Elsevier Academic Press.
Hagoort, Peter, and Colin Brown. 1994. Brain responses to lexical ambiguity resolution and parsing. In Charles Clifton, Jr., Lyn Frazier and Keith Rayner (eds.), *Perspectives on Sentence Processing*, 45–80. Hillsdale, NJ: Lawrence Erlbaum.
Hagoort, Peter, Colin Brown and Jolanda Groothusen. 1993. The syntactic positive shift (SPS) as an ERP measure of syntactic processing. *Language and Cognitive Processes* 8(4): 439–483. DOI http://dx.doi.org/10.1080/01690969308407585.
Hahn, Michael, Judith Degen, Noah Goodman, Dan Jurafsky and Richard Futrell. 2018. An information-theoretic explanation of adjective ordering preferences. In *Proceedings of the 40th Annual Meeting of the Cognitive Science Society (CogSci)*, 1766–1771. URL https://cogsci.mindmodeling.org/2018/papers/0339/index.html.
Hahn, Michael, Judith Degen and Richard Futrell. 2021. Modeling word and morpheme order in natural language as an efficient tradeoff of memory and surprisal. *Psychological Review* 128(4): 726–756. DOI https://doi.org/10.1037/rev0000269.
Haig, Geoffrey. 2018. The grammaticalization of object pronouns: Why differential object indexing is an attractor state. *Linguistics* 56(4): 781–818. DOI https://doi.org/10.1515/ling-2018-0011.
Haig, Geoffrey, and Stefan Schnell. 2016. The discourse basis of ergativity revisited. *Language* 92(3): 591–618.
Haig, Geoffrey, and Hanna Thiele. 2016. Northern Kurdish. In Geoffrey Haig and Stefan Schnell (eds.), *Multi-CAST: Multilingual Corpus of Annotated Spoken Texts*, Version 2108. https://multicast.aspra.uni-bamberg.de/, accessed 5 April 2022.
Haiman, John. 1983. Iconic and economic motivation. *Language* 59(4): 781–819.

1985. *Natural Syntax: Iconicity and Erosion*. Cambridge: Cambridge University Press.

1994. Ritualization and the development of language. In William Pagliuca (ed.), *Perspectives on Grammaticalization*, 3–28. Amsterdam: John Benjamins.

Hale, John. 2001. A probabilistic early parser as a psycholinguistic model. In *Proceedings of the 2nd Conference of the North American Chapter of the Association for Computational Linguistics, Vol. 2*, 159–166. Pittsburgh, PA: ACL.

Hale, Kenneth. 1973. Person marking in Walbiri. In Stephen R. Anderson and Paul Kiparsky (eds.), *A Festschrift for Morris Halle*, 308–344. New York: Holt, Rinehart and Winston.

Hall, Matthew L., Rachel I. Mayberry and Victor S. Ferreira. 2013. Cognitive constraints on constituent order: Evidence from elicited pantomime. *Cognition* 129 (1): 1–17 DOI https://doi.org/10.1016/j.cognition.2013.05.004.

Hall, Matthew L., Y. Danbi Ahn, Rachel I. Mayberry and Victor S. Ferreira. 2015. Production and comprehension show divergent constituent order preferences: Evidence from elicited pantomime. *Journal of Memory and Language* 81: 16–33. DOI https://doi.org/10.1016/j.jml.2014.12.003.

Hampe, Beate. 2011. Metaphor, constructional ambiguity and the causative resultatives. In Sandra Handl and Hans-Jörg Schmid (eds.), *Windows to the Mind*, 185–215. Berlin, Mouton de Gruyter.

Harmon, Zara, and Vsevolod Kapatsinski. 2017. Putting old tools to novel uses: The role of form accessibility in semantic extension. *Cognitive Psychology* 98: 22–24. DOI https://doi.org/10.1016/j.cogpsych.2017.08.002.

Haspelmath, Martin. 1993. More on the typology of inchoative/causative verb alternations. In Bernard Comrie and Maria Polinsky (eds.), *Causatives and Transitivity*, 87–120. Amsterdam: John Benjamins.

1999. Why is grammaticalization irreversible? *Linguistics* 37: 1043–1068.

2006. Against markedness (and what to replace it with). *Journal of Linguistics* 42(1): 25–70. DOI https://doi.org/10.1017/S0022226705003683.

2008a. A frequentist explanation of some universals of reflexive marking. *Linguistic Discovery* 6(1): 40–63. DOI https://doi.org/10.1349/PS1.1537-0852.A.331.

2008b. Creating economical morphosyntactic patterns in language change. In Jeff Good (ed.), *Language Universals and Language Change*, 185–214. Oxford: Oxford University Press.

2008c. Frequency vs. iconicity in explaining grammatical asymmetries. *Cognitive Linguistics* 19(1): 1–33. DOI https://doi.org/10.1515/COG.2008.001.

2010. Comparative concepts and descriptive categories in cross-linguistic studies. *Language* 86(3): 663–687.

2013a. Argument indexing: A conceptual framework for the syntactic status of bound person forms. In Dik Bakker and Martin Haspelmath (eds.), *Languages Across Boundaries*, 197–226. Berlin: De Gruyter Mouton.

2013b. On the cross-linguistic distribution of same-subject and different-subject 'want' complements: Economic vs. iconic motivation. *SKY Journal of Linguistics* 26: 41–69.

2014. On system pressure competing with economic motivation. In Brian MacWhinney, Andrej Malchukov and Edith Moravcsik (eds.), *Competing Motivations in Grammar and Usage*, 197–208. Oxford: Oxford University Press.

2017. Explaining alienability contrasts in adpossessive constructions: Predictability vs. iconicity. *Zeitschrift für Sprachwissenschaft* 36(2): 193–231. DOI https://doi.org/10.1515/zfs-2017-0009.

2019. Differential place marking and differential object marking. *STUF – Language Typology and Universals* 72(3): 313–334. DOI https://doi.org/10.1515/stuf-2019-0013.

2021a. Explaining grammatical coding asymmetries: Form–frequency correspondences and predictability. *Journal of Linguistics* 57(3): 605–633. DOI https://doi.org/10.1017/S0022226720000535.

2021b. Role-reference associations and the explanation of argument coding splits. *Linguistics* 59(1): 123–174. DOI https://doi.org/10.1515/ling-2020-0252.

Haspelmath, Martin, and Andres Karjus. 2017. Explaining asymmetries in number marking: Singulatives, pluratives and usage frequency. *Linguistics* 55(6): 1213–1235.

Haspelmath, Martin, Andreea Calude, Michael Spagnol, Heiko Narrog and Elif Bamyacı. 2014. Coding causal–noncausal verb alternations: A form–frequency correspondence explanation. *Journal of Linguistics* 50(3): 587–625.

Haude, Katharina, and Alena Witzlack-Makarevich. 2016. Referential hierarchies and alignment: An overview. *Linguistics* 54(4): 433–441.

Havelka, Jiří. 2007. Beyond projectivity: Multilingual evaluation of constraints and measures on non-projective structures. In *Proceedings of the 45th Annual Meeting of the Association of Computational Linguistics*, 608–615. Prague: ACL.

Hawkins, John A. 1986. *A Comparative Typology of English and German: Unifying the Contrasts*. London: Croom Helm.

1994. *A Performance Theory of Order and Constituency* (Cambridge Studies in Linguistics, 73). Cambridge: Cambridge University Press.

2004. *Efficiency and Complexity in Grammars*. Oxford: Oxford University Press.

2014. *Cross-Linguistic Variation and Efficiency*. Oxford: Oxford University Press.

2019. Word-external properties in a typology of Modern English: A comparison with German. *English Language and Linguistics* 23(3): 701–727. DOI https://doi.org/10.1017/S1360674318000060.

Hay, Jennifer. 2001. Lexical frequency in morphology: Is everything relative? *Linguistics* 39(6): 1041–1070.

Heilbron, Micha, Benedikt Ehinger, Peter Hagoort and Floris P. de Lange. 2019. Tracking naturalistic linguistic predictions with deep neural language models. In *Proceedings of the 2019 Conference on Cognitive Computational Neuroscience*, 424–427. DOI https://doi.org/10.32470/CCN.2019.1096-0.

Heine, Bernd. 2002. On the role of context in grammaticalization. In Ilse Wischer and Gabriele Diewald (eds.), *New Reflections on Grammaticalization*, 83–101. Amsterdam: John Benjamins.

Heine, Bernd, Ulrike Claudi and Friederike Hünnemeyer. 1991. *Grammaticalization: A Conceptual Framework*. Chicago, IL: University of Chicago Press.

Helmbrecht, Johannes, Lukas Denk, Sarah Thanner and Ilenia Tonetti. 2018. Morphosyntactic coding of proper names and its implications for the animacy hierarchy. In Sonia Cristofaro and Fernando Zúñiga (eds.), *Typological Hierarchies in Synchrony and Diachrony*, 377–401. Amsterdam: John Benjamins.

Hengeveld, Kees, and Sterre Leufkens. 2018. Transparent and non-transparent languages. *Folia Linguistica* 52(1): 139–175. DOI https://doi.org/10.1515/flin-2018-0003.

Hilpert, Martin. 2012. *Constructional Change in English: Developments in Allomorphy, Word Formation, and Syntax*. Cambridge: Cambridge University Press.

Himmelmann, Nikolaus P. 2014. Asymmetries in the prosodic phrasing of function words: Another look at the suffixing preference. *Language* 90: 927–960.

Hockett, Charles F. 1967. Where the tongue slips, there slip I. In *To Honor Roman Jakobson: Essays on the Occasion of His 70th Birthday, 11. October 1966*, Vol. 2, 910–936. The Hague: Mouton.

Holler, Judith, and Stephen C. Levinson. 2019. Multimodal language processing in human communication. *Trends in Cognitive Sciences* 23(8): 639–652. DOI https://doi.org/10.1016/j.tics.2019.05.006.

Holler, Judith, Kobin H. Kendrick and Stephen C. Levinson. 2018. Processing language in face-to-face conversation: Questions with gestures get faster responses. *Psychonomic Bulletin & Review* 25(5): 1900–1908. DOI https://doi.org/10.3758/s13423-017-1363-z.

Hollmann, Willem B. 2003. *Synchrony and Diachrony of English Periphrastic Causatives: A Cognitive Perspective*. PhD dissertation. Manchester: University of Manchester.

Hooper, Joan B. 1976. Word frequency in lexical diffusion and the source of morphophonological change. In William M. Christie (ed.), *Current Progress in Historical Linguistics*, 96–105. Amsterdam: North Holland.

Hopper, Paul J., and Sandra A. Thompson. 1980. Transitivity in grammar and discourse. *Language* 56(2): 251–299.

Hopper, Paul J., and Elizabeth C. Traugott. 1993. *Grammaticalization*. Cambridge: Cambridge University Press.

Horn, Laurence R. 1984. Towards a new taxonomy for pragmatic inference: Q-based and R-based implicature. In Deborah Schiffrin (ed.), *Georgetown University Round Table on Languages and Linguistics*, 11–42. Washington, DC: Georgetown University Press.

  2009. Implying and inferring. In Keith Allan and Kasia M. Jaszczolt (eds.), *The Cambridge Handbook of Pragmatics*, 69–86. Cambridge: Cambridge University Press.

Howes, Davis. 1968. Zipf's law and Miller's random-monkey model. *The American Journal of Psychology* 81(2): 269–272.

Howes, Davis, and Richard L. Solomon. 1951. Visual duration threshold as a function of word-probability. *Journal of Experimental Psychology* 41(6): 401–410. DOI https://doi.org/10.1037/h0056020.

Huang, Yan. 2007. *Pragmatics*. Oxford: Oxford University Press.

Huddleston, Rodney, and Geoffrey K. Pullum. 2002. *The Cambridge Grammar of the English Language*. Cambridge: Cambridge University Press.

Hudson Kam, Carla L., and Elissa L. Newport. 2009. Getting it right by getting it wrong: When learners change languages. *Cognitive Psychology* 59: 30–66. DOI https://doi.org/10.1016/j.cogpsych.2009.01.001.

Humboldt, Wilhelm von. 1836. *Über die Verschiedenheit des menschlichen Sprachbaues und ihren Einfluss auf die geistige Entwicklung des Menschengeschlechts*. Berlin: Dümmler.

Hupp, Julie M., Vladimir M. Sloutsky and Peter W. Culicover. 2009. Evidence for a domain-general mechanism underlying the suffixation preference in language.

Language and Cognitive Processes 24: 876–909. DOI https://doi.org/10.1080/01690960902719267.

Hyman, Larry. 1971. Consecutivization in Fe'fe'. *Journal of African Languages* 10(2): 29–43.

Hömke, Paul, Judith Holler and Stephen C. Levinson. 2017. Eye blinking as addressee feedback in face-to-face conversation. *Research on Language and Social Interaction* 50(1): 54–70. DOI https://doi.org/10.1080/08351813.2017.1262143.

Iemmolo, Giorgio. 2010. Topicality and differential object marking. Evidence from Romance and beyond. *Studies in Language* 34(2): 239–272. DOI https://doi.org/10.1075/sl.34.2.01iem.

Isaacs, Ellen A., and Herbert H. Clark. 1987. References in conversation between experts and novices. *Journal of Experimental Psychology: General* 116(1): 26–37.

Jaeger, T. Florian. 2006. *Redundancy and Syntactic Reduction in Spontaneous Speech*. PhD thesis. Stanford, CA: Stanford University.

2010. Redundancy and reduction: Speakers manage syntactic information density. *Cognitive Psychology* 61 (1): 23–62. DOI https://doi.org/10.1016/j.cogpsych.2010.02.002.

Jaeger, T. Florian, and Esteban Buz. 2017. Signal reduction and linguistic encoding. In Eva M. Fernández and Helen Smith Cairns (eds.), *Handbook of Psycholinguistics*, 38–81. Oxford: Wiley-Blackwell.

Jakobson, Roman. 1971 [1932]. Zur Structur des russischen Verbums. In Roman Jakobson, *Selected Writings. Vol. II. Word and Language*, 3–15. Berlin: De Gruyter Mouton.

1971 [1960]. Linguistics and poetics. In Roman Jakobson, *Selected Writings*. Vol. III. Poetry of Grammar and Grammar of Poetry, 18–51. Berlin: De Gruyter Mouton.

Just, Erika, and Slavomir Čéplö. 2019. A corpus based analysis of differential object indexing in Maltese. Paper presented at the 7th International Conference on Maltese Linguistics. Jagiellonian University Kraków, 10–11 July 2019.

Just, Erika, and Alena Witzlack-Makarevich. Forthcoming. A corpus-based analysis of P indexing in Ruuli. *South African Journal of African Languages* 42(2).

Kahneman, Daniel. 2011. *Thinking, Fast and Slow*. London: Penguin Books.

Kanwal, Jasmeen, Kenny Smith, Jennifer Culbertson and Simon Kirby. 2017. Zipf's Law of Abbreviation and the Principle of Least Effort: Language users optimise a miniature lexicon for efficient communication. *Cognition* 165: 45–52. DOI https://doi.org/10.1016/j.cognition.2017.05.001.

Keenan, Edward L. 1975. Variation in Universal Grammar. In Ralph Fasold and Roger Shuy (eds.), *Analyzing Variation in Language*, 136–148. Washington, DC: Georgetown University Press.

Keenan, Edward L., and Bernard Comrie. 1977. Noun phrase accessibility and Universal Grammar. *Linguistic Inquiry* 8(1): 63–99.

Keller, Rudi. 1994. *On Language Change: The Invisible Hand in Language*. London: Routledge.

Kemmer, Susanne, and Arie Verhagen. 1994. The grammar of causatives and the conceptual structure of events. *Cognitive Linguistics* 5: 115–156.

Kemp, Charles, Yang Xu and Terry Regier. 2018. Semantic typology and efficient communication. *Annual Review of Linguistics* 4: 109–128. DOI https://doi.org/10.1146/annurev-linguistics-011817-045406.

Kim, Taeho. 2008. *Subject and Object Markings in Conversational Korean*. PhD dissertation. Buffalo, NY: The State University of New York.

Kiparsky, Paul. 1996. The shift to head-initial VP in Germanic. In Höskuldur Thráinsson, Samuel D. Epstein and Steve Peter (eds.), *Studies in Comparative Germanic Syntax II*, 140–179. Dordrecht: Kluwer.

Kirby, Simon, Hannah Cornish and Kenny Smith. 2008. Cumulative cultural evolution in the laboratory: An experimental approach to the origins of structure in human language. *PNAS* 105: 10681–10686. DOI https://doi.org/10.1073/pnas.0707835105.

Kirby, Simon, Tom Griffiths and Kenny Smith. 2014. Iterated learning and the evolution of language. *Current Opinion in Neurobiology* 28: 108–114. DOI https://doi.org/10.1016/j.conb.2014.07.014.

Kirby, Simon, Monica Tamariz, Hannah Cornish and Kenny Smith. 2015. Compression and communication in the cultural evolution of linguistic structure. *Cognition* 141: 87–102. DOI https://doi.org/10.1016/j.cognition.2015.03.016.

Konieczny, Lars. 2000. Locality and parsing complexity. *Journal of Psycholinguistic Research* 29: 627–645.

König, Ekkehard, and Letizia Vezzosi. 2004. The role of predicate meaning in the development of reflexivity. In Walter Bisang, Nikolaus Himmelmann and Björn Wiemer (eds.), *What Makes Grammaticalization? A Look from Its Fringes and Its Components*, 213–244. Berlin: Mouton de Gruyter.

Koplenig, Alexander, Peter Meyer, Sascha Wolfer and Carolin Müller-Spitzer. 2017. The statistical trade-off between word order and word structure: Large-scale evidence for the Principle of Least Effort. *PLoS ONE* 12(3): e0173614. DOI https://doi.org/10.1371/journal.pone.0173614.

Koptjevskaja-Tamm, Maria. 1996. Possessive noun phrases in Maltese: Alienability, iconicity, and grammaticalization. *Rivista di Linguistica* 8(1): 245–274.

Krug, Manfred. 2000. *Emerging English Modals: A Corpus-Based Study of Grammaticalization*. Berlin: Mouton de Gruyter.

Kulikov, Leonid I. 2001. Causatives. In Martin Haspelmath, Ekkehard König, Wolfgang Oesterreicher and Wolfgang Raible (eds.), *Language Typology and Language Universals: An International Handbook*, 886–898. Berlin: Mouton de Gruyter.

Kurumada, Chigusa, and T. Florian Jaeger. 2015. Communicative efficiency in language production: Optional case-marking in Japanese. *Journal of Memory and Language* 83: 152–178. DOI https://doi.org/10.1016/j.jml.2015.03.003.

Kurumada, Chigusa, and Scott Grimm. 2019. Predictability of meaning in grammatical encoding: Optional plural marking. *Cognition* 191: 103953. DOI https://doi.org/10.1016/j.cognition.2019.04.022.

Kwon, Song-Nim, and Anne Zribi-Hertz. 2008. Differential function marking, case, and information structure: Evidence from Korean. *Language* 84(2): 258–299.

Lambrecht, Knud. 1994. *Information Structure and Sentence Form: Topic, Focus, and the Mental Representation of Discourse Referents*. Cambridge: Cambridge University Press.

Langacker, Ronald W. 2011. Grammaticalization and Cognitive Grammar. In Heiko Narrog and Bernd Heine (eds.), *The Oxford Handbook of Grammaticalization*, 79–91. Oxford: Oxford University Press.

References

LaPolla, Randy J., and Chenglong Huang. 2003. *A Grammar of Qiang with Annotated Texts and Glossary*. Berlin: De Gruyter Mouton.

Lastra, Yolanda, and Pedro Martin Butragueño. 2010. Futuro perifrástico y future morfológico en el Corpus Sociolingüístico de la ciudad de México. *Oralia* 13: 145–171.

Leben, William. 1973. *Suprasegmental Phonology*. PhD dissertation. Cambridge, MA: MIT.

Lee, Hanjung. 2009. Quantitative variation in Korean case ellipsis: Implications for Case Theory. In Helen de Hoop and Peter de Swart (eds.), *Differential Subject Marking*, 41–61. New York: Springer.

Lehmann, Christian. 2015. *Thoughts on Grammaticalization*, 3rd edn. Berlin: Language Science Press.

Levelt, Willem J.M. 1989. *Speaking: From Intention to Articulation*. Cambridge, MA: MIT Press.

Levinson, Stephen C. 2000. *Presumptive Meanings: The Theory of Generalized Conversational Implicature*. Cambridge, MA: MIT Press.

Levshina, Natalia. 2011. *Doe wat je niet laten kan [Do what you cannot let]: A usage-based study of Dutch causatives*. PhD dissertation. Leuven: University of Leuven.

2015. European analytic causatives as a comparative concept: Evidence from a parallel corpus of film subtitles. *Folia Linguistica* 49(2): 487–520.

2016. Why we need a token-based typology: A case study of analytic and lexical causatives in fifteen European languages. *Folia Linguistica* 50(2): 507–542.

2018a. Anybody (at) home? Communicative efficiency knocking on the Construction Grammar door. *Yearbook of the German Cognitive Linguistics Association* 6: 71–90. DOI https://doi.org/10.1515/gcla-2018-0004.

2018b. Probabilistic grammar and constructional predictability: Bayesian generalized additive models of *help* + (to) Infinitive in varieties of web-based English. *Glossa* 3(1): 55. DOI https://doi.org/10.5334/gjgl.294.

2018 [2016]. Finding the best fit for direct and indirect causation: A typological study. *Lingua Posnaniensis* 58(2): 65–83.

2019a. Linguistic Frankenstein, or How to test universal constraints without real languages. In Karsten Schmidtke-Bode, Natalia Levshina, Susanne M. Michaelis and Ilja Seržant (eds.), *Explanation in Linguistic Typology: Diachronic Sources, Functional Motivations and the Nature of the Evidence*, 203–223. Berlin: Language Science Press. https://langsci-press.org/catalog/book/220 (open access).

2019b. Token-based typology and word order entropy. *Linguistic Typology* 23(3): 533–572. DOI https://doi.org/10.1515/lingty-2019-0025.

2019c. Universal Dependencies in a galaxy far, far away... What makes Yoda's English truly alien. In *Proceedings of the Third Workshop on Universal Dependencies (UDW, SyntaxFest 2019)*, 35–45. Paris: ACL. www.aclweb.org/anthology/W19-8005.pdf.

2020a. Conditional inference trees and random forests. In Magali Paquot and Stefan Th. Gries (eds.), *A Practical Handbook of Corpus Linguistics*, 611–643. Cham: Springer. DOI https://doi.org/10.1007/978-3-030-46216-1_25.

2020b. How tight is your language? A semantic typology based on Mutual Information. In *Proceedings of the 19th International Workshop on Treebanks and*

Linguistic Theories, 70–78. Düsseldorf: ACL. www.aclweb.org/anthology/2020 .tlt-1.7.pdf.

2021a. Communicative efficiency and differential case marking: A reverse-engineering approach. *Linguistics Vanguard* 7(s3): 20190087. DOI https://doi.org/10.1515/lingvan-2019-0087.

2021b. Cross-linguistic trade-offs and causal relationships between cues to grammatical subject and object, and the problem of efficiency-related explanations. *Frontiers in Psychology*. DOI https://doi.org/10.3389/fpsyg.2021.648200.

2022a. Comparing Bayesian and frequentist models of language variation: The case of help + (to) Infinitive. In Ole Schützler and Julia Schlüter (eds.), *Data and Methods in Corpus Linguistics*, 224–258. Cambridge: Cambridge University Press.

2022b. Frequency, informativity and word length: Insights from typologically diverse corpora. *Entropy* 24(2): 280. DOI https://doi.org/10.3390/e24020280.

Levshina, Natalia, and Steven Moran. 2021. Efficiency in human languages: corpus evidence for universal principles. *Linguistics Vanguard* 7(s3): 20200081. DOI https://doi.org/10.1515/lingvan-2020-0081.

Levy, Elena T., and David McNeill. 1992. Speech, gesture and discourse. *Discourse Processes* 15: 277–301.

Levy, Roger. 2008. Expectation-based syntactic comprehension. *Cognition* 106: 1126–1177. DOI https://doi.org/10.1016/j.cognition.2007.05.006.

Levy, Roger, and T. Florian Jaeger. 2007. Speakers optimize information density through syntactic reduction. In Bernhard Schlökopf, John Platt and Thomas Hoffman (eds.), *Advances in Neural Information Processing Systems (NIPS)*, Vol. 19, 849–856. Cambridge, MA: MIT Press.

Levy, Roger, Evelina Fedorenko and Edward Gibson. 2013. The syntactic complexity of Russian relative clauses. *Journal of Memory and Language* 69: 461–495. DOI https://doi.org/10.1016/j.jml.2012.10.005.

Lewis, Richard L. 1996. Interference in short-term memory: The magical number two (or three) in sentence processing. *Journal of Psycholinguistic Research* 25(1): 93–115.

Lin, Wan-hua. 2009. Preferred Argument Structure in Chinese: A comparison among conversations, narratives and written texts. In Yun Xiao (ed.), *Proceedings of the 21st North American Conference on Chinese Linguistics (NACCL-21)*, Vol. 2, 341–357. Smithfield, RI: Bryant University.

Lind, Age. 1983. The variant forms of *help to/help Ø*. *English Studies* 64: 263–275.

Lindblom, Björn. 1984. Economy of speech gestures. In Peter F. MacNeilage (ed.), *The Production of Speech*, 217–245. New York: Springer.

1990. Explaining phonetic variation: A sketch of the H & H theory. In W.J. Hardcastle and A. Marchal (eds.), *Speech Production and Speech Modeling*, 403–439. Dordrecht: Kluwer Academic.

Little, Hannah, Kerem Eryılmaz and Bart de Boer. 2017. Signal dimensionality and the emergence of combinatorial structure. *Cognition* 168: 1–15. DOI https://doi.org/10.1016/j.cognition.2017.06.011.

Liu, Haitao. 2008. Dependency distance as a metric of language comprehension difficulty. *Journal of Cognitive Science* 9(2): 159–191.

References

Liu, Zoey. 2020. Mixed evidence for crosslinguistic dependency length minimization. *STUF – Linguistic Typology and Universals* 73(4): 605–633. DOI https://doi.org/10.1515/stuf-2020-1020.

Lohmann, Arne. 2011. *Help* vs. *help to*: A multifactorial, mixed-effects account of infinitive marker omission. *English Language and Linguistics* 15(3): 499–521. DOI https://doi.org/10.1017/S1360674311000141.

Lowrey, Brian. 2012. Early English causative constructions and the 'second agent' factor. *Varieng: Studies in Variation, Contacts and Change in English* 10. https://varieng.helsinki.fi/series/volumes/10/lowrey/.

Luraghi, Silvia. 2003. Definite referential null objects in Ancient Greek. *Indogermanische Forschungen* 108: 169–196.

MacDonald, Maryellen C. 2013. How language production shapes language form and comprehension. *Frontiers in Psychology* 4: 226. DOI https://doi.org/10.3389/fpsyg.2013.00226.

MacKay, Donald G. 1987. *The Organization of Perception and Action: A Theory for Language and Other Cognitive Skills*. New York: Springer.

MacWhinney, Brian. 1977. Starting points. *Language* 53(1): 152–168.

MacWhinney, Brian, Andrej Malchukov and Edith A. Moravcsik (eds). 2014. *Competing Motivations in Grammar and Usage*. Oxford: Oxford University Press.

Mahowald, Kyle, Evelina Fedorenko, Steven T. Piantadosi and Edward Gibson. 2013. Info/information theory: Speakers choose shorter words in predictive contexts. *Cognition* 126: 313–318.

Mair, Christian. 2002. Three changing patterns of verb complementation in Late Modern English: A real-time study based on matching text corpora. *English Language and Linguistics* 6(1): 105–131.

Malchukov, Andrej L. 2008. Animacy and asymmetries in differential case marking. *Lingua* 118(2): 203–221.

Manin, Dmitrii Yu. 2006. Experiments on predictability of word in context and information rate in natural language. *Information Processes* 6(3): 229–236. www.jip.ru.

2012. The right word in the left place: Measuring lexical foregrounding in poetry and prose. *Scientific Study of Literature* 2(2): 273–300.

Martin, Alexander, and Jennifer Culbertson. 2020. Revisiting the suffixing preference: Native-language affixation patterns influence perception of sequences. *Psychological Science* 31(9): 1107–1116.

Martinet, André. 1963. *Grundzüge der Allgemeinen Sprachwissenschaft*. Stuttgart: Kohlhammer.

Maslova, Elena. 2003. *A Grammar of Kolyma Yukaghir* (Mouton Grammar Library 27). Berlin: De Gruyter Mouton.

Maurits, Luke. 2011. *Representation, Information Theory and Basic Word Order*. PhD dissertation. Adelaide: University of Adelaide.

McCawley, James D. 1978. Conversational implicature and the lexicon. In Peter Cole (ed.), *Syntax and Semantics*, Vol. 9. Pragmatics, 245–259. New York: Academic Press.

McEnery, Anthony, and Zhonghua Xiao. 2005. HELP or HELP to: What do corpora have to say? *English Studies* 86(2): 161–187.

McGregor, William B. 2008. Indexicals as sources of case markers in Australian languages. In Folke Josephson and Ingmar Söhrman (eds), *Interdependence of Diachronic and Synchronic Analyses*, 299–321. Amsterdam: John Benjamins.

2018. Emergence of optional accusative case marking in Khoe languages. In Ilja Seržant and Alena Witzlack-Makarevich (eds.), *Diachrony of Differential Argument Marking*, 243–279. Berlin: Language Science Press.

McWhorter, John. 2007. *Language Interrupted: Signs of Non-Native Acquisition in Standard Language Grammars*. Oxford: Oxford University Press.

Meakins, Felicity. 2008. *Case-Marking in Contact: The Development and Function of Case Morphology in Gurindji Kriol, an Australian Mixed Language*. PhD dissertation. Melbourne: University of Melbourne.

Meillet, Antoine. 1958. *Linguistique historique et linguistique générale*. Paris: Champion.

Merkx, Danny, and Stefan L. Frank. 2020. Human sentence processing: Recurrence or attention? In *Proceedings of the Workshop on Cognitive Modeling and Computational Linguistics (CMCL) 2021*. DOI https://doi.org/10.18653/v1/2021.cmcl-1.2.

Meylan, Stephan, and Tom Griffiths. 2021. The challenges of large-scale, web-based language datasets: Word length and predictability revisited. *Cognitive Science* 45(6): e12983. DOI https://doi.org/0.1111/cogs.12983.

Michaelis, Susanne M. 2017. Asymmetry in path coding: Creole data support a universal trend. Paper presented at the SPCL meeting Tampere, June 2017. DOI https://doi.org/10.5281/zenodo.1456803.

2019. Support from creole languages for functional adaptation in grammar: Dependent and independent possessive person-forms. In Karsten Schmidtke-Bode, Natalia Levshina, Susanne M. Michaelis and Ilja Seržant (eds.), *Explanation in Typology: Diachronic Sources, Functional Motivations and the Nature of the Evidence*, 179–201. Berlin: Language Science Press.

Miller, George A. 1951. *Language and Communication*. New York: McGraw Hill.

1957. Some effects of intermittent silence. *The American Journal of Psychology* 70(2): 311–314.

Mithun, Marianne. 1987. Is basic word order universal? In Russell S. Tomlin (ed.), *Coherence and Grounding in Discourse: Outcome of a Symposium, Eugene, Oregon, June 1984*, 281–328. Amsterdam: John Benjamins.

2002. An invisible hand at the root of causation: The role of lexicalization in the grammaticalization of causatives. In Ilse Wischer and Gabriele Diewald (eds.), *New Reflections on Grammaticalization*, 237–257. Amsterdam: John Benjamins.

Mondorf, Britta. 2003. Support for *more*-support. In Günter Rohdenburg and Britta Mondorf (eds.), *Determinants of Grammatical Variation in English*, 251–304. Berlin: Mouton de Gruyter.

2014. (Apparently) competing motivations in morpho-syntactic variation. In Edith A. Moravcsik, Andrej Malchukov and Brian MacWhinney (eds.), *Competing Motivations in Grammar and Usage*, 209–228. Oxford: Oxford University Press.

Montaut, Annie. 2018. The rise of differential object marking in Hindi and related languages. In Ilja Seržant and Alena Witzlack-Makarevich (eds.), *Diachrony of Differential Argument Marking*, 281–313. Berlin: Language Science Press.

Moriya, Akira. 2017. Causative 'make' in the King James Bible (1611): Possible factors influencing the choice of bare and *to*-infinitives. *Zephyr* 29: 44–58. DOI https://doi.org/10.14989/227415.

Mosel, Ulrike and Schnell, Stefan. 2016. Teop. In Geoffrey Haig and Stefan Schnell (eds.), *Multi-CAST: Multilingual Corpus of Annotated Spoken Texts*, Version 2108. https://multicast.aspra.uni-bamberg.de/, accessed 5 April 2022.

Müller-Gotama, Franz. 1994. *Grammatical Relations: A Cross-Linguistic Perspective on Their Syntax and Semantics*. Berlin: Mouton de Gruyter.

Napoli, Donna Jo, and Stephanie Liapis. 2019. Effort reduction in articulation in sign languages and dance. *Journal of Cultural Cognitive Science* 3: 31–61. https://link.springer.com/article/10.1007/s41809-019-00027-3.

Napoli, Donna Jo, Nathan Sanders, and Rebecca Wright. 2014. On the linguistic effects of articulatory ease, with a focus on sign languages. *Language* 90(2): 424–456.

Næss, Åshild. 2007. *Prototypical Transitivity*. Amsterdam: John Benjamins.

Nedjalkov, Vladimir P., and Galina A. Otaina. 2013. *A Syntax of the Nivkh Language: The Amur Dialect*. Amsterdam: John Benjamins.

Newman, John, and Sally Rice. 2006. Transitivity schemas of English EAT and DRINK in the BNC. In Stefan Th. Gries and Anatol Stefanowitsch (eds.), *Corpora in Cognitive Linguistics: Corpus-Based Approaches to Syntax and Lexis*, 225–260. Amsterdam: John Benjamins.

Newmeyer, Frederick J. 2003. Grammar is grammar and usage is usage. *Language* 79: 682–707.

Nieuwland, Mante S., Tali Ditman and Gina R. Kuperberg. 2010. On the incrementality of pragmatic processing: An ERP investigation of informativeness and pragmatic abilities. *Journal of Memory and Language* 63: 324–346. DOI https://doi.org/10.1016/j.jml.2010.06.005.

Nivre, Joakim, and Jens Nilsson. 2005. Pseudo-projective dependency parsing. In *Proceedings of the 43rd Annual Meeting on Association for Computational Linguistics, ACL'05*, 99–106, Stroudsburg, PA: ACL.

Norcliffe, Elisabeth, Agnieszka E. Konopka, Penelope Brown and Stephen C. Levinson. 2015. Word order affects the time course of sentence formulation in Tzeltal. *Language, Cognition and Neuroscience* 30(9): 1187–1208. DOI https://doi.org/10.1080/23273798.2015.1006238.

Nordlinger, Rachel, Gabriela Garrido Rodriguez and Evan Kidd. 2022. Sentence planning and production in Murrinhpatha, an Australian 'free word order' language. *Language* 98(2): 187–220.

Okrand, Marc. 1977. *Mutsun Grammar*. PhD dissertation. Berkeley, CA: University of California.

Olawsky, Knut. 2006. *A Grammar of Urarina* (Mouton Grammar Library 37). Berlin: Mouton de Gruyter.

Osborne, Timothy, and Kim Gerdes. 2019. The status of function words in dependency grammar: A critique of Universal Dependencies (UD). *Glossa: A Journal of General Linguistics* 4(1): 17. DOI http://doi.org/10.5334/gjgl.537.

Osterhout, Lee, Phillip J. Holcomb and David A. Swinney. 1994. Brain potentials elicited by garden-path sentences: Evidence of the application of verb information during parsing. *Journal of Experimental Psychology: Learning, Memory, and Cognition* 20(4): 786–803.

Pate, John K., and Sharon Goldwater. 2015. Talkers account for listener and channel characteristics to communicate efficiently. *Journal of Memory and Language* 78: 1–17. DOI https://doi.org/10.1016/j.jml.2014.10.003/.

Petré, Peter. 2017. The extravagant progressive: An experimental corpus study on the history of emphatic [*be* Ving]. *English Language and Linguistics* 21(2): 227–250. DOI https://doi.org/10.1017/S1360674317000107.

Piaget, Jean. 1952. *The Origins of Intelligence in Children*. New York: International Universities Press.

Piantadosi, Steven, Harry Tily and Edward Gibson. 2011. Word lengths are optimized for efficient communication. *PNAS* 108(9): 3526. DOI https://doi.org/10.1073/pnas.1012551108.

2012. The communicative function of ambiguity in language. *Cognition* 122: 280–291. DOI https://doi.org/10.1016/j.cognition.2011.10.004.

Pickering, Martin J., and Holly P. Branigan. 1998. The representation of verbs: Evidence from syntactic priming in language production. *Journal of Memory and Language* 39(4): 633–651.

Pickering, Martin J., and Victor S. Ferreira. 2008. Structural priming: A critical review. *Psychological Bulletin* 134(3): 427–459. DOI https://doi.org/10.1037/0033-2909.134.3.427.

Pierrehumbert, Janet. 2001. Exemplar dynamics: Word frequency, lenition, and contrast. In Joan Bybee and Paul Hopper (eds.), *Frequency and the Emergence of Linguistic Structure*, 137–157. Amsterdam: John Benjamins.

Poplack, Shana, and Sali Tagliamonte. 1996. Nothing in context: Variation, grammaticization and past time marking in Nigerian Pidgin English. In Philip Baker and Anand Syea (eds.), *Changing Meanings, Changing Functions. Papers related to grammaticalization in contact languages*, 71–94. Westminster, UK: University Press.

Pullum, Geoffrey K. 1990. Constraints on intransitive quasi-serial verb constructions in modem colloquial English. *The Ohio State University Working Papers in Linguistics* 39: 218–239.

R Core Team. 2020. *R: A Language and Environment for Statistical Computing*. R Foundation for Statistical Computing, Vienna, Austria. www.R-project.org/.

Rayner, Keith, and Susan A. Duffy. 1986. Lexical complexity and fixation times in reading: Effects of word frequency, verb complexity, and lexical ambiguity. *Memory and Cognition* 14: 191–201.

Reali, Florencia, and Morten H. Christiansen. 2007. Processing of relative clauses is made easier by frequency of occurrence. *Journal of Memory and Language* 57: 1–23. DOI https://doi.org/10.1016/j.jml.2006.08.014.

Regel, Stefanie. 2009. *The Comprehension of Figurative Language: Electrophysiological Evidence on the Processing of Irony*. PhD dissertation. Leipzig: Max Planck Institute for Human Cognitive and Brain Sciences.

Resnik, Philip. 1996. Selectional constraints: An information-theoretic model and its computational realization. *Cognition* 61: 127–159.

Roelofs, Ardi. 1992. A spreading-activation theory of lemma retrieval in speaking. *Cognition.* 42(1-3): 107–142. DOI https://doi.org/10.1016/0010-0277(92)90041-f.

Rohde, Hannah, Richard Futrell and Christopher G. Lucas. 2021. What's new? A comprehension bias in favor of informativity. *Cognition* 209: 104491. DOI https://doi.org/10.1016/j.cognition.2020.104491.

Rohdenburg, Günter. 1996. Cognitive complexity and increased grammatical explicitness in English. *Cognitive Linguistics* 7(2): 149–182.

2003. *Horror aequi* and cognitive complexity as factors determining the use of interrogative clause linkers. In Günter Rohdenburg and Britta Mondorf (eds.), *Determinants of Grammatical Variation in English*, 205–250. Berlin: Mouton de Gruyter.

2009. Grammatical divergence between British and American English in the nineteenth and early twentieth centuries. In Ingrid Tieken-Boon van Ostade and Wim van der Wurff (eds.), *Current Issues in Late Modern English* (Linguistic Insights 77), 301–330. Bern: Peter Lang.

Royen, Gerlach. 1929. *Die nominalen Klassifikations-Systeme in den Sprachen der Erde. Historische Studie, mit besonderer Berücksichtigung des Indogermanischen.* Vienna: Anthropos.

Saldana, Carmen, Yohei Oseki and Jennifer Culbertson. 2021. Cross-linguistic patterns of morpheme order reflect cognitive biases: An experimental study of case and number morphology. *Journal of Memory and Language* 118: 104204. DOI https://doi.org/10.1016/j.jml.2020.104204.

Sapir, Edward. 1921. *Language: An Introduction to the Study of Speech.* New York: Harcourt.

Schiborr, Nils Norman. 2016. English. In Geoffrey Haig and Stefan Schnell (eds.), *Multi-CAST: Multilingual Corpus of Annotated Spoken Texts*, Version 2108. https://multicast.aspra.uni-bamberg.de/, accessed 5 April 2022.

Schlüter, Julia. 2003. Phonological determinants of grammatical variation in English: Chomsky's worst possible case. In Günter Rohdenburg and Britta Mondorf (eds.), *Determinants of Grammatical Variation in English*, 69–118. Berlin: Mouton de Gruyter.

2009. The conditional subjunctive. In Günter Rohdenburg and Julia Schlüter (eds.), *One Language, Two Grammars? Differences between British and American English*, 277–305. Cambridge: Cambridge University Press.

Schmid, Hans-Jörg. 2000. *English Abstract Nouns as Conceptual Shells: From Corpus to Cognition*. Berlin: Mouton de Gruyter.

Schmid, Hans-Jörg, and Helmut Küchenhoff. 2013. Collostructional analysis and other ways of measuring lexicogrammatical attraction: Theoretical premises, practical problems and cognitive underpinnings. *Cognitive Linguistics* 24(3): 531–577. DOI https://doi.org/10.1515/cog-2013-0018.

Schmidtke-Bode, Karsten, and Natalia Levshina. 2018. Reassessing scale effects on differential case marking: Methodological, conceptual and theoretical issues in the quest for a universal. In Ilja A. Seržant and Alena Witzlack-Makarevich (eds.), *Diachrony of Differential Argument Marking*, 509–537. Berlin: Language Science Press.

Schnadt, Michael J., and Martin Corley. 2006. The influence of lexical, conceptual and planning based factors on disfluency production. In *Proceedings of the Annual Meeting of the Cognitive Science Society 28*. https://escholarship.org/uc/item/9337x2hk.

Schnell, Stefan. 2016. Vera'a. In Geoffrey Haig and Stefan Schnell (eds.), *Multi-CAST: Multilingual Corpus of Annotated Spoken Texts*, Version 2108. https://multicast.aspra.uni-bamberg.de/, accessed 5 April 2022.

Schnell, Stefan, Nils N. Schiborr and Geoffrey Haig. 2021. Efficiency in discourse processing: Does morphosyntax adapt to accommodate new referents? *Linguistics Vanguard* 7(3s): 20190064. DOI https://doi.org/10.1515/lingvan-2019-0064.

Scholz, Melanie N., Maarten F. Bobbert, A.J. Van Soest, James R. Clark, and Johan van Heerden. 2008. Running biomechanics: Shorter heels, better economy. *Journal of Experimental Biology* 211(20): 3266–3271. DOI https://doi.org/10.1242/jeb.018812.

Schriefers, Herbert, Antje S. Meyer and Willem J.M. Levelt. 1990. Exploring the time course of lexical access in language production: Picture–word interference studies. *Journal of Memory and Language* 29: 86–102.

Seiler, Walter. 1984. *The Main Structures of Imonda: A Papuan Language*. PhD dissertation. Canberra: Australian National University.

Selten, Reinhard, and Massimo Warglien. 2007. The emergence of simple languages in an experimental coordination game. *PNAS* 104(18): 7361–7366. DOI https://doi.org/10.1073/pnas.0702077104.

Seržant, Ilja. 2019. Weak universal forced: The discriminatory function of case in differential object marking systems. In Karsten Schmidtke-Bode, Natalia Levshina, Susanne M. Michaelis and Ilja Seržant (eds.), *Explanation in Typology: Diachronic Sources, Functional Motivations and the Nature of the Evidence*, 149–178. Berlin: Language Science Press.

Seyfarth, Scott. 2014. Word informativity influences acoustic duration: Effects of contextual predictability on lexical representation. *Cognition* 133(1): 140–155. DOI https://doi.org/10.1016/j.cognition.2014.06.013.

Seyfarth, Scott, Esteban Buz and T. Florian Jaeger. 2016. Dynamic hyperarticulation of coda voicing contrasts. *Journal of the Acoustical Society of America* 139(2): EL31–37. DOI https://doi.org/10.1121/1.4942544.

Shannon, Claude E. 1948. A mathematical theory of communication. *Bell System Technical Journal* 27(3): 379–423, and (4): 623–656.

Shibatani, Masayoshi, and Prashant Pardeshi. 2002. The causative continuum. In Masayoshi Shibatani (ed.), *The Grammar of Causation and Interpersonal Manipulation*, 85–126. Amsterdam: John Benjamins.

Shklovsky, Viktor. 2017. *Viktor Shklovsky: A Reader* (ed. and transl. by Alexandra Berlina). New York: Bloomsbury.

Shosted, Ryan K. 2006. Correlating complexity: A typological approach. *Linguistic Typology* 10(1): 1–40. DOI https://doi.org/10.1515/LINGTY.2006.001.

Siewierska, Anna. 2004. *Person*. Cambridge: Cambridge University Press.

Sikos, Les, Noortje J. Venhuizen, Heiner Drenhaus and Matthew W. Crocker. 2021. Reevaluating pragmatic reasoning in language games. *PLoS ONE* 16(3): e0248388. DOI https://doi.org/10.1371/journal.pone.0248388.

Silverman, Laura B., Loisa Bennetto, Ellen Campana and Michael K. Tanenhaus. 2010. Speech-and-gesture integration in high functioning autism. *Cognition* 115(3): 380–393. DOI https://doi.org/10.1016/j.cognition.2010.01.002.

Silverstein, Michael. 1976. Hierarchy of features and ergativity. In R.M.W. Dixon (ed.), *Grammatical Categories in Australian Languages*, 112—171. Canberra: Australian Institute for Aboriginal Studies, Canberra.

Sinnemäki, Kaius. 2008. Complexity trade-offs in core argument marking. In Matti Miestamo, Kaius Sinnemäki and Fred Karlsson (eds.), *Language Complexity: Typology, Contact, Change*, 67–88. Amsterdam: John Benjamins.

2010. Word order in zero-marking languages. *Studies in Language* 34(4): 869–912. DOI https://doi.org/10.1075/sl.34.4.04sin.

2014. A typological perspective on Differential Object Marking. *Linguistics* 52(2): 281–313. DOI https://doi.org/10.1515/ling-2013-0063.

Shopen, Timothy. 1971. Caught in the act: An intermediate stage in a would-be historical process providing syntactic evidence for the psychological reality of paradigms. *Papers from the Seventh Regional Meeting of the Chicago Linguistic Society* 7: 254–263.

Slobin, Dan I. 1987. Thinking for speaking. In Jon Aske, Natasha Beery, Laura Michaelis and Hana Filip (eds.), *Proceedings of the Thirteenth Annual Meeting of the Berkeley Linguistics Society*, 435–445. Berkeley, CA: Berkeley Linguistics Society.

Slonimska, Anita, Aslı Özyürek and Olga Capirci. 2020. The role of iconicity and simultaneity for efficient communication: The case of Italian Sign Language (LIS). *Cognition* 200: 104246. DOI https://doi.org/10.1016/j.cognition.2020.104246.

Smith, Kenny, and Jennifer Culbertson. 2020. Communicative pressures shape language during communication (not learning): Evidence from casemarking in artificial languages. *PsyArXiv*. August 18. https://psyarxiv.com/5nwhq/.

Smith, Kenny, and Elizabeth Wonnacott. 2010. Eliminating unpredictable variation through iterated learning. *Cognition* 116: 444–449. DOI https://doi.org/10.1016/j.cognition.2010.06.004.

Smith, Kenny, Amy Perfors, Olga Fehér, Anna Samara, Kate Swoboda and Elizabeth Wonnacott. 2017. Language learning, language use and the evolution of linguistic variation. *Philosophical Transactions of the Royal Society B* 372: 20160051. DOI https://doi.org/10.1098/rstb.2016.0051.

Smith, Mark, and Linda Wheeldon. 2004. Horizontal information flow in spoken sentence production. *Journal of Experimental Psychology: Learning, Memory, and Cognition* 30(3): 675–686. DOI https://doi.org/10.1037/0278-7393.30.3.675.

Smith, Nathaniel J., and Roger Levy. 2013. The effect of word predictability on reading time is logarithmic. *Cognition* 128(3): 302–319. DOI https://doi.org/10.1016/j.cognition.2013.02.013.

Sommer, Noëlle, and Natalia Levshina. 2021. *Cross-Linguistic Differential and Optional Marking Database* (v1.0.0). Zenodo. DOI https://doi.org/10.5281/zenodo.4896007.

Song, Jae Jung. 1996. *Causatives and Causation: A Universal-Typological Perspective*. London: Addison Wesley Longman.

Sóskuthy, Márton. 2017. Generalised additive mixed models for dynamic analysis in linguistics: a practical introduction. *ArXiv*. DOI https://doi.org/10.48550/arXiv.1703.05339.

Sperber, Dan, and Deirdre Wilson. 1995. *Relevance: Communication and Cognition*. Oxford: Blackwell.

Spirtes, Peter, Clark Glymour and Richard Scheines. 2000. *Causation, Prediction, and Search*, 2nd edn. Cambridge, MA: MIT Press.

Stallings, Lynne M., and Maryellen C. MacDonald. 2011. It's not just the 'heavy NP': Relative phrase length modulates the production of heavy-NP shift. *Journal of Psycholinguistic Research* 40: 177–187. DOI https://doi.org/10.1007/s10936-010-9163-x.

Stefanowitsch, Anatol, and Stefan Th. Gries. 2003. Collostructions: Investigating the interaction between words and constructions. *International Journal of Corpus Linguistics* 8(2): 209–243. DOI https://doi.org/10.1075/ijcl.8.2.03ste.

Stent, Amanda J., Marie K. Huffman and Susan E. Brennan. 2008. Adapting speaking after evidence of misrecognition: Local and global hyperarticulation. *Speech Communication* 50(3): 163–178. DOI https://doi.org/10.1016/j.specom.2007.07.005.

Stephens, Greg J., Lauren J. Silbert and Uri Hasson. 2010. Speaker–listener neural coupling underlies successful communication. *PNAS* 107(32): 14425–14430. DOI https://doi.org/10.1073/pnas.1008662107.

Sun, Linlin, and Walter Bisang. 2020. Grammaticalization changes in Chinese. In Walter Bisang and Andrej Malchukov (eds.), *Grammaticalization Scenarios: Cross-Linguistic Variation and Universal Tendencies*, Vol. 1, 609–658. Berlin: De Gruyter Mouton.

Sutherland-Smith, Wendy. 1996. Spoken narrative and Preferred Argument Structure: Evidence from modern Hebrew discourse. *Studies in Language* 20(1): 163–189.

Szmrecsanyi, Benedikt. 2003. *Be going to* versus *will/shall*: Does syntax matter? *Journal of English Linguistics* 31(4): 295–323. DOI https://doi.org/10.1177/0075424203257830.

2006. *Morphosyntactic Persistence in Spoken English: A Corpus Study at the Intersection of Variationist Sociolinguistics, Psycholinguistics, and Discourse Analysis*. Berlin: Mouton de Gruyter.

2009. Typological parameters of intralingual variability: Grammatical analyticity versus syntheticity in varieties of English. *Language Variation and Change* 21(3): 319–353. DOI https://doi.org/10.1017/S0954394509990123.

Tagliamonte, Sally, and R. Harald Baayen. 2012. Models, forests and trees of York English: *Was/were* variation as a case study for statistical practice. *Language Variation and Change* 24(2): 135–178. DOI https://doi.org/10.1017/S0954394512000129.

Tal, Shira, Kenny Smith, Jennifer Culbertson, Eitan Grossman and Inbal Arnon. 2022. The impact of information structure on the emergence of differential object marking: An experimental study. *Cognitive Science* 46(3): e13119.

Talmy, Leonard. 2000. *Toward a Cognitive Semantics*, Vol. 1. Cambridge, MA: MIT Press.

Tamariz, Monica. 2016. Experimental studies on the cultural evolution of language. *Annual Review of Linguistics* 3: 389–407. DOI https://doi.org/10.1146/annurev-linguistics-011516-033807.

Tanaka, Mikihiro N., Holly P. Branigan, Janet F. McLean and Martin J. Pickering. 2011. Conceptual influences on word order and voice in sentence production: Evidence from Japanese. *Journal of Memory and Language* 65(3): 318–330. DOI https://doi.org/10.1016/j.jml.2011.04.009.

Taylor, John R. 2012. *Mental Corpus: How Language Is Represented in the Mind*. Oxford: Oxford University Press.

Temperley, David. 2008. Dependency-length minimization in natural and artificial languages. *Journal of Quantitative Linguistics* 15(3): 256–282. DOI https://doi.org/10.1080/09296170802159512.

Thomson, Alexander. 1909. Beiträge zur Kasuslehre. *Indogermanische Forschungen* 24: 293–307.

Tiersma, Peter Meijes. 1982. Local and general markedness. *Language* 58(4): 832–849.

Tily, Harry. 2010. *The Role of Processing Complexity in Word Order Variation and Change*. PhD dissertation. Stanford, CA: Stanford University.

Tily, Harry, and Steven Piantadosi. 2009. Refer efficiently: Use less informative expressions for more predictable meanings. In Kees van Deemter, Albert Gatt, Roger van Gompel and Emiel Krahmer (eds.), *Proceedings of the Workshop on the*

Production of Referring Expressions (PRE-Cogsci 2009): Bridging the Gap between Computational and Empirical Approaches to Reference. https://pre2009.uvt.nl/pdf/tilypiantadosi.pdf.

Tosco, Mauro. 1994. On case marking in the Ethiopian language area (with special reference to the subject marking in East Cushitic). In Vermondo Brugnatelli (ed.), *Sem, Cam, Iafet Atti della 7a Giornata di Studi Camito-Semitica e Indeuropei*, 225–244. Milan: Centro Studi Camito-Semitici.

Traugott, Elizabeth C. 2010. Revisiting subjectification and intersubjectification. In Kristin Davidse, Lieven Vandelanotte and Hubert Cuyckens (eds.), *Subjectification, Intersubjectification and Grammaticalization*, 29–71. Berlin: De Gruyter Mouton.

Trudgill, Peter. 2011. *Sociolinguistic Typology: Social Determinants of Linguistic Complexity*. Oxford: Oxford University Press.

Turnbull, Rory, 2019. Listener-oriented phonetic reduction and theory of mind. *Language, Cognition and Neuroscience* 34(6): 747–768. DOI https://doi.org/10.1080/23273798.2019.1579349.

Vajrabhaya, Prakaywan. 2016. *Cross-Modal Reduction: Repetition of Words and Gestures*. PhD dissertation. Eugene, OR: University of Oregon.

van der Horst, Joop M. 1998. *Doen* in Old and Early Middle Dutch: A comparative approach. In Ingrid Tieken-Boon van Ostade, Marijke van der Wal and Arjan van Leuvensteijn (eds.), *'Do' in English, Dutch and German: History and present-day variation*, 53–64. Münster: Nodus Publicationen.

Van Dyke, Jilie M., and Brian McElree. 2011. Cue-dependent interference in comprehension. *Journal of Memory and Language* 65(3): 247–263. DOI https://doi.org/10.1016/j.jml.2011.05.002.

Vanlangendonck, Flora, Roel M. Willems and Peter Hagoort. 2018. Taking common ground into account: Specifying the role of the mentalizing network in communicative language production. *PLoS ONE* 13(10): e0202943. DOI https://doi.org/10.1371/journal.pone.0202943.

Vasishth, Shravan, and Richard L. Lewis. 2006. Argument-head distance and processing complexity: Explaining both locality and antilocality effects. *Language* 82(4): 767–794.

Venhuizen, Noortje, Matthew W. Crocker and Harm Brouwer. 2019. Expectation-based comprehension: Modeling the interaction of world knowledge and linguistic experience. *Discourse Processes* 56(3): 229–255. DOI https://doi.org/10.1080/0163853X.2018.1448677.

Verhagen, Arie, and Suzanne Kemmer. 1997. Interaction and causation: Causative constructions in modern standard Dutch. *Journal of Pragmatics* 27: 61–82.

Verhoef, Tessa. 2012. The origins of the duality of patterning in artificial whistled languages. *Language and Cognition* 4(4): 357–380. DOI https://doi.org/10.1515/langcog-2012-0019.

von Heusinger, Klaus, and Georg A. Kaiser. 2007. Differential object marking and the lexical semantics of verbs in Spanish. In Georg A. Kaiser and Manuel Leonetti (eds.), *Proceedings of the Workshop 'Definiteness, Specificity and Animacy in Ibero-Romance Languages'*, 83–109. Universität Konstanz: Fachbereich Sprachwissenschaft.

von Heusinger, Klaus, and Edgar Onea Gáspár. 2008. Triggering and blocking effects in the diachronic development of DOM in Romanian. *Probus* 20(1): 67–110. DOI doi.org/10.1515/PROBUS.2008.003.

Walter, Mary Ann, and T. Florian Jaeger. 2008. Constraints on optional *that*: A strong word form OCP effect. In Rodney L. Edwards, Patrick J. Midtlyng, Colin L. Sprague and Kjersti G. Stensrud (eds.), *Proceedings from the Annual Meeting of the Chicago Linguistic Society*, 505–519. Chicago, IL: Chicago Linguistic Society.

Wang, Lin, Marcel Bastiaansen, Yufang Yang and Peter Hagoort. 2010. The influence of information structure on the depth of semantic processing: How focus and pitch accent determine the size of the N400 effect. *Neuropsychologia* 49: 813–820. DOI https://doi.org/10.1016/j.neuropsychologia.2010.12.035.

Warren, Tessa, and Edward Gibson. 2002. The influence of referential processing on sentence complexity. *Cognition* 85: 79–112. DOI https://doi.org/10.1016/S0010-0277(02)00087-2.

Wasow, Thomas. 1997. End-weight from the speaker's perspective. *Journal of Psycholinguistic Research* 26(3): 347–361.

2002. *Postverbal Behavior*. Stanford, CA: CSLI Publications.

2015. Ambiguity avoidance is overrated. In Susanne Winkler (ed.), *Ambiguity: Language and Communication*, 29–47. Berlin: De Gruyter Mouton.

Wasow, Thomas, T. Florian Jaeger and David M. Orr. 2011. Lexical variation in relativizer frequency. In Horst J. Simon and Heike Wiese (eds.), *Expecting the Unexpected: Exceptions in Grammar*, 175–195. Berlin: De Gruyter Mouton.

Wasow, Thomas, Roger Levy, Robin Melnick, Hanzhi Zhu and Tom Juzek. 2015. Processing, prosody, and optional *to*. In Lyn Frazier and Edward Gibson (eds.), *Explicit and Implicit Prosody in Sentence Processing*, 133–158. New York: Springer.

Weiner, E. Judith, and William Labov. 1983. Constraints on the agentless passive. *Journal of Linguistics* 19: 29–58.

Wheeldon, Linda R., and Stephen Monsell. 1994. Inhibition of spoken word production by priming a semantic competitor. *Journal of Memory and Language* 33(3): 332–356. DOI https://doi.org/10.1006/jmla.1994.1016.

Whitney, William Dwight. 1875. *The Life and Growth of Language*. London: Henry S. King & Co. https://archive.org/details/lifeandgrowthla01whitgoog.

Wieling, Martijn. 2018. Analyzing dynamic phonetic data using generalized additive mixed modeling: A tutorial focusing on articulatory differences between L1 and L2 speakers of English. *Journal of Phonetics* 70: 86–116. DOI https://doi.org/10.1016/j.wocn.2018.03.002.

Wierzbicka, Anna. 2006. *English: Meaning and Culture*. Oxford: Oxford University Press.

Wilcox, Ethan G., Jon Gauthier, Jennifer Hu, Peng Qian and Roger P. Levy. 2020. On the predictive power of neural language models for human real-time comprehension behavior. In *Proceedings of CogSci 2020*. DOI https://doi.org/10.48550/arXiv.2006.01912.

Wilkes-Gibbs, Deanna, and Herbert H. Clark. 1992. Coordinating beliefs in conversation. *Journal of Memory and Language* 31: 183–194.

Wilson, Deirdre, and Dan Sperber. 1993. Linguistic form and relevance. *Lingua* 90: 1–25.

2004. Relevance Theory. In Laurence R. Horn and Gregory Ward (eds.), *The Handbook of Pragmatics*, 607–632. Oxford: Blackwell.

Wingfield, Arthur. 1968. Effects of frequency on identification and naming of objects. *The American Journal of Psychology* 81(2): 226–234.

Witkowski, Stanley R., and Cecil H. Brown. 1983. Marking-reversals and cultural importance. *Language* 59(3): 569–582.

Witzlack-Makarevich, Alena, and Ilja Seržant. 2018. Differential argument marking: Patterns of variation. In Ilja Seržant and Alena Witzlack-Makarevich (eds.), *Diachrony of Differential Argument Marking*, 1–40. Berlin: Language Science Press.

Wood, Simon N. 2006. *Generalized Additive Models: An Introduction with R*. Boca Raton, FL: Chapman and Hall/CRC.

Wulff, Stefanie. 2006. *Go*-V vs. *go-and*-V in English: A case of constructional synonymy? In Stefan Th. Gries and Anatol Stefanowitsch (eds.), *Corpora in Cognitive Linguistics. Corpus-Based Approaches to Syntax and Lexis*, 101–125. Berlin: Mouton de Gruyter.

Yadav, Himanshu, Samar Husain and Richard Futrell. 2021. Do dependency lengths explain constraints on crossing dependencies? *Linguistics Vanguard* 7 (s3): 20190070. DOI https://doi.org/10.1515/lingvan-2019-0070.

Yamashita, Hiroko, and Franklin Chang. 2001. 'Long before short' preference in the production of a head-final language. *Cognition* 81: B45–B55.

Yang, Suying. 1995. *The Aspectual System of Chinese*. PhD dissertation. Victoria: University of Victoria.

Ye, Jingting, 2020. Independent and dependent possessive person forms: Three universals. *Studies in Language* 44(2): 363–406. DOI https://doi.org/10.1075/sl.19020.ye.

Yngve, Victor H. 1960. A model and an hypothesis for language structure. *Proceedings of the American Philosophical Society* 104(5): 444–466.

Zach, Reto. 1979. Shell dropping: Decision-making and optimal foraging in Northwestern crows. *Behaviour* 68: 106–117. DOI https://doi.org/10.1163/156853979X00269.

Zehentner, Eva. 2022. Ambiguity avoidance as a factor in the rise of the English dative alternation. *Cognitive Linguistics* 33(1): 3–33. DOI https://doi.org/10.1515/cog-2021-0018.

Zeman, Daniel, Joakim Nivre, Mitchell Abrams et al. 2020. *Universal Dependencies 2.6*, LINDAT/CLARIAH-CZ digital library at the Institute of Formal and Applied Linguistics (ÚFAL), Faculty of Mathematics and Physics, Charles University. http://hdl.handle.net/11234/1-3226. See also http://universaldependencies.org.

Zemskaja, Elena L., and L.A. Kapanadze (eds.). 1978. *Russkaja Razgovornaja Reč. Teksty [Russian Colloquial Speech. Texts]*. Moscow: Nauka.

Zipf, George K. 1965 [1935]. *The Psychobiology of Language: An Introduction to Dynamic Philology*. Cambridge, MA: MIT Press.

1949. *Human Behavior and the Principle of Least Effort*. Cambridge, MA: Addison-Wesley.

Index

accessibility, 18–19
  and common ground, 20, 39
  and competing referents, 39
  and markedness, 47
  and previous discourse, 38
  and syntactic functions, 38
  and thematic roles, 38
  in poetry vs. prose, 22
  in Relevance Theory, 19
  of coreferential and disjoint-reference objects, 46
  of referents, 19
  of syntactic constituents, 19
  of syntactic structures, 28
  quantitative measures, 20
Accessibility Hierarchy, 53
Accessibility Theory, 142
agreement (indexing), 145
alignment of conceptual representations, 34
ambiguity, 16–17, 139
ambiguity avoidance, 206
analogy, 136
analytic causatives. *See* causatives
analytic support, 98–99
anticausative (inchoative) alternation, 129
anticausatives, 129
argument omission, 39–40
  and agreement (indexing), 43
  and habitual actions, 42
  and politeness, 42
  Deprofiled Object Construction, 42
  Implicit Theme Construction, 42
  object omission, 40–43
  omission of objects of *win*, 41
  subject omission, 44, 141
  subject omission and indexing, 141
argument prominence, scale of, 45
articulation costs, 12, 102
artificial language learning, 111, 118, 187, 226
  and communication, 226–227
Attraction, 231

audience design, 32–33, 62, 64
  cognitive load, 33
automatization of articulation, 125
avoidance of identity. *See* horror aequi

binomial expressions, 70, 73
'buying time', 63

case marking, 145, *see also* differential case marking
causation
  Causee, role of, 157
  curative, 157, 186–187
  direct and indirect, 156–158, 165, 180
  implicative and non-implicative, 178
  intentional and accidental, 158
  permissive, 157
  with involved Causer, 174
causative alternation, 129
causative continuum, 155–156
causatives, 129, 165
  'default', 163, 178
  analytic vs. lexical, 173
  analytic/periphrastic, 128, 155, 157
  and I- and M-implicatures, 160
  and iconicity, 159, 167, 191
  Causee marking, 191
  diachronic sources, 182–183
  formal compactness, 161
  lexical, 155, 157
  morphological, 155, 157
  morphological vs. lexical, 173
  productivity, 176
  semantic generalization, 185
  with auxiliaries *doen* and *laten* in Dutch, 185–186
  with auxiliary *make*, 183
chunking, 125
cognitive complexity. *See* principle of (reduction of) cognitive complexity
cognitive effects, 8–9, 103, 114

Index

competing motivations, 136
  systemic pressure, 48
complementizers, 51
  that, 52
compositionality, 128–129
conditional inference trees, 172
conditional probability, 211
  Feature given Role, 209–210, 213, 218, *see also* differential case marking
  Role given Feature, 210, 216, 220, 222, *see also* differential case marking
connectors
  causal and concessive, 51
  omission of, 51
  particle *to*, 52
constant information rate, 20–21, 75, 85
Construction Grammar and efficiency, 244
conventional implicatures, 51
Cooperative Principle, 29
coreferentiality, 45
  and self-directed vs. other-directed verbs, 45
  and verb semantics, 45
coronavirus. See COVID-19 pandemic
COVID-19 pandemic, 4
cross-register doublets, 97

dative alternation, 49–50, 71
  and accessibility of arguments, 71
defamiliarization, 92
dependency locality theory, 67, 77
differential case marking, 193
  and distance from the verb, 206
  and iconicity of markedness, 206, 210, 221
  and TAM categories, 203
  and topicality, 225
  and word order, 205, 226, 228
  as expectation management, 205
  differential object marking, 48, 193, 195, 202, 207
  differential place (locative) marking, 48
  differential recipient marking, 49
  differential subject marking, 193, 196, 202, 207
  distinguishing/disambiguating function, 203, 205, 207–209, 222
  global and local, 203, 223
  identifying/indexing function, 207
  probabilistic/optional, 204
  referential features as cues, 204
  source-based explanation, 224
  universal scale effects, problem of, 196, 202
differential enhancement, 111–112, 223
differential inhibition, 115
differential object indexing, 44
differential reduction, 109–110, 184, 223

disjoint reference. *See* coreferentiality
double centre-embedded clauses, 67, 101

Easy First bias, 28, 72
entropy of order, 147
equal complexity, assumption of, 150
evolution, biological, 3
extraposed prepositional phrases, 86

Fast Causal Inference (FCI), 149
figure-first preference, 71
force of diversification, 15
force of unification, 15
formal enhancement, 108, 111, 114
formal reduction, 107–110, 119, 125–126, *see also* phonetic reduction
frequency, 47, 49, 122–123, 125–127, 130
Funes the Memorious, 128
future, 114

garden path sentences, 29, 72
gender differences in language processing, 247
gender-equal language, 11–12
Generalized Additive Models (GAMs), 242
Gestalts, multimodal, 144
gestures, 23, 144
'good-enough' efficiency, 31, 65
'good-enough' processing, 72
Google Books Ngrams, 237
grammaticalization, 109, 119, *see also* formal reduction
  and word-order correlations, 130
  of going to/gonna, 120
  of zero, 116
  paths, 124
  semantic bleaching, 120–121
  unidirectionality, 120
Greenberg's Universal 25, 89
Greenberg's Universal 41, 146

heavy-NP shift, 76
hierarchy of explicitness, 37
horror aequi, 100, 146
hyperarticulation, 62, 65
Hypothesis of Construction–Lexeme Accessibility and Formal Length, 230

I-implicatures, 25–27, 97
inequality in communication, 248
information locality, 68, 75–76, 80, 82–83
informativity, 230, *see also* Law of Abbreviation
integration of new referents, 102

interference due to similarity, 96, 100–101
'invisible hand', 133–134

kinship terms, 137, 140

Law of Abbreviation, 6, 57, 122
  and informativity, 58, 60
law of growing constituents, 7, 77
learnability, 246
Leipzig Corpora Collection, 147
letting in Anglo-Saxon culture, 174
lexical causatives. *See* causatives
linguistic distance, scale of, 175
'loose-fit' and 'tight-fit' languages, 146

male bias in language, 11
markedness, 46
  and frequency, 47
  global and local, 47
  reversal, 47
Maximize On-line Processing, 72
memory costs. *See* processing costs
M-implicatures, 26–27, 97
minimization of dependency distances, 67, 76–77
  and language change, 131
Minimize Domains, 77–78
modalities, synergy of, 144
morphological causatives. *See* causatives
Mutual Information
  of roles and cases, 148
  of roles and lexemes, 148

Neuralink, 249
noisy channel, 9
number, 117
  plural, 48, 117–118, 136
  singular, 48
  singular vs. plural, 46–47, 107
  singulative, 48, 117, 136

'old before new', 74
order of adjectives in NP, 80
order of derivational and inflectional morphemes, 82
overspecification, 31

Pareto frontier, 137
phonetic reduction, 119, *see also* formal reduction
  and accessibility, 61
  as loss of phonetic detail, 61
  due to automatization, 63
  due to contextual predictability, 63
phonological reduction, scale of, 45

Plan Reuse principle, 28, 72, 131
politeness, 12
polysemy, 123
possessive constructions, 48, 109, 116
  alienable and inalienable possession, 49
possessive determiners, 110
Preferred Argument Structure, 102
present progressive, 114–115
principle of (reduction of) cognitive complexity, 53, 69, 184, 236
Principle of Communicative Efficiency, 30
principle of dependency locality, 67
Principle of Economical Permutation, 124
Principle of Economical Specialization, 124
principle of extravagance, 114
Principle of Immediate Mention, 28
Principle of Least Collaborative Effort, 18
Principle of Least Effort, 7, 122
processing complexity, 98–99, 101
processing costs, 10, 28, 102
  comprehension costs, 13
  indicators, 13–14
  memory costs, 5, 13–14, 23, 67, 70–71, 84–85, 87
  pragmatic processing, 14
  production costs, 13
  surprisal, 85
pro-drop. *See* argument omission

Q-implicatures, 26

Rational Artisan, 121–122, 124
reducing contexts, 125
redundancy, 150
referential scales, 195. *See* differential case marking
reflexive pronouns, 111–113
relative clauses
  subject vs. object, 54
relativizers, 51
Relevance Theory
  accessibility, 19
  cognitive effects, 8
  conceptual vs. procedural information, 50
Reliance, 231
renewal, 114, 120
resumptive pronouns, 53
  and Accessibility Hierarchy, 54
  and accessibility of referents, 55
routinization of articulation, 125

same-subject and different-subject constructions, 55
  and verb semantics, 56
  with *want*, 56

Index

selectional preference strength, 43
semantic bleaching, 125, *see also* grammaticalization
  and habituation, 126
  as an additive effect, 126
semantic extensions, 124
semantic principle of linear order, 73
semantics as a cue to grammatical roles, 146
'short before long', 78
signed languages, 23
similarity-based interference. *See* interference due to similarity
singulative. *See* number
Smooth Signal Redundancy Hypothesis, 21
social costs of communication, 11
subjectification and intersubjectification, 121
suffixing preference, 80–82
suppletion, 128
surprisal, 68, 96

teleology and language evolution, 132
time as communication costs, 10, 28, 70

trade-offs, 137–138, 142
  as negative correlations, 142
  between word order and case marking, 143–144
  directionality, 142, 144, 149
transparency, 99–100, 136
Trump, Donald, 4

Uniform Information Density Hypothesis, 21, 52, 75
Universal Dependencies, 147

verb-medial order, 145, 148

word order correlations, 87
  and branching direction, 87
  and harmonic orders, 87
  and learnability, 89

Yoda's word order, 90

Zipf's Law of Abbreviation. *See* Law of Abbreviation

For EU product safety concerns, contact us at Calle de José Abascal, 56–1°,
28003 Madrid, Spain or eugpsr@cambridge.org.

www.ingramcontent.com/pod-product-compliance
Lightning Source LLC
LaVergne TN
LVHW011802060526
838200LV00053B/3654